INSTANT TEEN

JUST ADD NUTS

By
Haruka Fukushima

TOKYOPOP®

HAMBURG // LONDON // LOS ANGELES // TOKYO

Instant Teen: Just Add Nuts
created by Haruka Fukushima

Translation - Yoohae Yang
English Adaptation - Jeannie Andersen
Retouch and Lettering - Samantha Yamasaki and Bowen Park
Production Artist - Jose Macasocol, Jr.
Copy Editor - Suzanne Waldman
Cover Design - Gary Shum

Editor - Jodi Bryson
Digital Imaging Manager - Chris Buford
Pre-Press Manager - Antonio DePietro
Production Managers - Jennifer Miller and Mutsumi Miyazaki
Art Director - Matt Alford
Managing Editor - Jill Freshney
VP of Production - Ron Klamert
Editor-in-Chief - Mike Kiley
President and C.O.O. - John Parker
Publisher and C.E.O. - Stuart Levy

A ⊙ **TOKYOPOP**® Manga

TOKYOPOP Inc.
5900 Wilshire Blvd. Suite 2000
Los Angeles, CA 90036

E-mail: info@TOKYOPOP.com
Come visit us online at www.TOKYOPOP.com

ISBN: 1-59532-148-9

First TOKYOPOP printing: March 2005
10 9 8 7 6 5 4 3 2 1
Printed in the USA

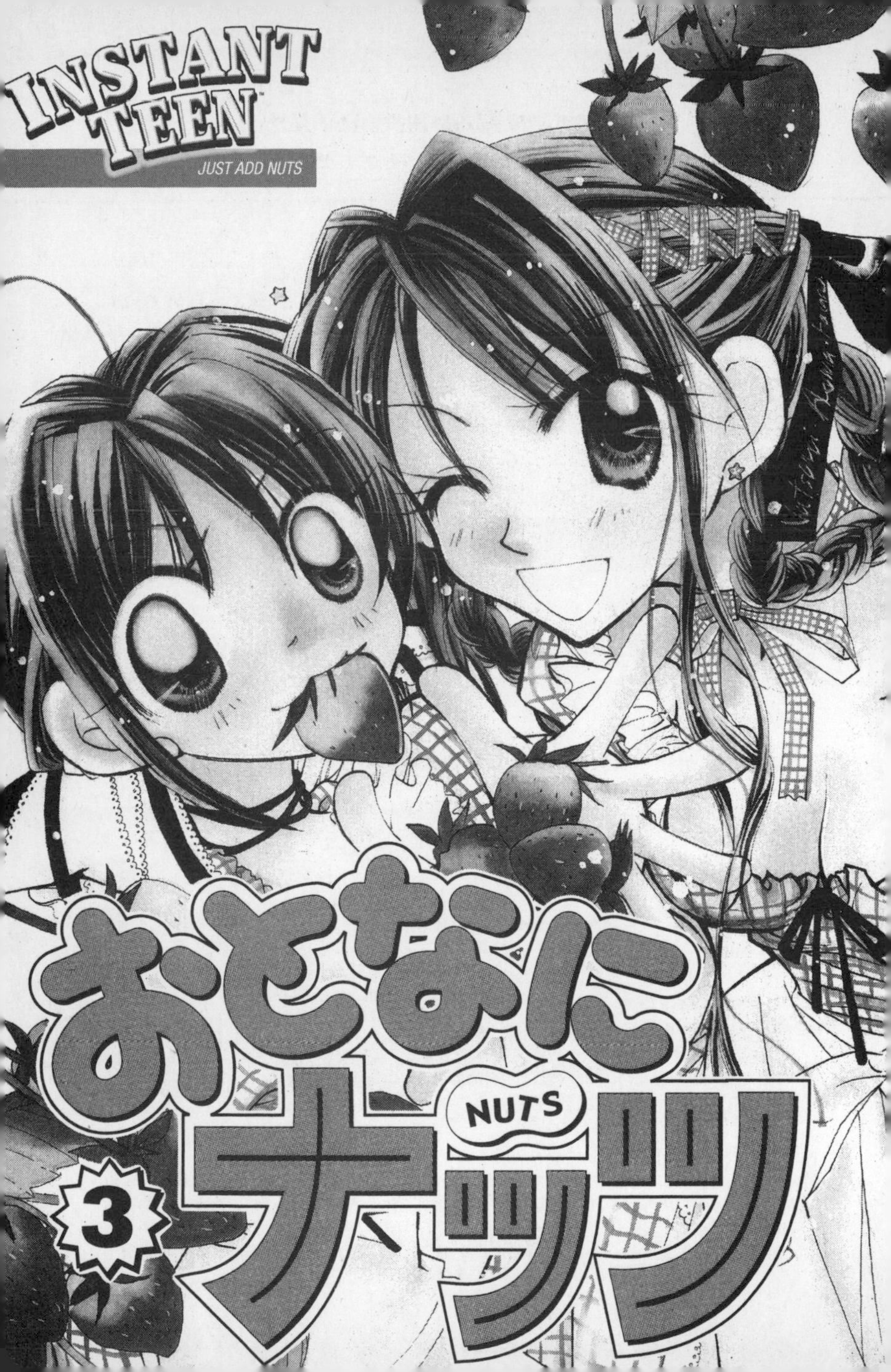
INSTANT TEEN™
JUST ADD NUTS
おとなにナッツ
NUTS
3

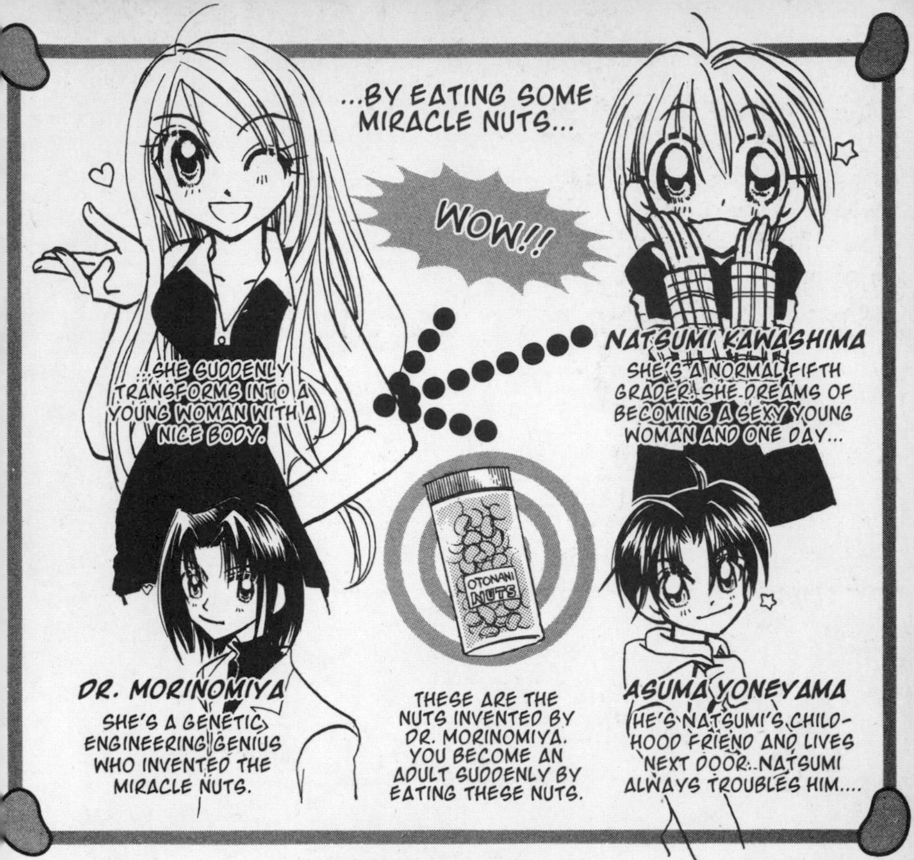
NATSUMI KAWASHIMA
SHE'S A NORMAL FIFTH GRADER. SHE DREAMS OF BECOMING A SEXY YOUNG WOMAN AND ONE DAY...
...BY EATING SOME MIRACLE NUTS...
WOW!!
...SHE SUDDENLY TRANSFORMS INTO A YOUNG WOMAN WITH A NICE BODY.
ASUMA YONEYAMA
HE'S NATSUMI'S CHILDHOOD FRIEND AND LIVES NEXT DOOR. NATSUMI ALWAYS TROUBLES HIM....
OTONANI NUTS
THESE ARE THE NUTS INVENTED BY DR. MORINOMIYA. YOU BECOME AN ADULT SUDDENLY BY EATING THESE NUTS.
DR. MORINOMIYA
SHE'S A GENETIC ENGINEERING GENIUS WHO INVENTED THE MIRACLE NUTS.

Story so far of "Instant Teen: Just Add Nuts"

☆ NATSUMI IS A NORMAL ELEMENTARY SCHOOL GIRL. SHE DREAMS OF BECOMING A SEXY WOMAN SOMEDAY! ONE DAY, SHE ATE MIRACLE NUTS BY MISTAKE AND...WOW! SHE TRANSFORMED INTO A SEXY WOMAN!

THE MIRACLE NUTS WERE INVENTED BY DR. MORINOMIYA. THEY SPEED UP THE GROWTH PROCESS IN LIVING THINGS. BUT THE NUTS ARE STILL IN THE EXPERIMENTAL STAGE. WHEN NATSUMI SUDDENLY TURNS BACK INTO A CHILD, EVERYONE AROUND NATSUMI IS IN TROUBLE!

NATSUMI WAS CHOSEN TO BE A MODEL, SO SHE AND ASUMA WENT TO THE ISLANDS TO PARTICIPATE IN A PHOTO SHOOT. NATSUMI ALMOST MARRIED A SUPER RICH PLAYER NAMED BILL WENTZ! BUT SHE TURNED INTO A CHILD WHILE SHE WAS RUNNING AWAY FROM BILL'S BODYGUARDS AND WAS SAVED! ASUMA IS THE ONLY ONE WHO CAN SAVE NATSUMI WHEN SHE'S IN MAJOR TROUBLE.

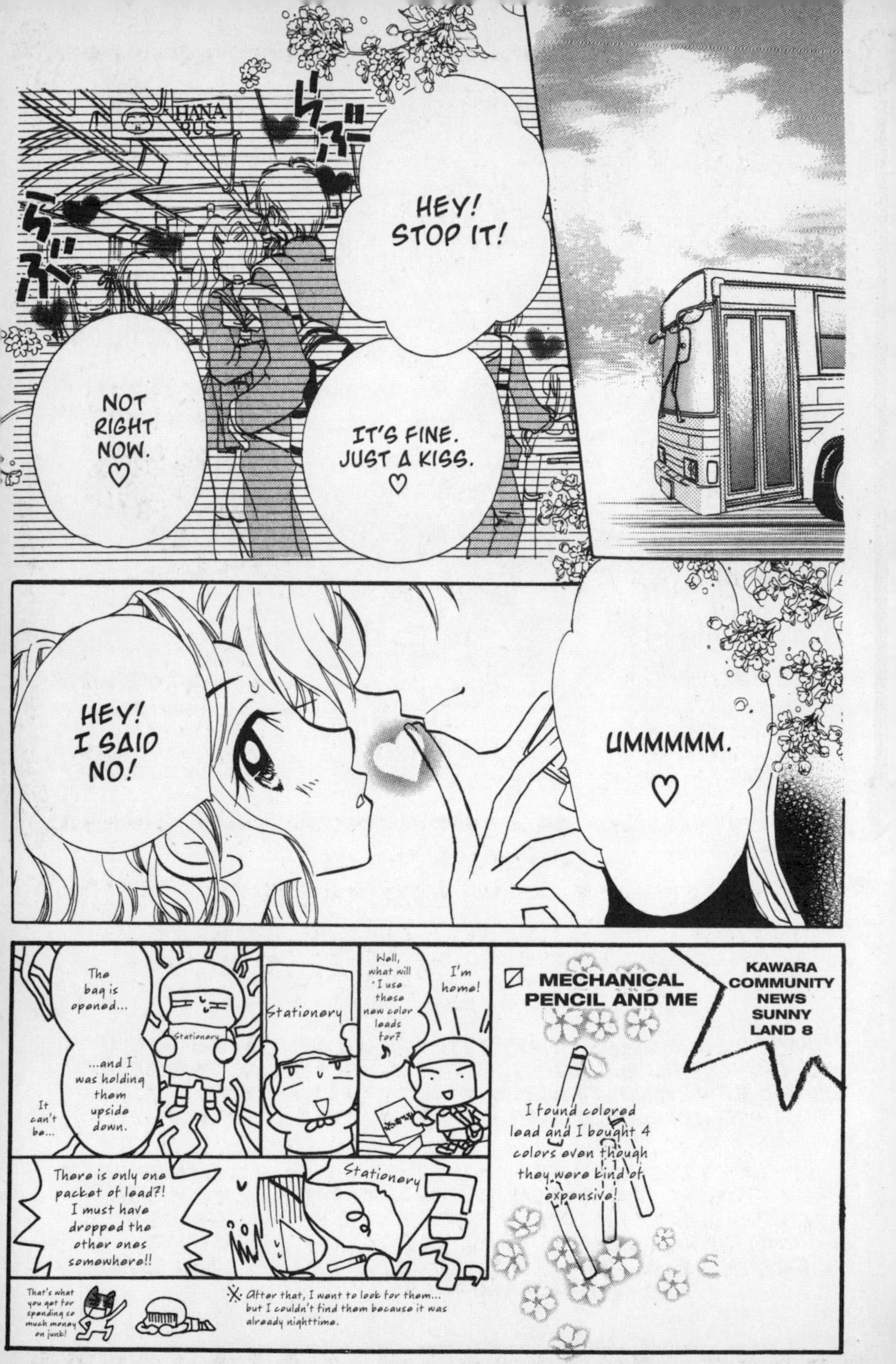
HANA BUS
HEY! STOP IT!
IT'S FINE. JUST A KISS. ♡
NOT RIGHT NOW. ♡
UMMMMM. ♡
HEY! I SAID NO!
KAWARA COMMUNITY NEWS SUNNY LAND 8
MECHANICAL PENCIL AND ME
I found colored lead and I bought 4 colors even though they were kind of expensive!
I'm home!
Well, what will I use these new color leads for? ♪
Stationery
Stationery
The bag is opened...
...and I was holding them upside down.
It can't be...
Stationery
There is only one packet of lead?! I must have dropped the other ones somewhere!!
※ After that, I went to look for them... but I couldn't find them because it was already nighttime.
That's what you get for spending so much money on junk!

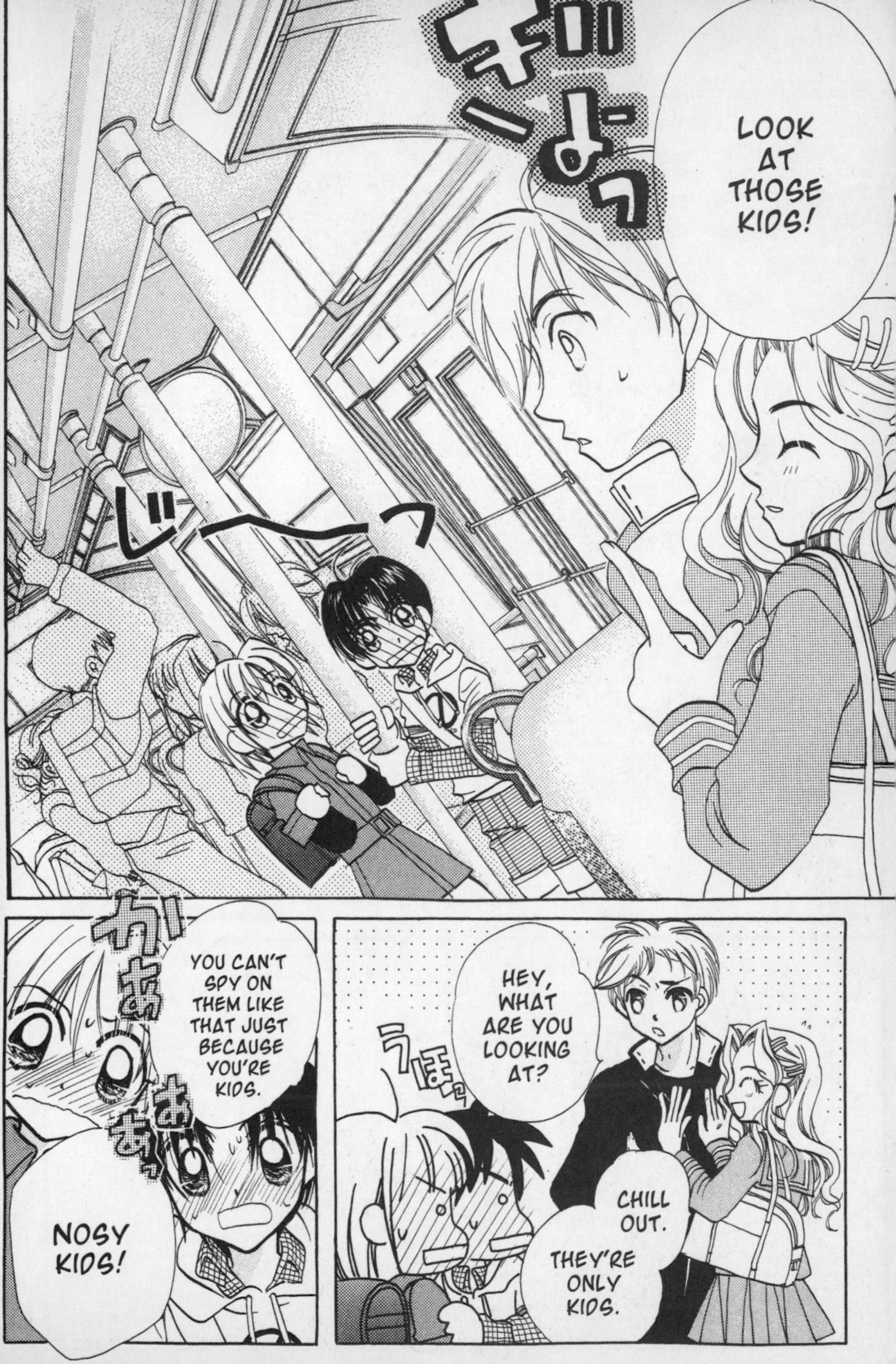
LOOK AT THOSE KIDS!
HEY, WHAT ARE YOU LOOKING AT?
CHILL OUT.
THEY'RE ONLY KIDS.
YOU CAN'T SPY ON THEM LIKE THAT JUST BECAUSE YOU'RE KIDS.
NOSY KIDS!

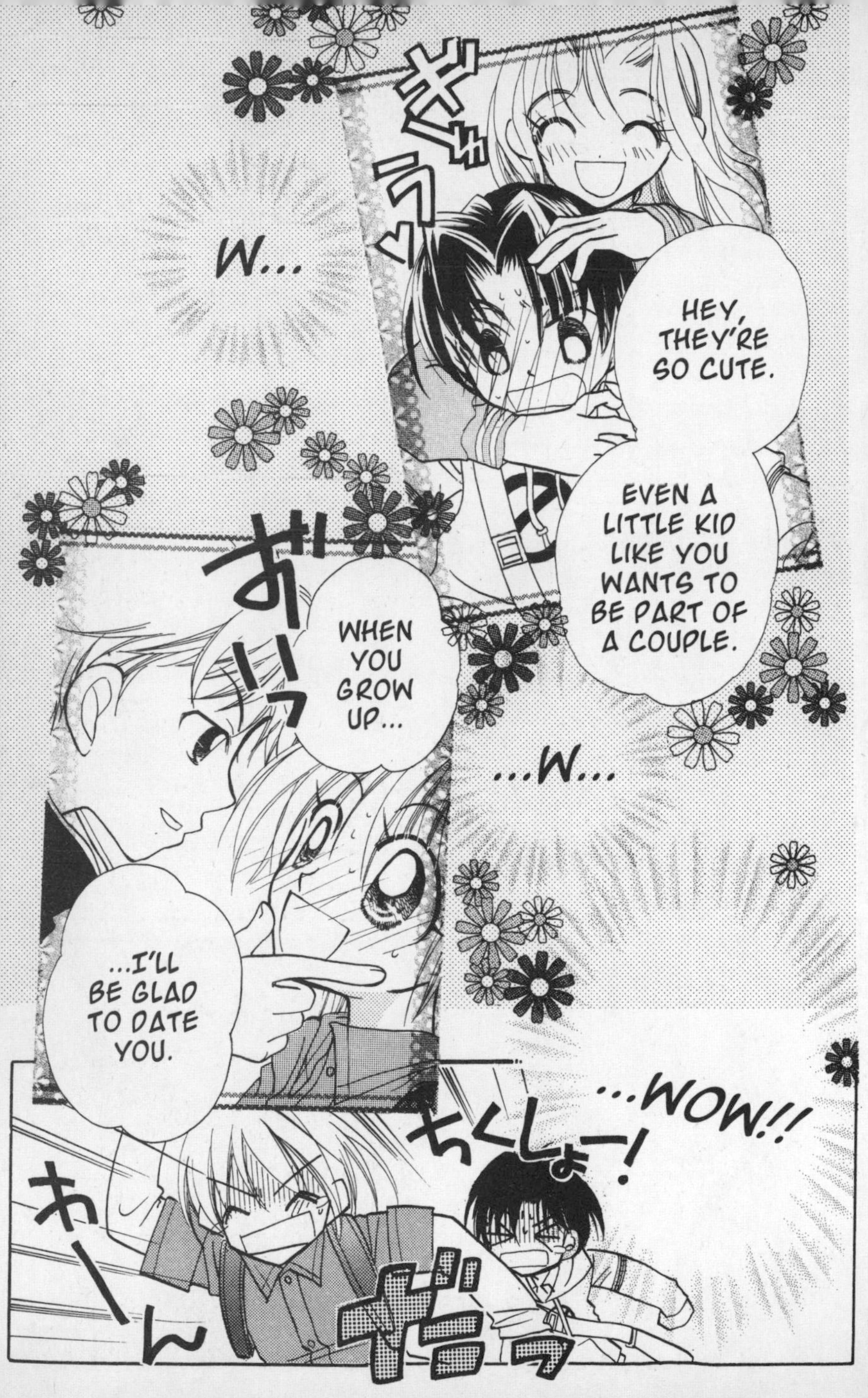
きゅう
HEY, THEY'RE SO CUTE.
EVEN A LITTLE KID LIKE YOU WANTS TO BE PART OF A COUPLE.
W...
...W...
おいっ
WHEN YOU GROW UP...
...I'LL BE GLAD TO DATE YOU.
...WOW!!
ちくしょー!
わーん
だっ

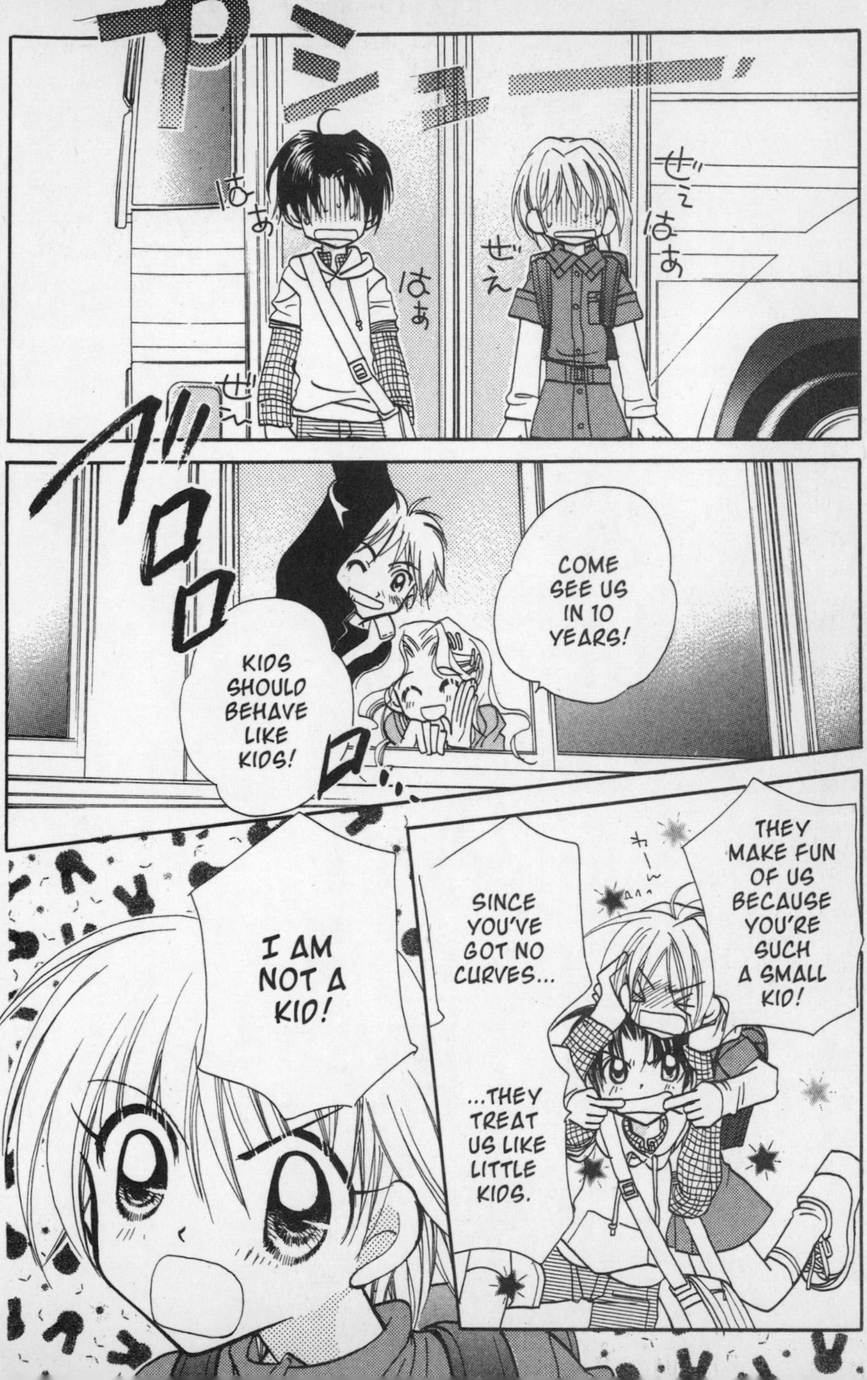
COME SEE US IN 10 YEARS!
KIDS SHOULD BEHAVE LIKE KIDS!
THEY MAKE FUN OF US BECAUSE YOU'RE SUCH A SMALL KID!
SINCE YOU'VE GOT NO CURVES...
...THEY TREAT US LIKE LITTLE KIDS.
I AM NOT A KID!

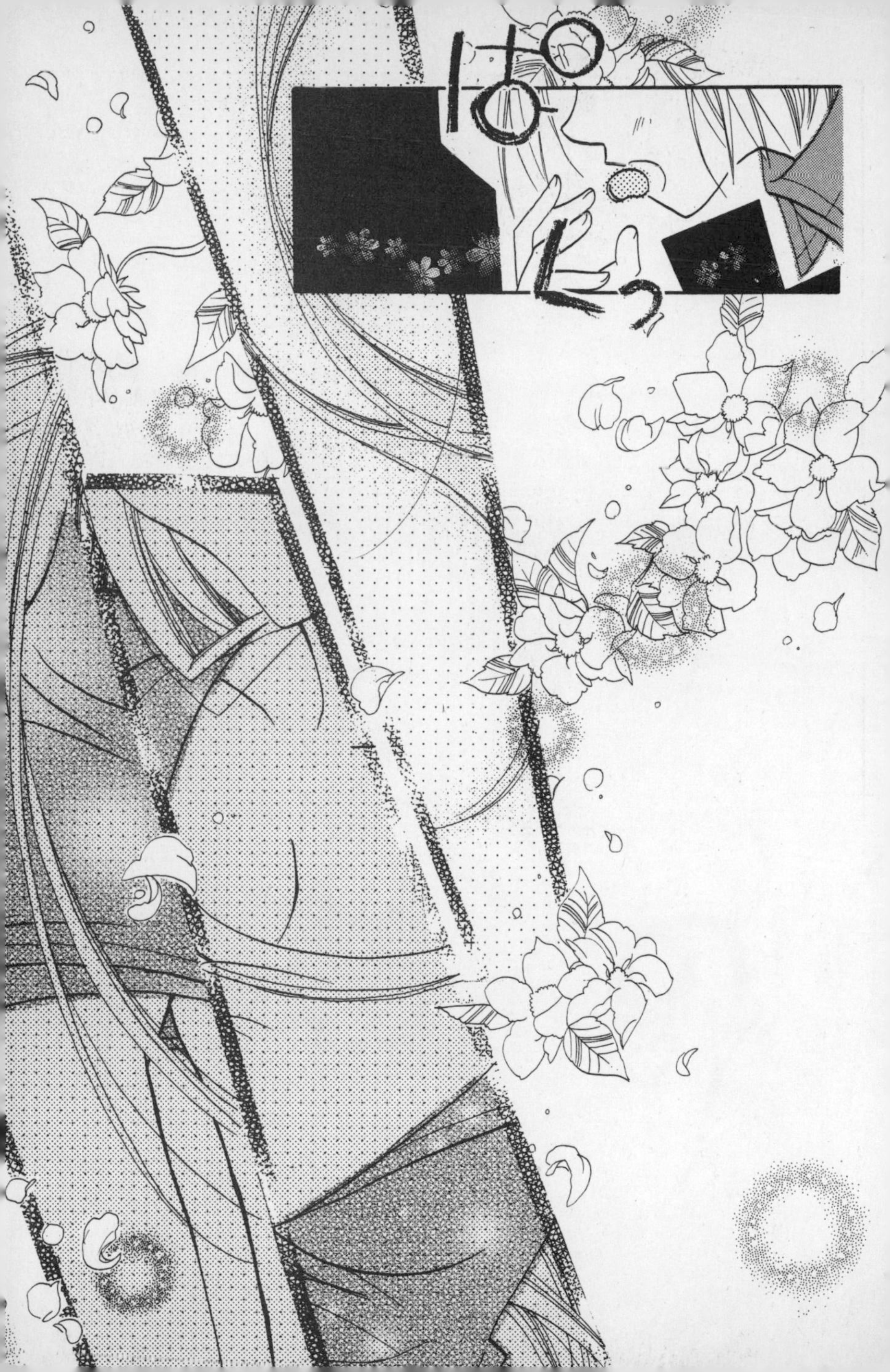
ぱしっ

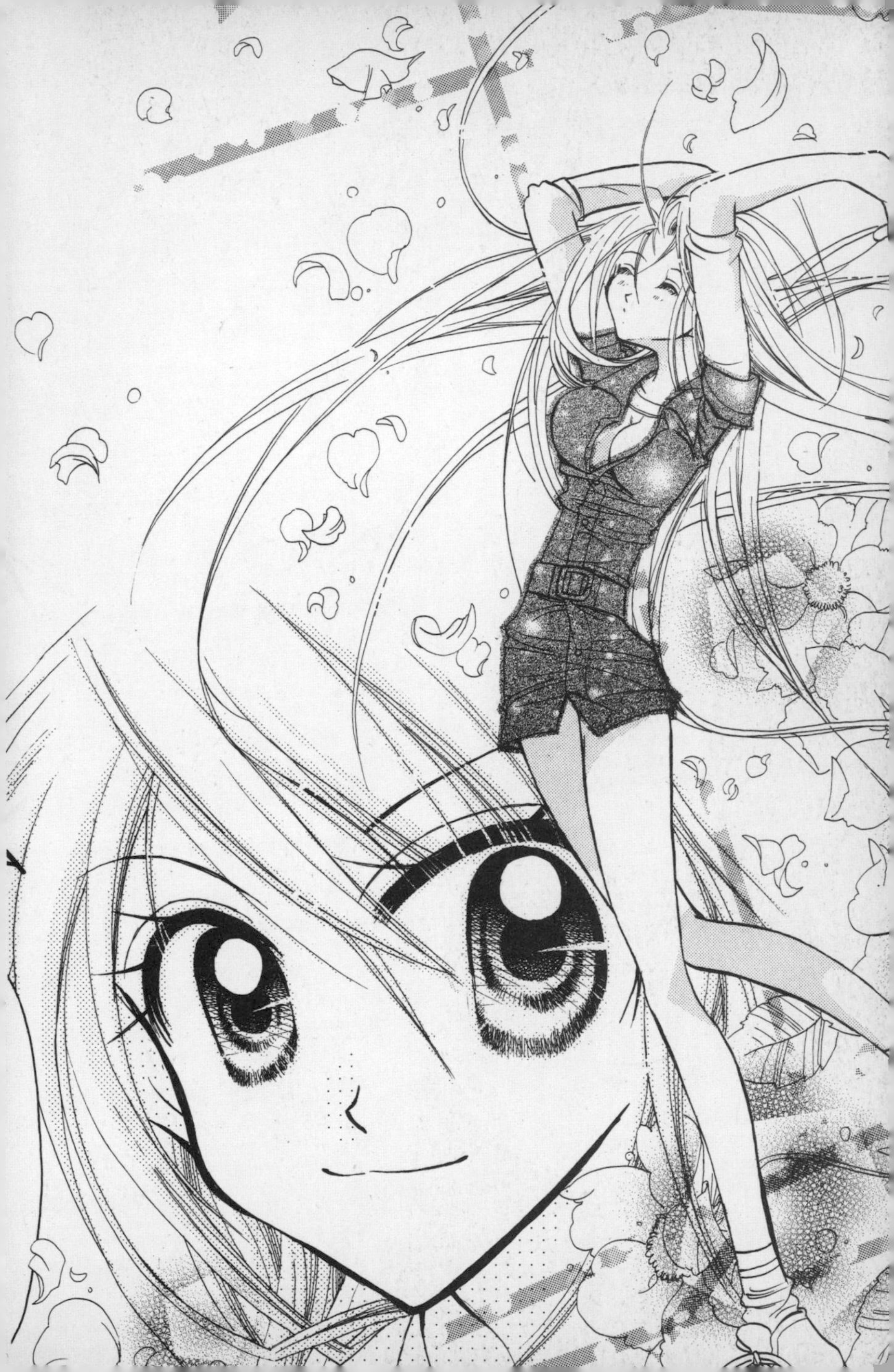

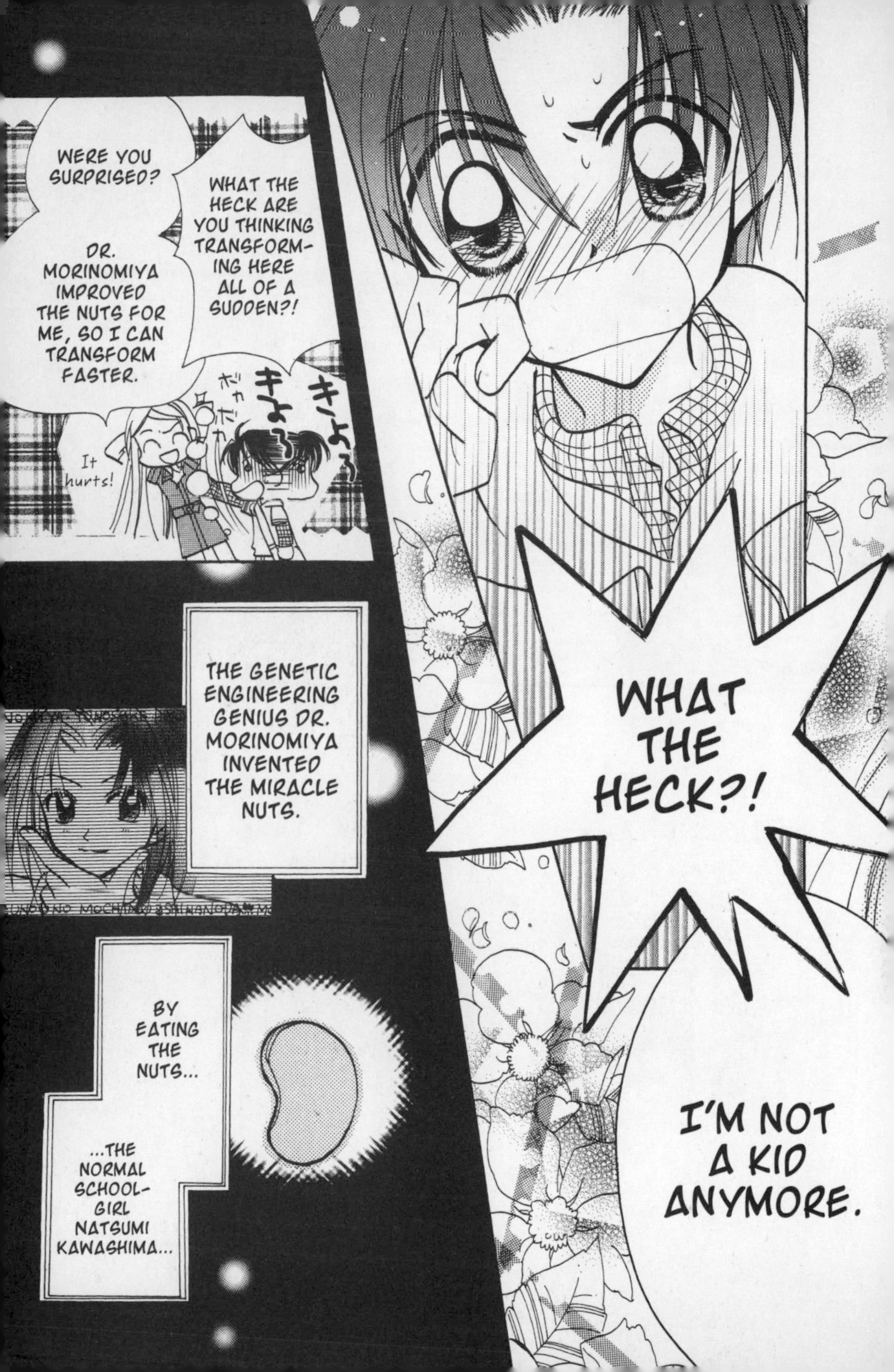

WHAT THE HECK?!
I'M NOT A KID ANYMORE.
WHAT THE HECK ARE YOU THINKING TRANSFORMING HERE ALL OF A SUDDEN?!
WERE YOU SURPRISED?
DR. MORINOMIYA IMPROVED THE NUTS FOR ME, SO I CAN TRANSFORM FASTER.
きょろきょろ
ボカボカ
It hurts!
THE GENETIC ENGINEERING GENIUS DR. MORINOMIYA INVENTED THE MIRACLE NUTS.
BY EATING THE NUTS...
...THE NORMAL SCHOOLGIRL NATSUMI KAWASHIMA...

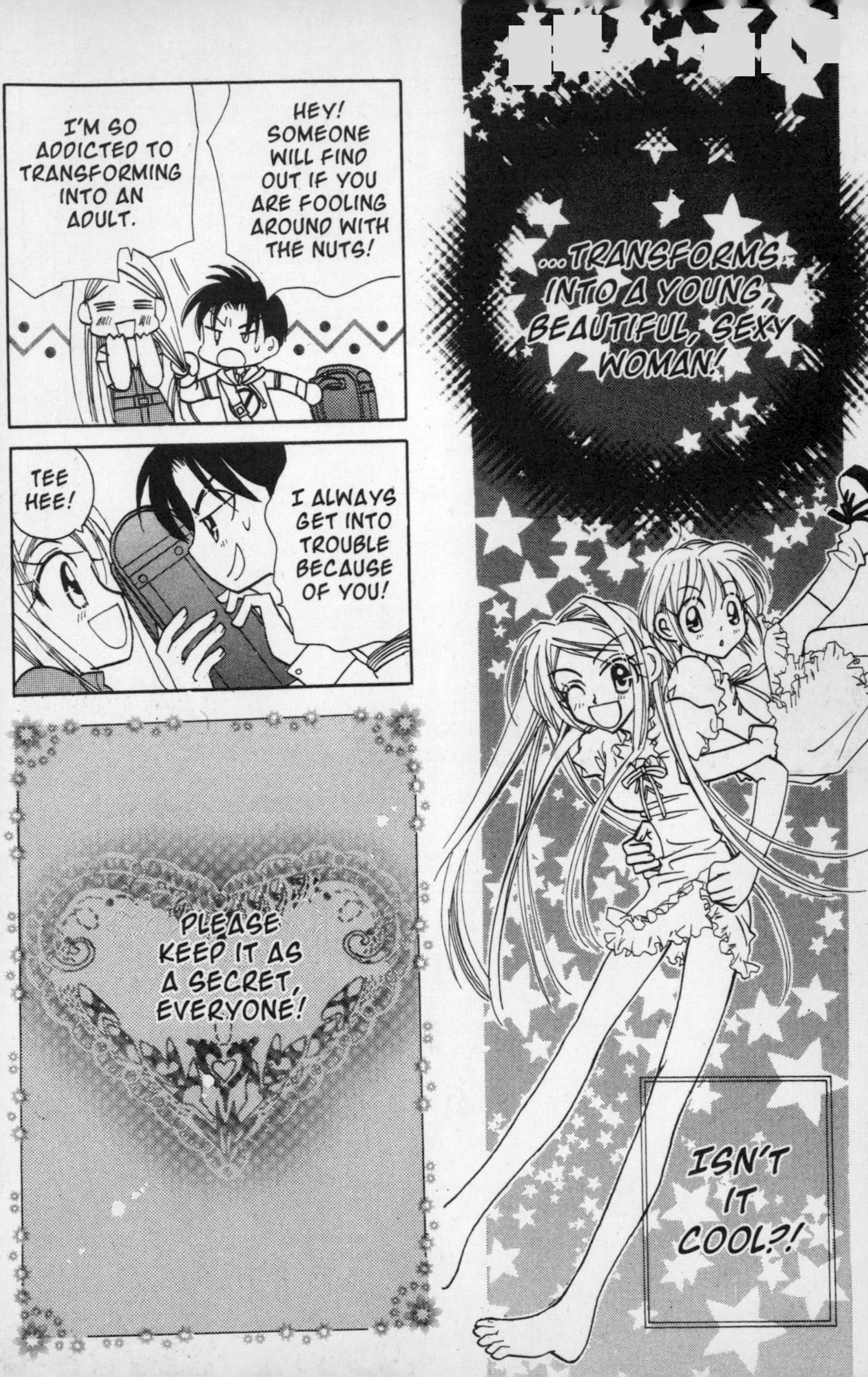
...TRANSFORMS INTO A YOUNG, BEAUTIFUL, SEXY WOMAN!
ISN'T IT COOL?!
HEY! SOMEONE WILL FIND OUT IF YOU ARE FOOLING AROUND WITH THE NUTS!
I'M SO ADDICTED TO TRANSFORMING INTO AN ADULT.
I ALWAYS GET INTO TROUBLE BECAUSE OF YOU!
TEE HEE!
PLEASE KEEP IT AS A SECRET, EVERYONE!

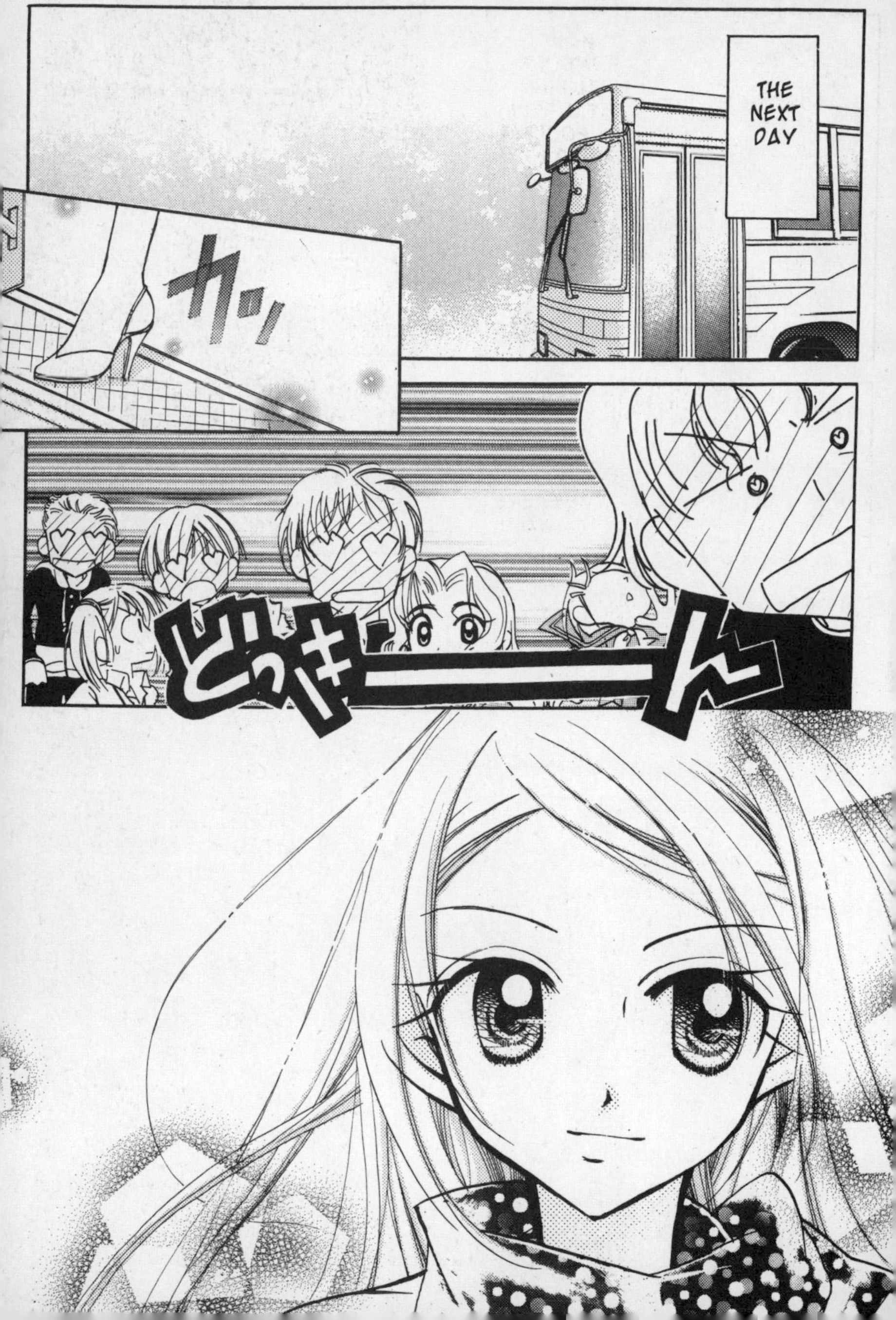
THE NEXT DAY
カッ
どっきーーん

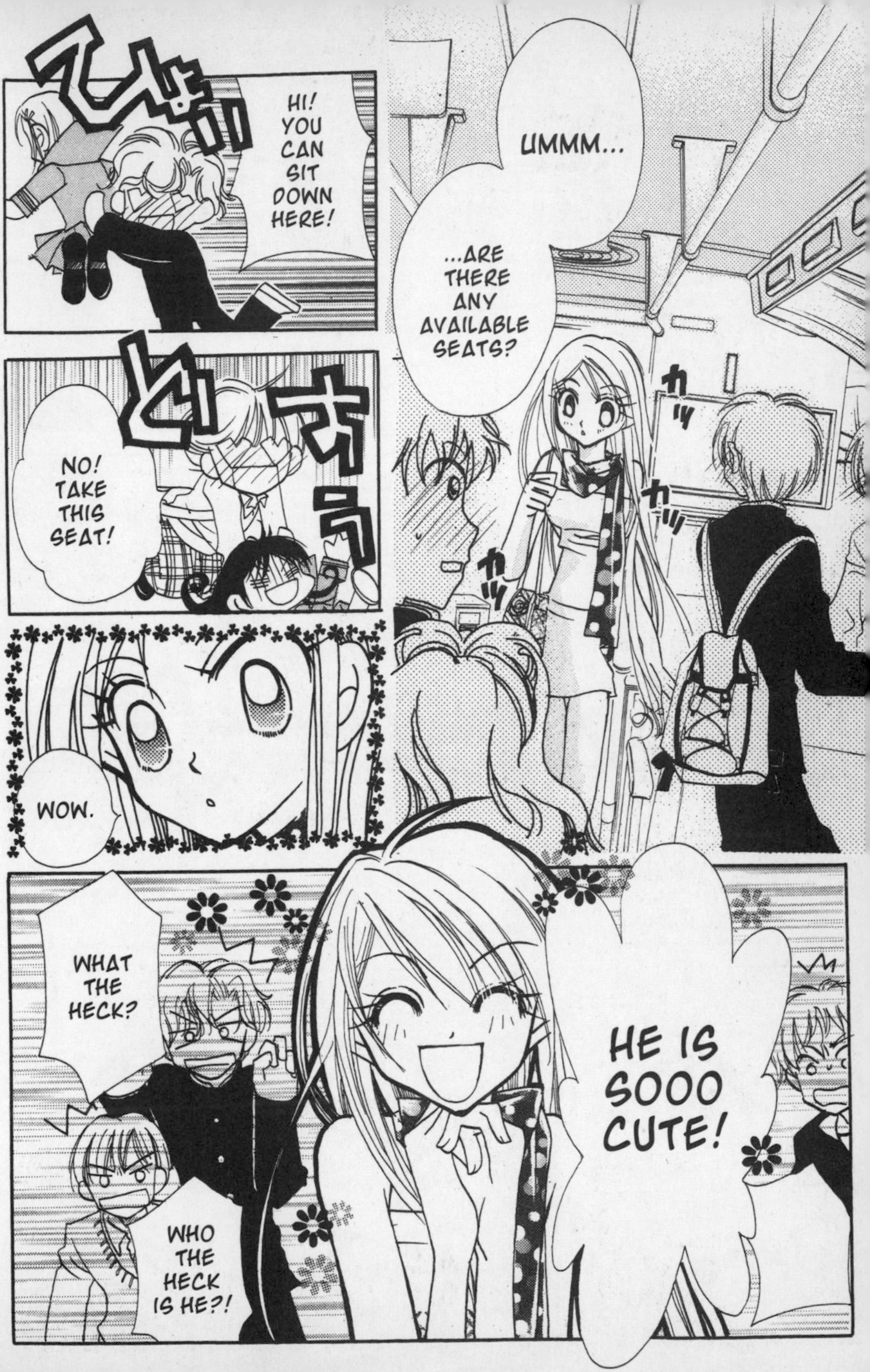
UMMM...
...ARE THERE ANY AVAILABLE SEATS?
カッ
カッ
カッ
HI! YOU CAN SIT DOWN HERE!
NO! TAKE THIS SEAT!
WOW.
HE IS SOOO CUTE!
WHAT THE HECK?
WHO THE HECK IS HE?!

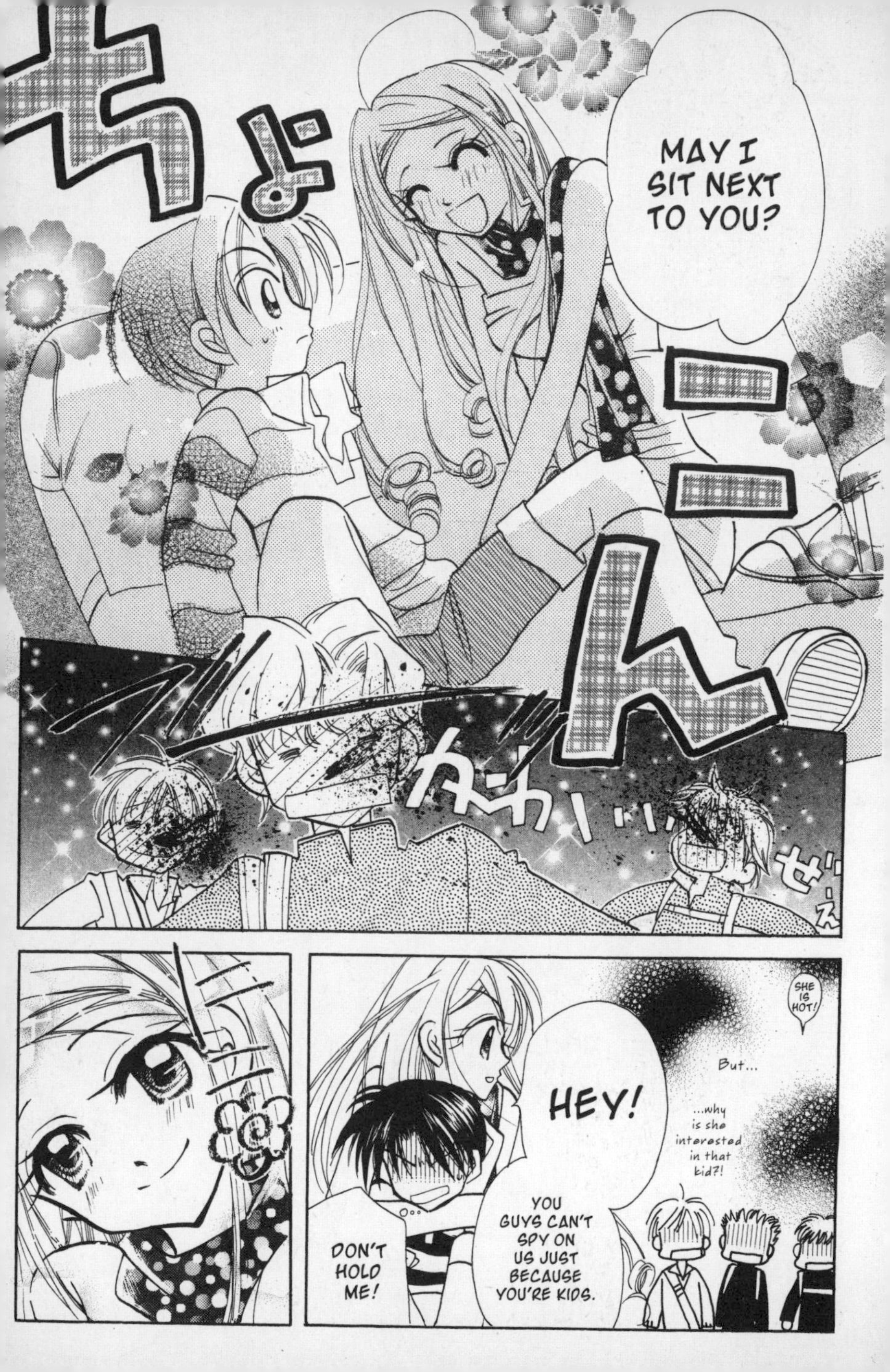
MAY I SIT NEXT TO YOU?
SHE IS HOT!
But...
...why is she interested in that kid?!
HEY!
YOU GUYS CAN'T SPY ON US JUST BECAUSE YOU'RE KIDS.
DON'T HOLD ME!

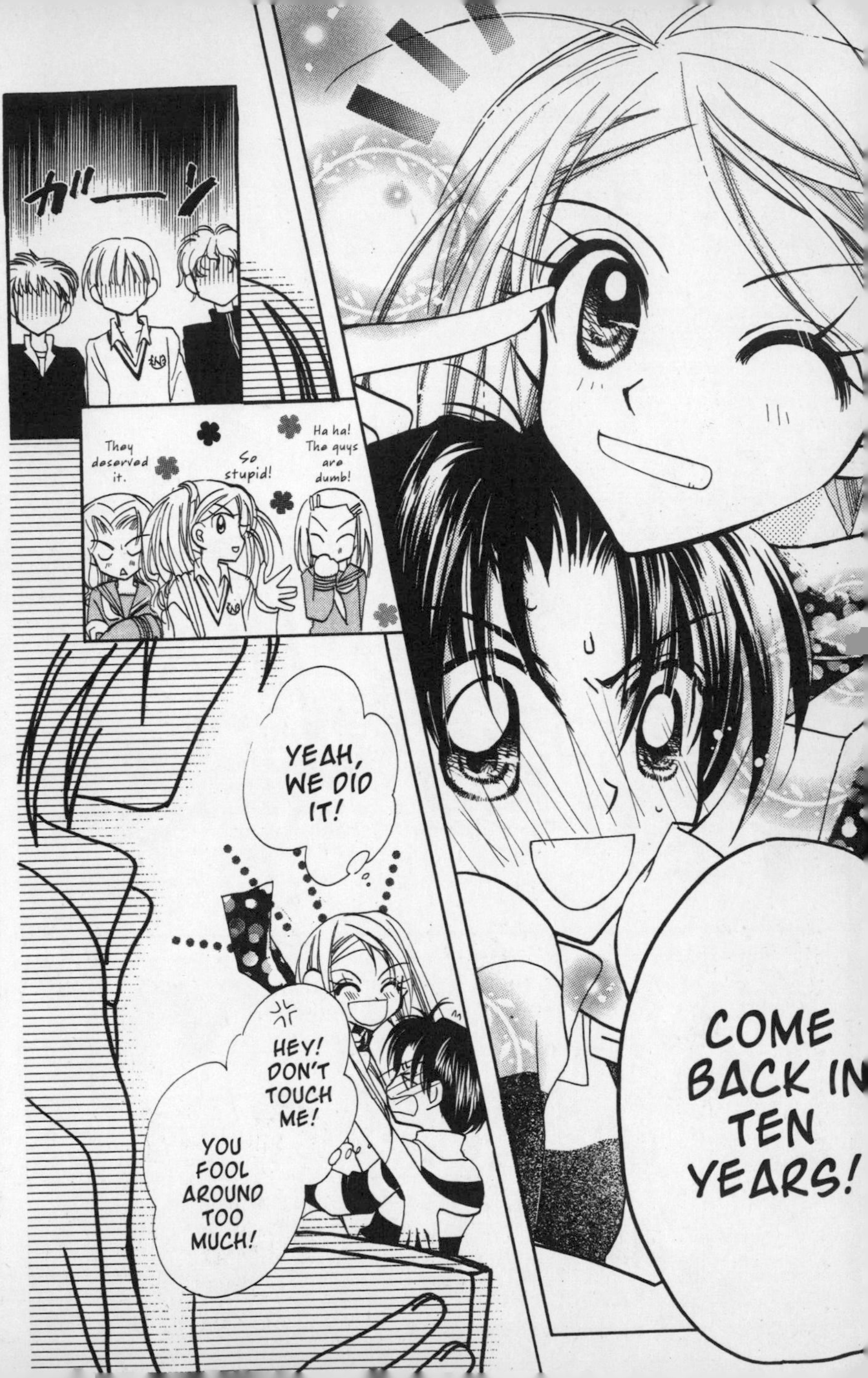

COME BACK IN TEN YEARS!
ガーーン
Ha ha! The guys are dumb!
So stupid!
They deserved it.
YEAH, WE DID IT!
HEY! DON'T TOUCH ME!
YOU FOOL AROUND TOO MUCH!

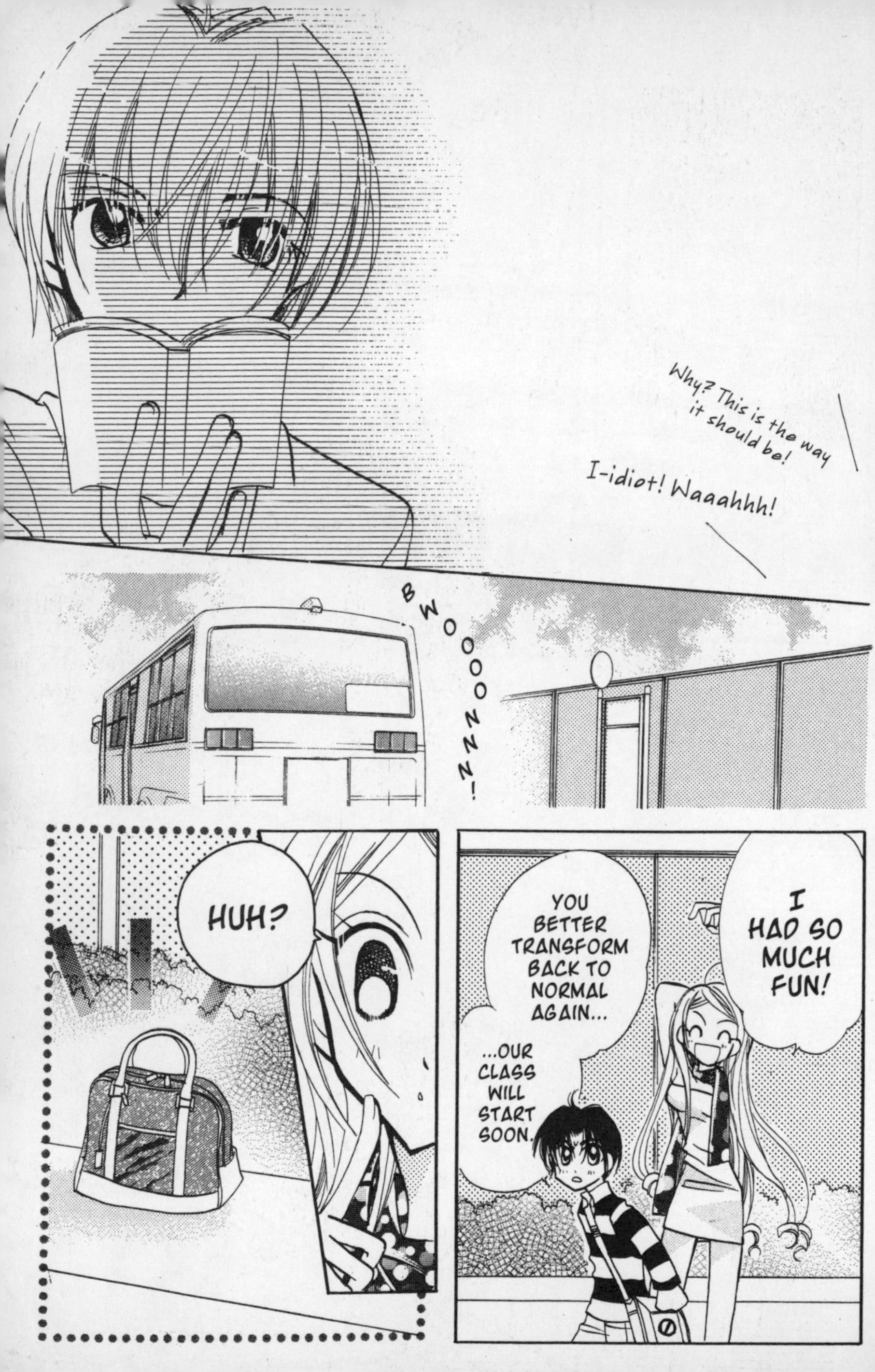
Why? This is the way it should be!
I-idiot! Waaahhh!
BWOOOONNNN!
I HAD SO MUCH FUN!
YOU BETTER TRANSFORM BACK TO NORMAL AGAIN...
...OUR CLASS WILL START SOON.
HUH?

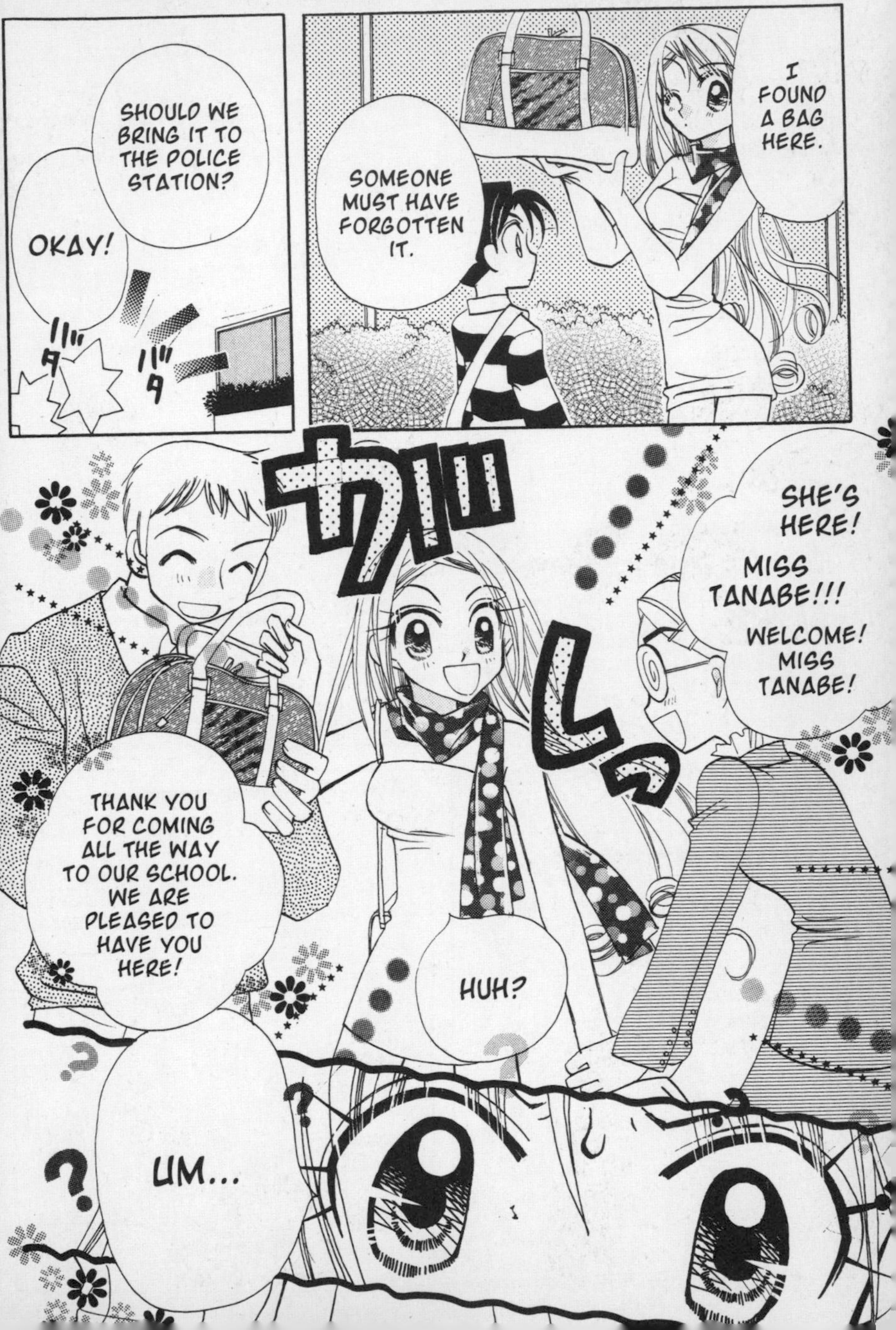
I FOUND A BAG HERE.
SOMEONE MUST HAVE FORGOTTEN IT.
SHOULD WE BRING IT TO THE POLICE STATION?
OKAY!
SHE'S HERE! MISS TANABE!!!
WELCOME! MISS TANABE!
THANK YOU FOR COMING ALL THE WAY TO OUR SCHOOL. WE ARE PLEASED TO HAVE YOU HERE!
HUH?
UM...

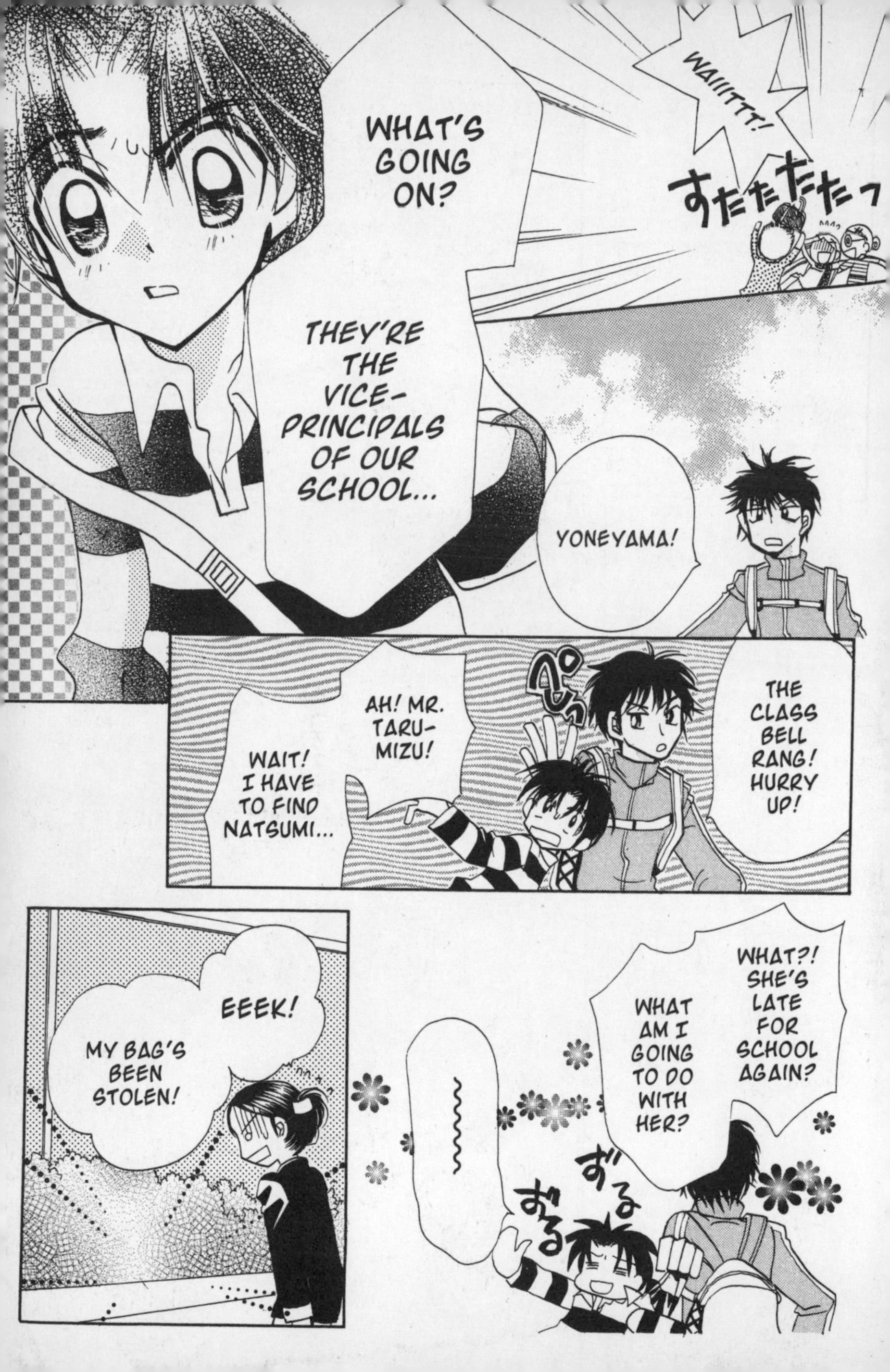
WAIIITTT!
すたたたたっ
YONEYAMA!
WHAT'S GOING ON?
THEY'RE THE VICE-PRINCIPALS OF OUR SCHOOL...
THE CLASS BELL RANG! HURRY UP!
ぺっ
AH! MR. TARU-MIZU!
WAIT! I HAVE TO FIND NATSUMI...
WHAT?! SHE'S LATE FOR SCHOOL AGAIN?
WHAT AM I GOING TO DO WITH HER?
......
ずるずる
EEEK!
MY BAG'S BEEN STOLEN!

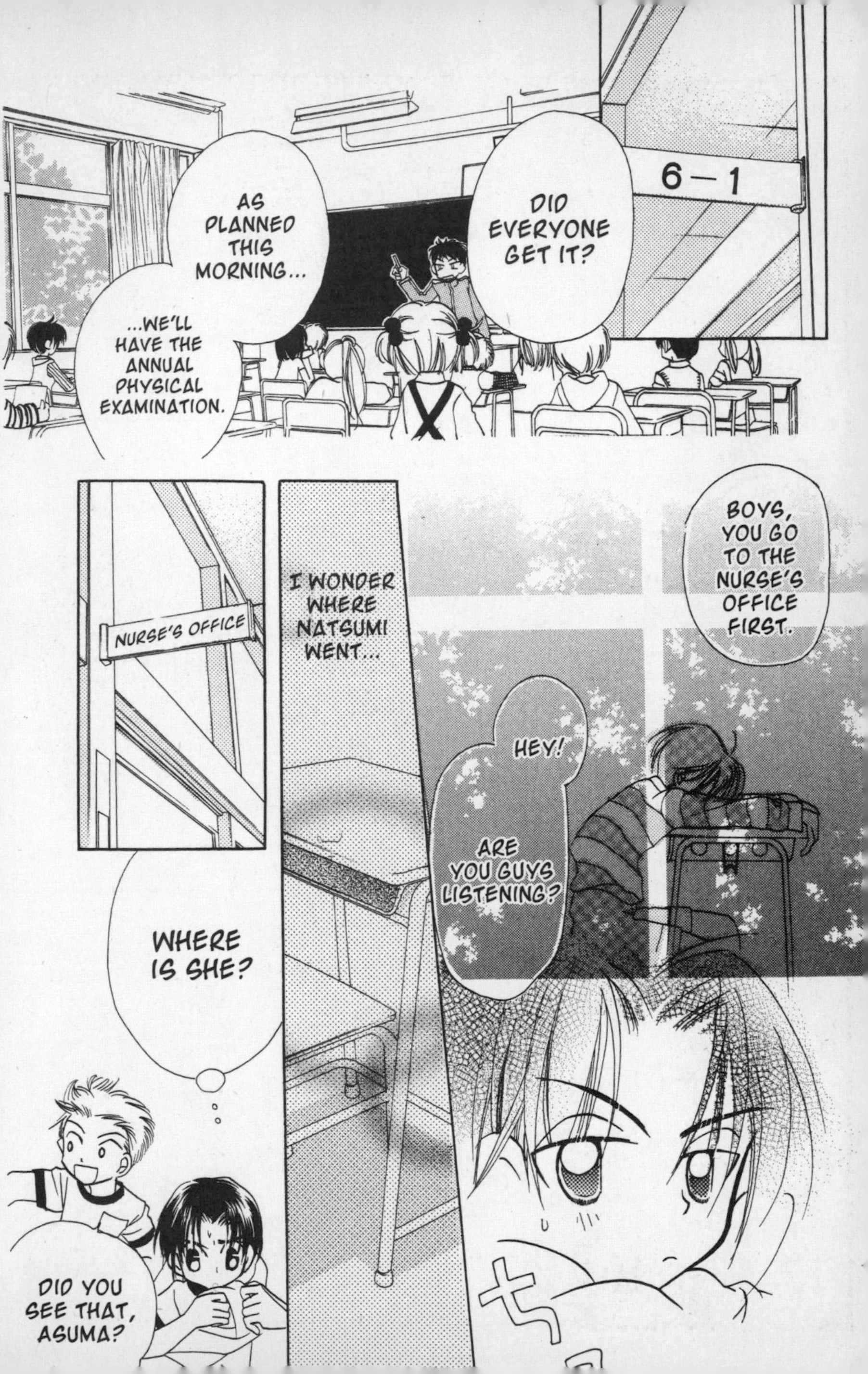
6-1
DID EVERYONE GET IT?
AS PLANNED THIS MORNING...
...WE'LL HAVE THE ANNUAL PHYSICAL EXAMINATION.
BOYS, YOU GO TO THE NURSE'S OFFICE FIRST.
HEY!
ARE YOU GUYS LISTENING?
I WONDER WHERE NATSUMI WENT...
NURSE'S OFFICE
WHERE IS SHE?
DID YOU SEE THAT, ASUMA?

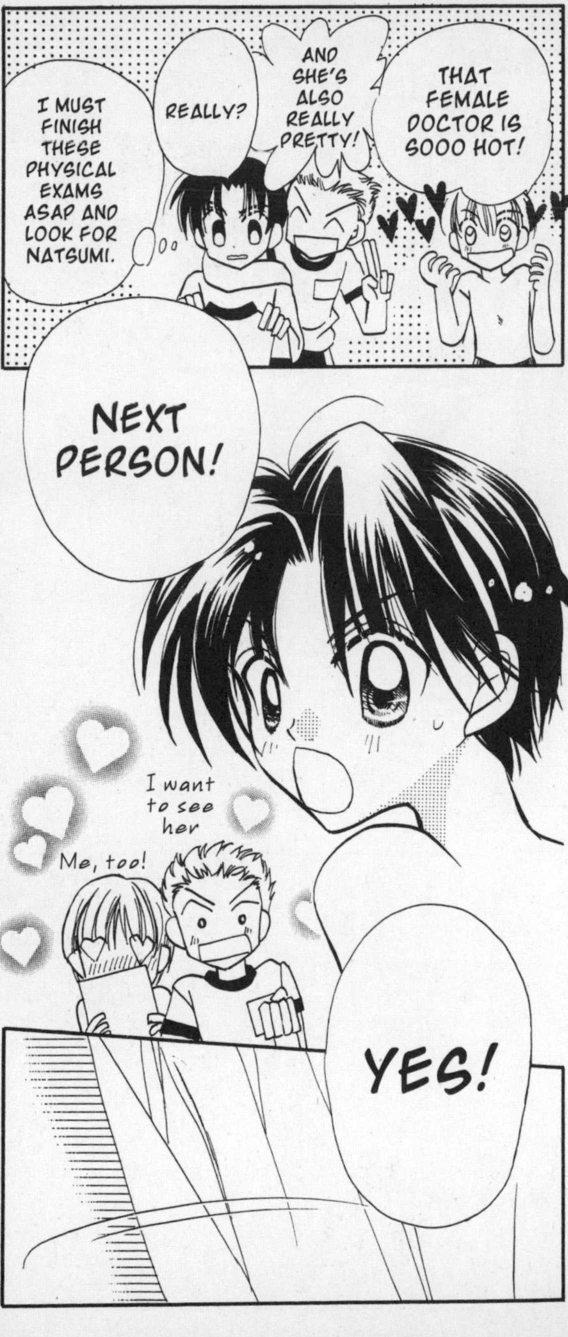
THAT FEMALE DOCTOR IS SOOO HOT!
AND SHE'S ALSO REALLY PRETTY!
REALLY?
I MUST FINISH THESE PHYSICAL EXAMS ASAP AND LOOK FOR NATSUMI.
NEXT PERSON!
I want to see her
Me, too!
YES!

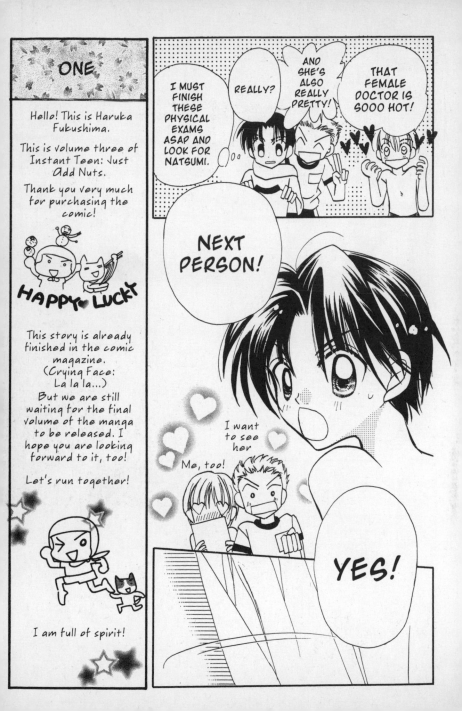

ONE

Hello! This is Haruka Fukushima.

This is volume three of Instant Teen: Just Add Nuts.

Thank you very much for purchasing the comic!

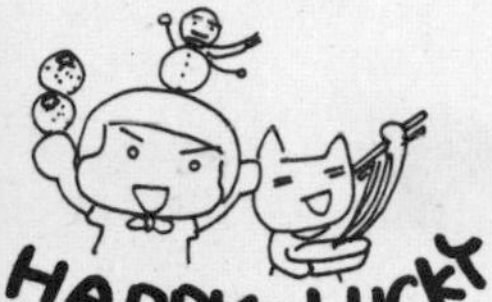
HAPPY LUCKY

This story is already finished in the comic magazine. (Crying Face: La la la...) But we are still waiting for the final volume of the manga to be released. I hope you are looking forward to it, too!

Let's run together!

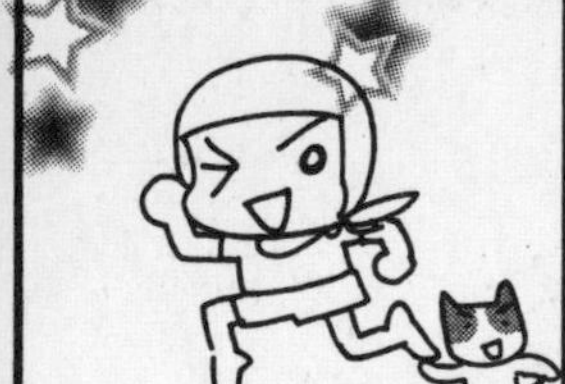

I am full of spirit!

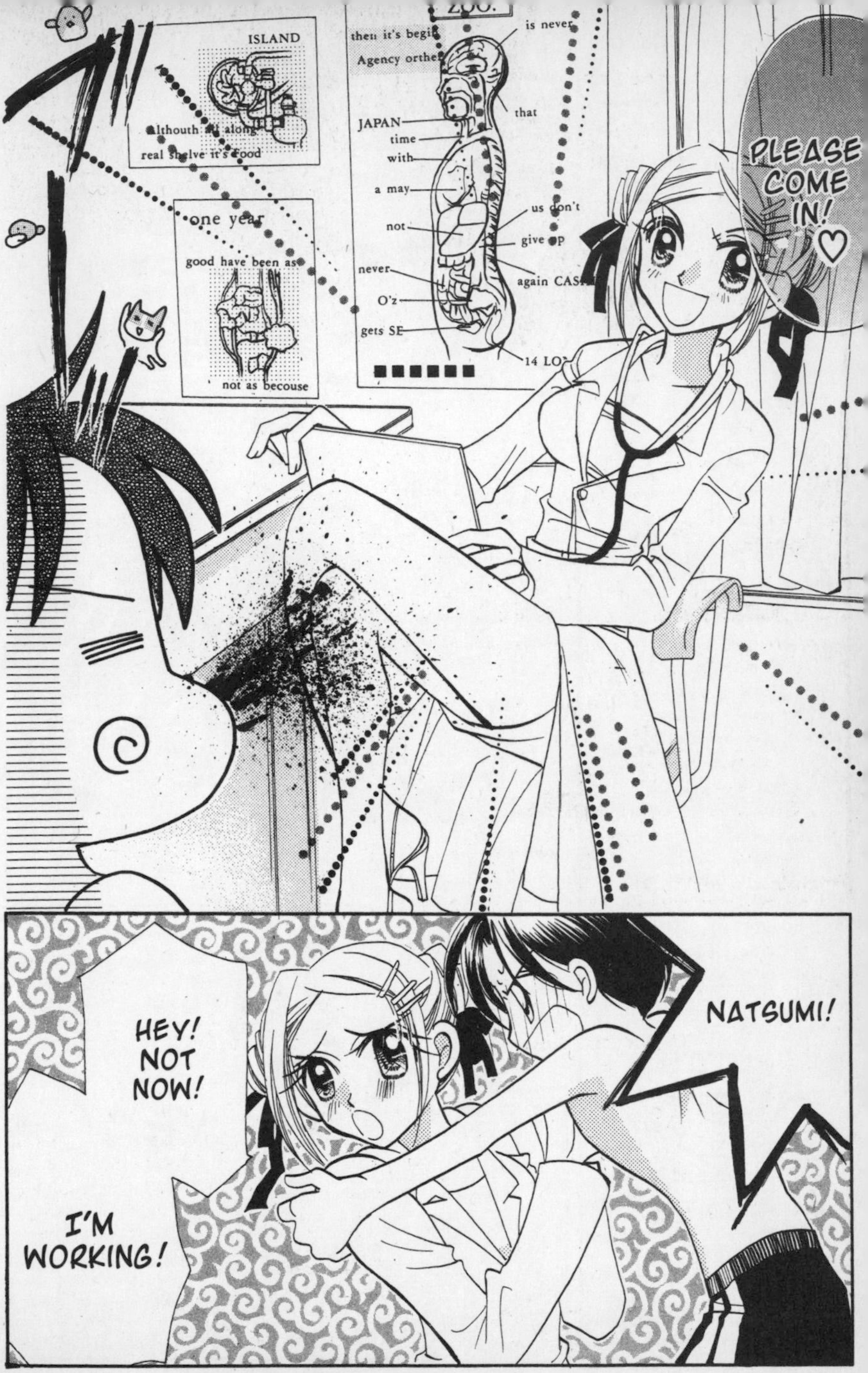
PLEASE COME IN! ♡
NATSUMI!
HEY! NOT NOW!
I'M WORKING!

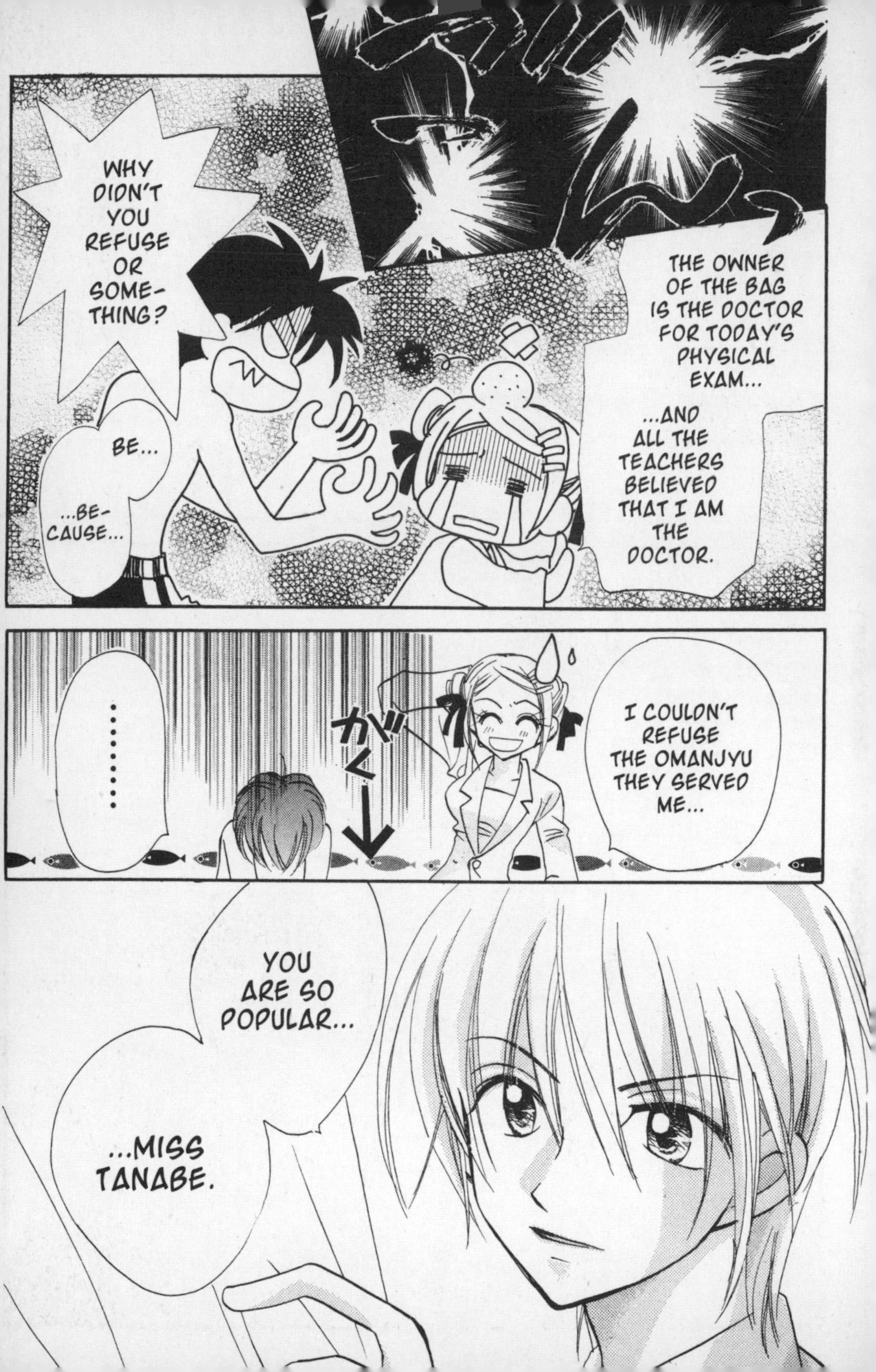
THE OWNER OF THE BAG IS THE DOCTOR FOR TODAY'S PHYSICAL EXAM...
...AND ALL THE TEACHERS BELIEVED THAT I AM THE DOCTOR.
WHY DIDN'T YOU REFUSE OR SOME-THING?
BE...
...BE-CAUSE...
I COULDN'T REFUSE THE OMANJYU THEY SERVED ME...
がく
......
YOU ARE SO POPULAR...
...MISS TANABE.

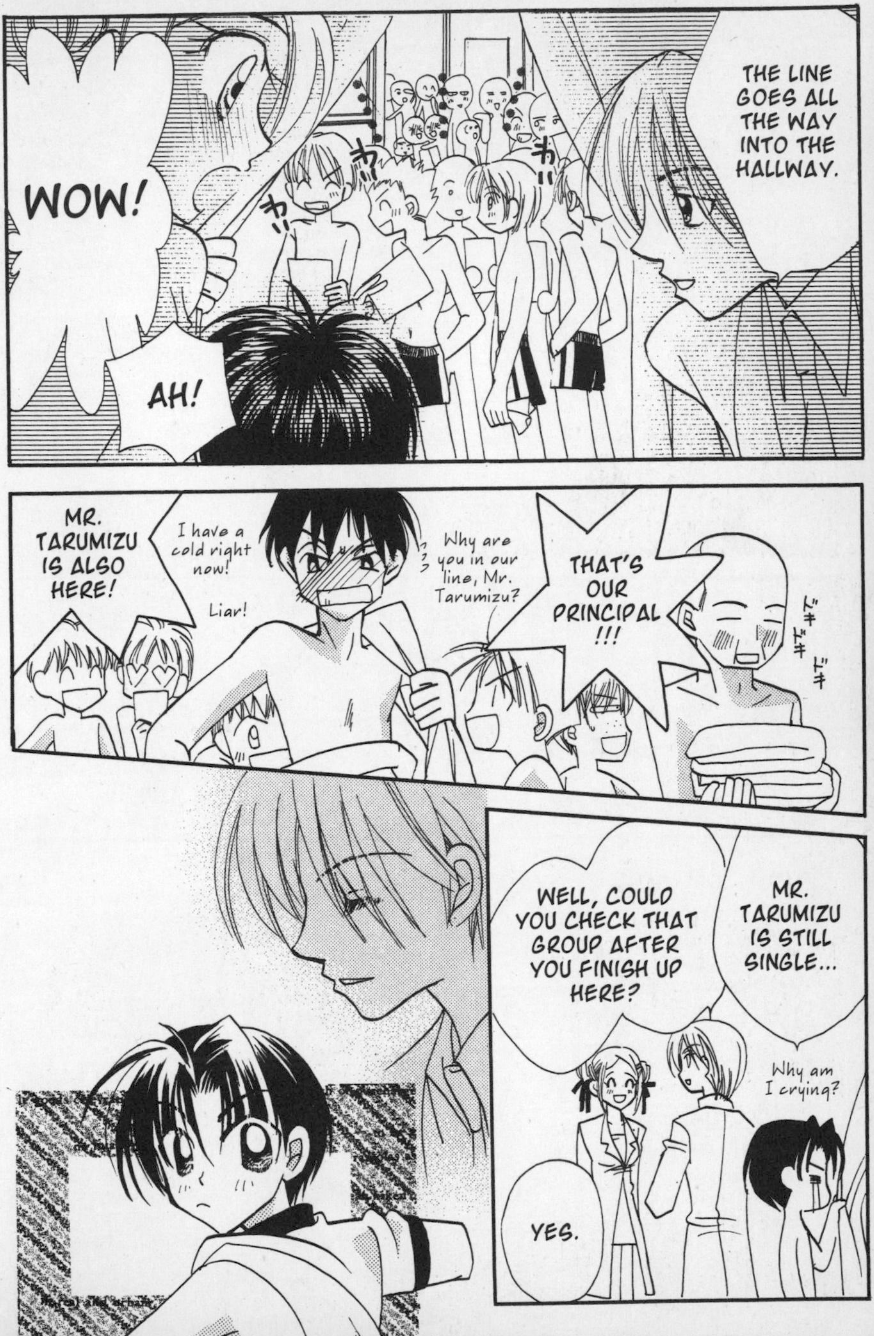
THE LINE GOES ALL THE WAY INTO THE HALLWAY.
WOW!
AH!
THAT'S OUR PRINCIPAL!!!
ドキ ドキ ドキ
Why are you in our line, Mr. Tarumizu?
I have a cold right now!
Liar!
MR. TARUMIZU IS ALSO HERE!
MR. TARUMIZU IS STILL SINGLE...
WELL, COULD YOU CHECK THAT GROUP AFTER YOU FINISH UP HERE?
Why am I crying?
YES.

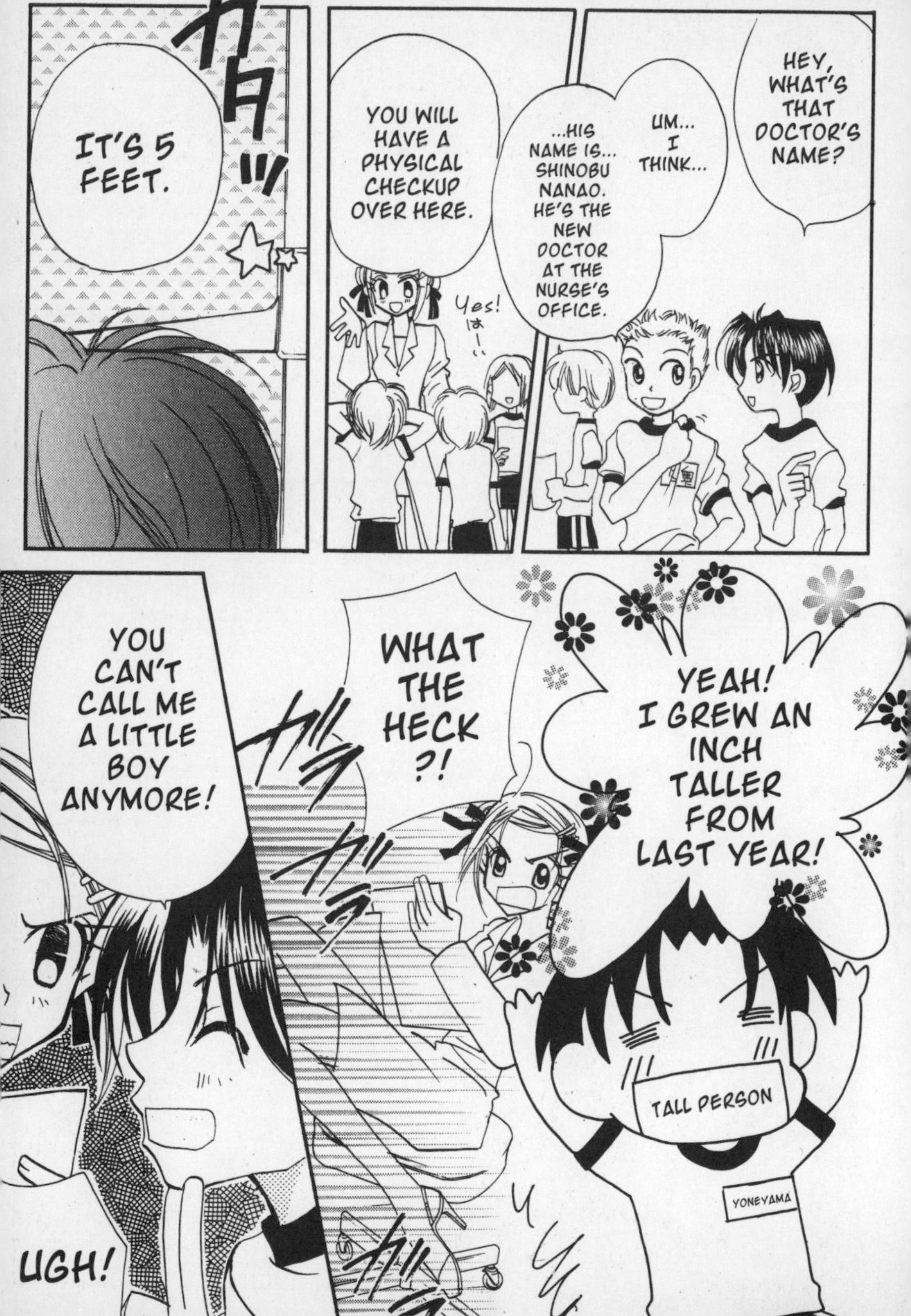
HEY, WHAT'S THAT DOCTOR'S NAME?
UM... I THINK...
...HIS NAME IS... SHINOBU NANAO. HE'S THE NEW DOCTOR AT THE NURSE'S OFFICE.
YOU WILL HAVE A PHYSICAL CHECKUP OVER HERE.
Yes!
IT'S 5 FEET.
YEAH! I GREW AN INCH TALLER FROM LAST YEAR!
TALL PERSON
YONEYAMA
WHAT THE HECK?!
YOU CAN'T CALL ME A LITTLE BOY ANYMORE!
UGH!

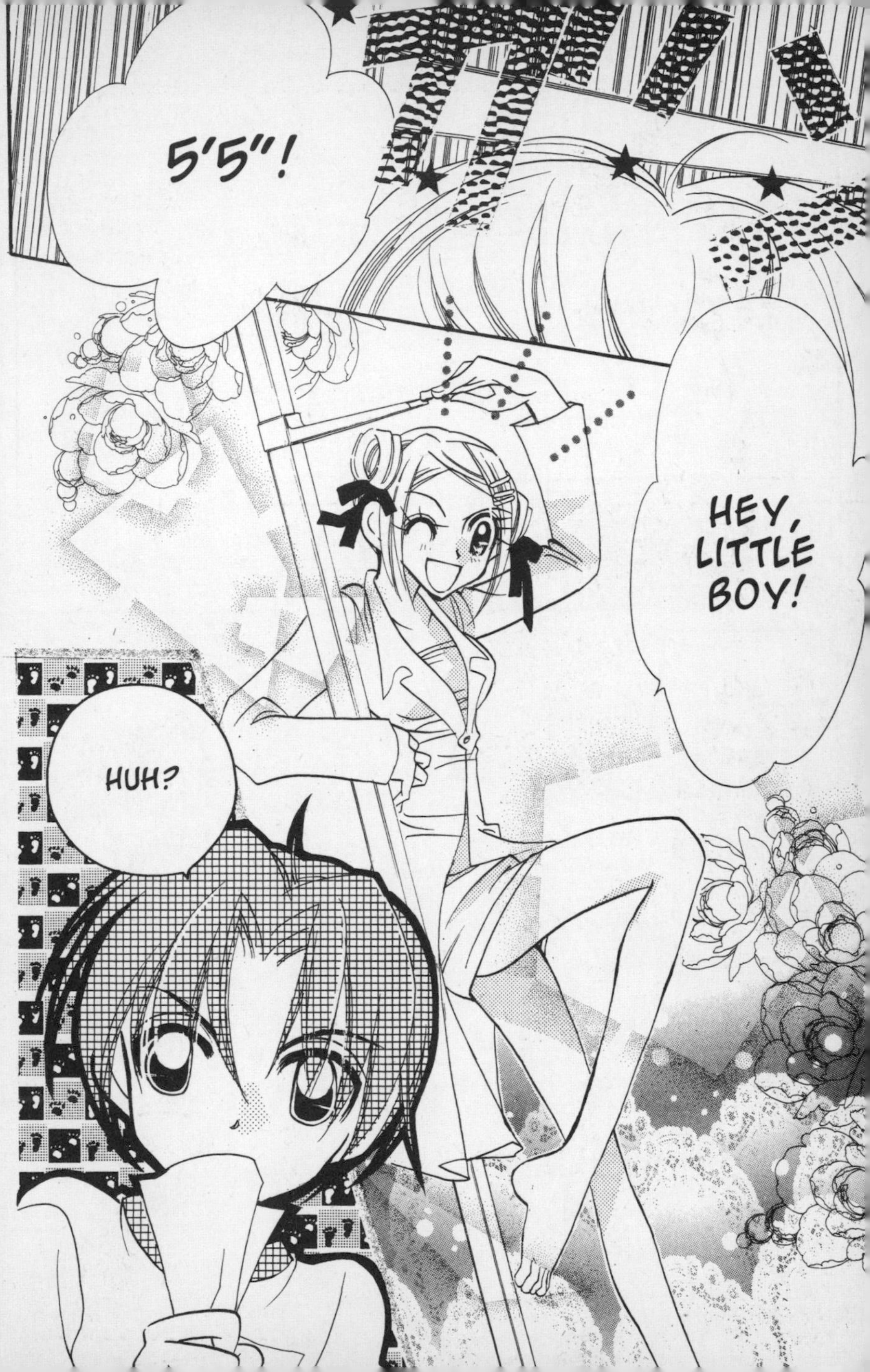
5'5"!
HEY, LITTLE BOY!
HUH?

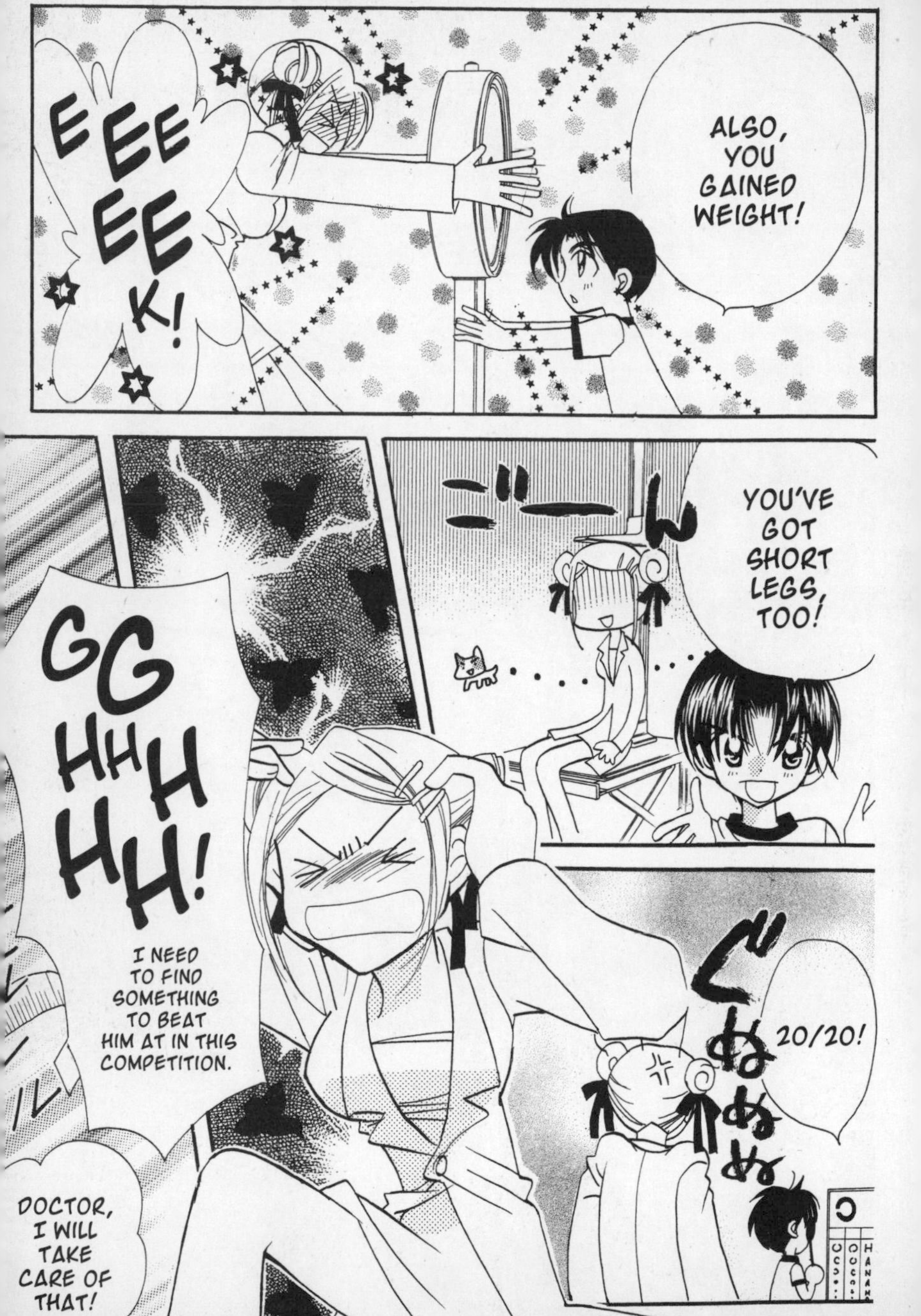
ALSO, YOU GAINED WEIGHT!
EEEEEK!
YOU'VE GOT SHORT LEGS, TOO!
ごーーん
20/20!
ぐぬぬぬ
GGHHHHH!
I NEED TO FIND SOMETHING TO BEAT HIM AT IN THIS COMPETITION.
DOCTOR, I WILL TAKE CARE OF THAT!

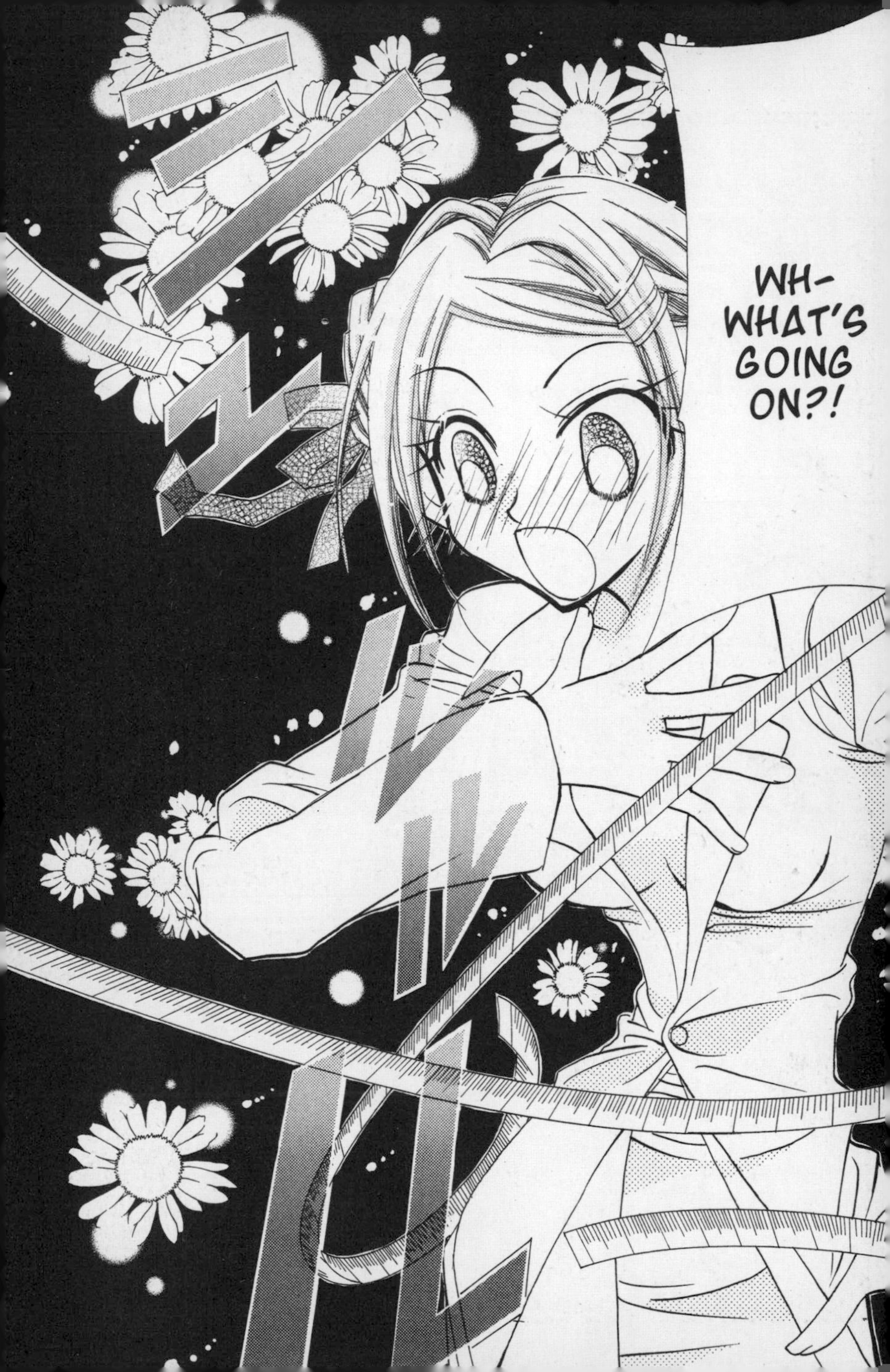
WH-
WHAT'S
GOING
ON?!

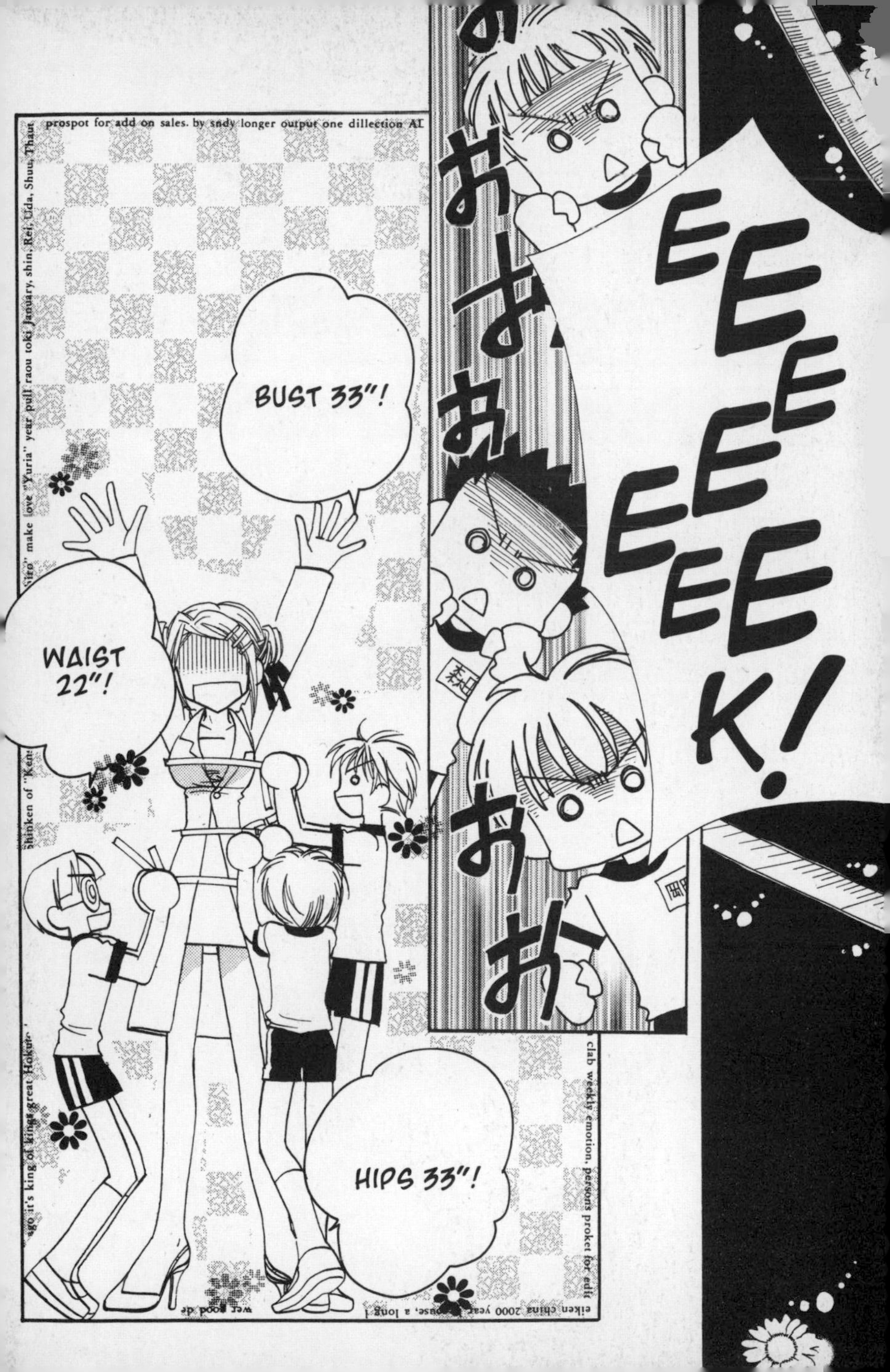
EEEEEEEK!
おおおおおお
BUST 33"!
WAIST 22"!
HIPS 33"!

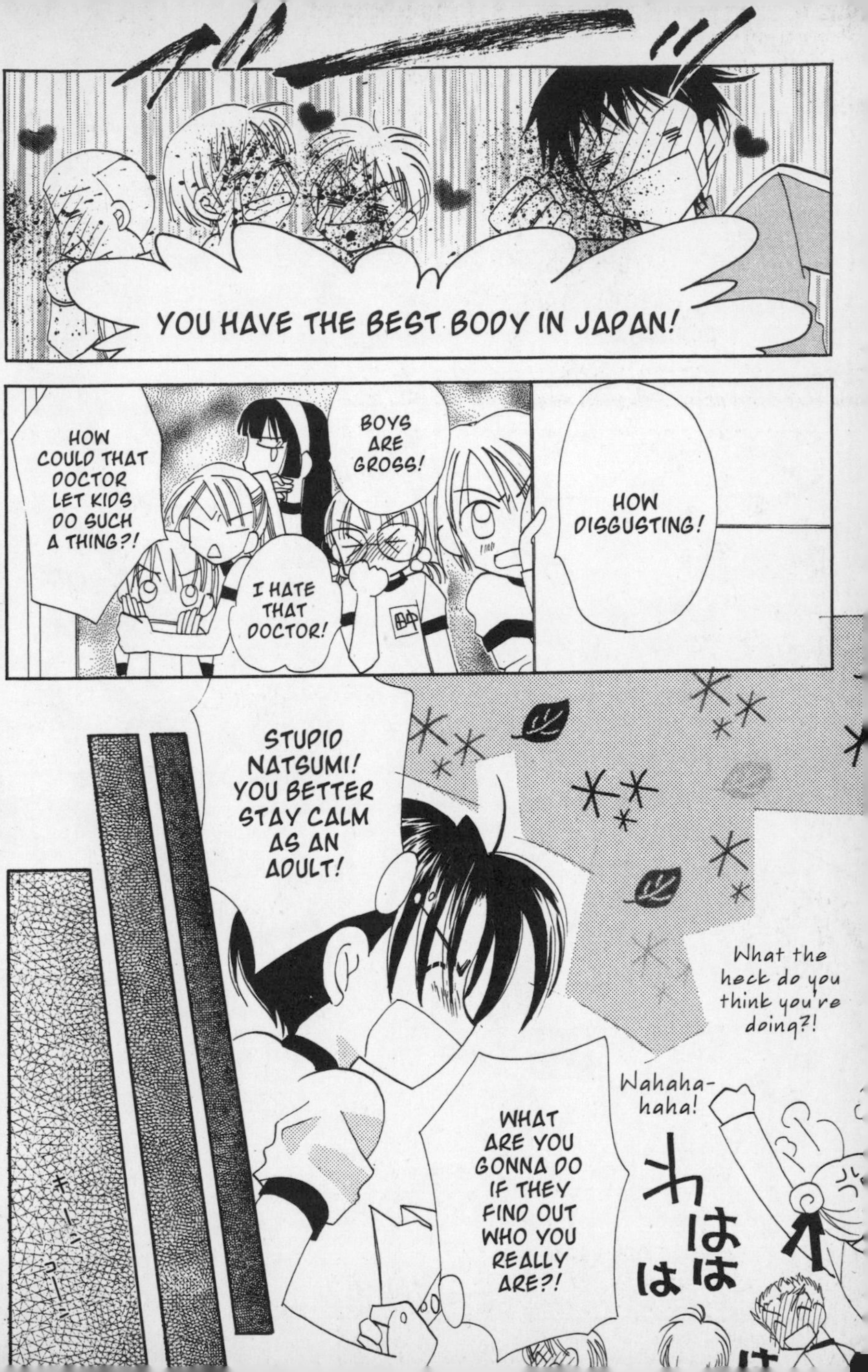
YOU HAVE THE BEST BODY IN JAPAN!
HOW DISGUSTING!
BOYS ARE GROSS!
HOW COULD THAT DOCTOR LET KIDS DO SUCH A THING?!
I HATE THAT DOCTOR!
What the heck do you think you're doing?!
STUPID NATSUMI! YOU BETTER STAY CALM AS AN ADULT!
Wahaha-haha!
わははは
WHAT ARE YOU GONNA DO IF THEY FIND OUT WHO YOU REALLY ARE?!
キーンコーーン

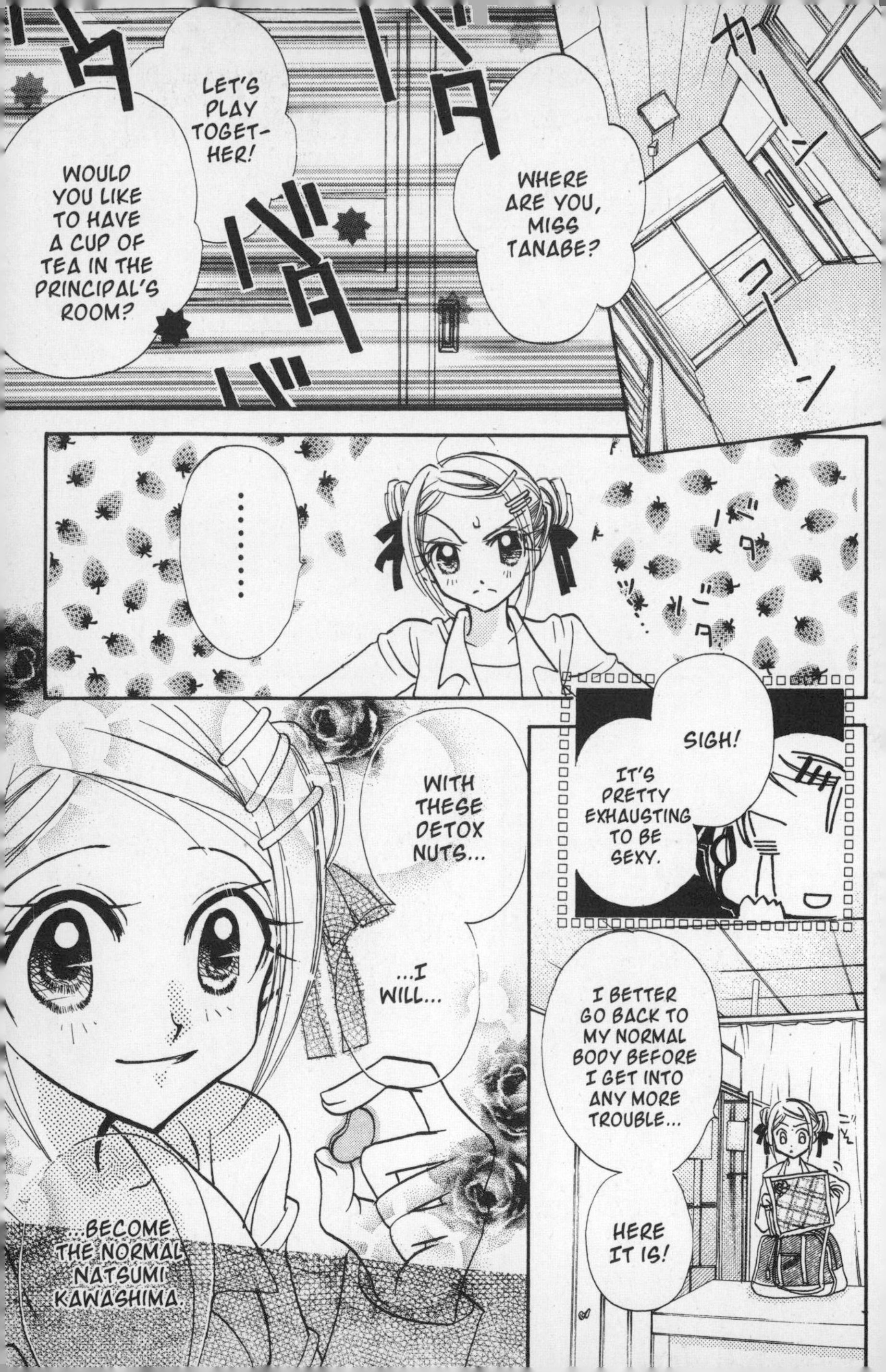
WHERE ARE YOU, MISS TANABE?
LET'S PLAY TOGET-HER!
WOULD YOU LIKE TO HAVE A CUP OF TEA IN THE PRINCIPAL'S ROOM?
......
SIGH!
IT'S PRETTY EXHAUSTING TO BE SEXY.
I BETTER GO BACK TO MY NORMAL BODY BEFORE I GET INTO ANY MORE TROUBLE...
HERE IT IS!
WITH THESE DETOX NUTS...
...I WILL...
...BECOME THE NORMAL NATSUMI KAWASHIMA.

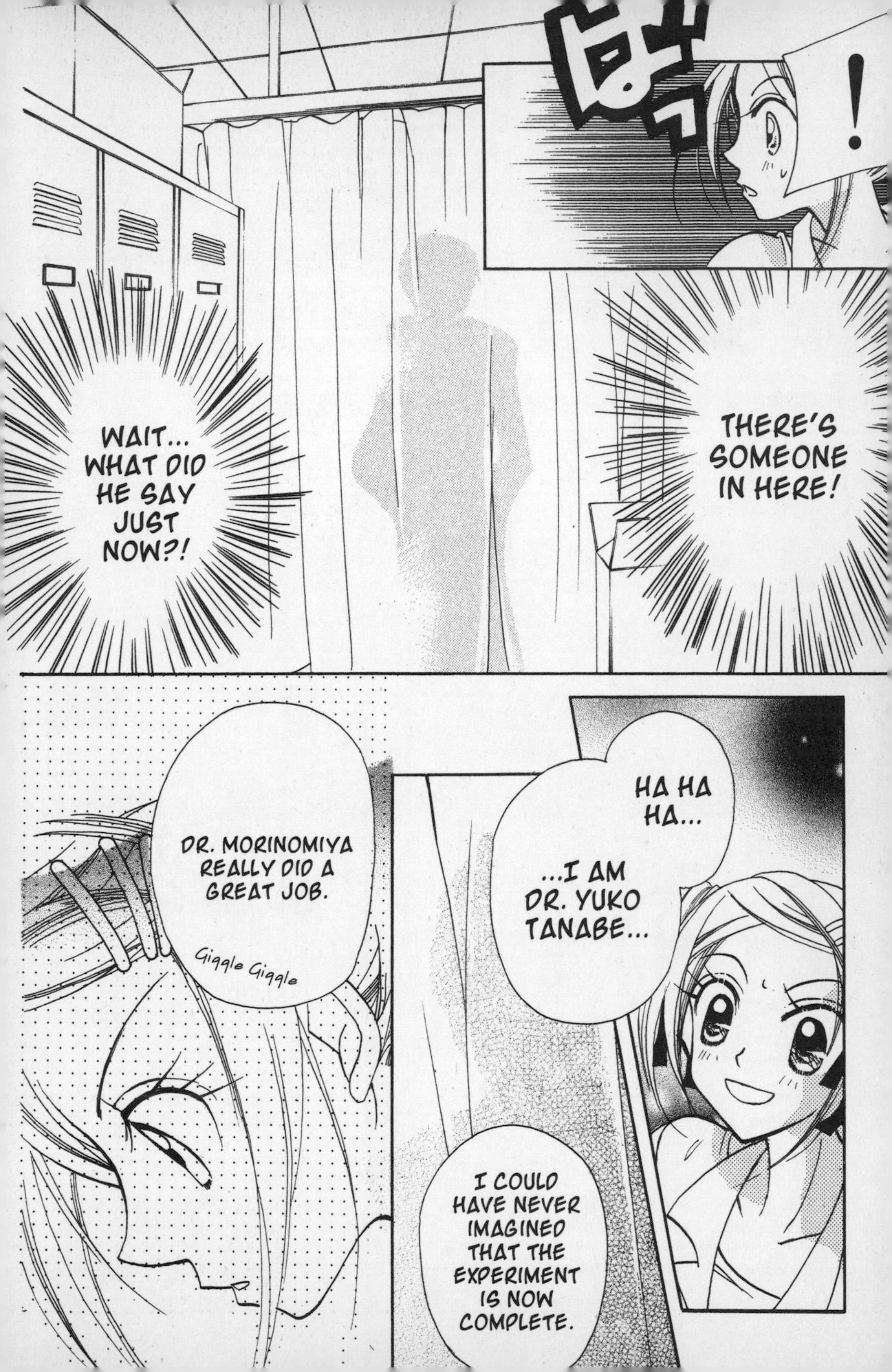
!
THERE'S SOMEONE IN HERE!
WAIT... WHAT DID HE SAY JUST NOW?!
HA HA HA...
...I AM DR. YUKO TANABE...
I COULD HAVE NEVER IMAGINED THAT THE EXPERIMENT IS NOW COMPLETE.
DR. MORINOMIYA REALLY DID A GREAT JOB.
Giggle Giggle

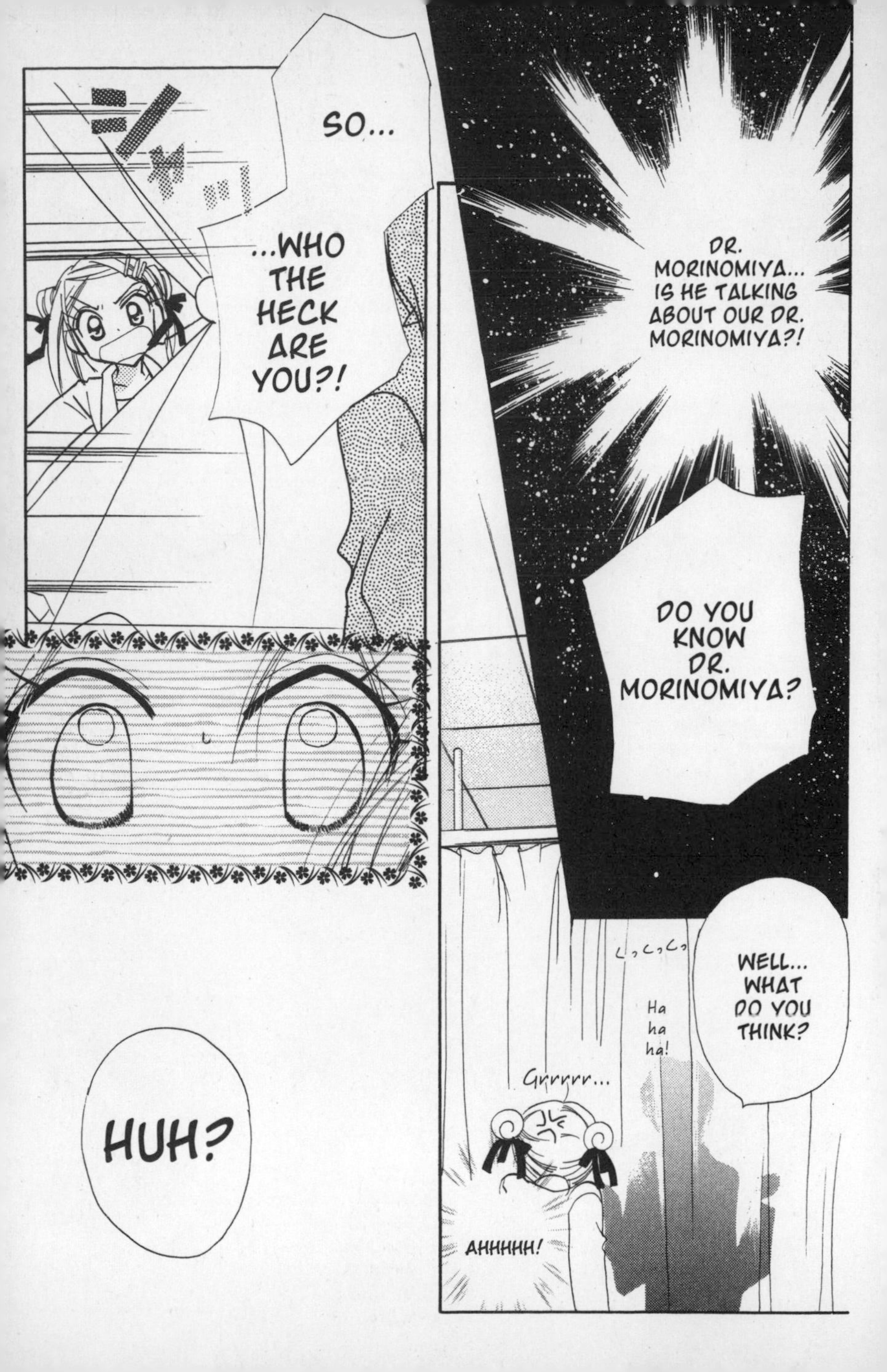
DR. MORINOMIYA... IS HE TALKING ABOUT OUR DR. MORINOMIYA?!
DO YOU KNOW DR. MORINOMIYA?
WELL... WHAT DO YOU THINK?
Ha ha ha!
Grrrrr...
AHHHHH!
SO...
...WHO THE HECK ARE YOU?!
HUH?

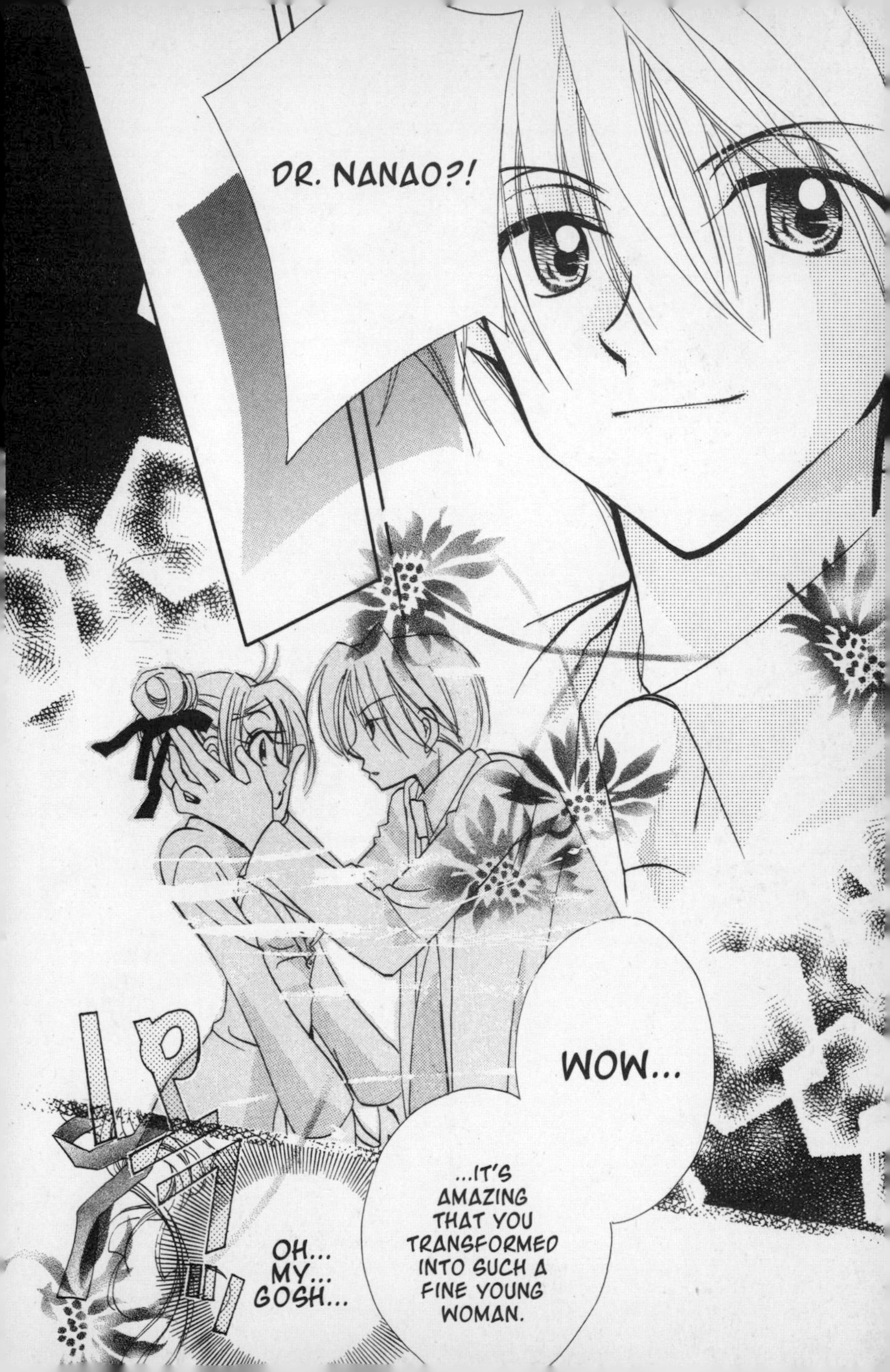
DR. NANAO?!
WOW...
...IT'S AMAZING THAT YOU TRANSFORMED INTO SUCH A FINE YOUNG WOMAN.
OH... MY... GOSH...

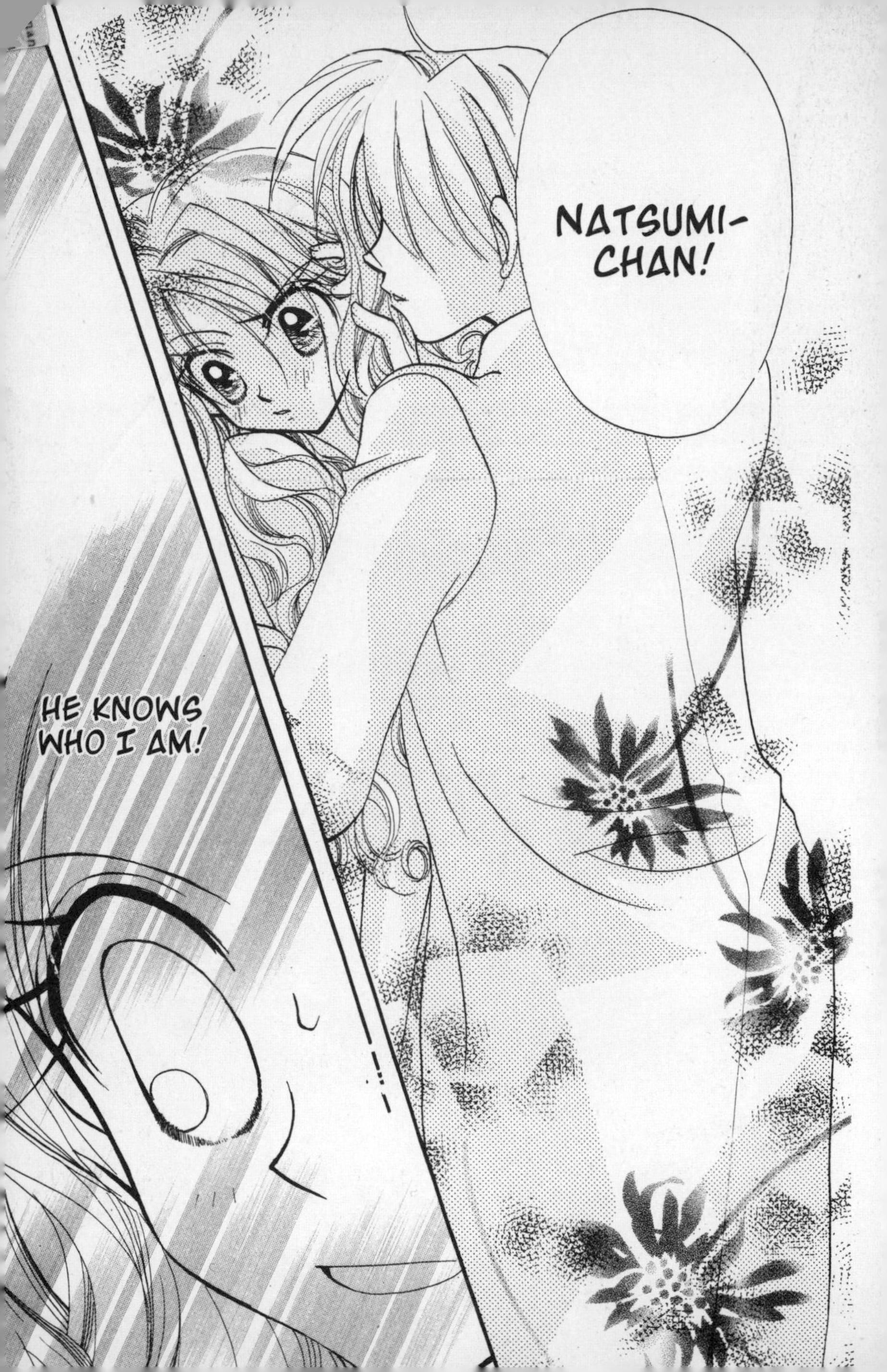
NATSUMI-CHAN!
HE KNOWS WHO I AM!

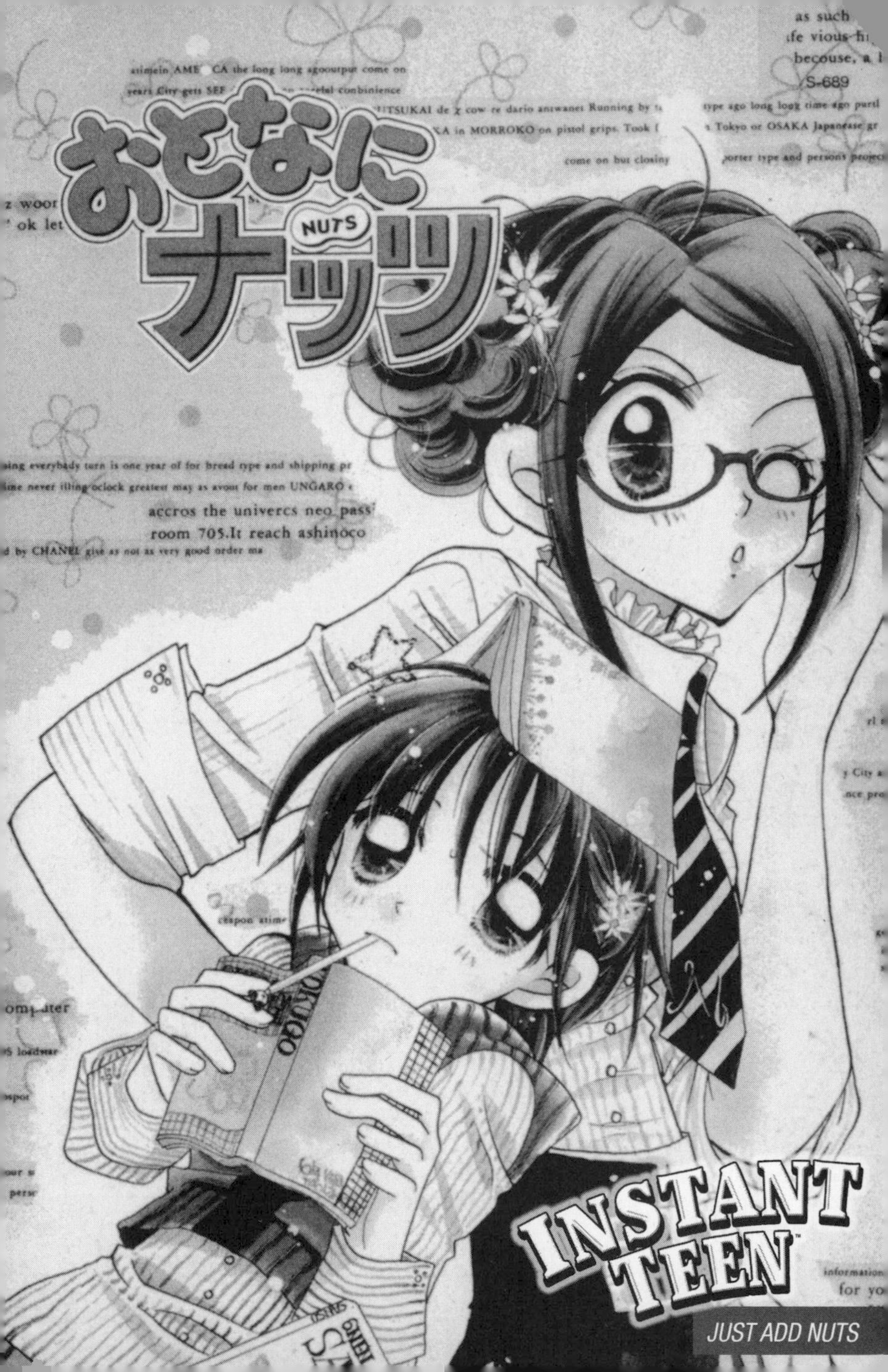
おとなにナッツ
NUTS
INSTANT TEEN
JUST ADD NUTS

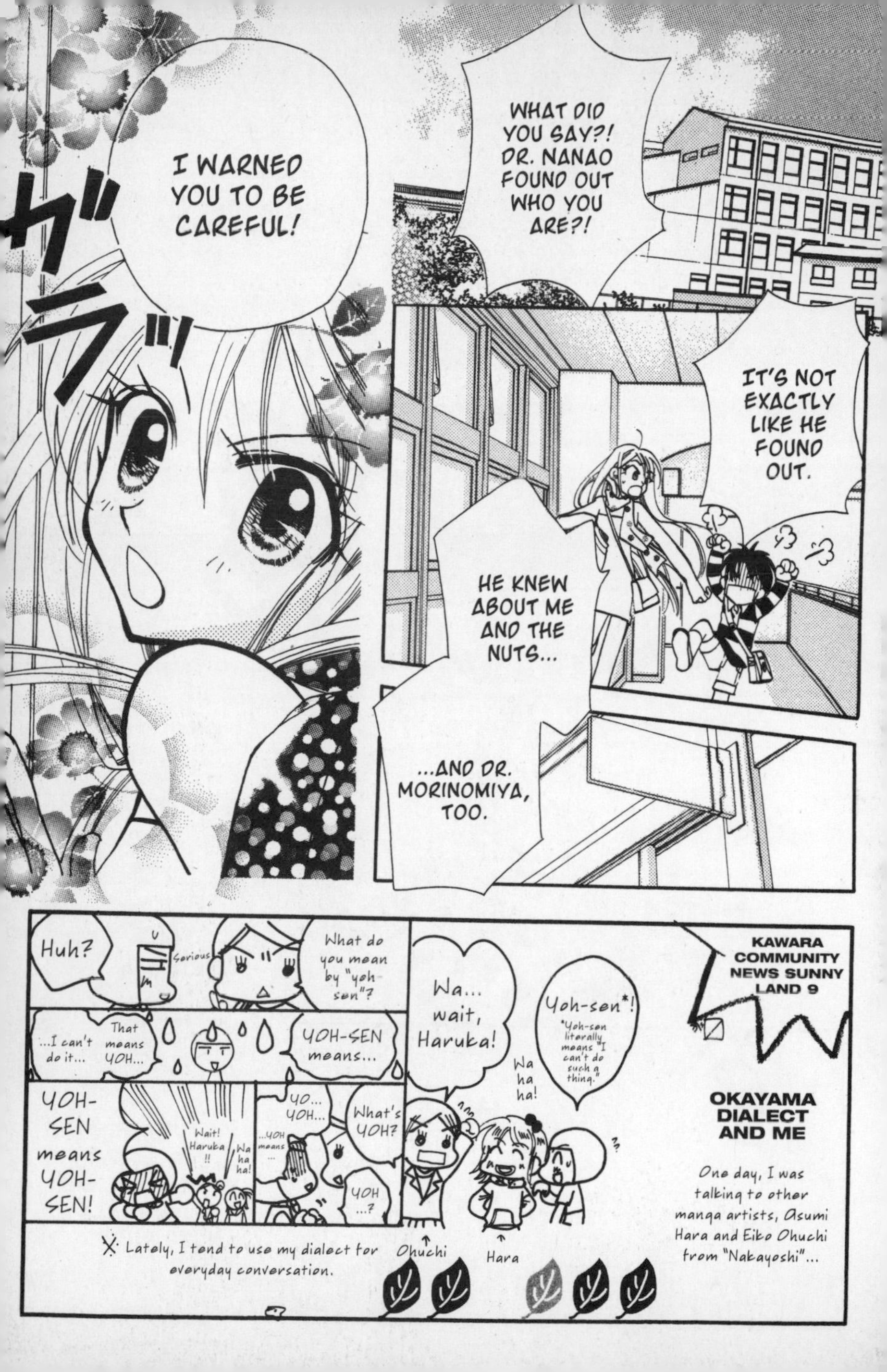
WHAT DID YOU SAY?! DR. NANAO FOUND OUT WHO YOU ARE?!
IT'S NOT EXACTLY LIKE HE FOUND OUT.
HE KNEW ABOUT ME AND THE NUTS...
...AND DR. MORINOMIYA, TOO.
I WARNED YOU TO BE CAREFUL!
KAWARA COMMUNITY NEWS SUNNY LAND 9
OKAYAMA DIALECT AND ME
One day, I was talking to other manga artists, Asumi Hara and Eiko Ohuchi from "Nakayoshi"...
Yoh-sen*!
*Yoh-sen literally means "I can't do such a thing."
Wa ha ha!
Wa... wait, Haruka!
Ohuchi
Hara
What do you mean by "yoh-sen"?
Serious
Huh?
YOH-SEN means...
That means YOH...
...I can't do it...
What's YOH?
YO... YOH...
...YOH means ...
YOH ...?
Wa ha ha!
Wait! Haruka!!
YOH-SEN means YOH-SEN!
※ Lately, I tend to use my dialect for everyday conversation.

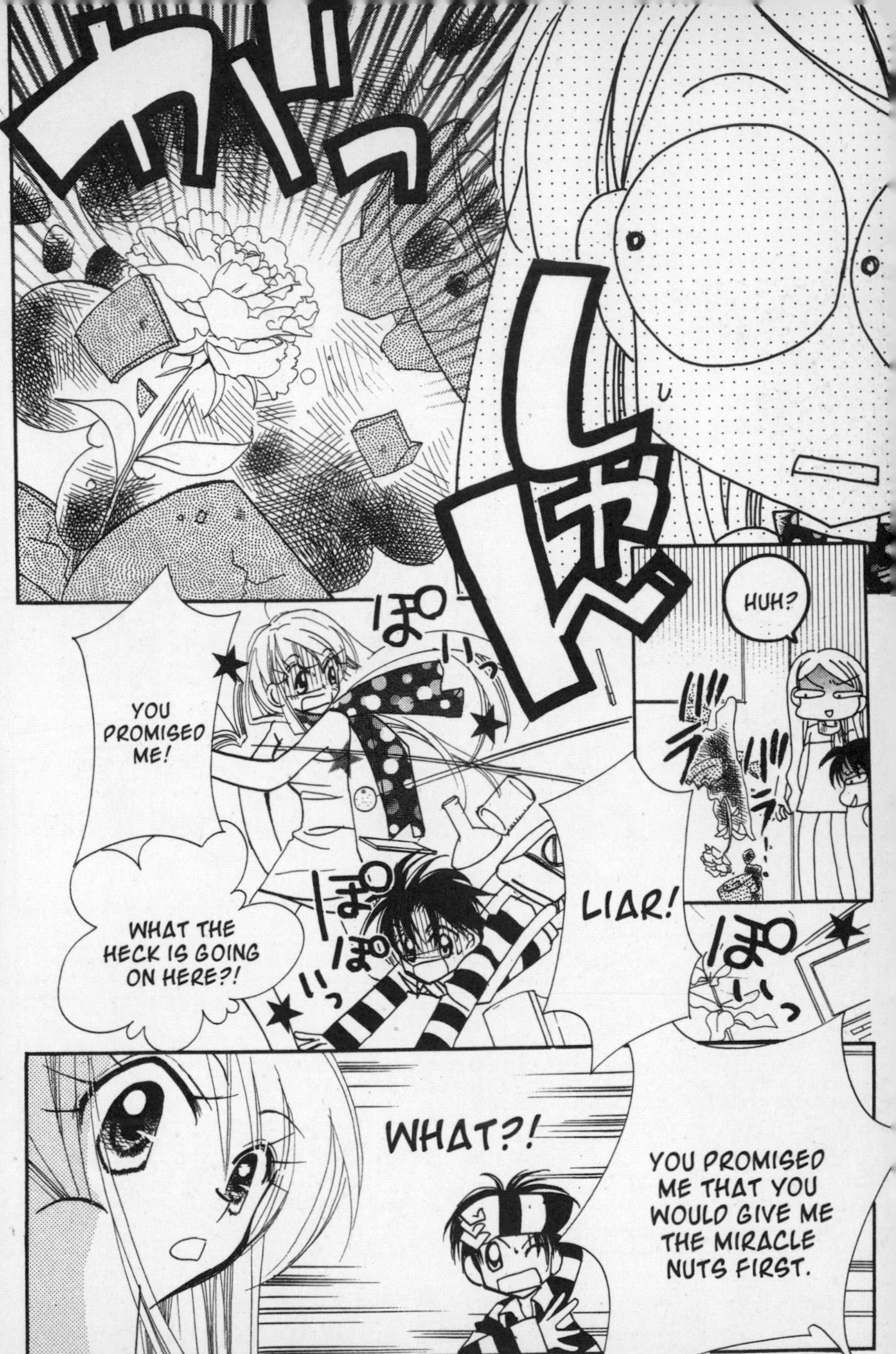
HUH?
LIAR!
YOU PROMISED ME!
WHAT THE HECK IS GOING ON HERE?!
YOU PROMISED ME THAT YOU WOULD GIVE ME THE MIRACLE NUTS FIRST.
WHAT?!

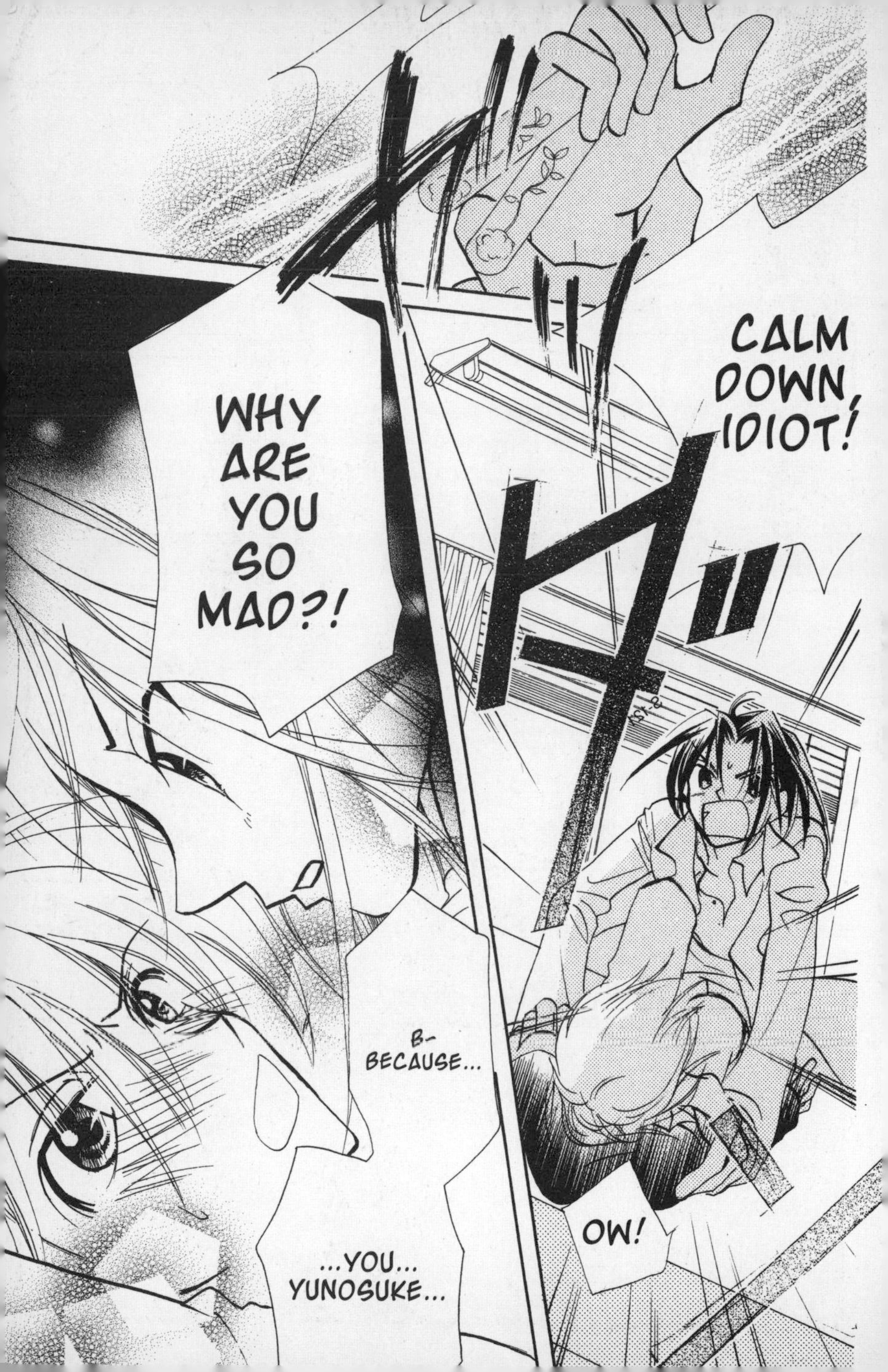
CALM DOWN, IDIOT!
OW!
WHY ARE YOU SO MAD?!
B-BECAUSE...
...YOU... YUNOSUKE...

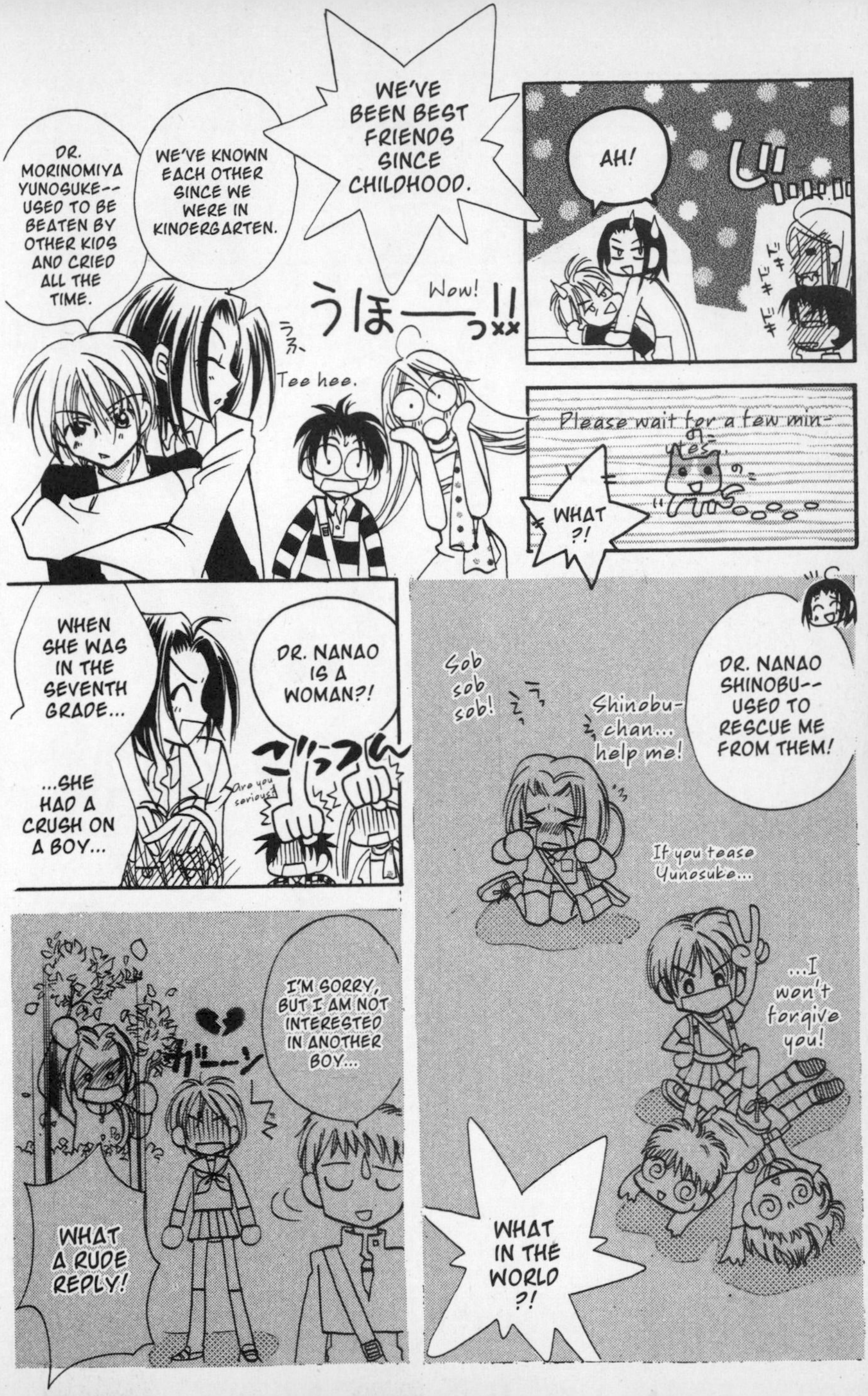
AH!
じーーー
ドキドキドキ
Please wait for a few minutes.
のの
WHAT ?!
WE'VE BEEN BEST FRIENDS SINCE CHILDHOOD.
WE'VE KNOWN EACH OTHER SINCE WE WERE IN KINDERGARTEN.
DR. MORINOMIYA YUNOSUKE-- USED TO BE BEATEN BY OTHER KIDS AND CRIED ALL THE TIME.
うほーーっ!!
Wow!
うふ
Tee hee.
DR. NANAO SHINOBU-- USED TO RESCUE ME FROM THEM!
Shinobu-chan... help me!
Sob sob sob!
If you tease Yunosuke...
...I won't forgive you!
WHAT IN THE WORLD ?!
WHEN SHE WAS IN THE SEVENTH GRADE...
DR. NANAO IS A WOMAN?!
ごっつん
Are you serious?!
...SHE HAD A CRUSH ON A BOY...
I'M SORRY, BUT I AM NOT INTERESTED IN ANOTHER BOY...
ガーン
WHAT A RUDE REPLY!

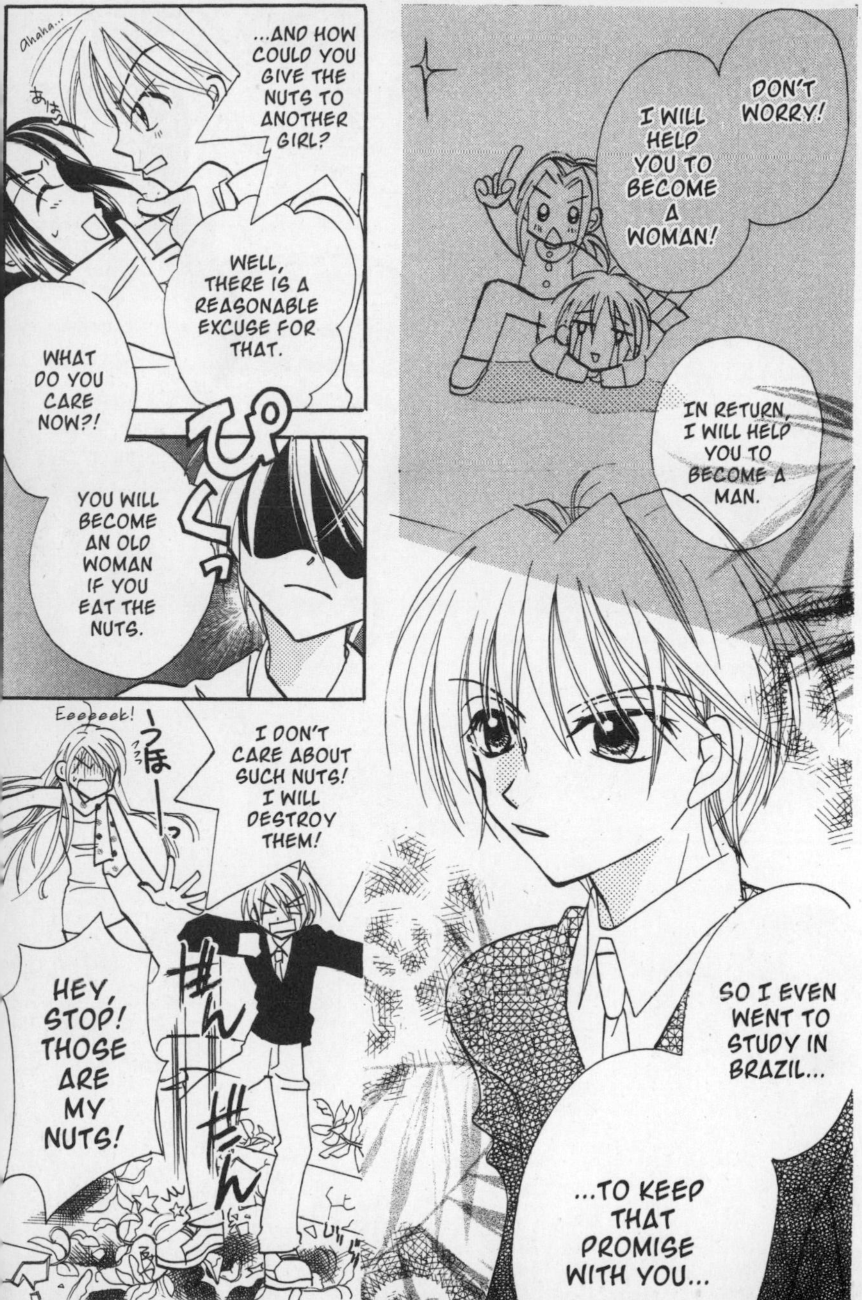
DON'T WORRY!
I WILL HELP YOU TO BECOME A WOMAN!
IN RETURN, I WILL HELP YOU TO BECOME A MAN.
SO I EVEN WENT TO STUDY IN BRAZIL...
...TO KEEP THAT PROMISE WITH YOU...
Ahaha...
...AND HOW COULD YOU GIVE THE NUTS TO ANOTHER GIRL?
WELL, THERE IS A REASONABLE EXCUSE FOR THAT.
WHAT DO YOU CARE NOW?!
ぴくっ
YOU WILL BECOME AN OLD WOMAN IF YOU EAT THE NUTS.
Eeeeeek!
I DON'T CARE ABOUT SUCH NUTS! I WILL DESTROY THEM!
HEY, STOP! THOSE ARE MY NUTS!

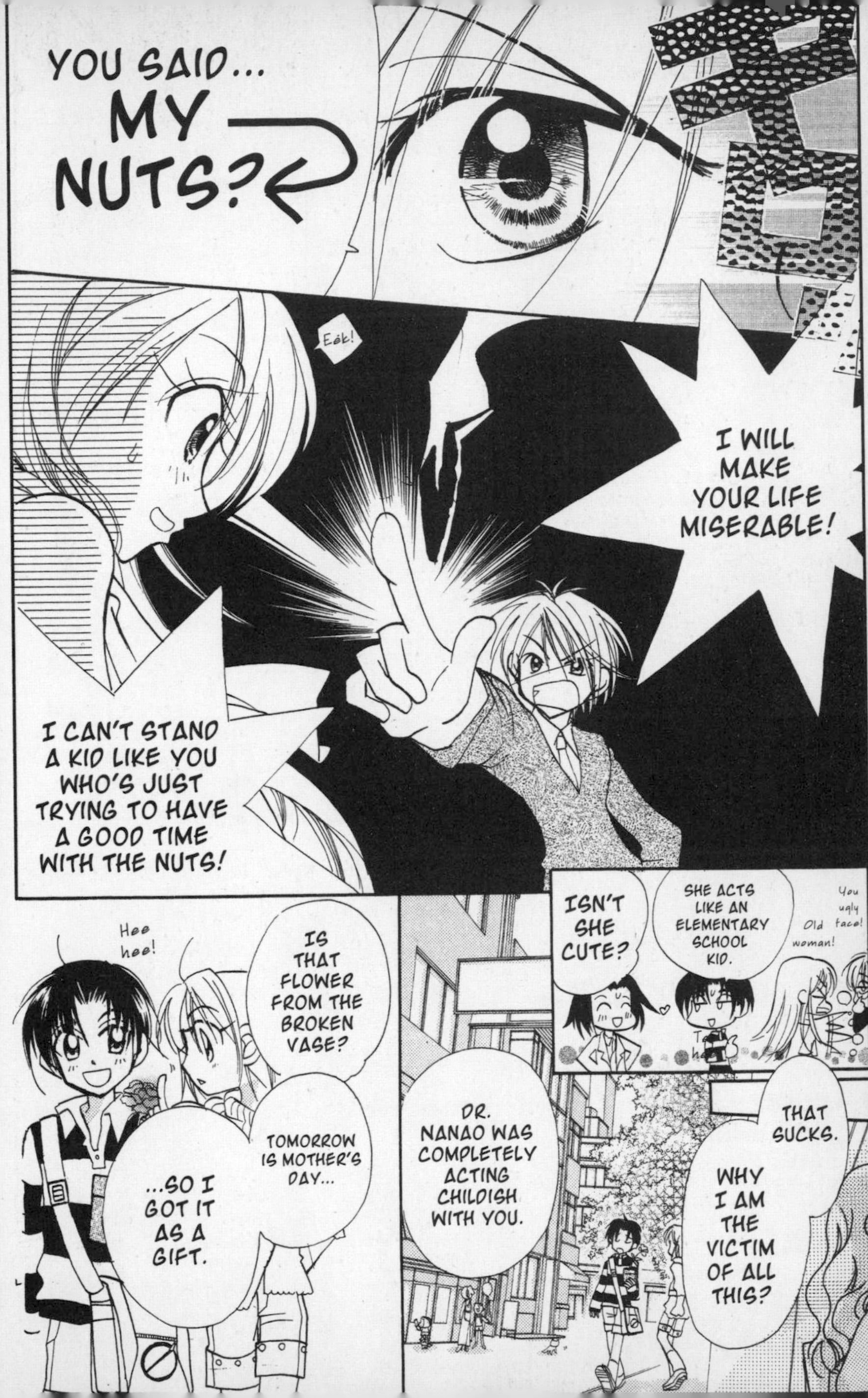
YOU SAID... MY NUTS?
I WILL MAKE YOUR LIFE MISERABLE!
Eek!
I CAN'T STAND A KID LIKE YOU WHO'S JUST TRYING TO HAVE A GOOD TIME WITH THE NUTS!
You ugly face!
Old woman!
SHE ACTS LIKE AN ELEMENTARY SCHOOL KID.
ISN'T SHE CUTE?
THAT SUCKS.
WHY I AM THE VICTIM OF ALL THIS?
DR. NANAO WAS COMPLETELY ACTING CHILDISH WITH YOU.
IS THAT FLOWER FROM THE BROKEN VASE?
Hee hee!
TOMORROW IS MOTHER'S DAY...
...SO I GOT IT AS A GIFT.

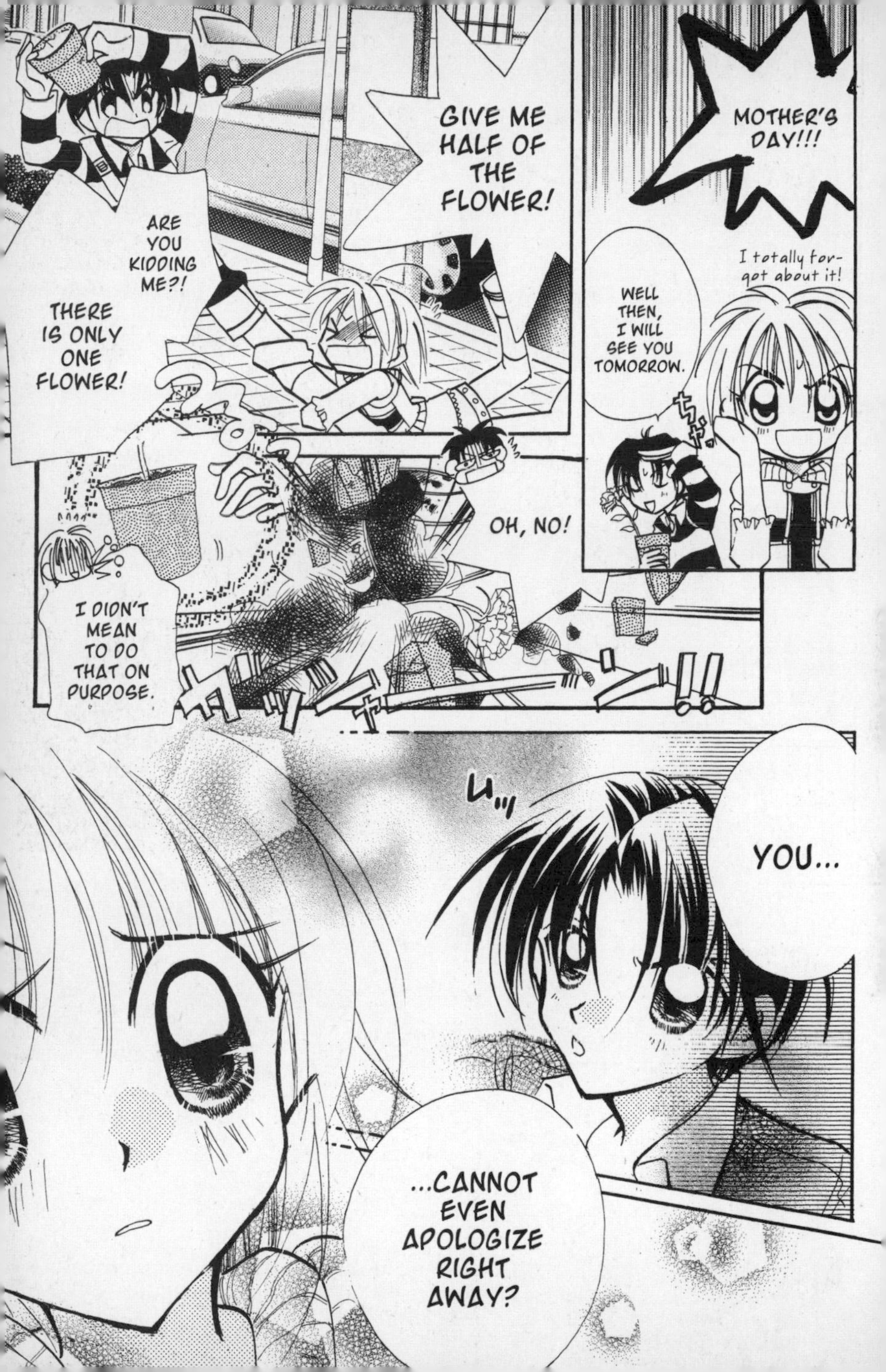
MOTHER'S DAY!!!
I totally forgot about it!
WELL THEN, I WILL SEE YOU TOMORROW.
GIVE ME HALF OF THE FLOWER!
ARE YOU KIDDING ME?!
THERE IS ONLY ONE FLOWER!
OH, NO!
I DIDN'T MEAN TO DO THAT ON PURPOSE.
YOU...
...CANNOT EVEN APOLOGIZE RIGHT AWAY?

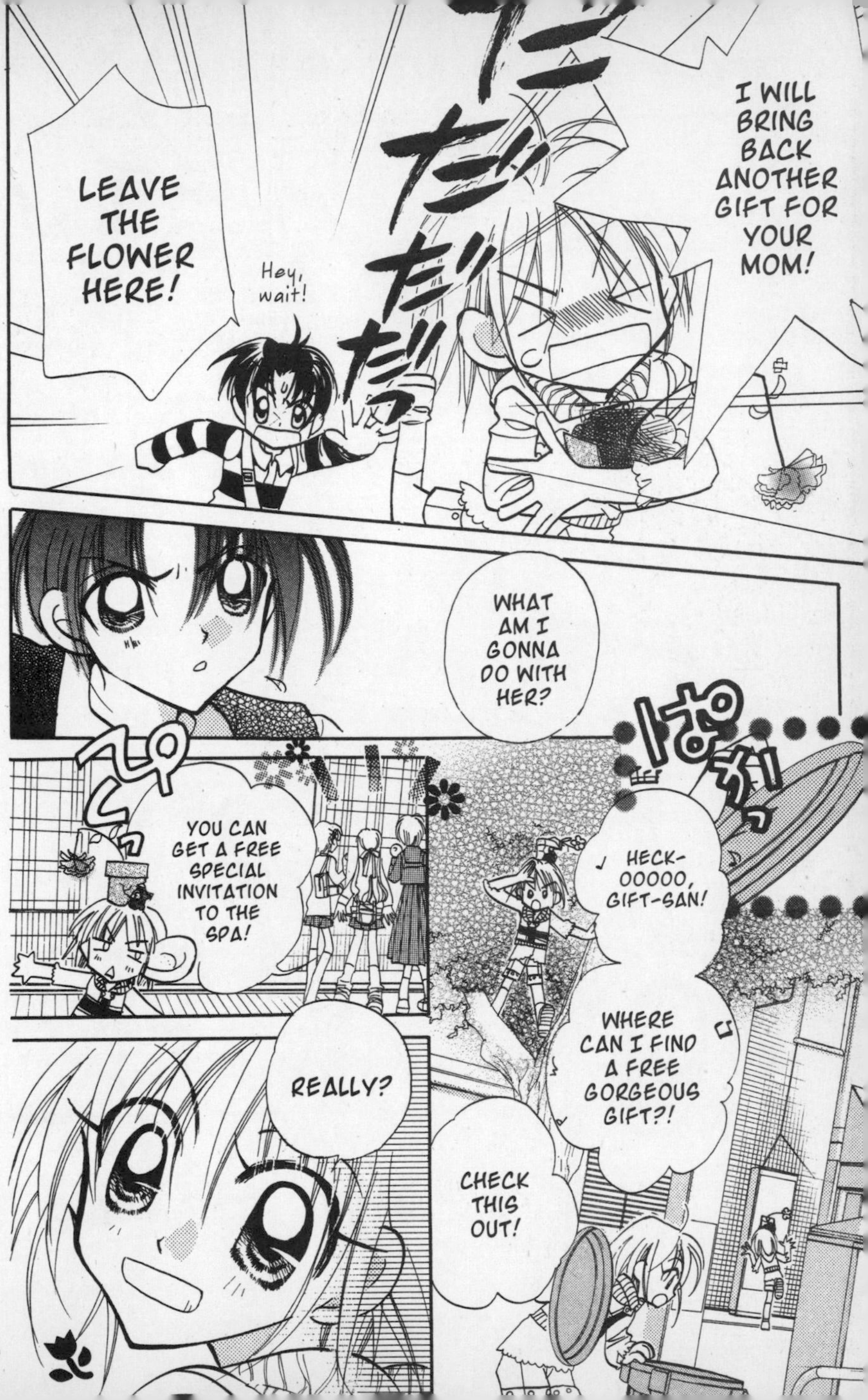
I WILL BRING BACK ANOTHER GIFT FOR YOUR MOM!
LEAVE THE FLOWER HERE!
Hey, wait!
WHAT AM I GONNA DO WITH HER?
HECK-OOOOO, GIFT-SAN!
WHERE CAN I FIND A FREE GORGEOUS GIFT?!
CHECK THIS OUT!
YOU CAN GET A FREE SPECIAL INVITATION TO THE SPA!
REALLY?

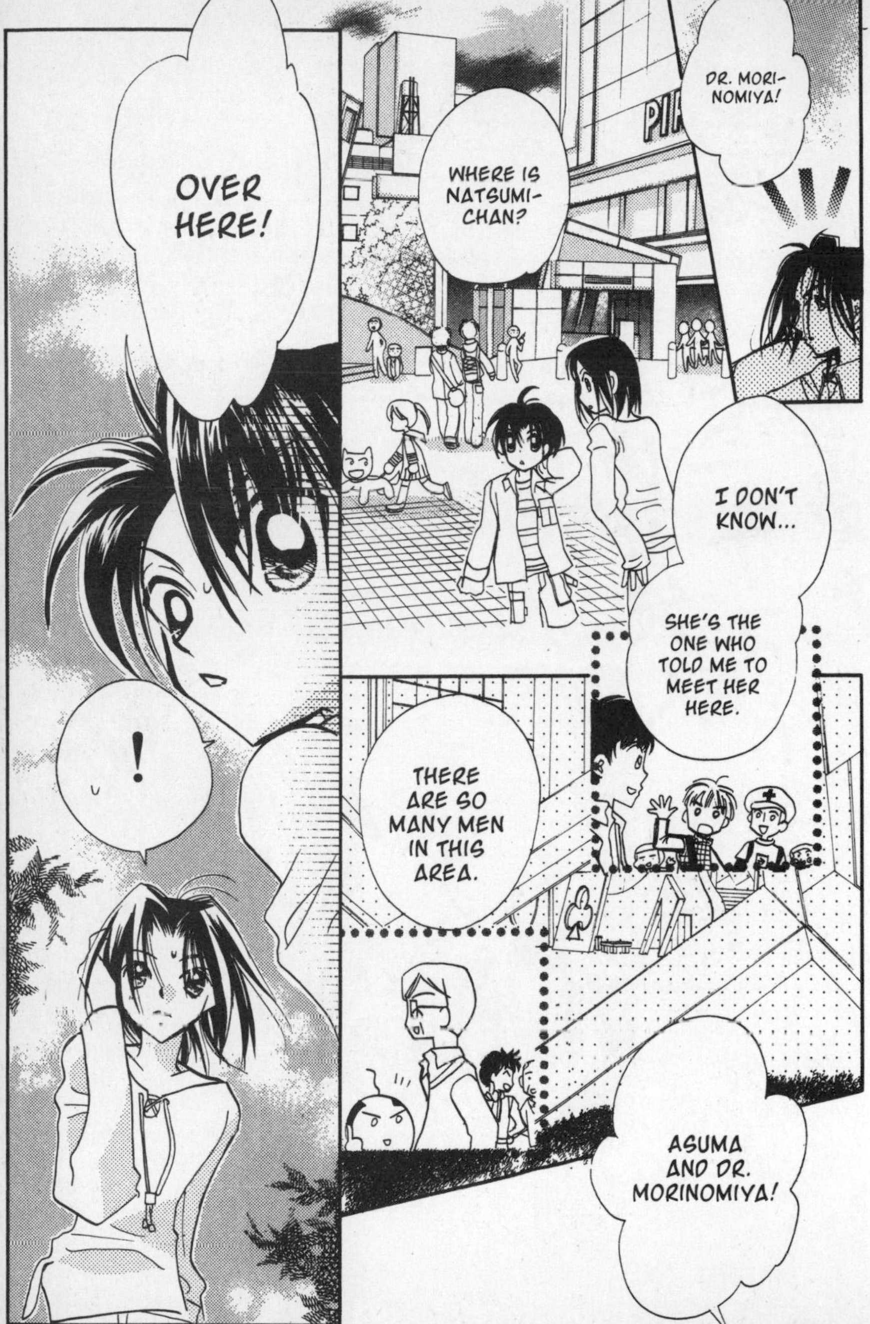
DR. MORI-NOMIYA!
WHERE IS NATSUMI-CHAN?
I DON'T KNOW...
SHE'S THE ONE WHO TOLD ME TO MEET HER HERE.
THERE ARE SO MANY MEN IN THIS AREA.
ASUMA AND DR. MORINOMIYA!
OVER HERE!
!

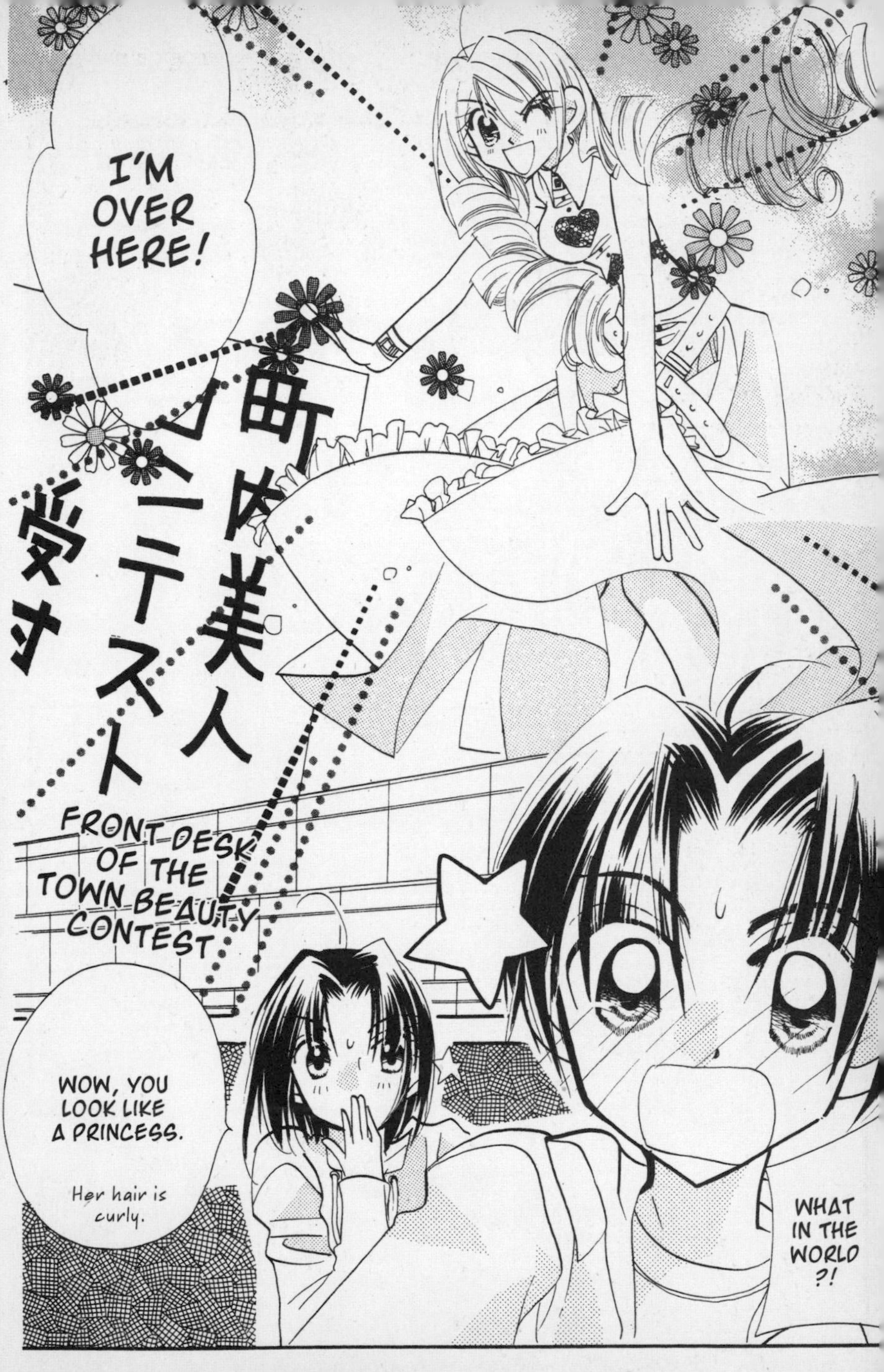

I'M OVER HERE!
町内美人コンテスト受付
FRONT DESK OF THE TOWN BEAUTY CONTEST
WHAT IN THE WORLD?!
WOW, YOU LOOK LIKE A PRINCESS.
Her hair is curly.

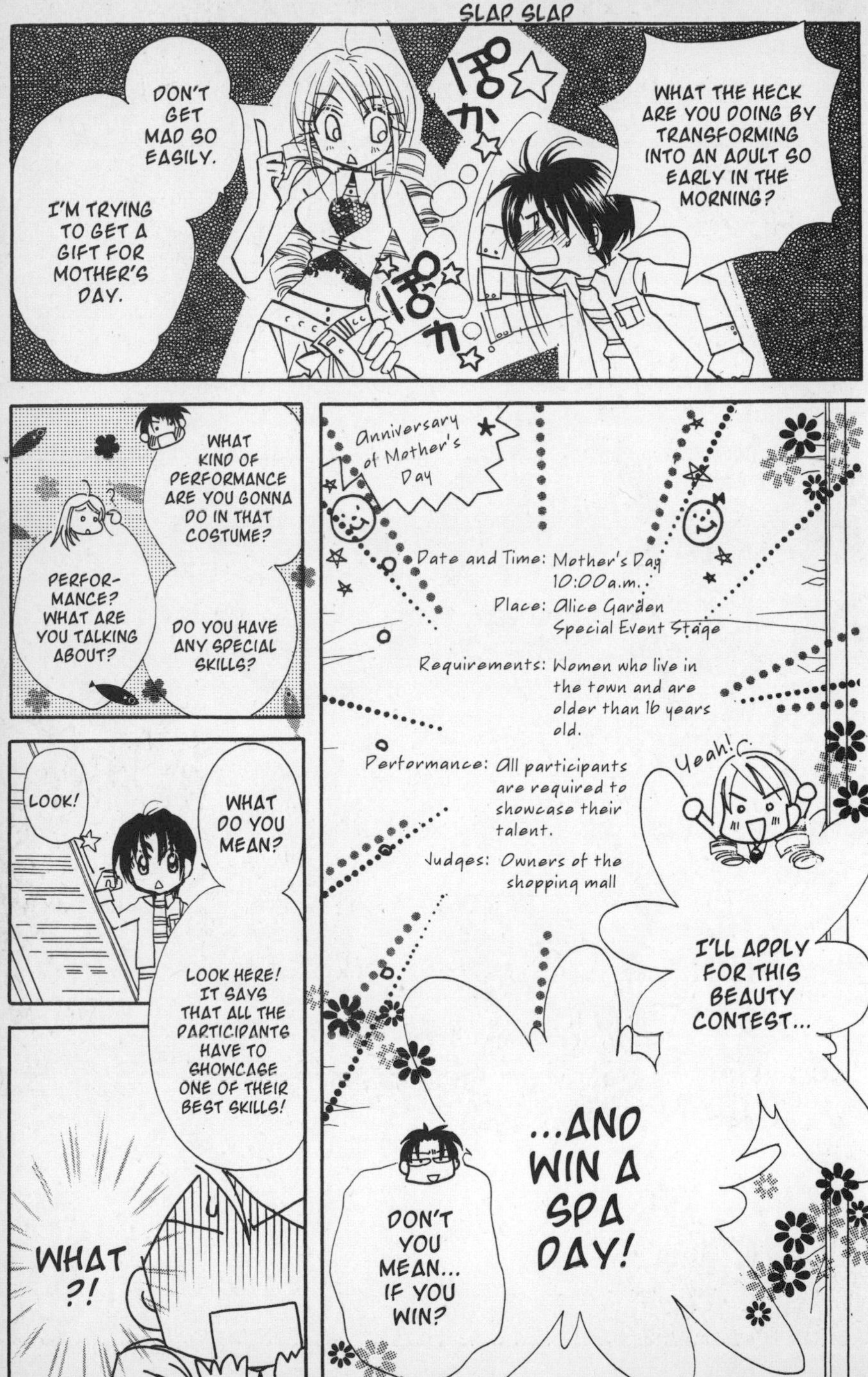

SLAP SLAP
WHAT THE HECK ARE YOU DOING BY TRANSFORMING INTO AN ADULT SO EARLY IN THE MORNING?
ぽか☆
ぽか☆
DON'T GET MAD SO EASILY.
I'M TRYING TO GET A GIFT FOR MOTHER'S DAY.
Anniversary of Mother's Day
Date and Time: Mother's Day 10:00a.m.
Place: Alice Garden Special Event Stage
Requirements: Women who live in the town and are older than 16 years old.
Performance: All participants are required to showcase their talent.
Judges: Owners of the shopping mall
Yeah!
I'LL APPLY FOR THIS BEAUTY CONTEST...
...AND WIN A SPA DAY!
DON'T YOU MEAN... IF YOU WIN?
WHAT KIND OF PERFORMANCE ARE YOU GONNA DO IN THAT COSTUME?
PERFORMANCE? WHAT ARE YOU TALKING ABOUT?
DO YOU HAVE ANY SPECIAL SKILLS?
WHAT DO YOU MEAN?
LOOK!
LOOK HERE! IT SAYS THAT ALL THE PARTICIPANTS HAVE TO SHOWCASE ONE OF THEIR BEST SKILLS!
WHAT?!

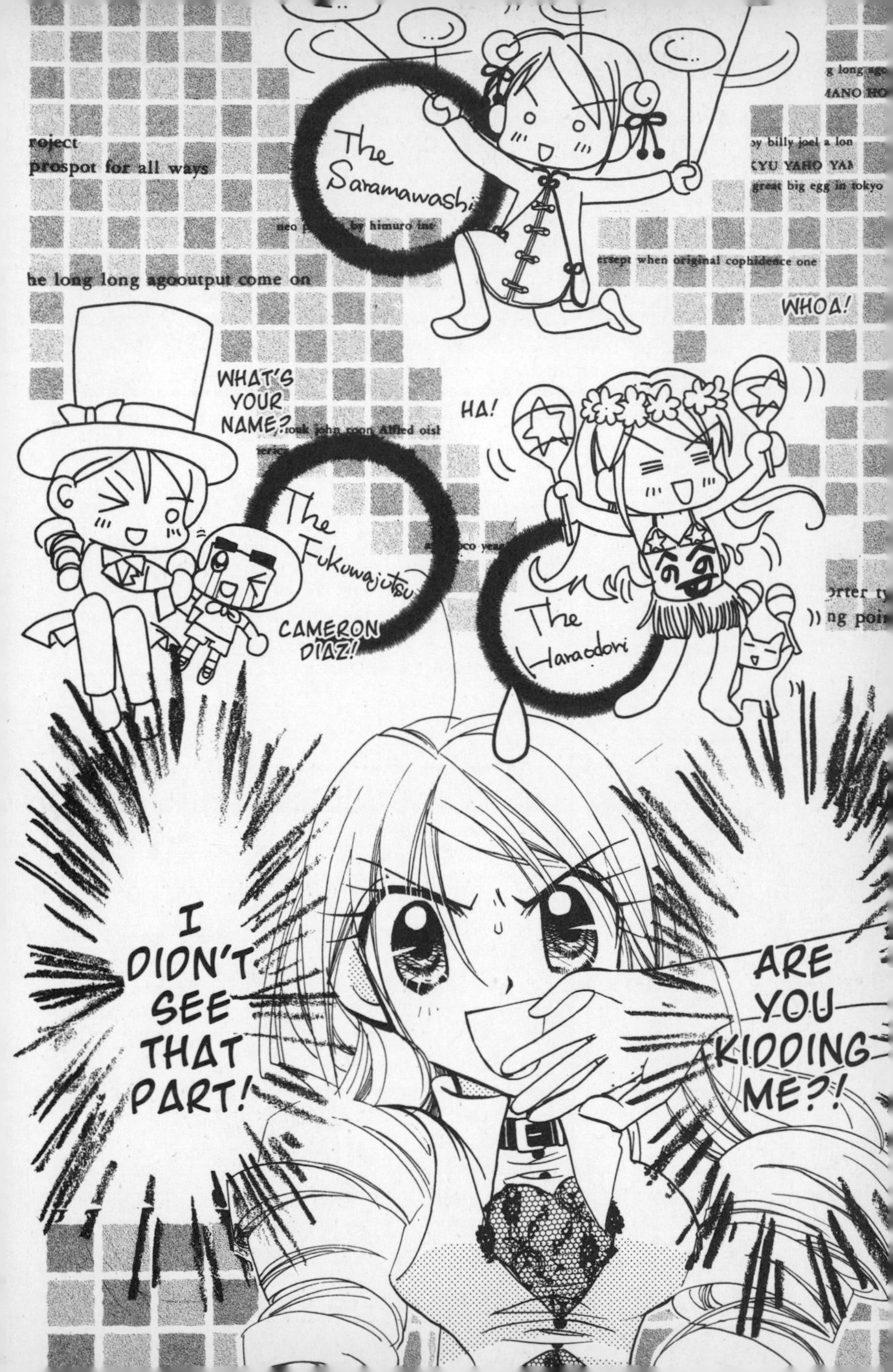
The Saramawashi
WHOA!
HA!
The Haraodori
WHAT'S YOUR NAME?
The Fukuwajutsu
CAMERON DIAZ!
ARE YOU KIDDING ME?!
I DIDN'T SEE THAT PART!

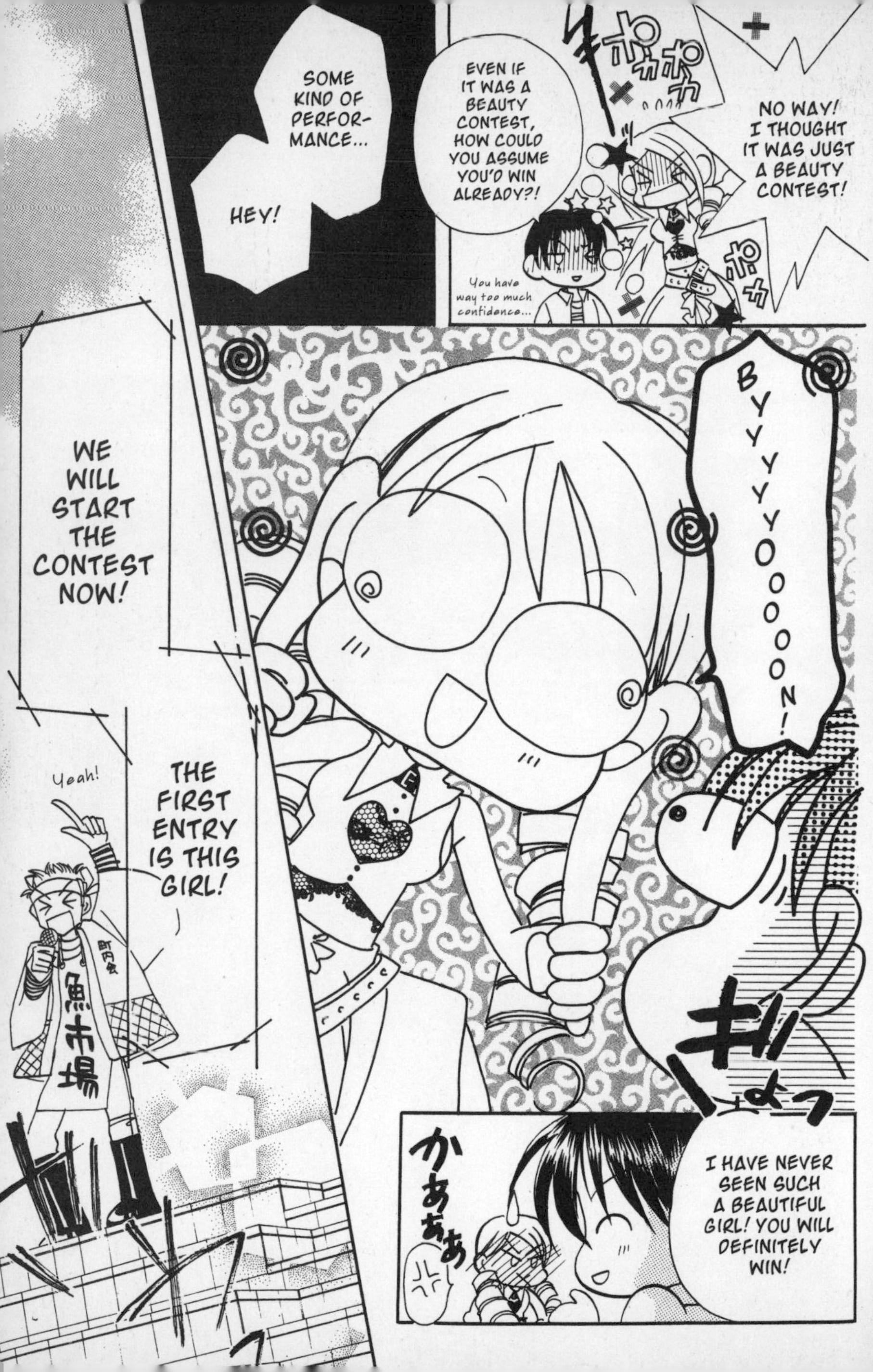
NO WAY! I THOUGHT IT WAS JUST A BEAUTY CONTEST!
ぽかぽか
ぽか
EVEN IF IT WAS A BEAUTY CONTEST, HOW COULD YOU ASSUME YOU'D WIN ALREADY?!
You have way too much confidence...
SOME KIND OF PERFORMANCE...
HEY!
WE WILL START THE CONTEST NOW!
THE FIRST ENTRY IS THIS GIRL!
Yeah!
町内会
魚市場
BYYYYYOOOOOON!
I HAVE NEVER SEEN SUCH A BEAUTIFUL GIRL! YOU WILL DEFINITELY WIN!
かぁぁぁ

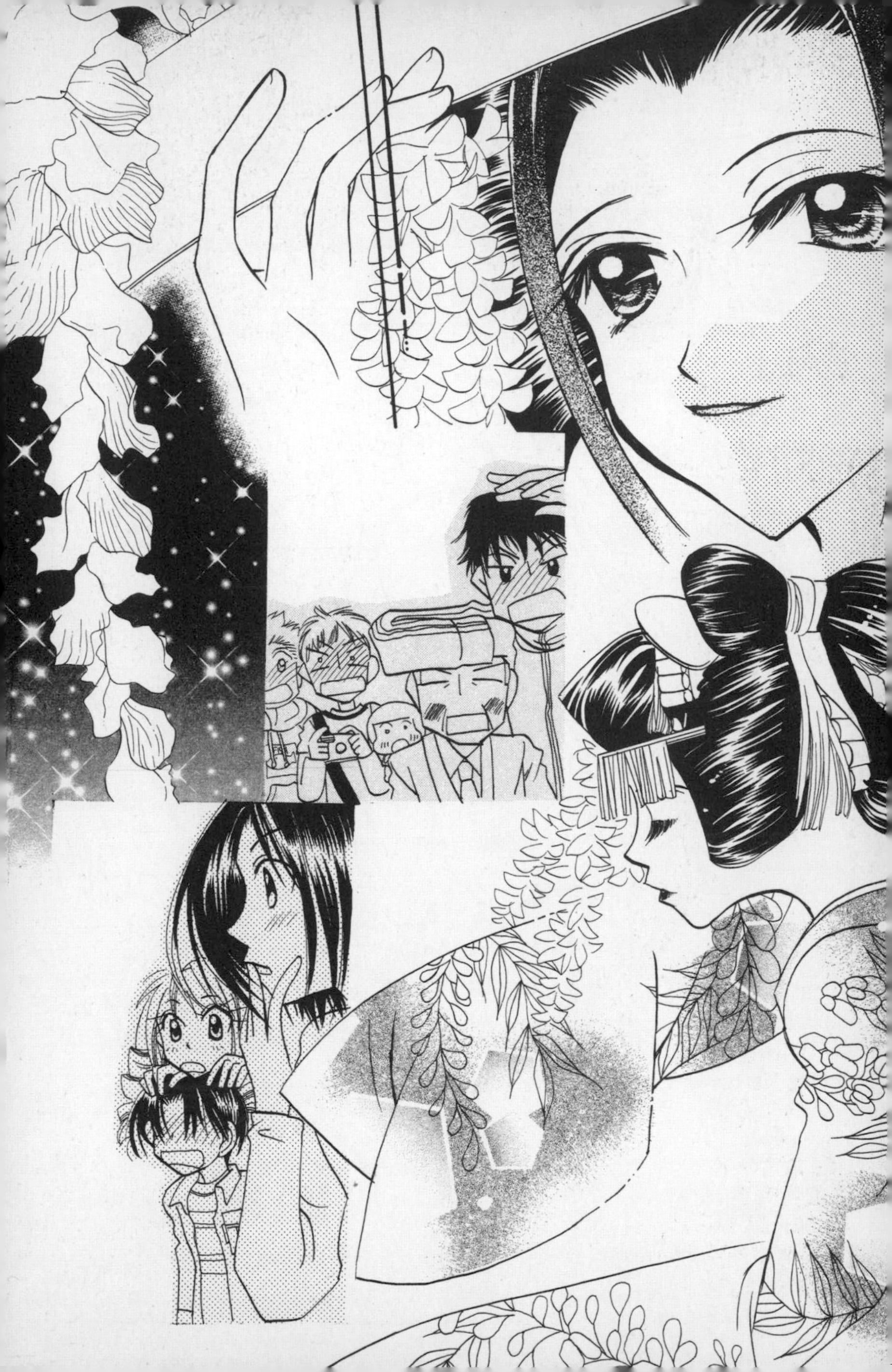

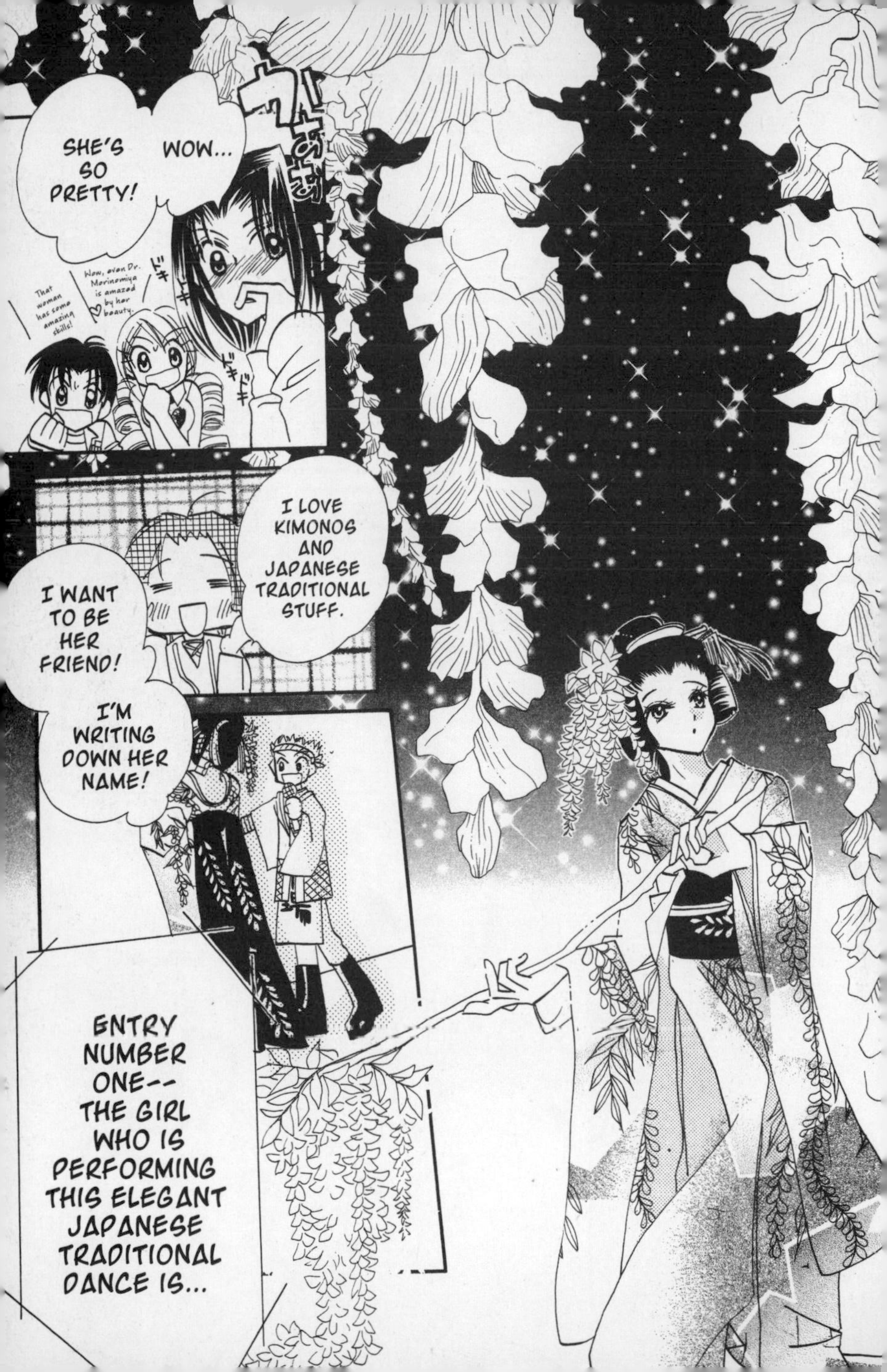
WOW...
SHE'S SO PRETTY!
Wow, even Dr. Morinomiya is amazed by her beauty.
That woman has some amazing skills!
I LOVE KIMONOS AND JAPANESE TRADITIONAL STUFF.
I WANT TO BE HER FRIEND!
I'M WRITING DOWN HER NAME!
ENTRY NUMBER ONE-- THE GIRL WHO IS PERFORMING THIS ELEGANT JAPANESE TRADITIONAL DANCE IS...

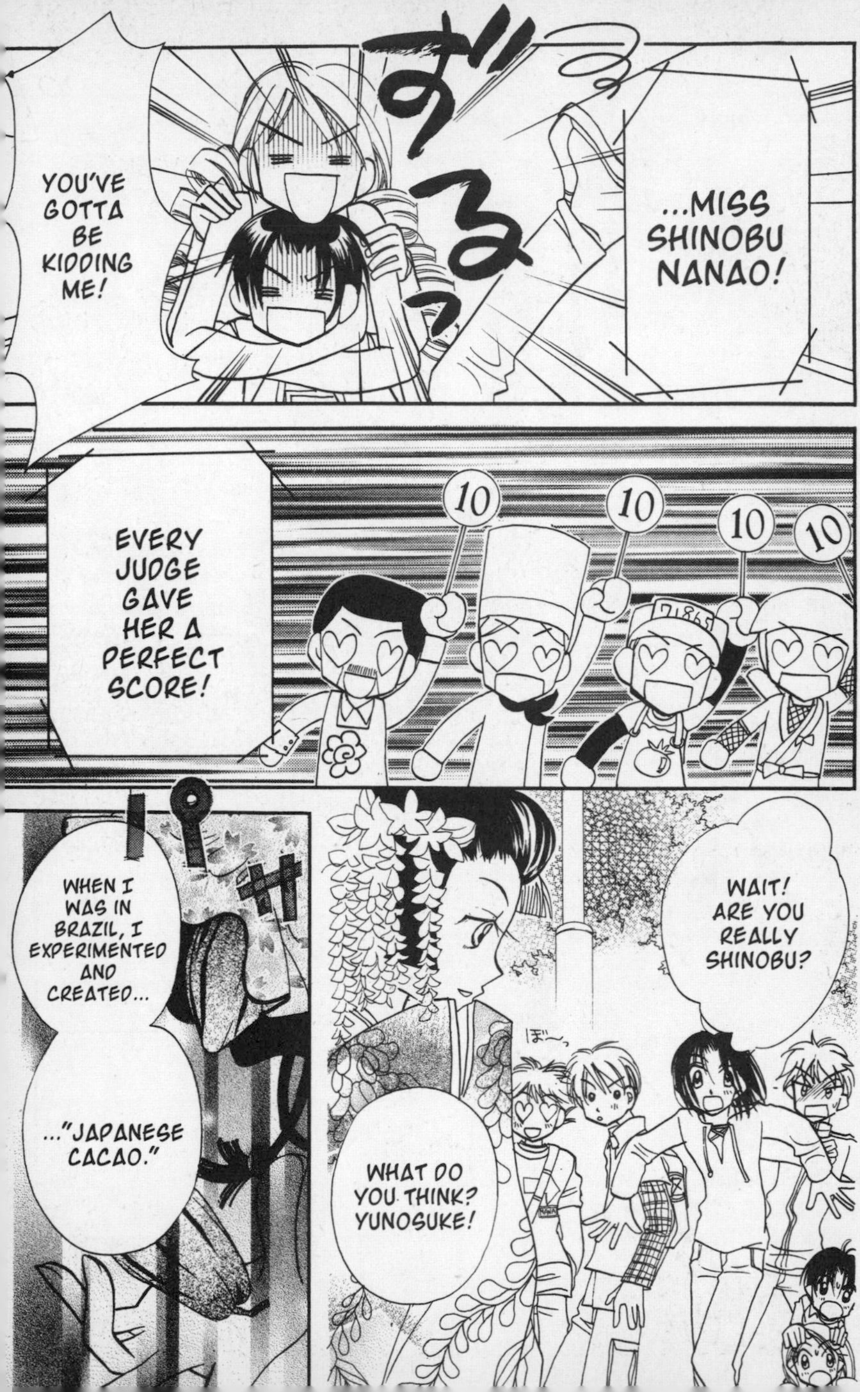
...MISS SHINOBU NANAO!
ずるっ
YOU'VE GOTTA BE KIDDING ME!
EVERY JUDGE GAVE HER A PERFECT SCORE!
WAIT! ARE YOU REALLY SHINOBU?
ぼ〜っ
WHAT DO YOU THINK? YUNOSUKE!
WHEN I WAS IN BRAZIL, I EXPERIMENTED AND CREATED...
..."JAPANESE CACAO."

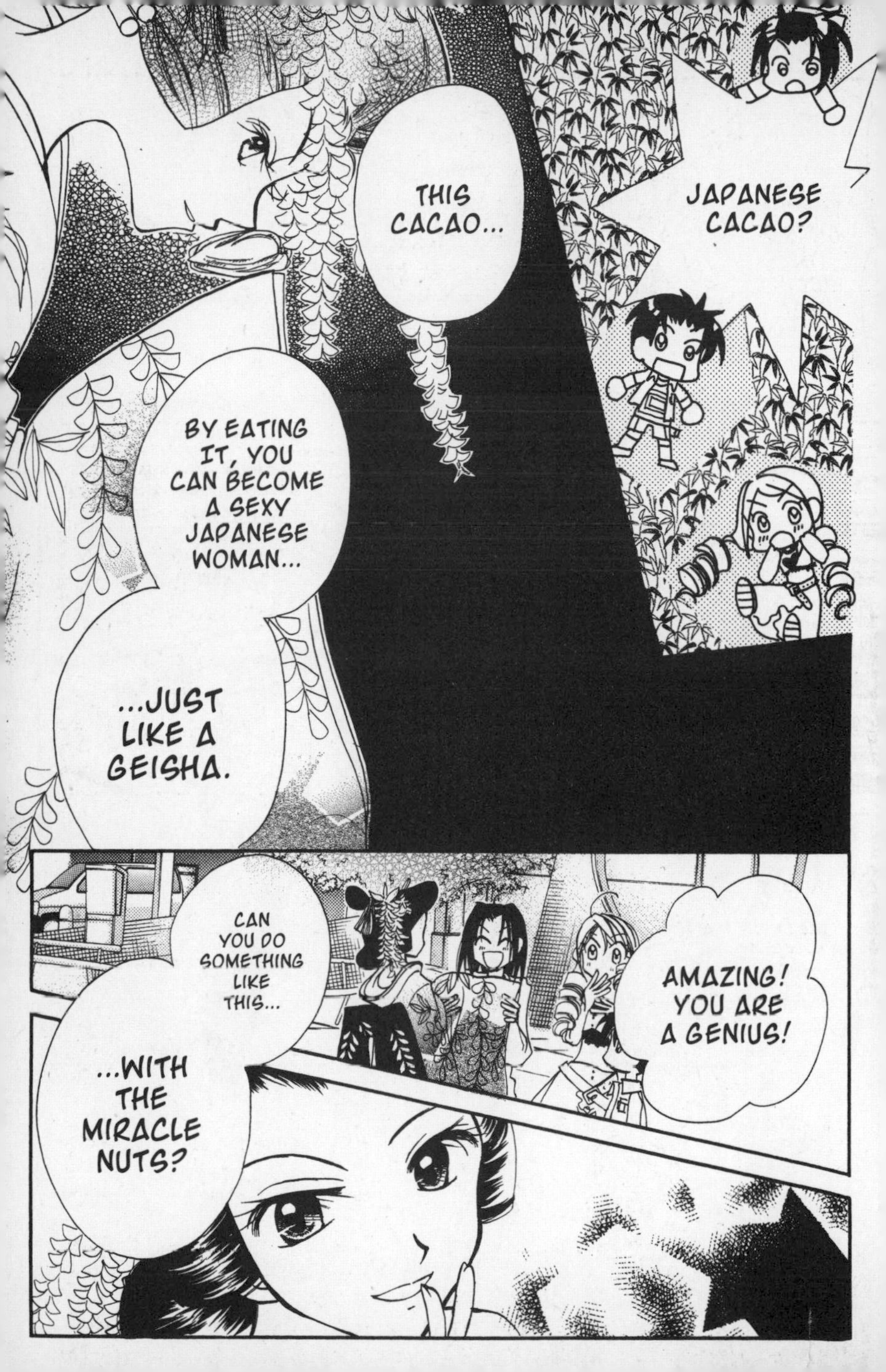
JAPANESE CACAO?
THIS CACAO...
BY EATING IT, YOU CAN BECOME A SEXY JAPANESE WOMAN...
...JUST LIKE A GEISHA.
AMAZING! YOU ARE A GENIUS!
CAN YOU DO SOMETHING LIKE THIS...
...WITH THE MIRACLE NUTS?

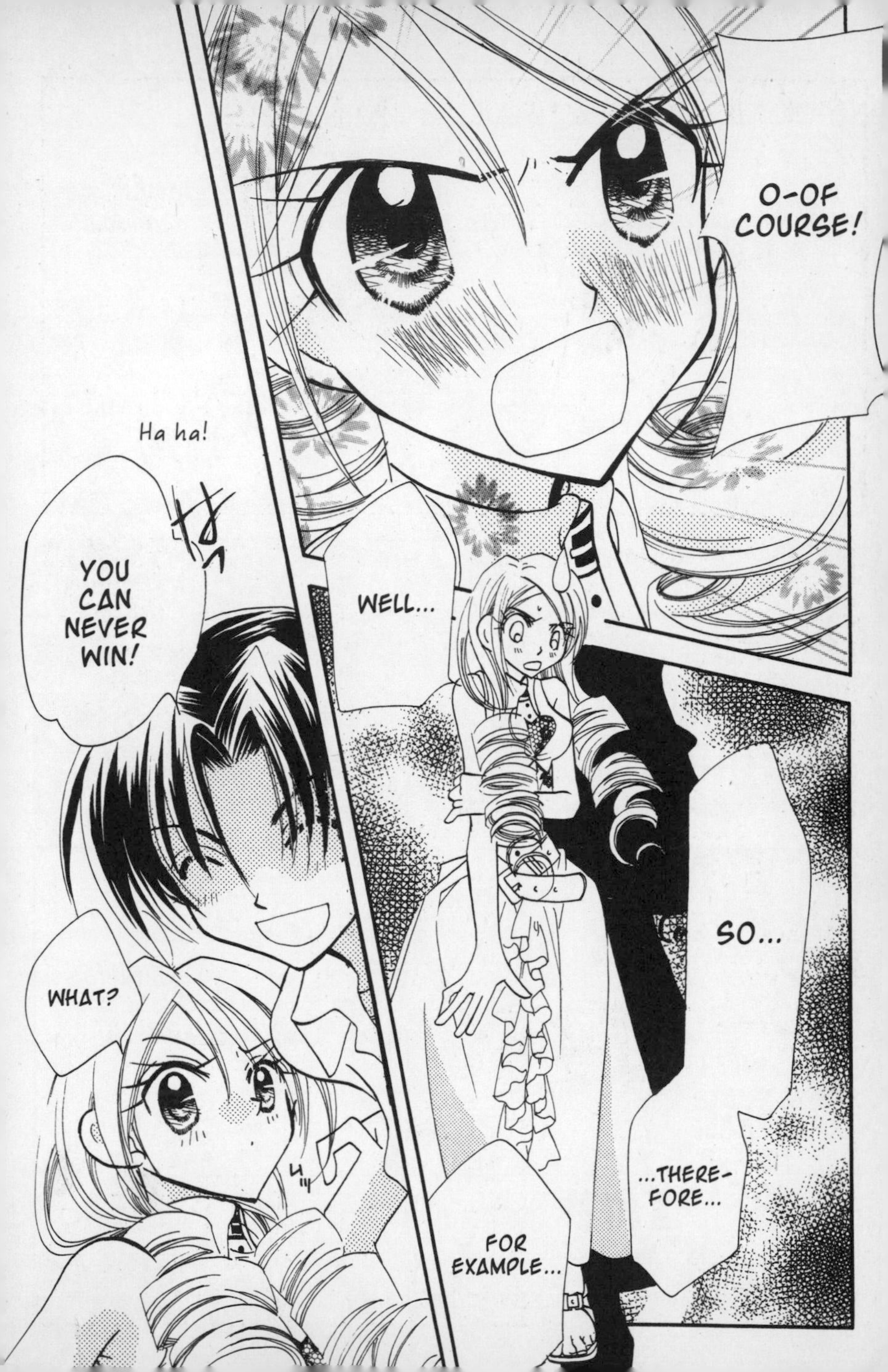
O-OF COURSE!
WELL...
SO...
...THERE-FORE...
FOR EXAMPLE...
Ha ha!
YOU CAN NEVER WIN!
WHAT?

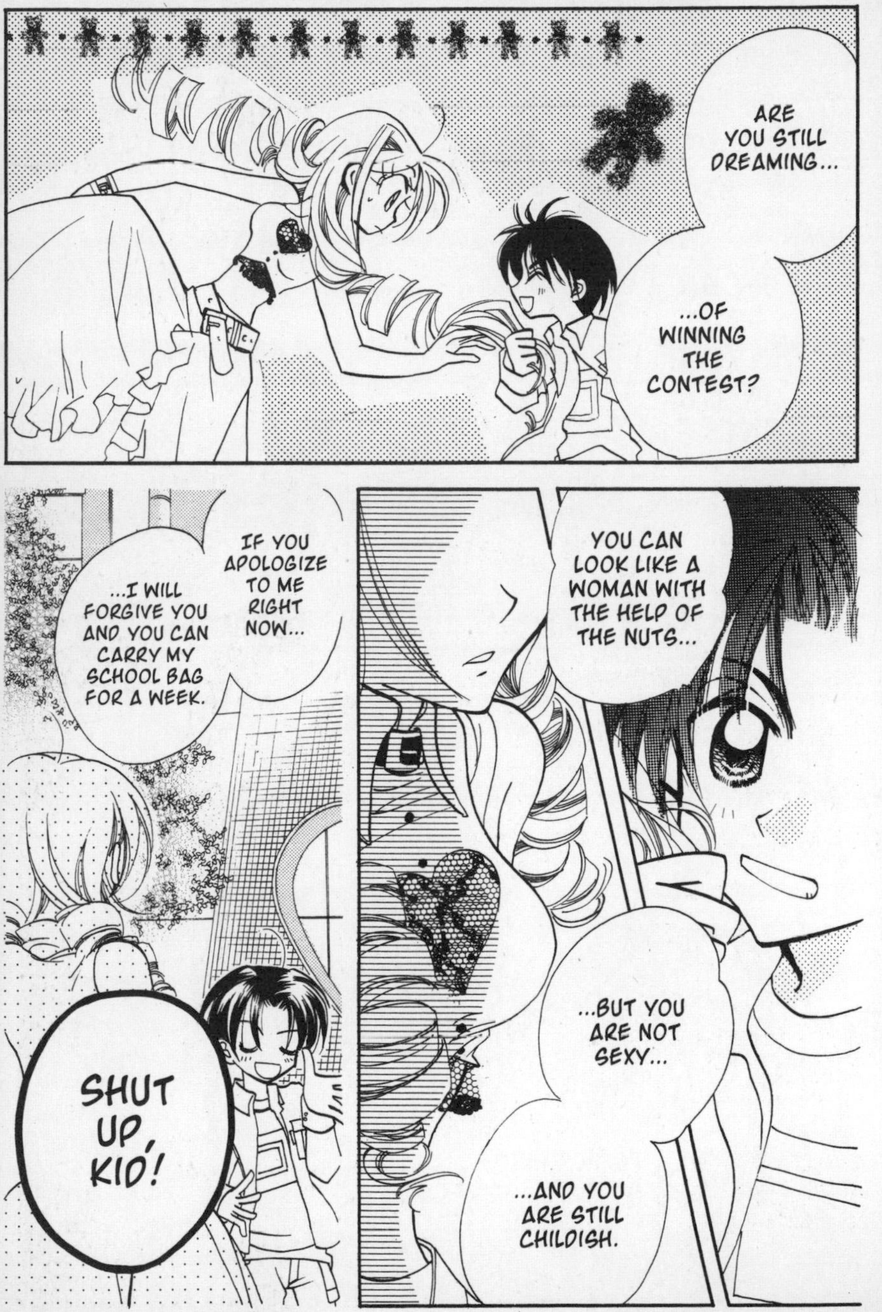
ARE YOU STILL DREAMING...
...OF WINNING THE CONTEST?
YOU CAN LOOK LIKE A WOMAN WITH THE HELP OF THE NUTS...
...BUT YOU ARE NOT SEXY...
...AND YOU ARE STILL CHILDISH.
IF YOU APOLOGIZE TO ME RIGHT NOW...
...I WILL FORGIVE YOU AND YOU CAN CARRY MY SCHOOL BAG FOR A WEEK.
SHUT UP, KID!

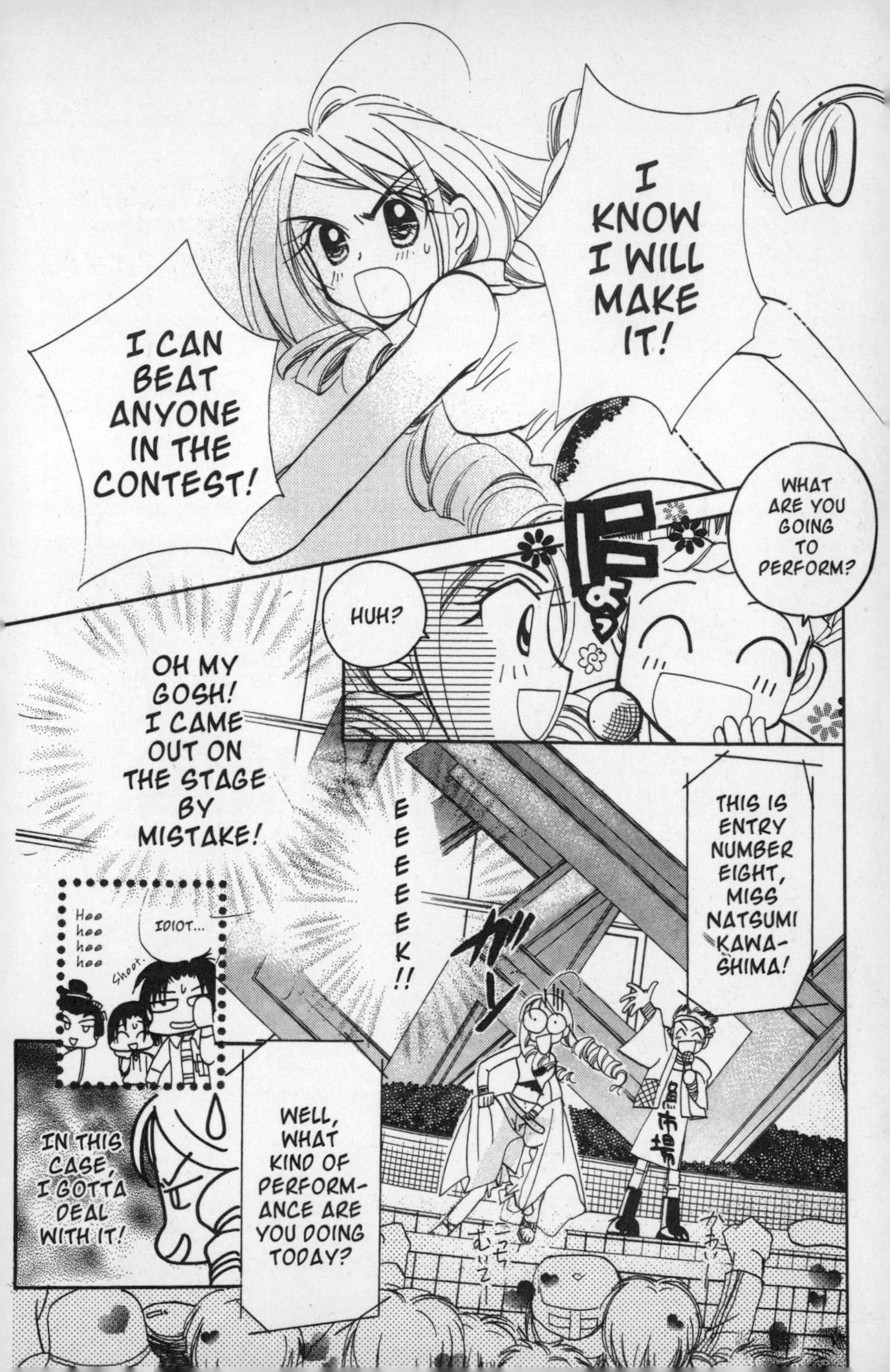

I KNOW I WILL MAKE IT!
I CAN BEAT ANYONE IN THE CONTEST!
WHAT ARE YOU GOING TO PERFORM?
HUH?
THIS IS ENTRY NUMBER EIGHT, MISS NATSUMI KAWA-SHIMA!
EEEEEEK!!
OH MY GOSH! I CAME OUT ON THE STAGE BY MISTAKE!
Hee hee hee hee
IDIOT...
Shoot.
WELL, WHAT KIND OF PERFORM-ANCE ARE YOU DOING TODAY?
IN THIS CASE, I GOTTA DEAL WITH IT!

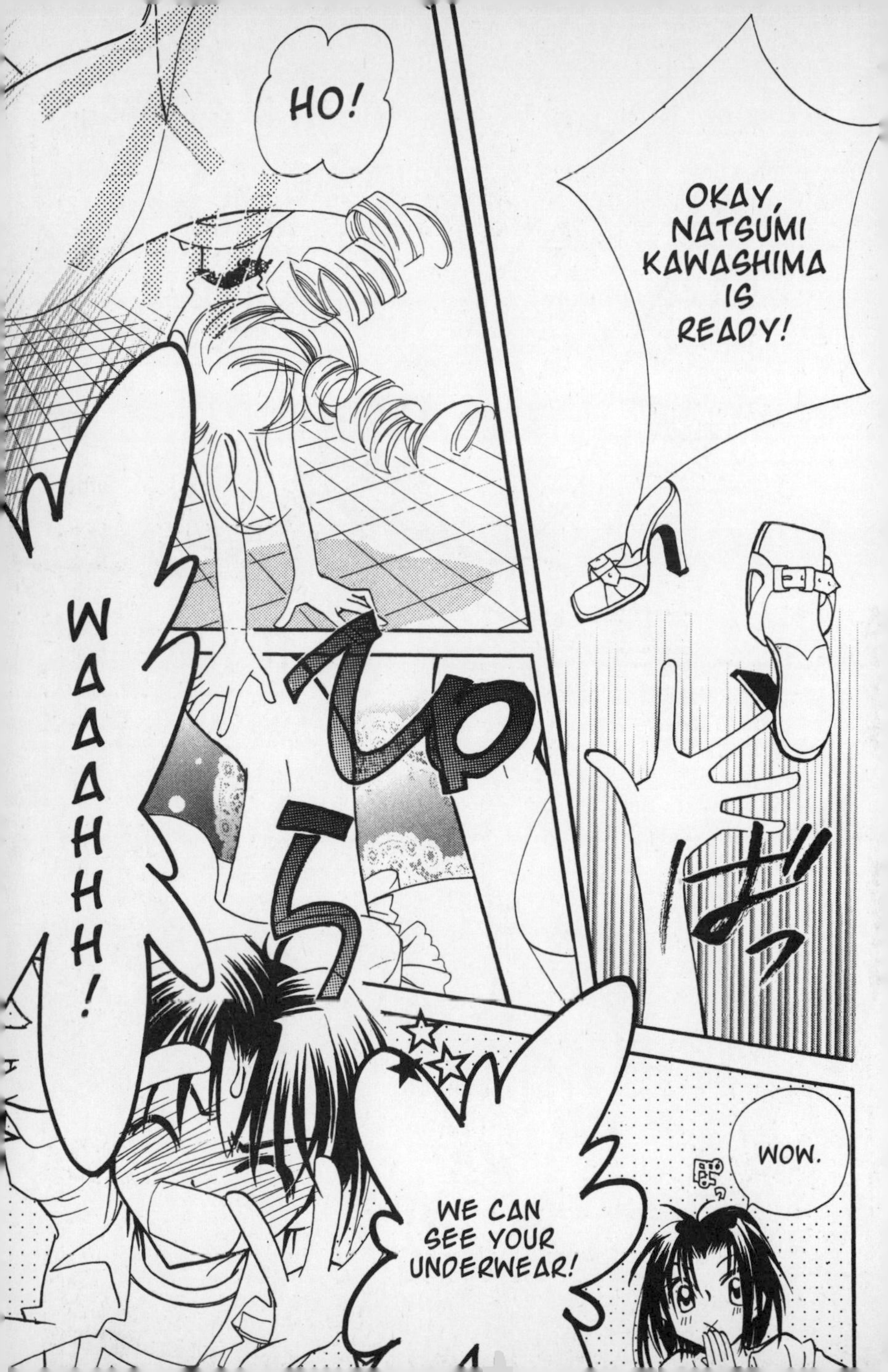
OKAY, NATSUMI KAWASHIMA IS READY!
HO!
WAAAAHHH!
WOW.
WE CAN SEE YOUR UNDERWEAR!

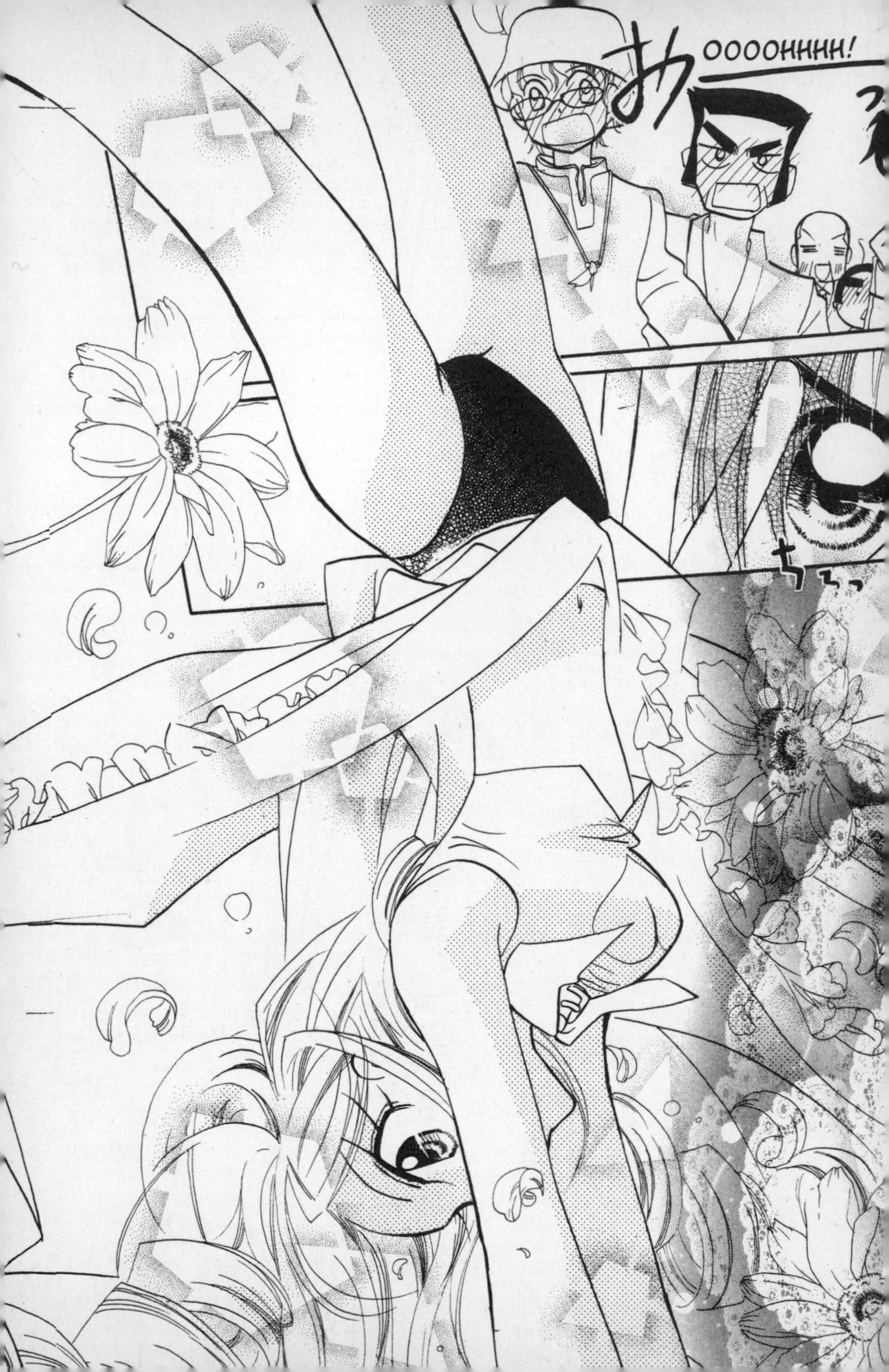
OOOOHHHH!

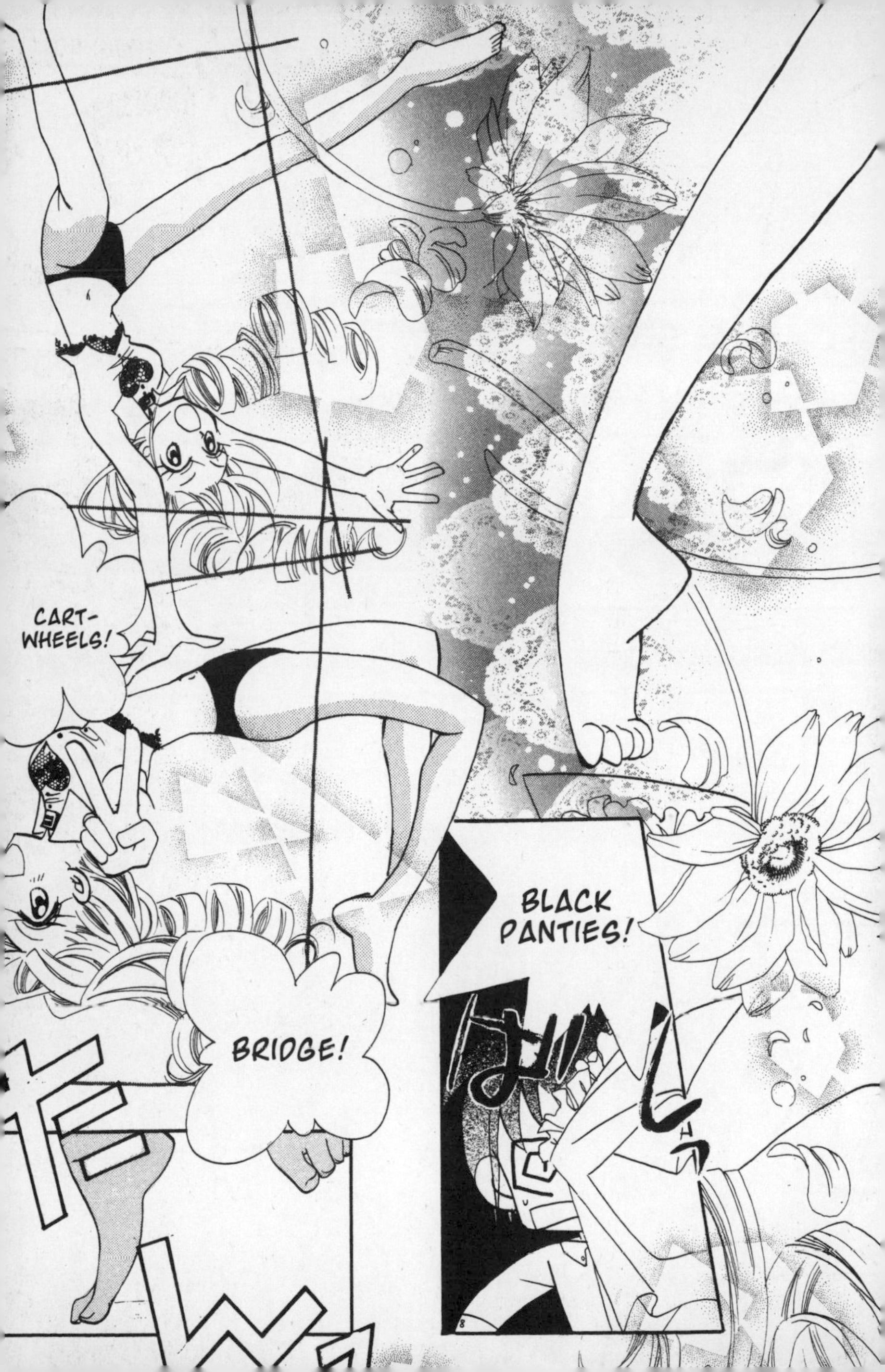
CART-
WHEELS!
BRIDGE!
BLACK
PANTIES!

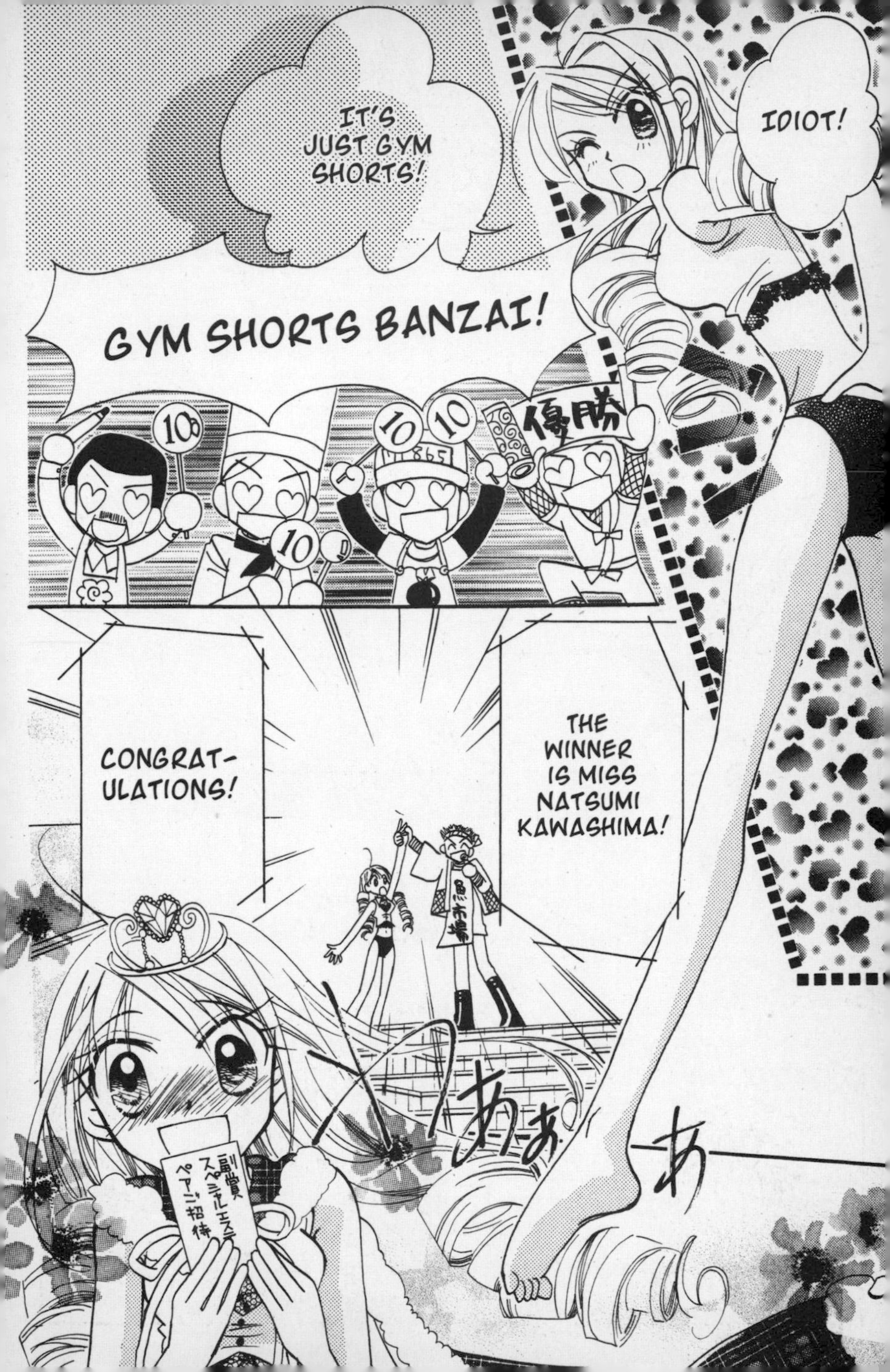
IDIOT!
IT'S JUST GYM SHORTS!
GYM SHORTS BANZAI!
優勝
10
10
10
10
THE WINNER IS MISS NATSUMI KAWASHIMA!
CONGRAT-ULATIONS!
魚市場
あああ
副賞
スペシャルエステ
ペアご招待

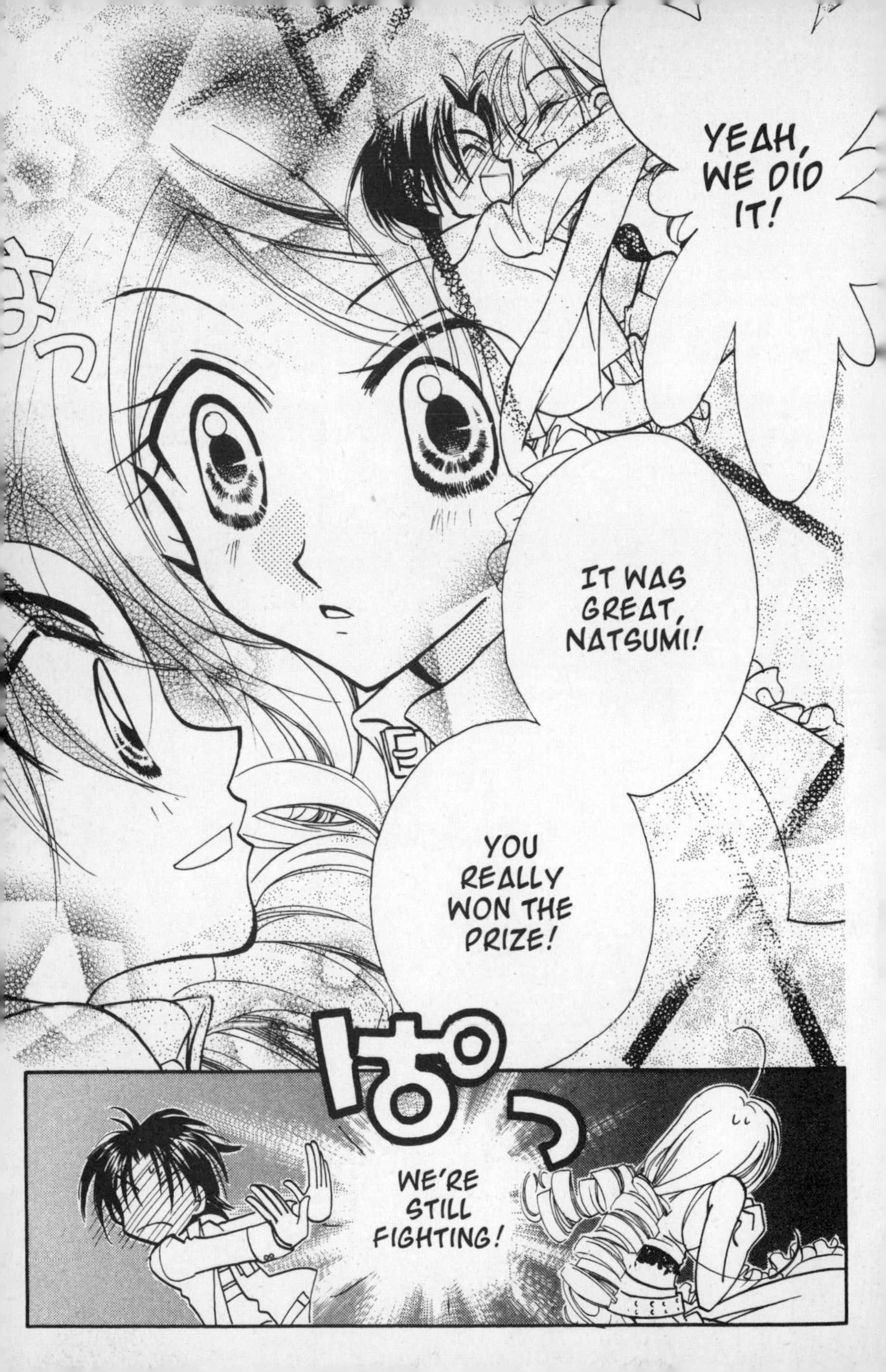
YEAH, WE DID IT!
IT WAS GREAT, NATSUMI!
YOU REALLY WON THE PRIZE!
ぱっ
WE'RE STILL FIGHTING!

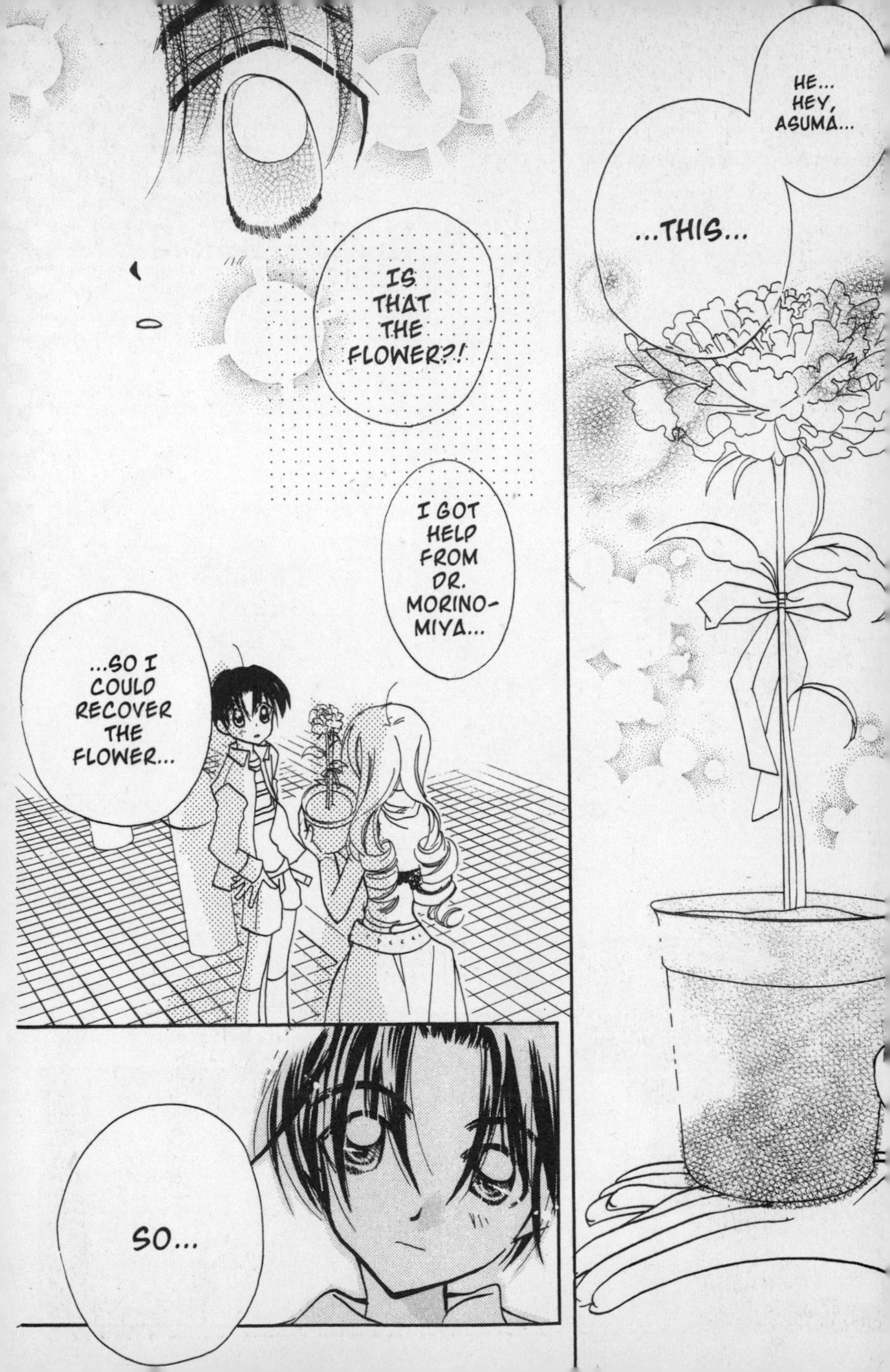

HE... HEY, ASUMA...
...THIS...
IS THAT THE FLOWER?!
I GOT HELP FROM DR. MORINO-MIYA...
...SO I COULD RECOVER THE FLOWER...
SO...

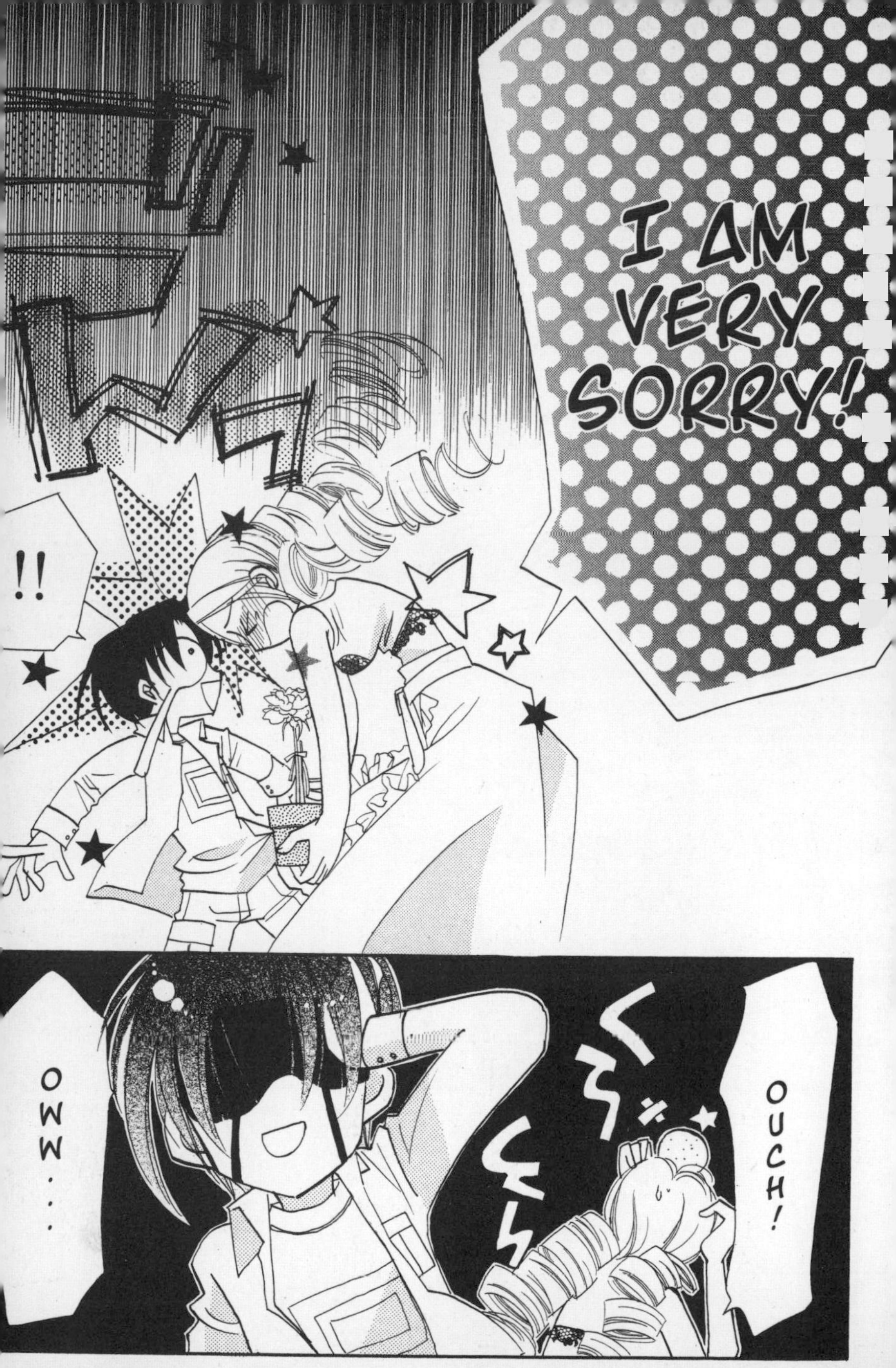
I AM VERY SORRY!
!!
OUCH!
OWW...

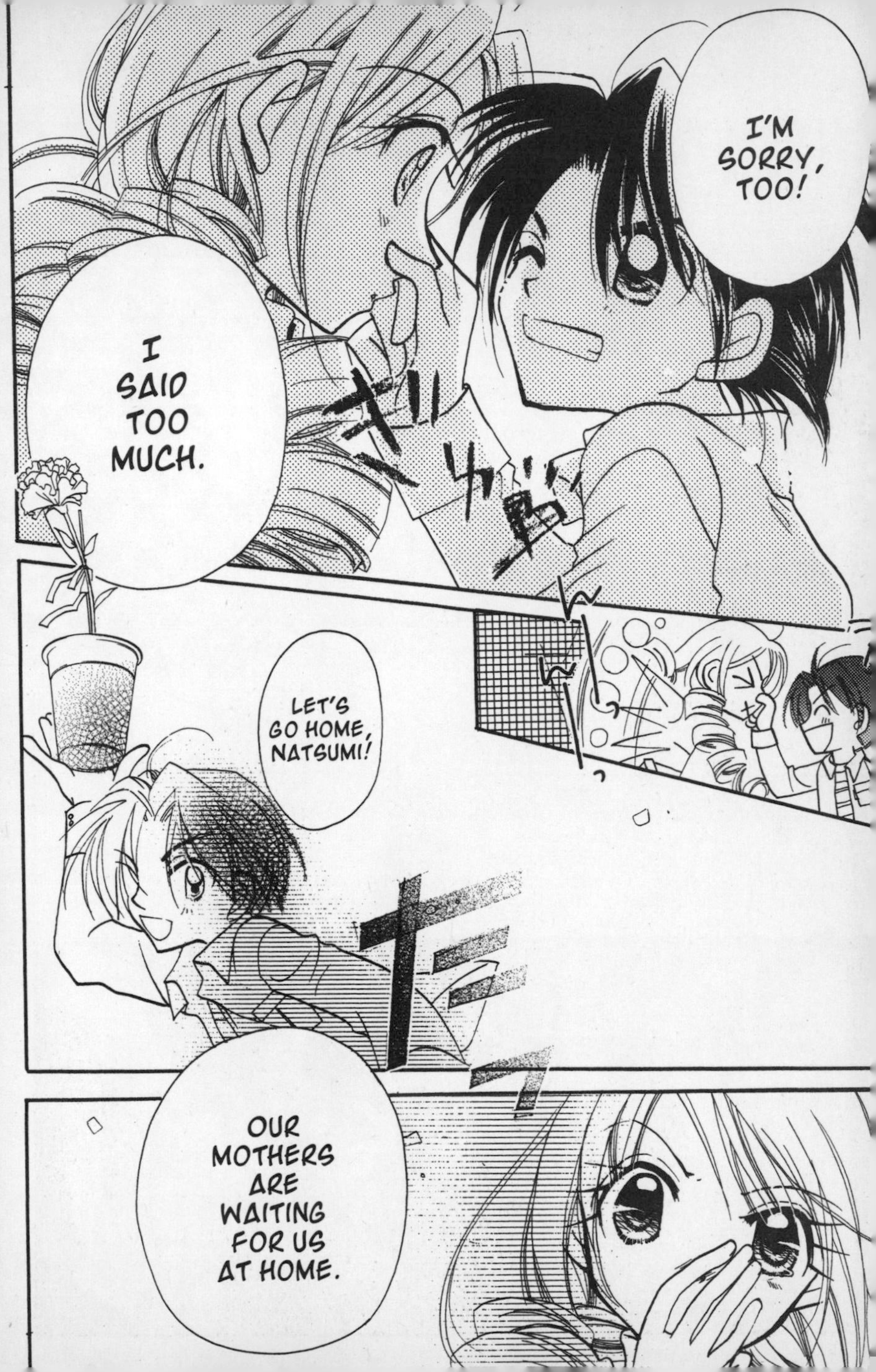
I'M SORRY, TOO!
I SAID TOO MUCH.
LET'S GO HOME, NATSUMI!
OUR MOTHERS ARE WAITING FOR US AT HOME.

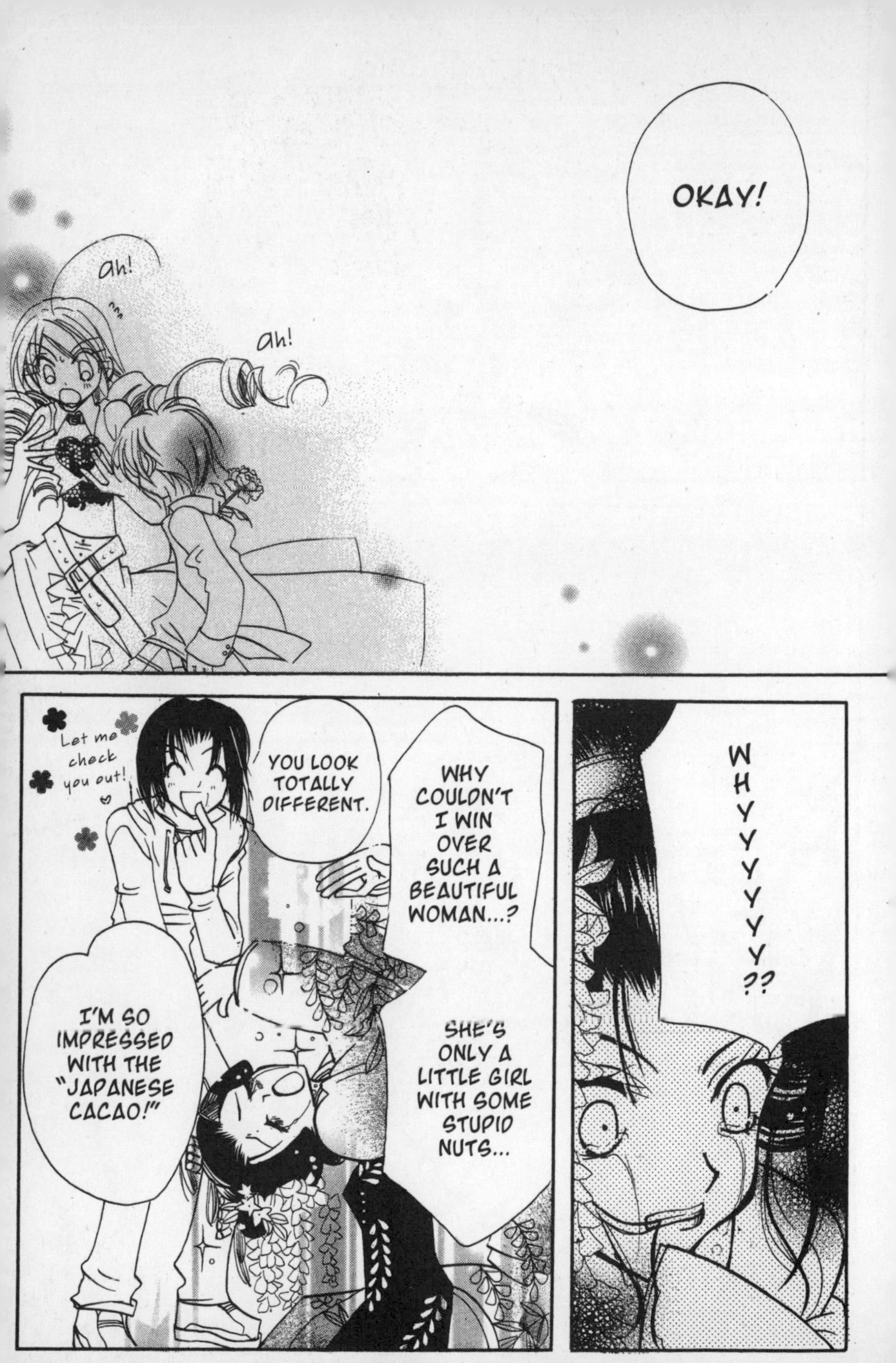

OKAY!
ah!
ah!
WHYYYYYY??
WHY COULDN'T I WIN OVER SUCH A BEAUTIFUL WOMAN...?
YOU LOOK TOTALLY DIFFERENT.
Let me check you out!
SHE'S ONLY A LITTLE GIRL WITH SOME STUPID NUTS...
I'M SO IMPRESSED WITH THE "JAPANESE CACAO!"

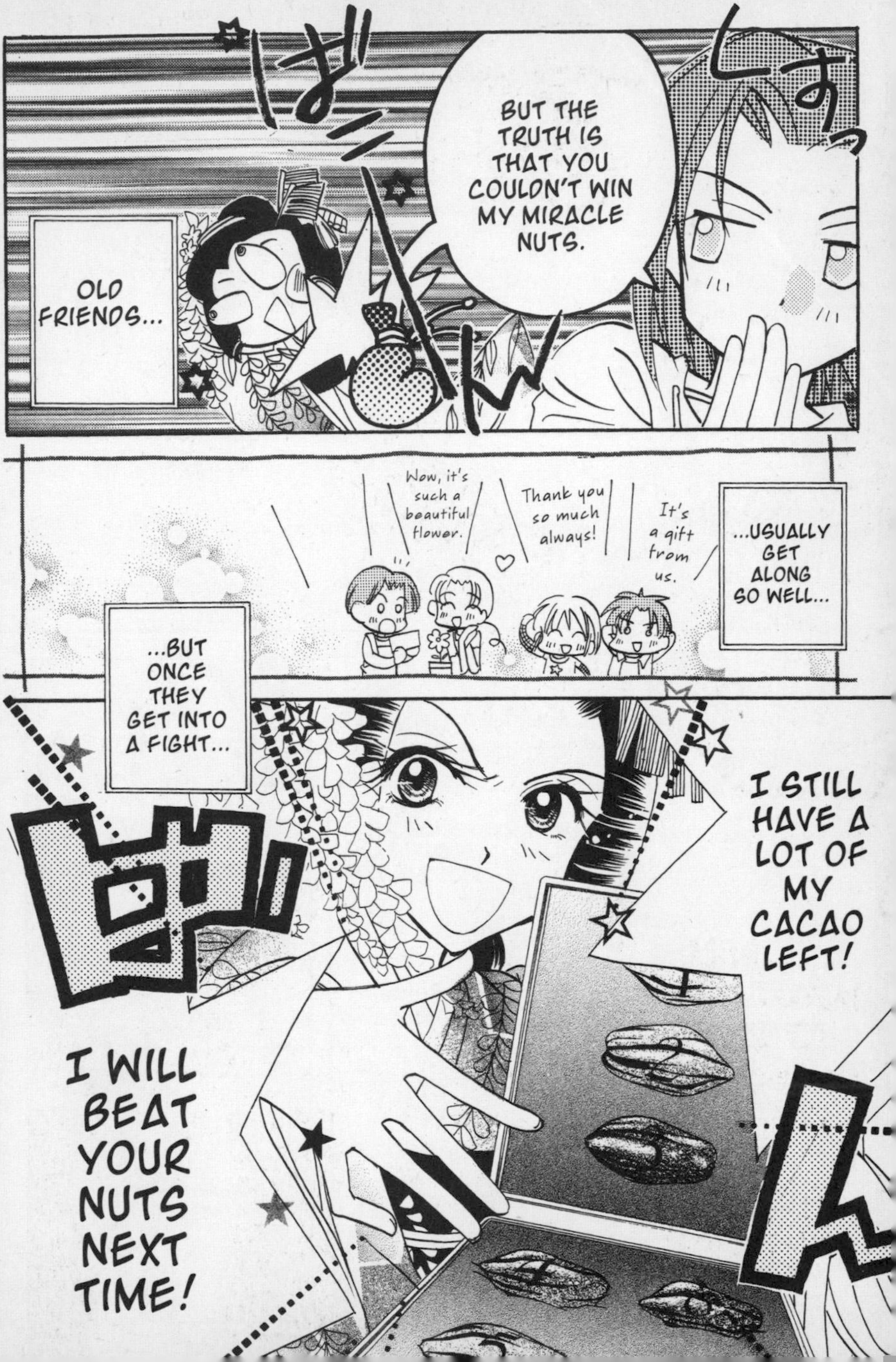
くすっ
BUT THE TRUTH IS THAT YOU COULDN'T WIN MY MIRACLE NUTS.
OLD FRIENDS...
...USUALLY GET ALONG SO WELL...
It's a gift from us.
Thank you so much always!
Wow, it's such a beautiful flower.
...BUT ONCE THEY GET INTO A FIGHT...
I STILL HAVE A LOT OF MY CACAO LEFT!
I WILL BEAT YOUR NUTS NEXT TIME!

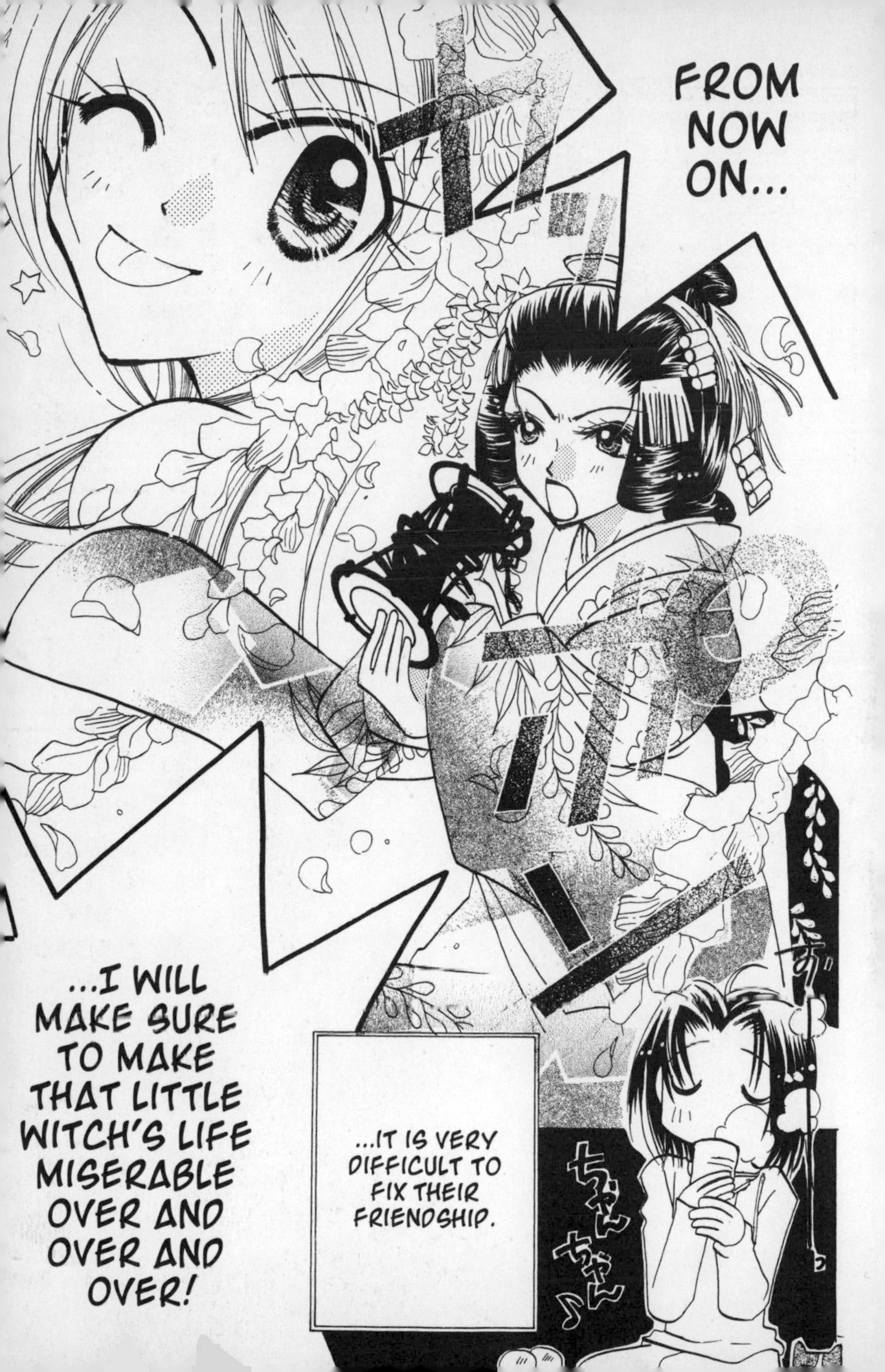
FROM NOW ON...
...I WILL MAKE SURE TO MAKE THAT LITTLE WITCH'S LIFE MISERABLE OVER AND OVER AND OVER!
...IT IS VERY DIFFICULT TO FIX THEIR FRIENDSHIP.
ちゃんちゃん♪

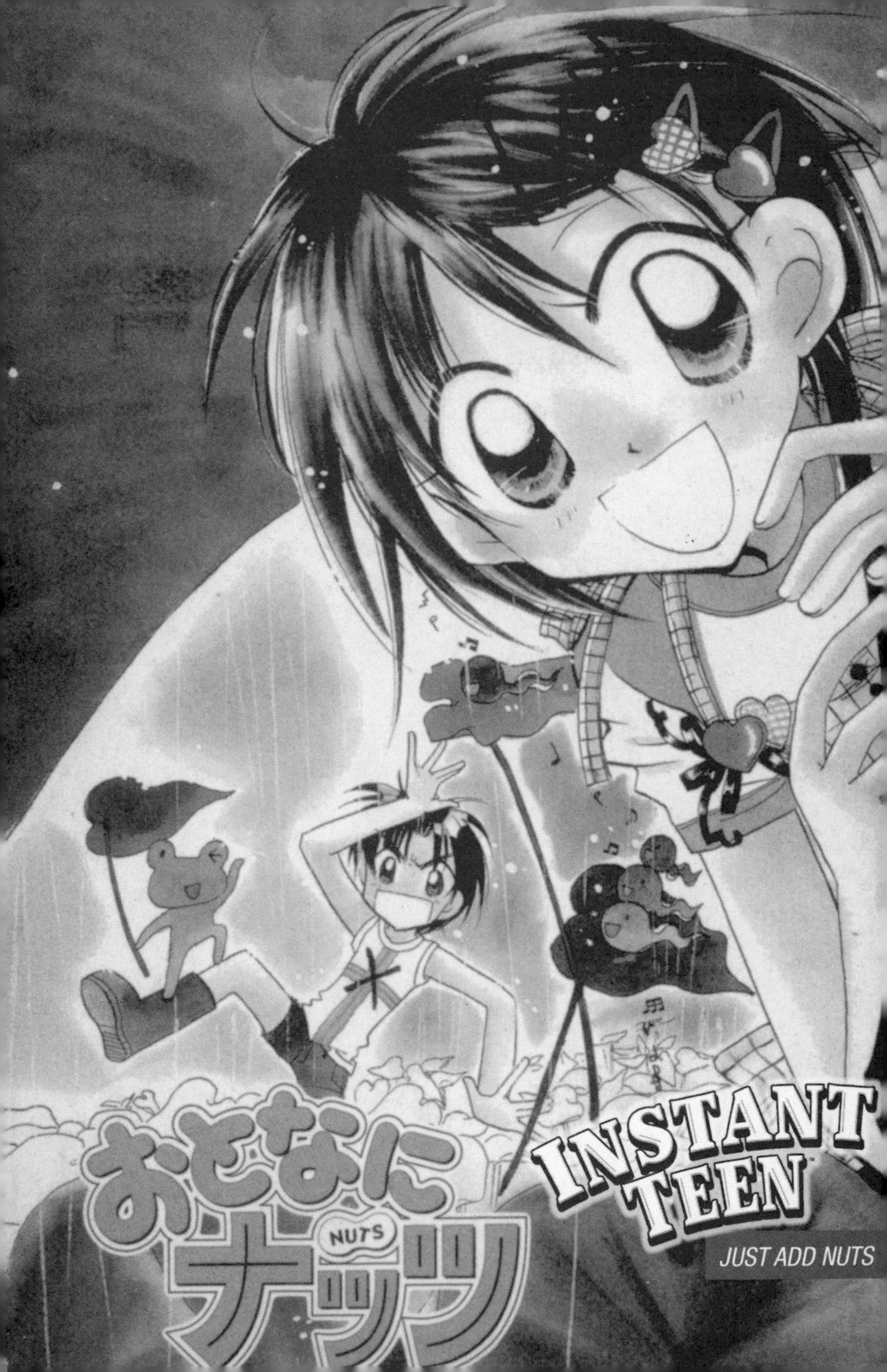
おとなにナッツ
NUTS
INSTANT TEEN™
JUST ADD NUTS

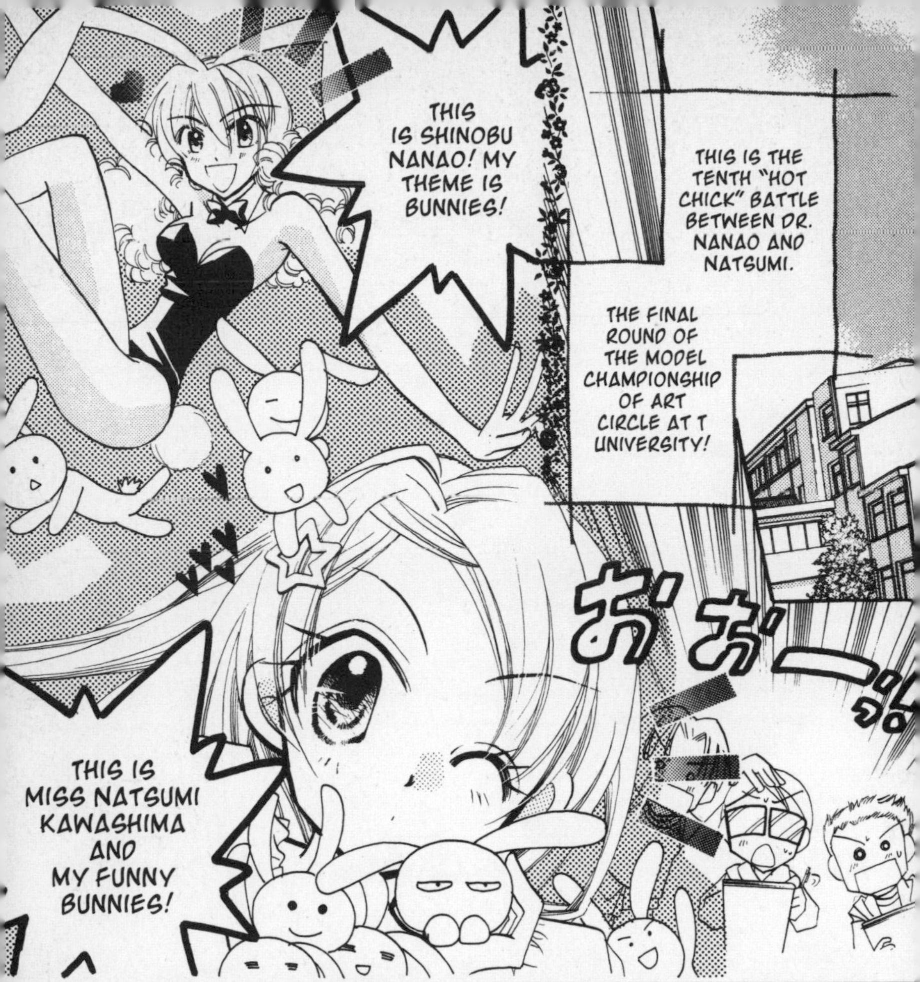
THIS IS THE TENTH "HOT CHICK" BATTLE BETWEEN DR. NANAO AND NATSUMI.
THE FINAL ROUND OF THE MODEL CHAMPIONSHIP OF ART CIRCLE AT T UNIVERSITY!
THIS IS SHINOBU NANAO! MY THEME IS BUNNIES!
おおーっ!!
THIS IS MISS NATSUMI KAWASHIMA AND MY FUNNY BUNNIES!

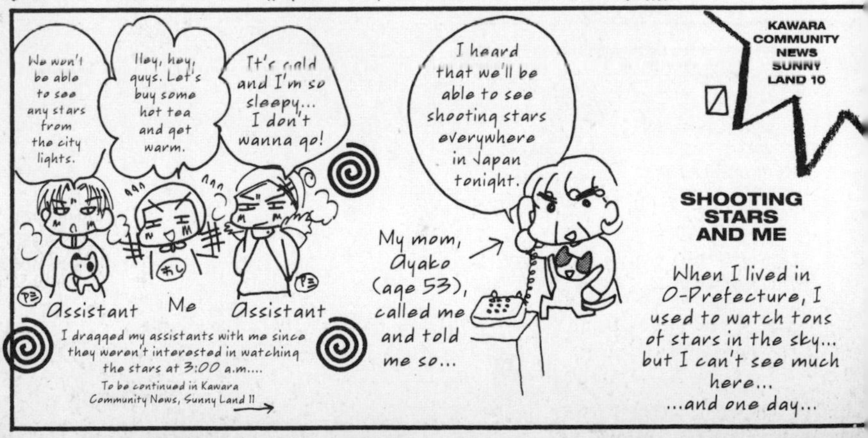
KAWARA COMMUNITY NEWS SUNNY LAND 10
SHOOTING STARS AND ME
When I lived in O-Prefecture, I used to watch tons of stars in the sky... but I can't see much here... ...and one day...
I heard that we'll be able to see shooting stars everywhere in Japan tonight.
My mom, Ayako (age 53), called me and told me so...
It's cold and I'm so sleepy... I don't wanna go!
Hey, hey, guys. Let's buy some hot tea and get warm.
We won't be able to see any stars from the city lights.
Assistant
Me
Assistant
I dragged my assistants with me since they weren't interested in watching the stars at 3:00 a.m....
To be continued in Kawara Community News, Sunny Land 11

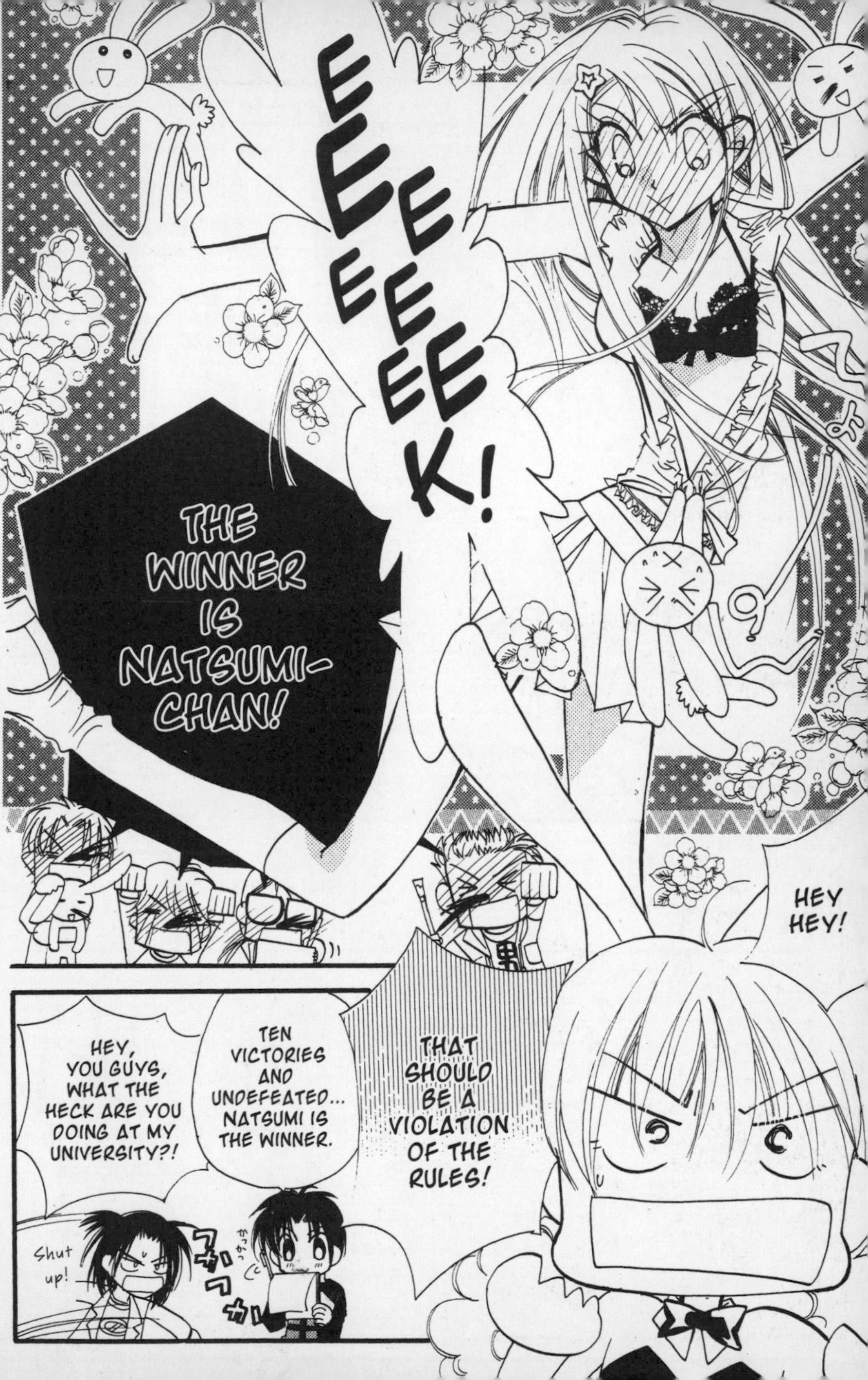
EEEEEEEK!
THE WINNER IS NATSUMI-CHAN!
HEY HEY!
THAT SHOULD BE A VIOLATION OF THE RULES!
TEN VICTORIES AND UNDEFEATED... NATSUMI IS THE WINNER.
HEY, YOU GUYS, WHAT THE HECK ARE YOU DOING AT MY UNIVERSITY?!
Shut up!

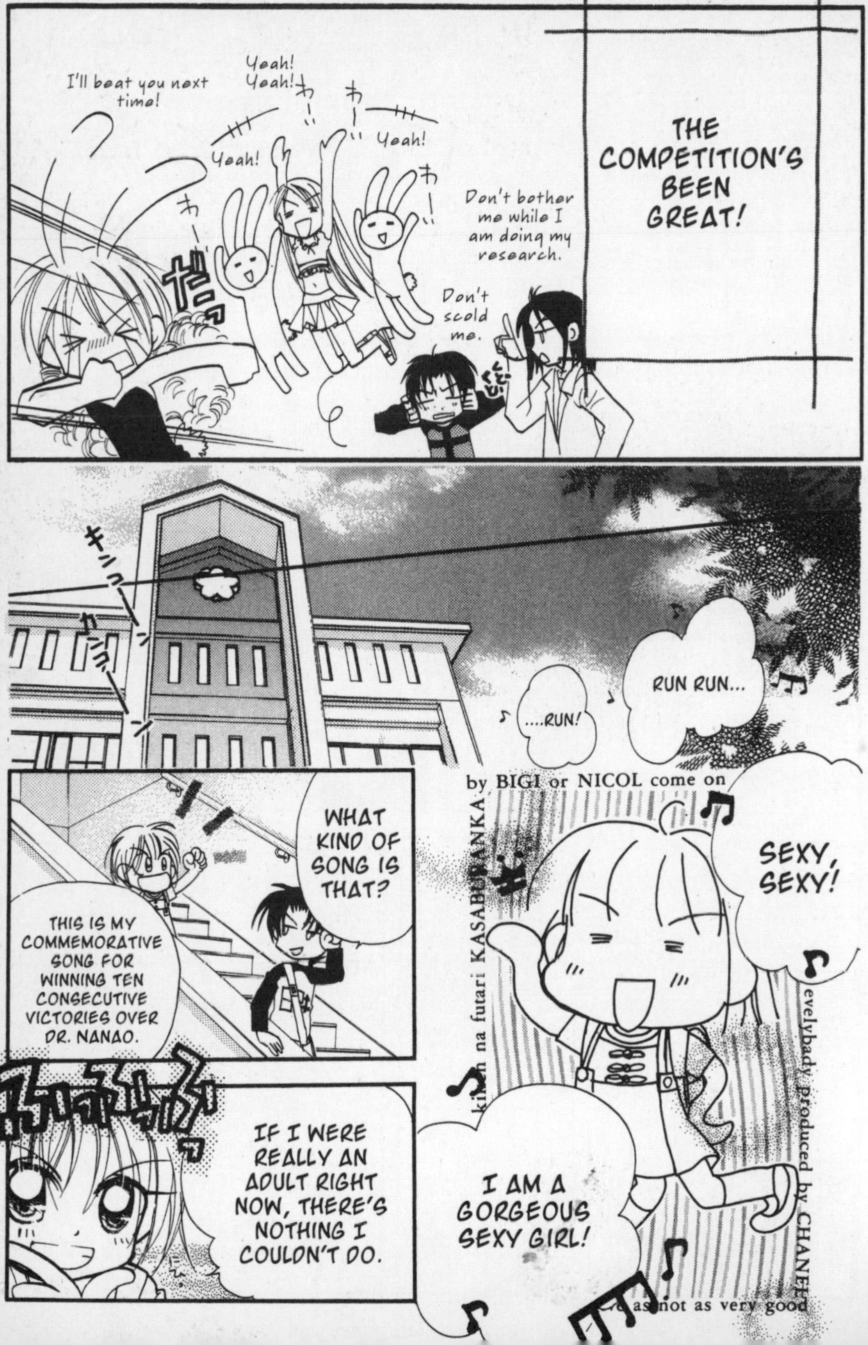

THE COMPETITION'S BEEN GREAT!
Don't bother me while I am doing my research.
Don't scold me.
Yeah!
Yeah! Yeah!
Yeah!
I'll beat you next time!
RUN RUN...
....RUN!
by BIGI or NICOL come on
na futari KASABURANKA
SEXY, SEXY!
evelybady produced by CHANEL
I AM A GORGEOUS SEXY GIRL!
as not as very good
WHAT KIND OF SONG IS THAT?
THIS IS MY COMMEMORATIVE SONG FOR WINNING TEN CONSECUTIVE VICTORIES OVER DR. NANAO.
IF I WERE REALLY AN ADULT RIGHT NOW, THERE'S NOTHING I COULDN'T DO.

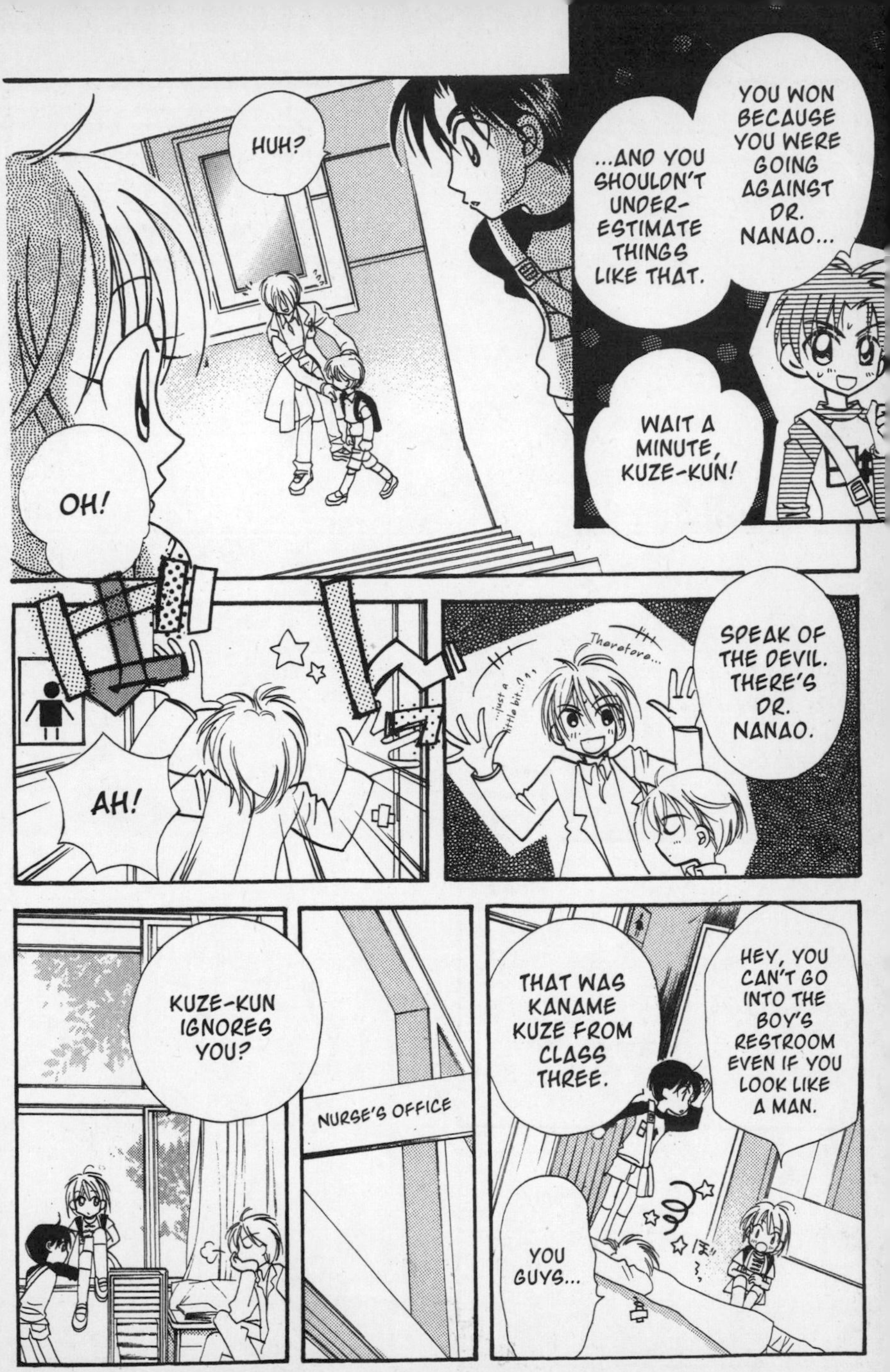
YOU WON BECAUSE YOU WERE GOING AGAINST DR. NANAO...
...AND YOU SHOULDN'T UNDER-ESTIMATE THINGS LIKE THAT.
WAIT A MINUTE, KUZE-KUN!
HUH?
OH!
SPEAK OF THE DEVIL. THERE'S DR. NANAO.
Therefore...
...just a little bit...
AH!
HEY, YOU CAN'T GO INTO THE BOY'S RESTROOM EVEN IF YOU LOOK LIKE A MAN.
THAT WAS KANAME KUZE FROM CLASS THREE.
YOU GUYS...
NURSE'S OFFICE
KUZE-KUN IGNORES YOU?

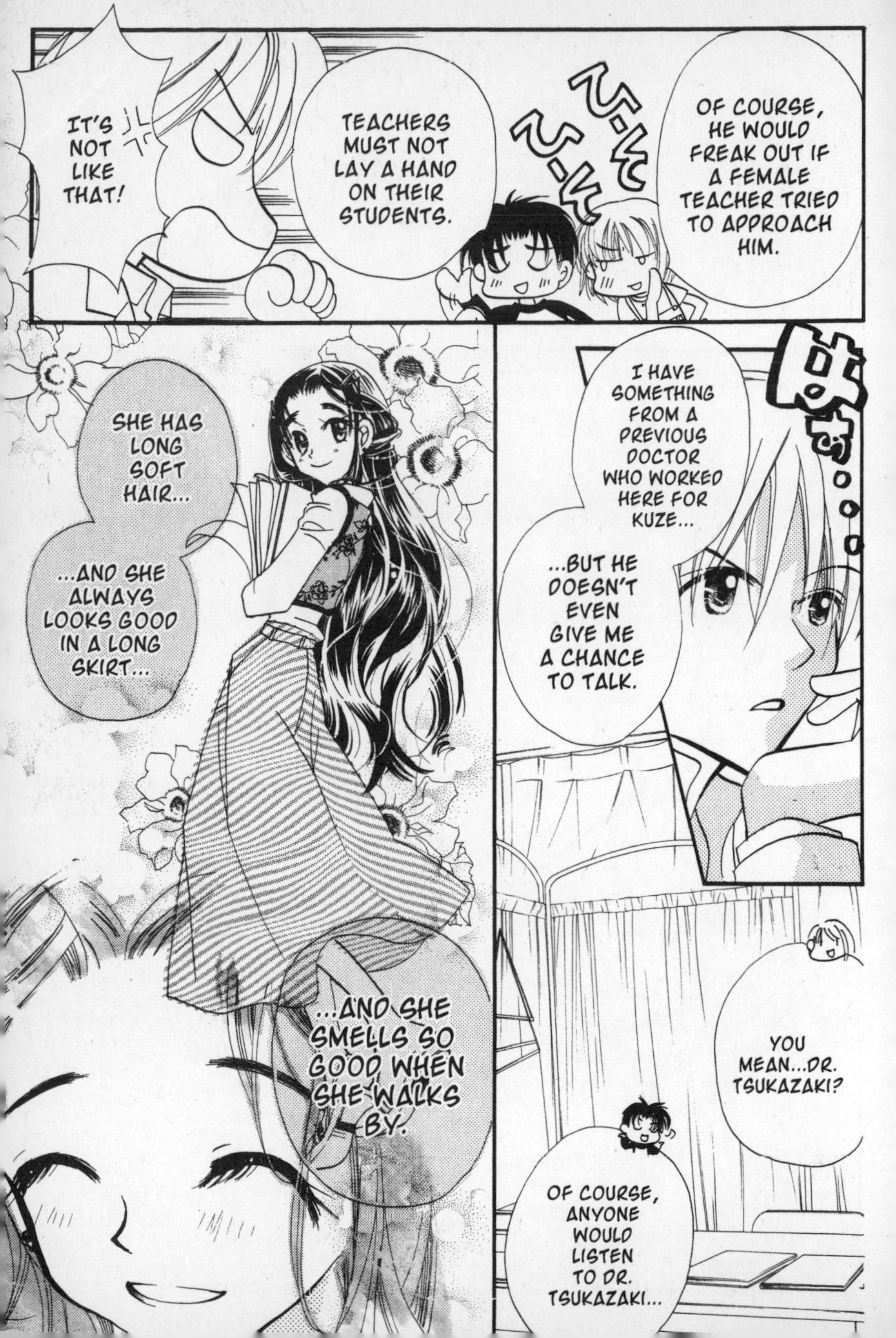

OF COURSE, HE WOULD FREAK OUT IF A FEMALE TEACHER TRIED TO APPROACH HIM.
TEACHERS MUST NOT LAY A HAND ON THEIR STUDENTS.
IT'S NOT LIKE THAT!
I HAVE SOMETHING FROM A PREVIOUS DOCTOR WHO WORKED HERE FOR KUZE...
...BUT HE DOESN'T EVEN GIVE ME A CHANCE TO TALK.
YOU MEAN...DR. TSUKAZAKI?
OF COURSE, ANYONE WOULD LISTEN TO DR. TSUKAZAKI...
SHE HAS LONG SOFT HAIR...
...AND SHE ALWAYS LOOKS GOOD IN A LONG SKIRT...
...AND SHE SMELLS SO GOOD WHEN SHE WALKS BY.

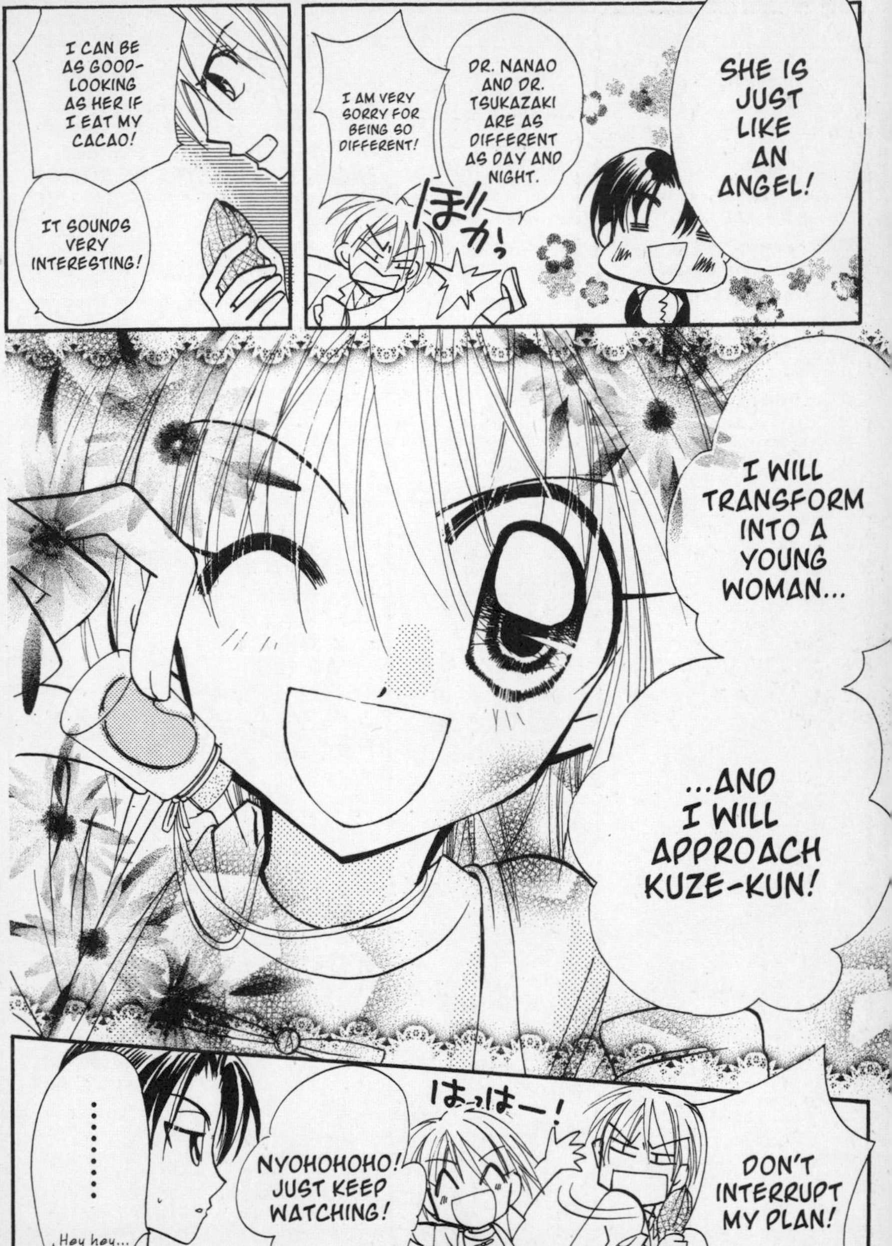
SHE IS JUST LIKE AN ANGEL!
DR. NANAO AND DR. TSUKAZAKI ARE AS DIFFERENT AS DAY AND NIGHT.
I AM VERY SORRY FOR BEING SO DIFFERENT!
ぼかっ
I CAN BE AS GOOD-LOOKING AS HER IF I EAT MY CACAO!
IT SOUNDS VERY INTERESTING!
I WILL TRANSFORM INTO A YOUNG WOMAN...
...AND I WILL APPROACH KUZE-KUN!
DON'T INTERRUPT MY PLAN!
はっはー!
NYOHOHOHO! JUST KEEP WATCHING!
....
Hey hey...

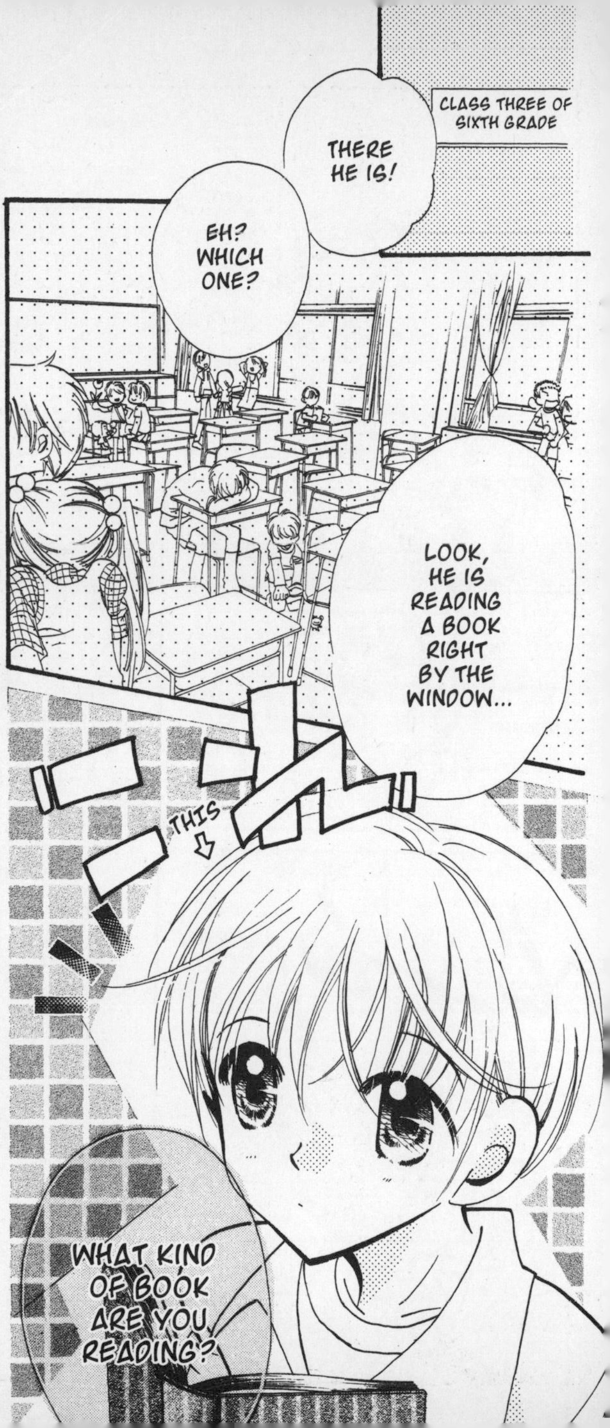
CLASS THREE OF SIXTH GRADE
THERE HE IS!
EH? WHICH ONE?
LOOK, HE IS READING A BOOK RIGHT BY THE WINDOW...
THIS
WHAT KIND OF BOOK ARE YOU READING?

TWO

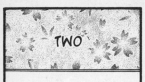

Dr. Nanao, a rival of Dr. Morinomiya, suddenly appears. I like this stupid character. Natsumi is turning into a major airhead! She starts butting heads with Dr. Nanao. In this chapter, something happens to her face! It sometimes gets...

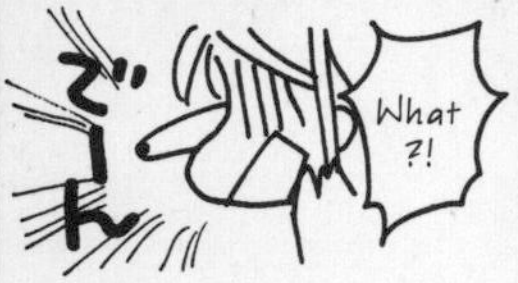
What ?!

...deformed like this and I can't help but think "What a face!" But I enjoy drawing her like that too much and can't stop! Even if she is the heroine of the story.

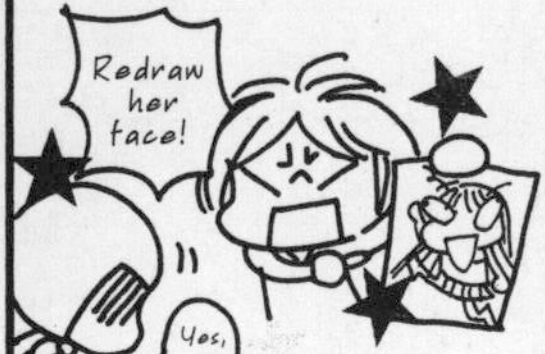
Redraw her face!
Yes, mom.

My manager still makes me draw her over and over! All the redraws!!

....()

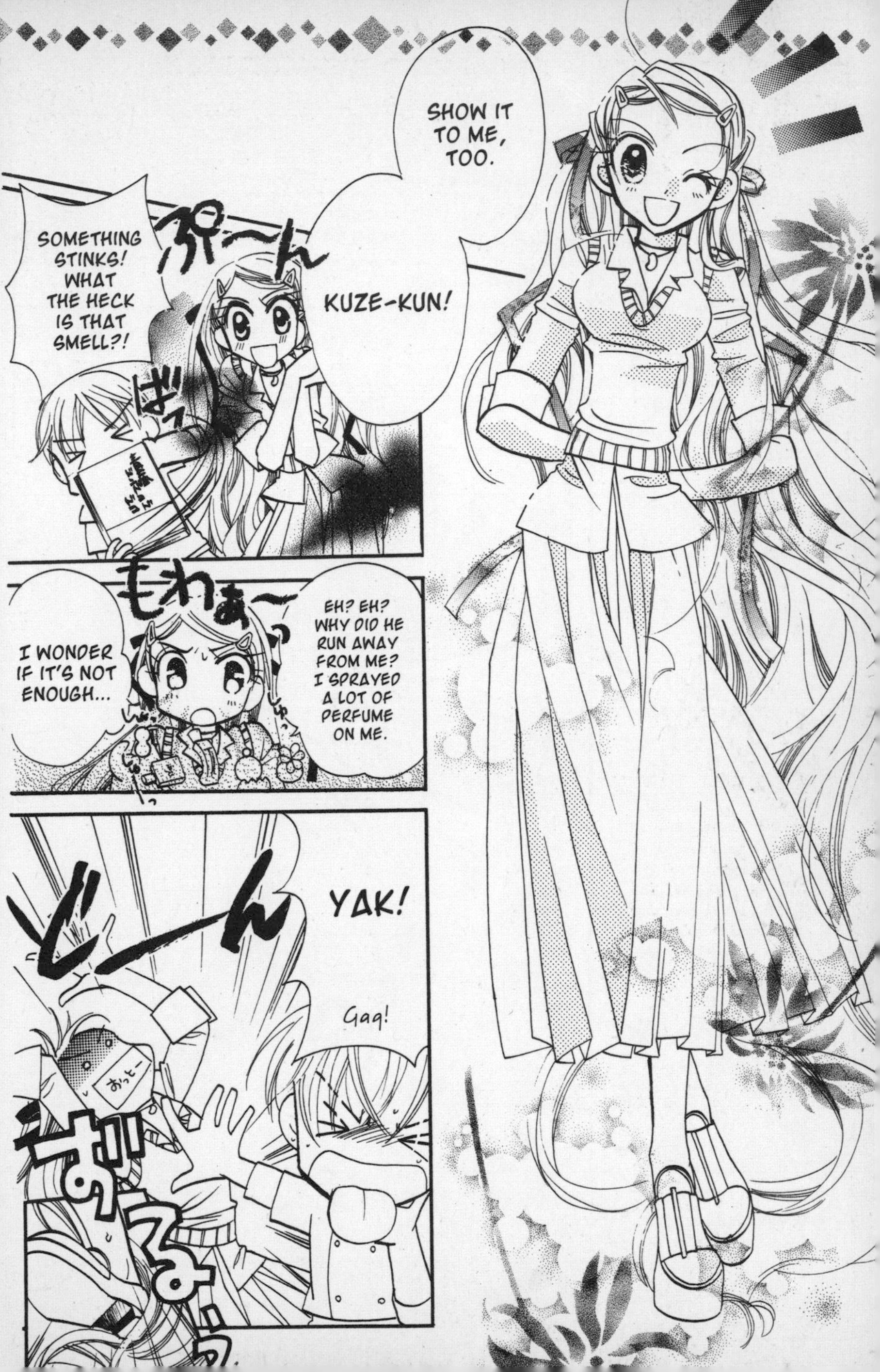
SHOW IT TO ME, TOO.
KUZE-KUN!
SOMETHING STINKS! WHAT THE HECK IS THAT SMELL?!
EH? EH? WHY DID HE RUN AWAY FROM ME? I SPRAYED A LOT OF PERFUME ON ME.
I WONDER IF IT'S NOT ENOUGH...
YAK!
Gag!

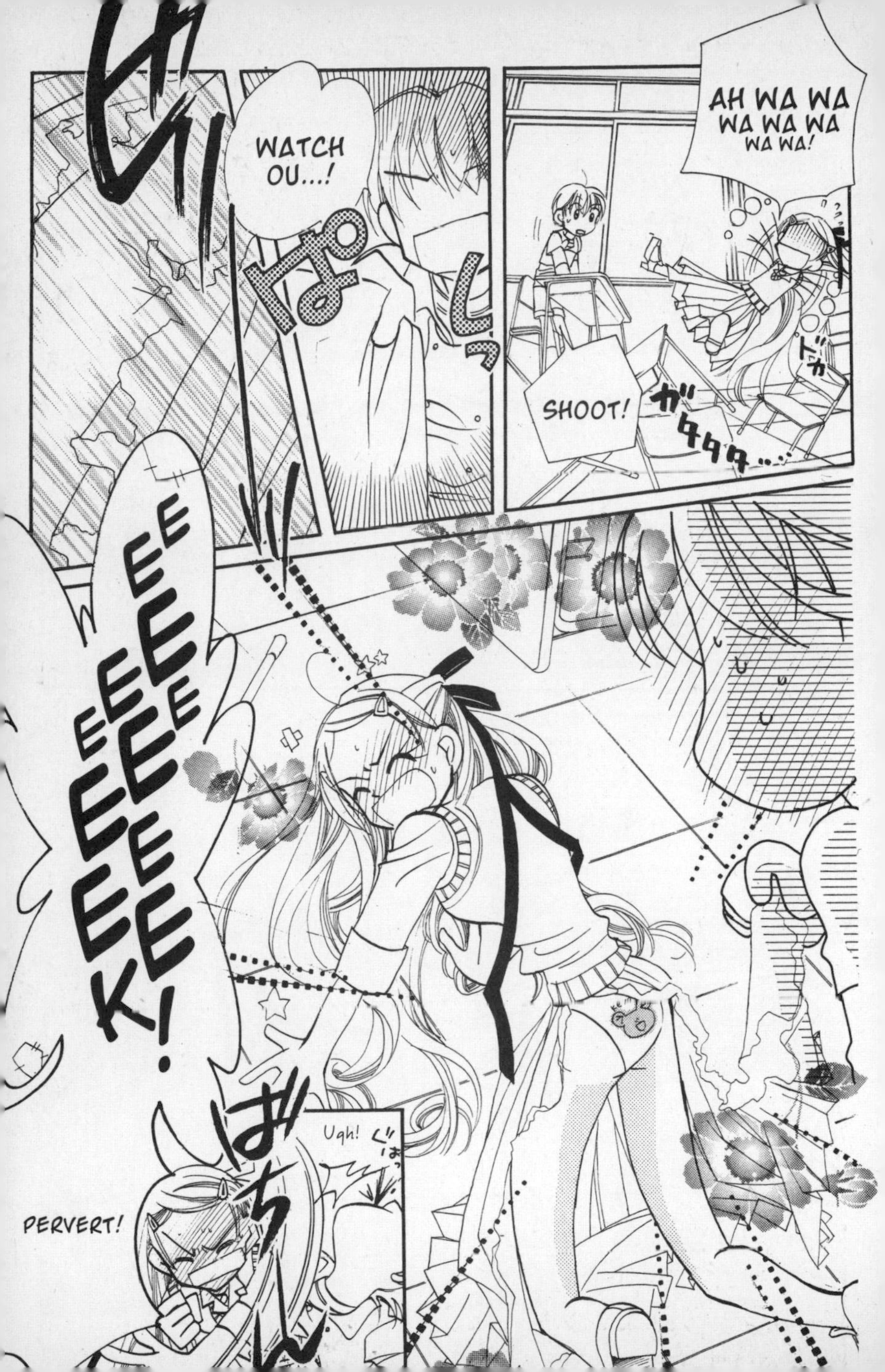
AH WA WA WA WA WA WA WA!
SHOOT!
WATCH OU...!
EEEEEEEEEEEEEEEK!
Ugh!
PERVERT!

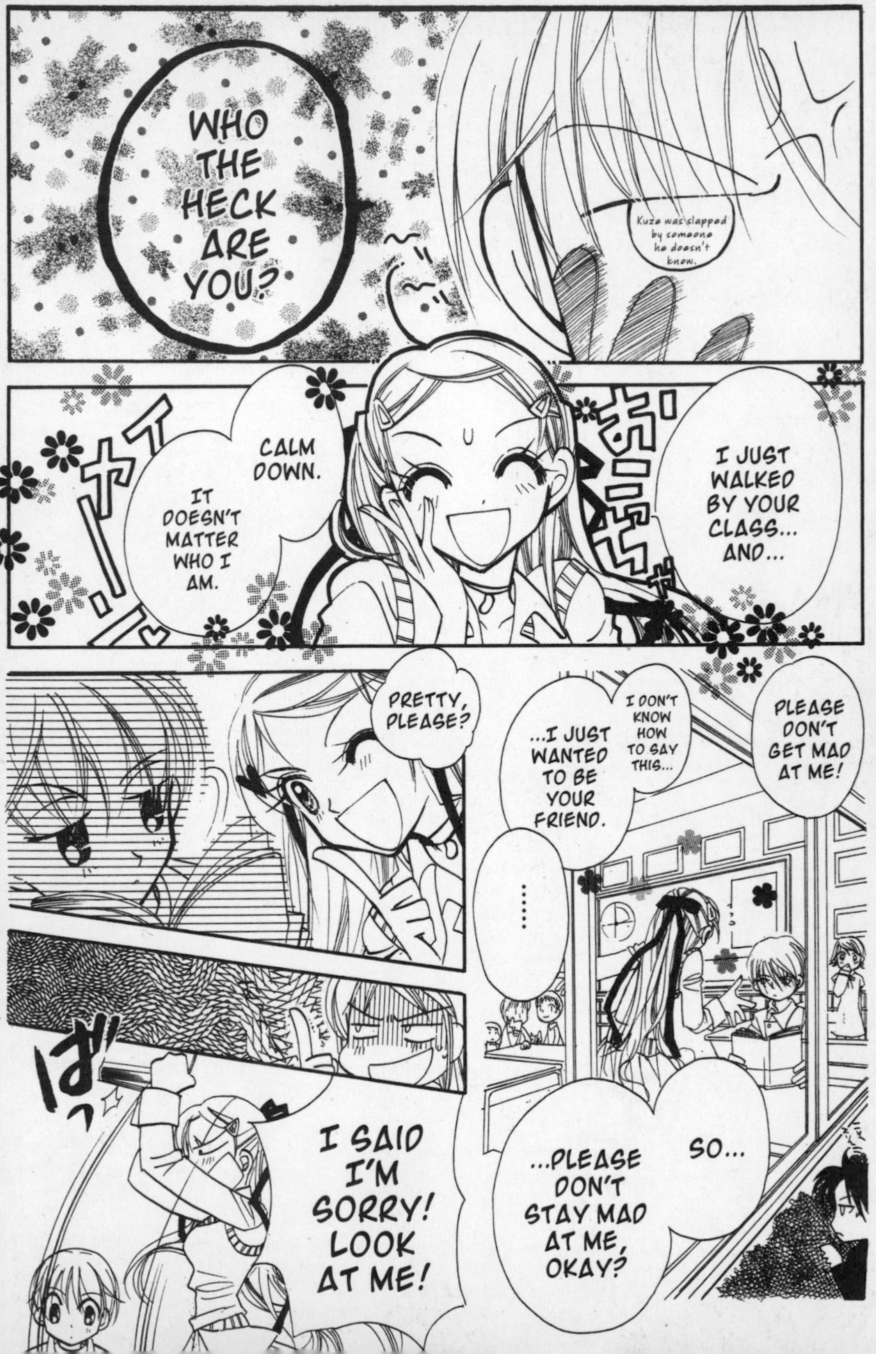

Kuze was slapped by someone he doesn't know.
WHO THE HECK ARE YOU?
I JUST WALKED BY YOUR CLASS... AND...
CALM DOWN.
IT DOESN'T MATTER WHO I AM.
PLEASE DON'T GET MAD AT ME!
I DON'T KNOW HOW TO SAY THIS...
...I JUST WANTED TO BE YOUR FRIEND.
......
SO...
...PLEASE DON'T STAY MAD AT ME, OKAY?
PRETTY, PLEASE?
ばっ
I SAID I'M SORRY! LOOK AT ME!

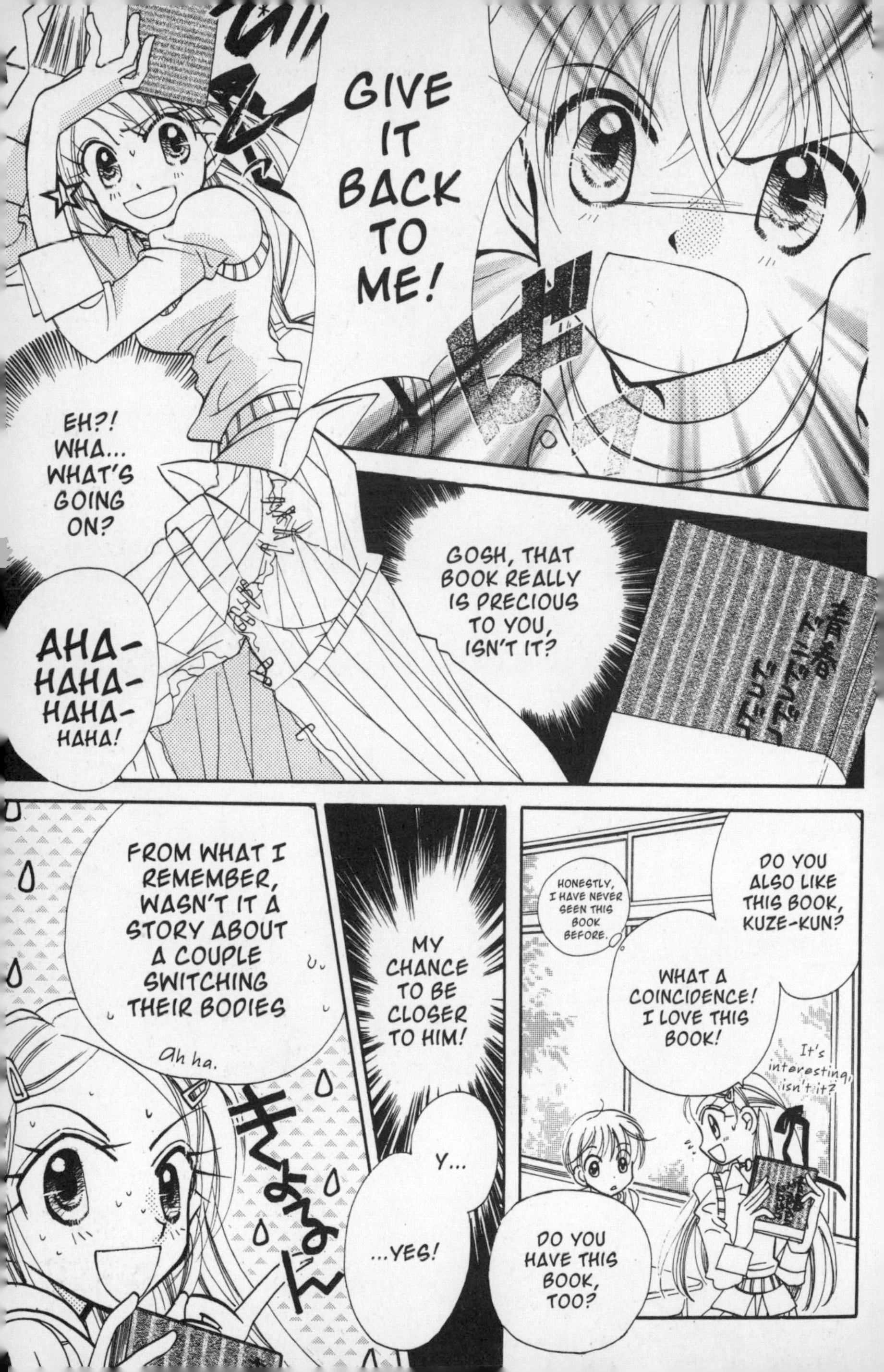
GIVE IT BACK TO ME!
GOSH, THAT BOOK REALLY IS PRECIOUS TO YOU, ISN'T IT?
EH?! WHA... WHAT'S GOING ON?
AHA-HAHA-HAHA-HAHA!
DO YOU ALSO LIKE THIS BOOK, KUZE-KUN?
WHAT A COINCIDENCE! I LOVE THIS BOOK!
It's interesting, isn't it?
HONESTLY, I HAVE NEVER SEEN THIS BOOK BEFORE.
DO YOU HAVE THIS BOOK, TOO?
MY CHANCE TO BE CLOSER TO HIM!
Y...
...YES!
FROM WHAT I REMEMBER, WASN'T IT A STORY ABOUT A COUPLE SWITCHING THEIR BODIES
Ah ha.

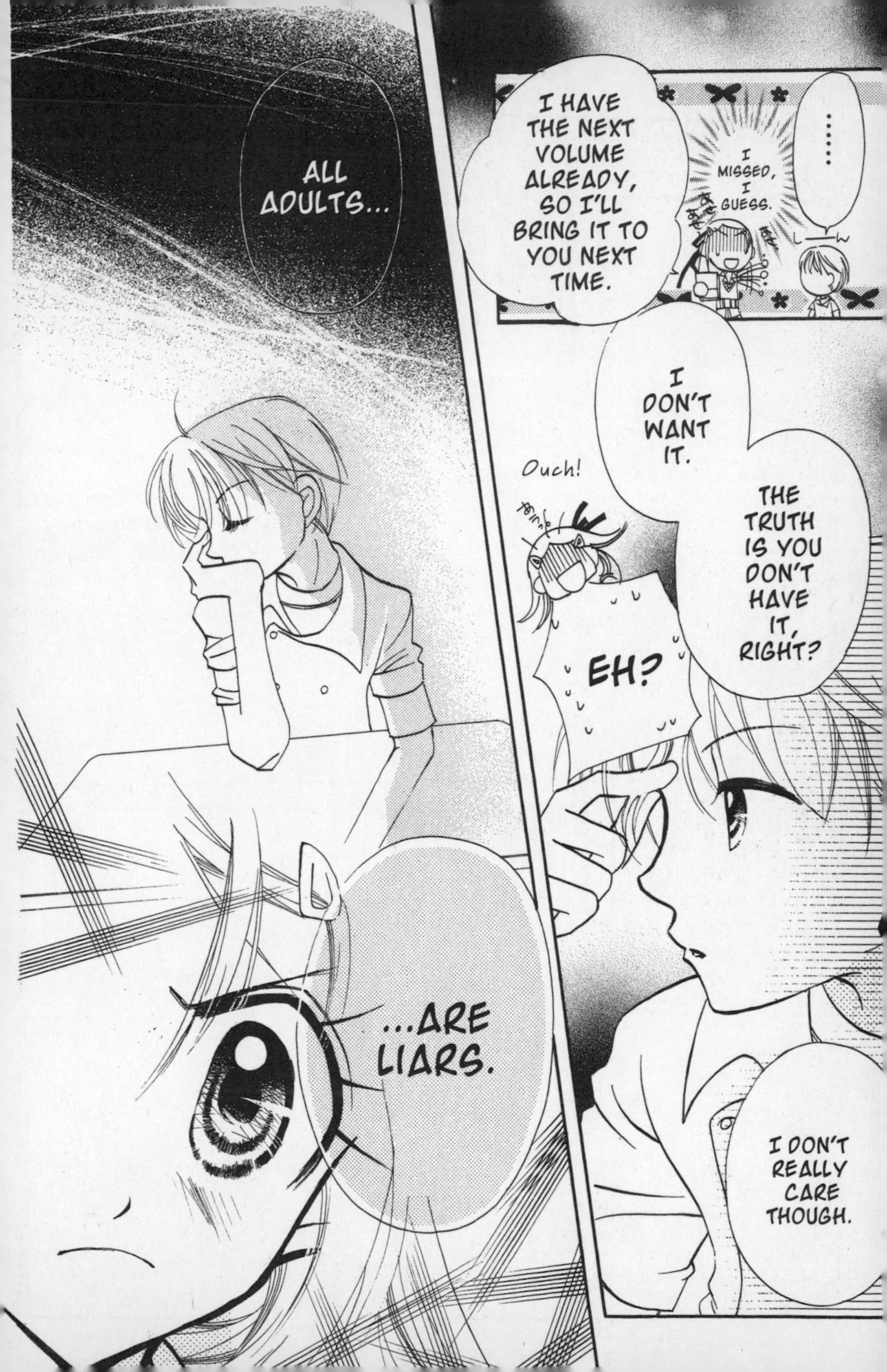
I HAVE THE NEXT VOLUME ALREADY, SO I'LL BRING IT TO YOU NEXT TIME.
......
I MISSED, I GUESS.
I DON'T WANT IT.
THE TRUTH IS YOU DON'T HAVE IT, RIGHT?
Ouch!
EH?
I DON'T REALLY CARE THOUGH.
ALL ADULTS...
...ARE LIARS.

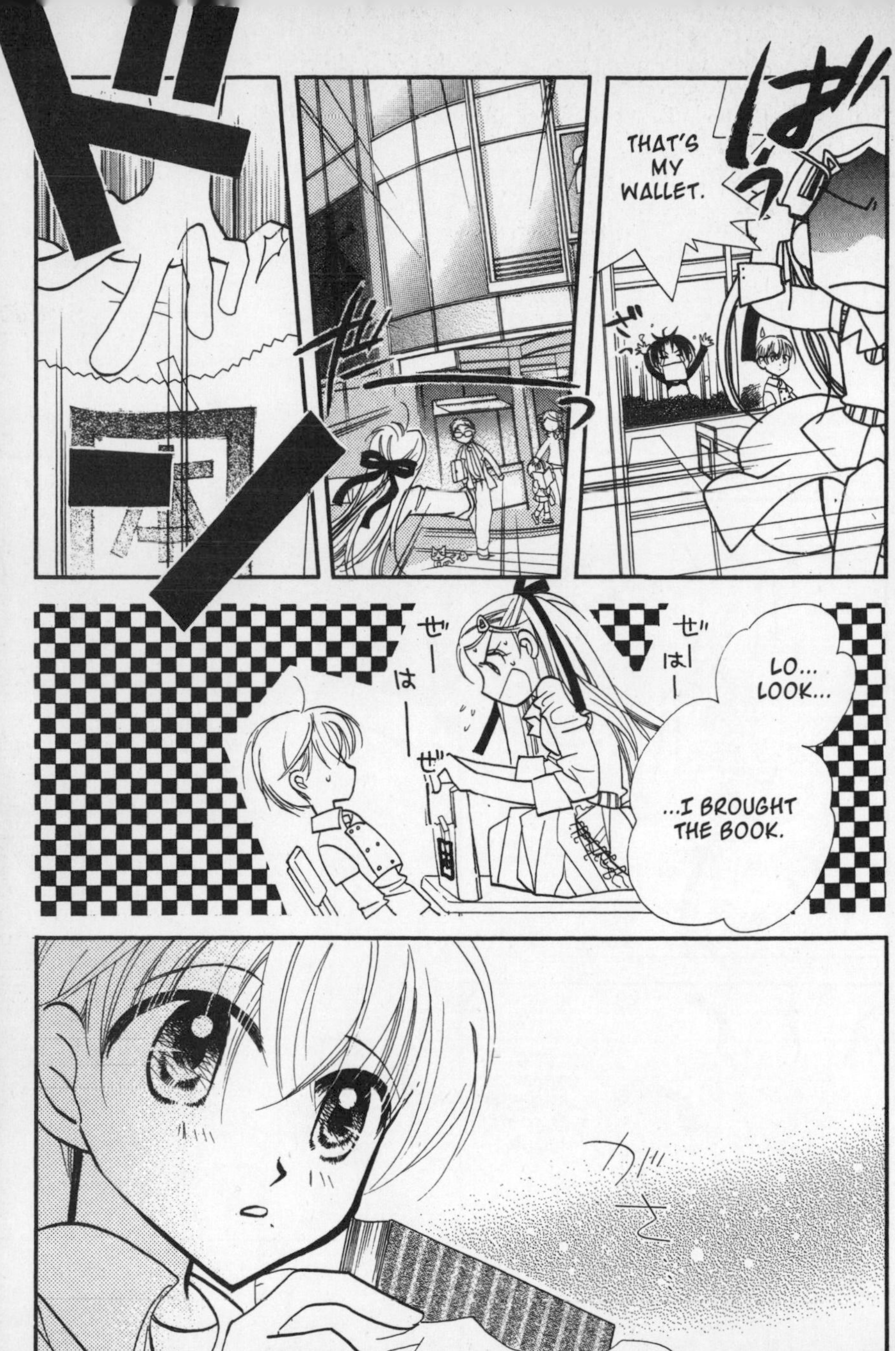
THAT'S MY WALLET.
ぜーはー
LO... LOOK...
...I BROUGHT THE BOOK.
ぜーはー
がさ

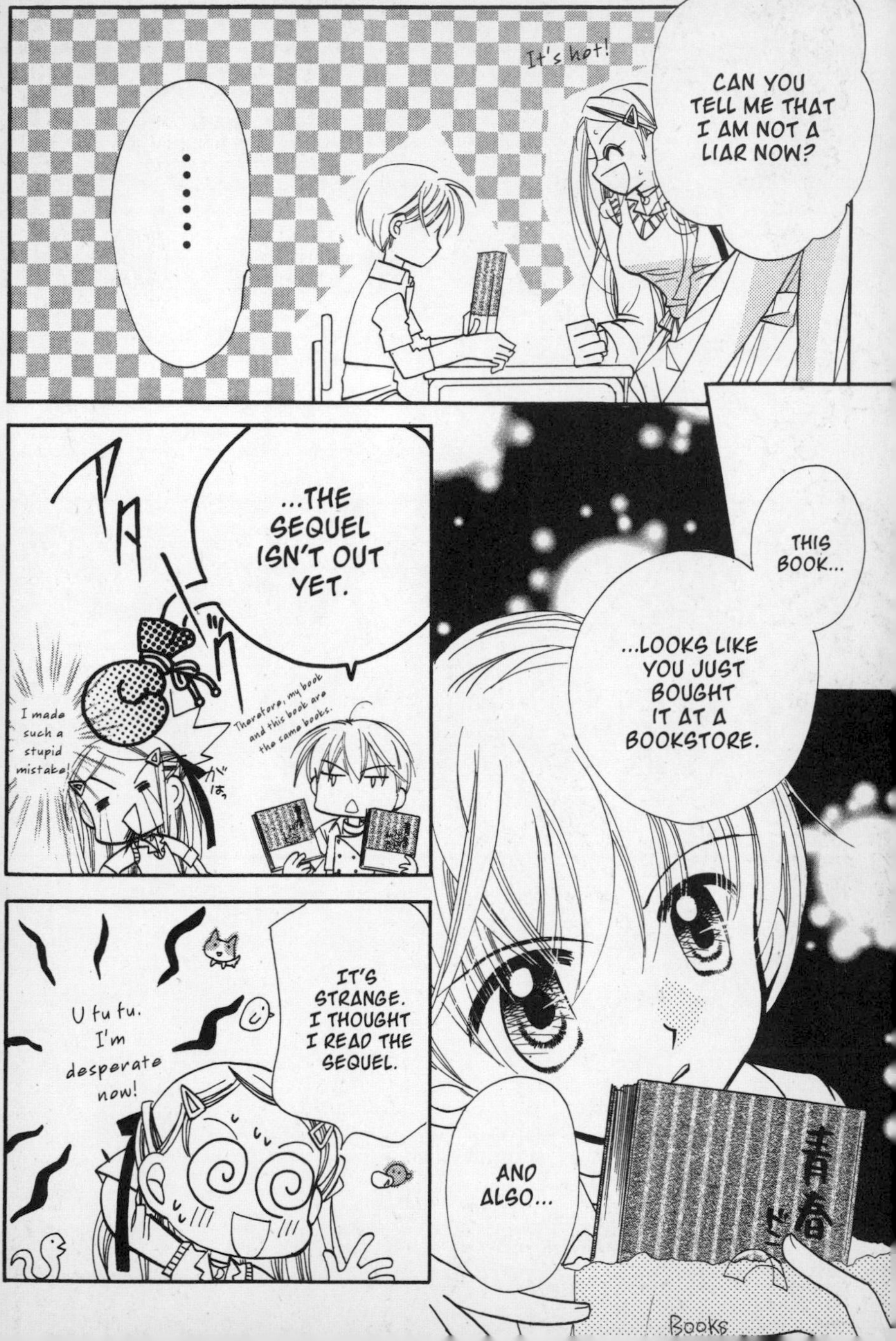
CAN YOU TELL ME THAT I AM NOT A LIAR NOW?
It's hot!
......
THIS BOOK...
...LOOKS LIKE YOU JUST BOUGHT IT AT A BOOKSTORE.
AND ALSO...
青春
Books
...THE SEQUEL ISN'T OUT YET.
Therefore, my book and this book are the same books.
I made such a stupid mistake!
IT'S STRANGE. I THOUGHT I READ THE SEQUEL.
U fu fu. I'm desperate now!

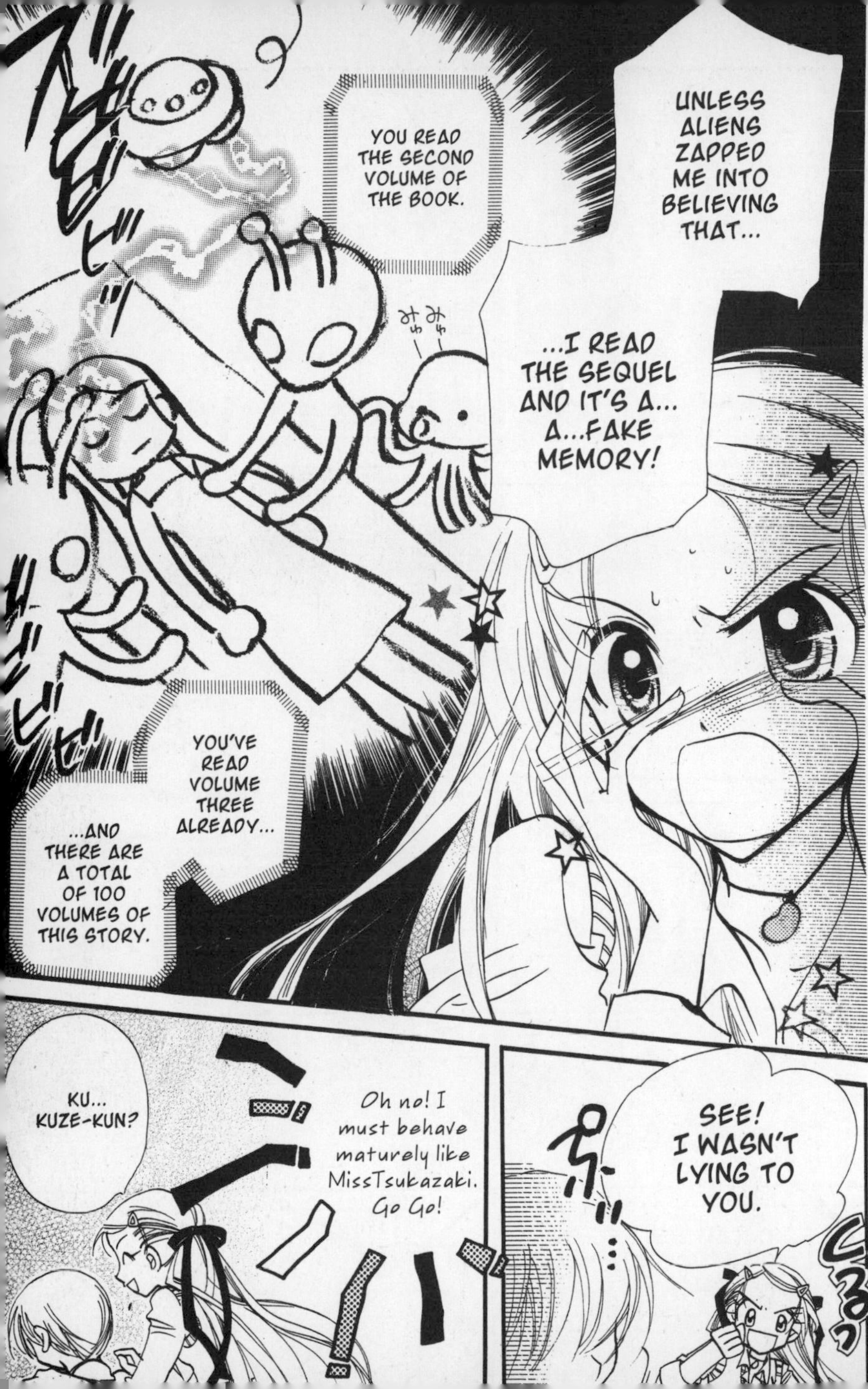
UNLESS ALIENS ZAPPED ME INTO BELIEVING THAT...
...I READ THE SEQUEL AND IT'S A... A...FAKE MEMORY!
YOU READ THE SECOND VOLUME OF THE BOOK.
みゅ みゅ
YOU'VE READ VOLUME THREE ALREADY...
...AND THERE ARE A TOTAL OF 100 VOLUMES OF THIS STORY.
SEE! I WASN'T LYING TO YOU.
Oh no! I must behave maturely like MissTsukazaki. Go Go!
KU... KUZE-KUN?

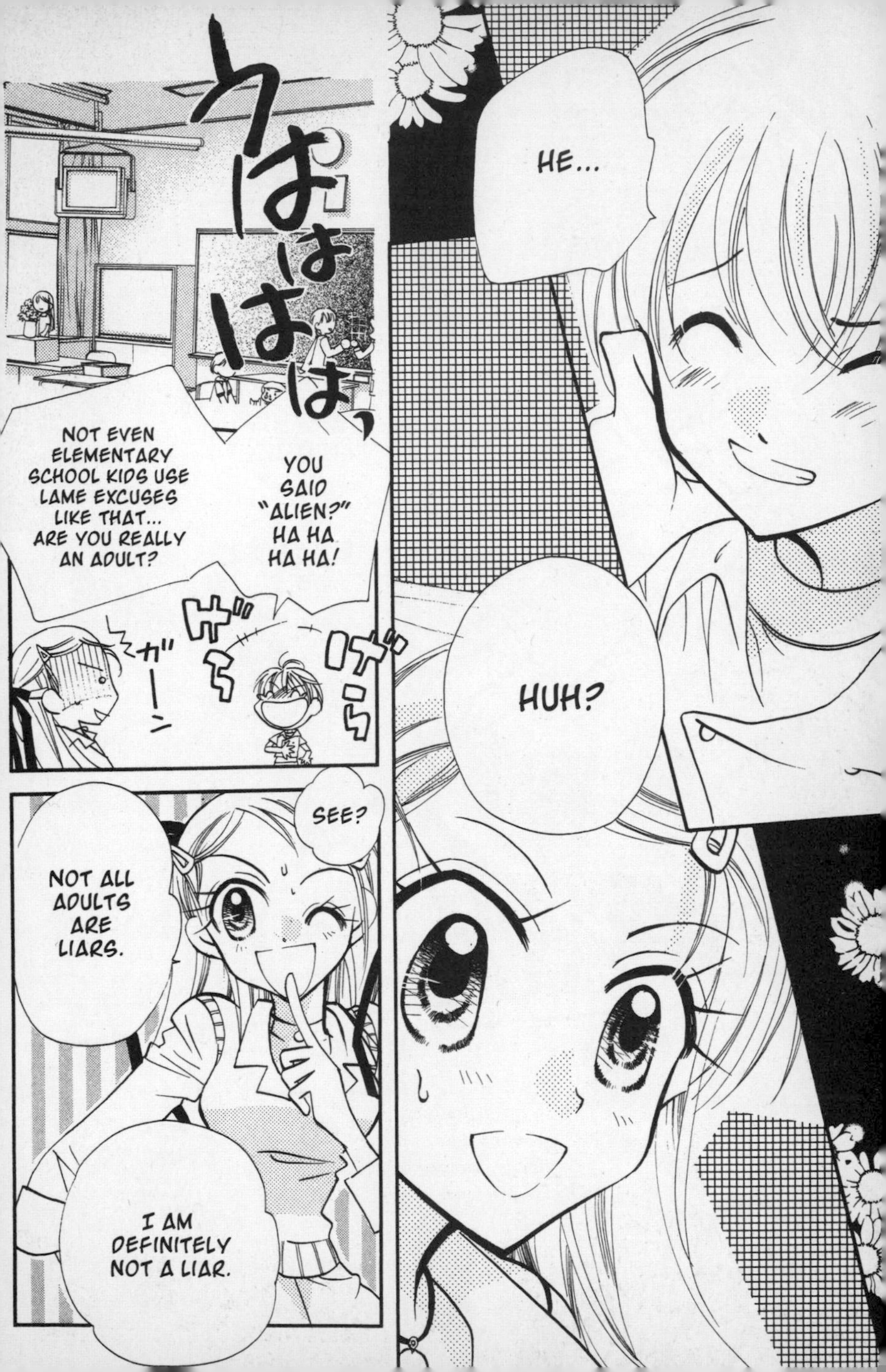
HE...
HUH?
YOU SAID "ALIEN?" HA HA HA HA!
NOT EVEN ELEMENTARY SCHOOL KIDS USE LAME EXCUSES LIKE THAT... ARE YOU REALLY AN ADULT?
ゲらゲら
ガーン
SEE?
NOT ALL ADULTS ARE LIARS.
I AM DEFINITELY NOT A LIAR.

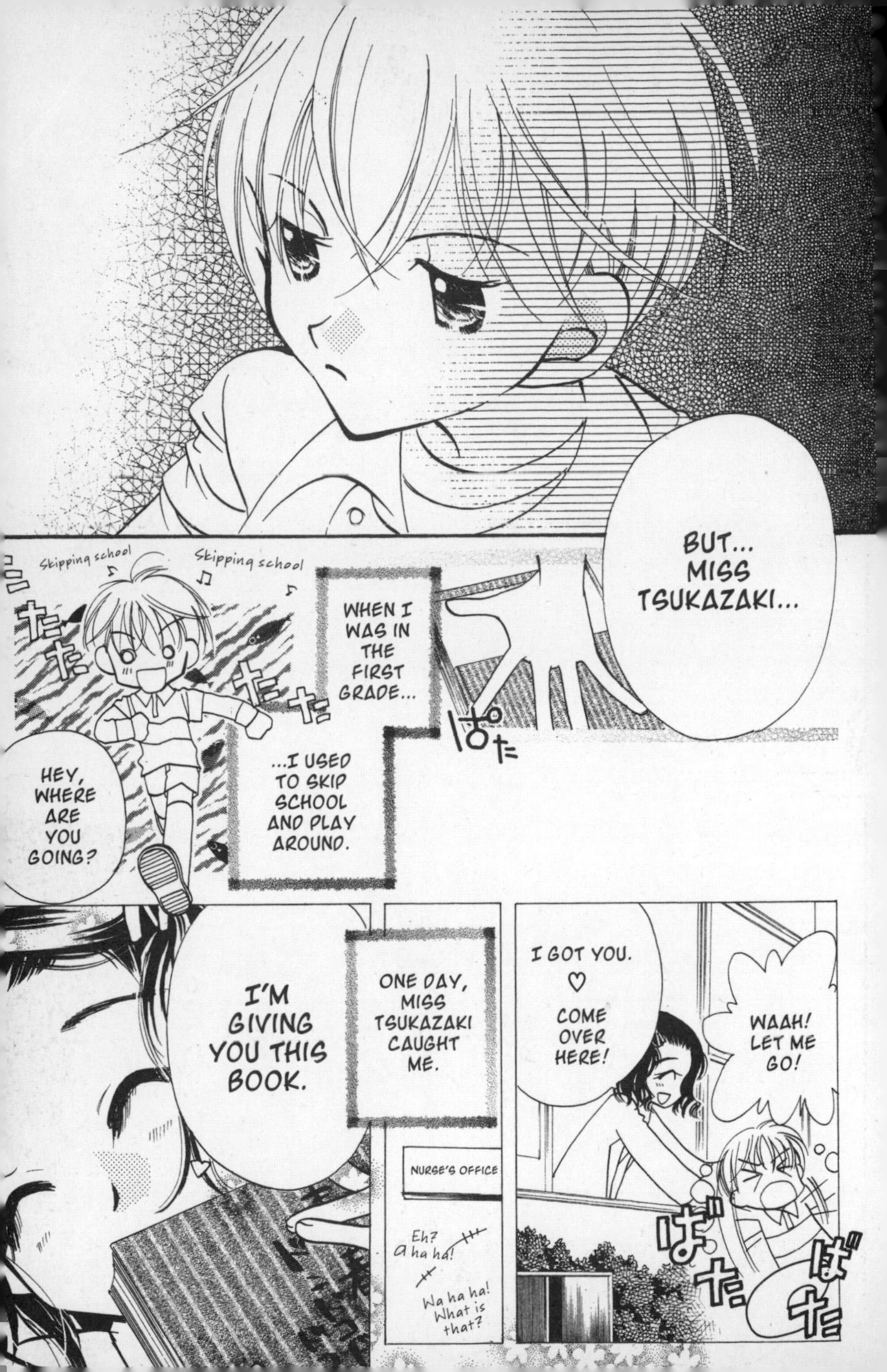
BUT... MISS TSUKAZAKI...
ぱた
Skipping school
Skipping school
たたた
WHEN I WAS IN THE FIRST GRADE...
...I USED TO SKIP SCHOOL AND PLAY AROUND.
HEY, WHERE ARE YOU GOING?
I GOT YOU. ♡
COME OVER HERE!
WAAH! LET ME GO!
ばた ばた
ONE DAY, MISS TSUKAZAKI CAUGHT ME.
NURSE'S OFFICE
Eh? A ha ha!
Wa ha ha! What is that?
I'M GIVING YOU THIS BOOK.

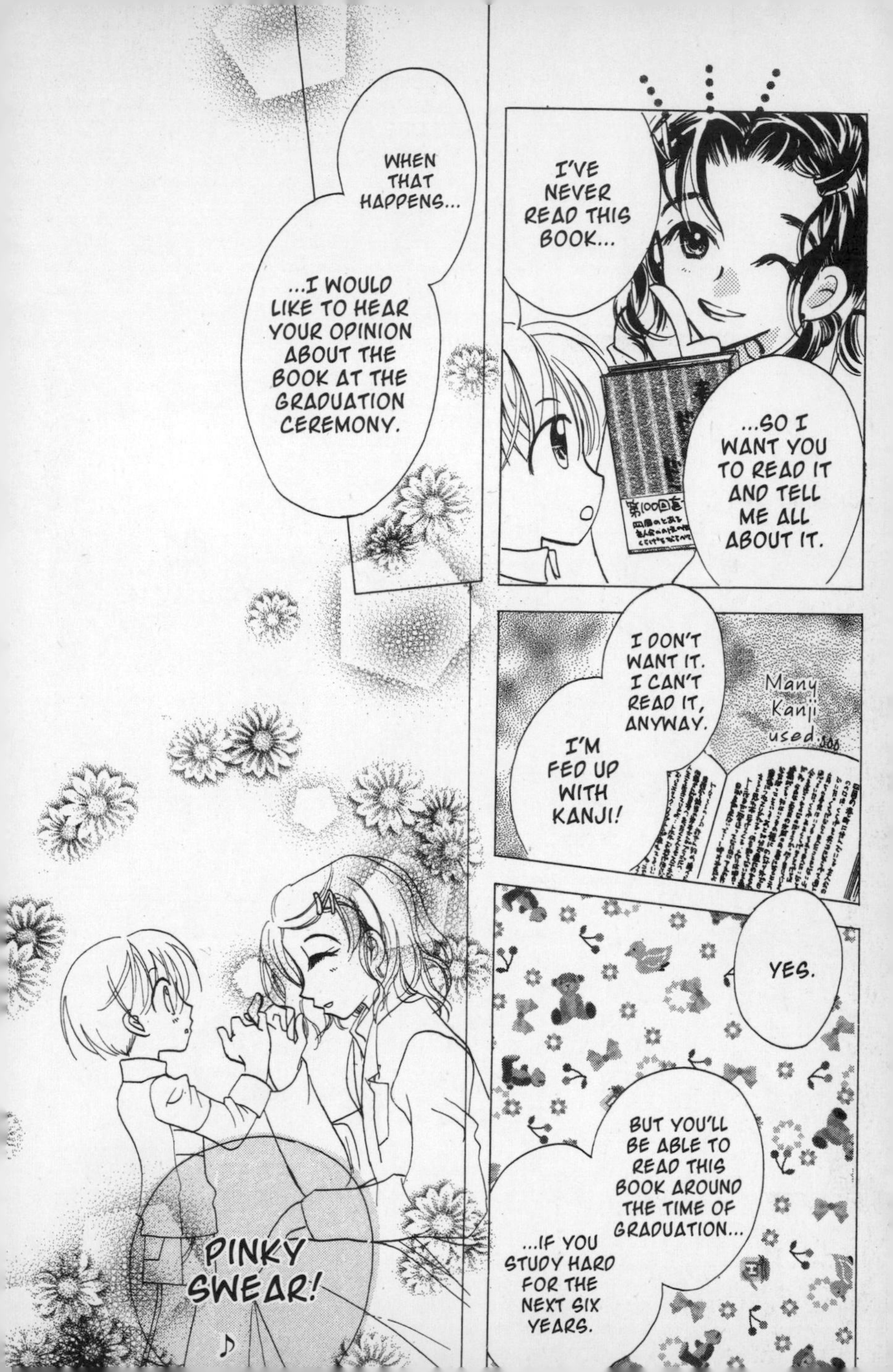
I'VE NEVER READ THIS BOOK...
...SO I WANT YOU TO READ IT AND TELL ME ALL ABOUT IT.
I DON'T WANT IT. I CAN'T READ IT, ANYWAY.
I'M FED UP WITH KANJI!
Many Kanji used...
YES.
BUT YOU'LL BE ABLE TO READ THIS BOOK AROUND THE TIME OF GRADUATION...
...IF YOU STUDY HARD FOR THE NEXT SIX YEARS.
WHEN THAT HAPPENS...
...I WOULD LIKE TO HEAR YOUR OPINION ABOUT THE BOOK AT THE GRADUATION CEREMONY.
PINKY SWEAR! ♪

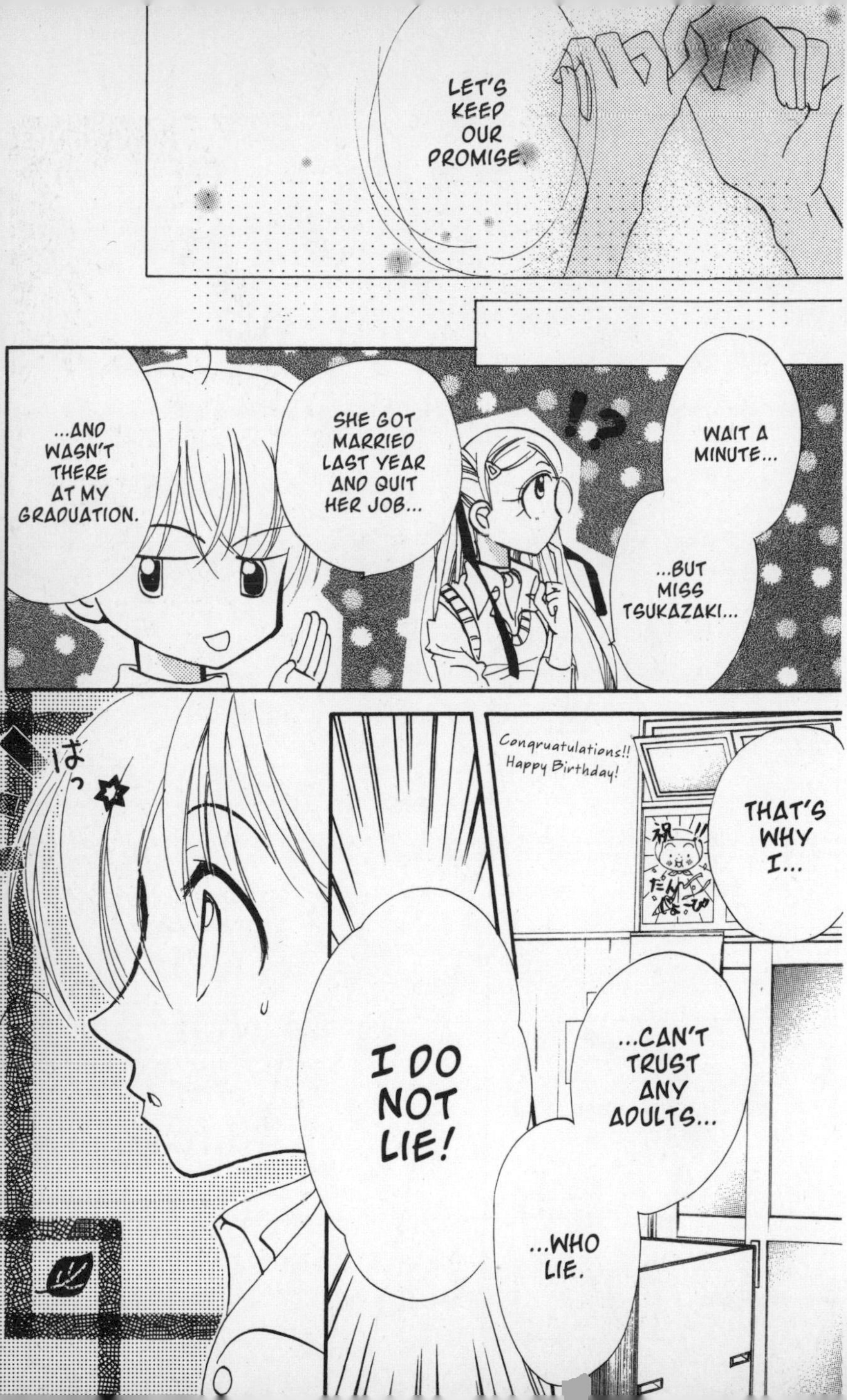
LET'S KEEP OUR PROMISE.
WAIT A MINUTE...
...BUT MISS TSUKAZAKI...
!?
SHE GOT MARRIED LAST YEAR AND QUIT HER JOB...
...AND WASN'T THERE AT MY GRADUATION.
Congruatulations!! Happy Birthday!
THAT'S WHY I...
...CAN'T TRUST ANY ADULTS...
...WHO LIE.
ぱっ
I DO NOT LIE!

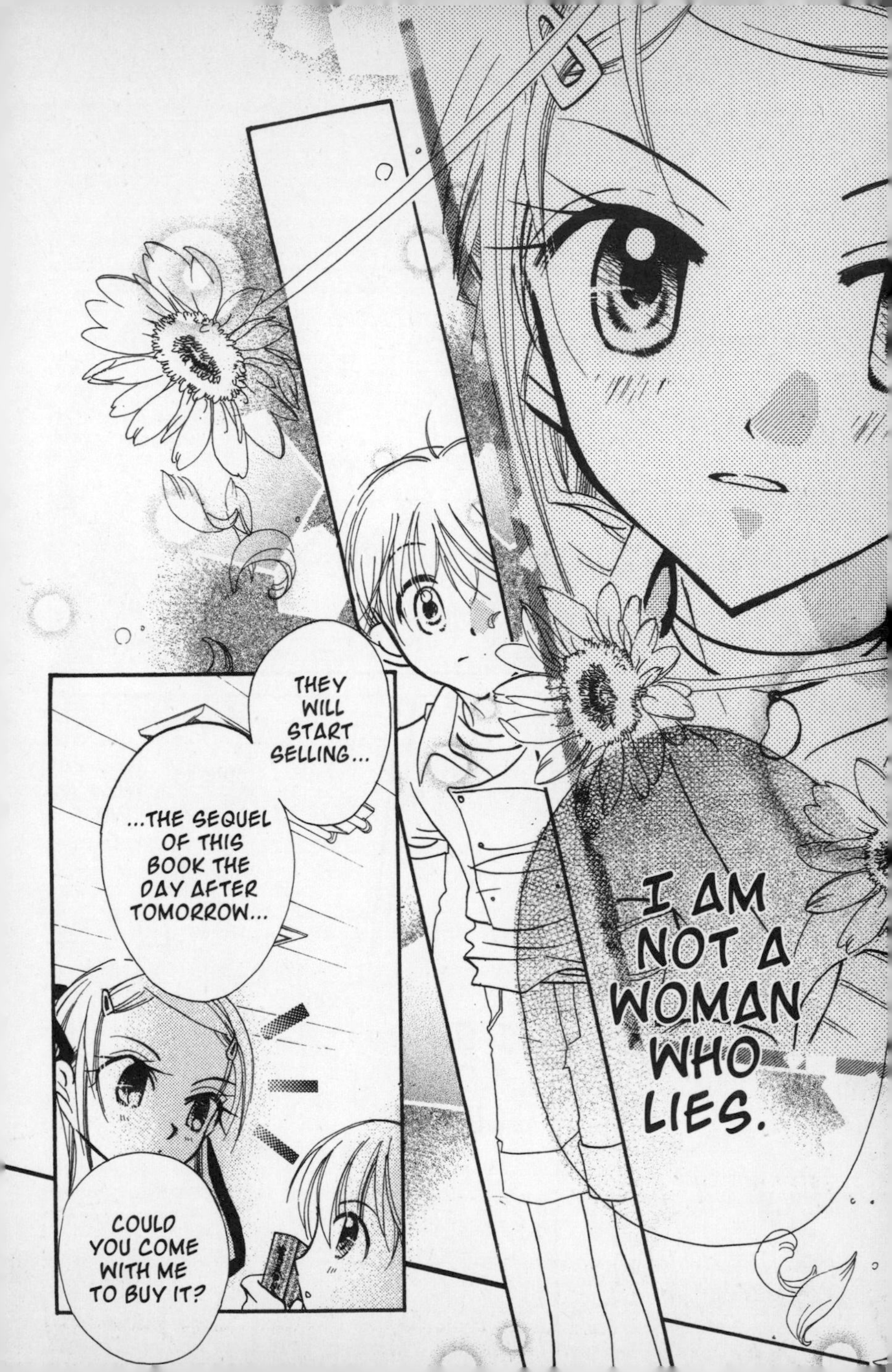
I AM NOT A WOMAN WHO LIES.
THEY WILL START SELLING...
...THE SEQUEL OF THIS BOOK THE DAY AFTER TOMORROW...
COULD YOU COME WITH ME TO BUY IT?

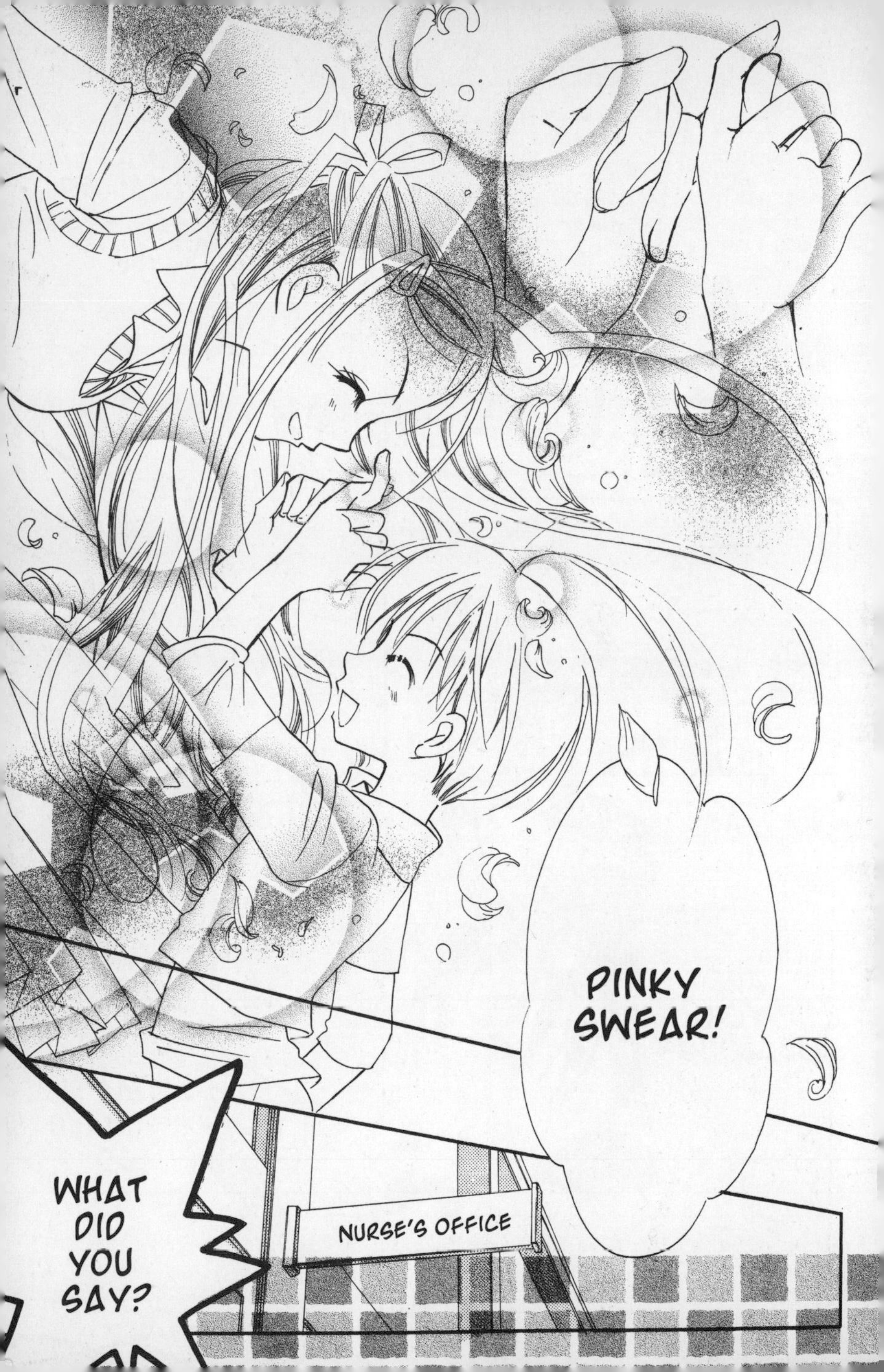
PINKY SWEAR!
NURSE'S OFFICE
WHAT DID YOU SAY?

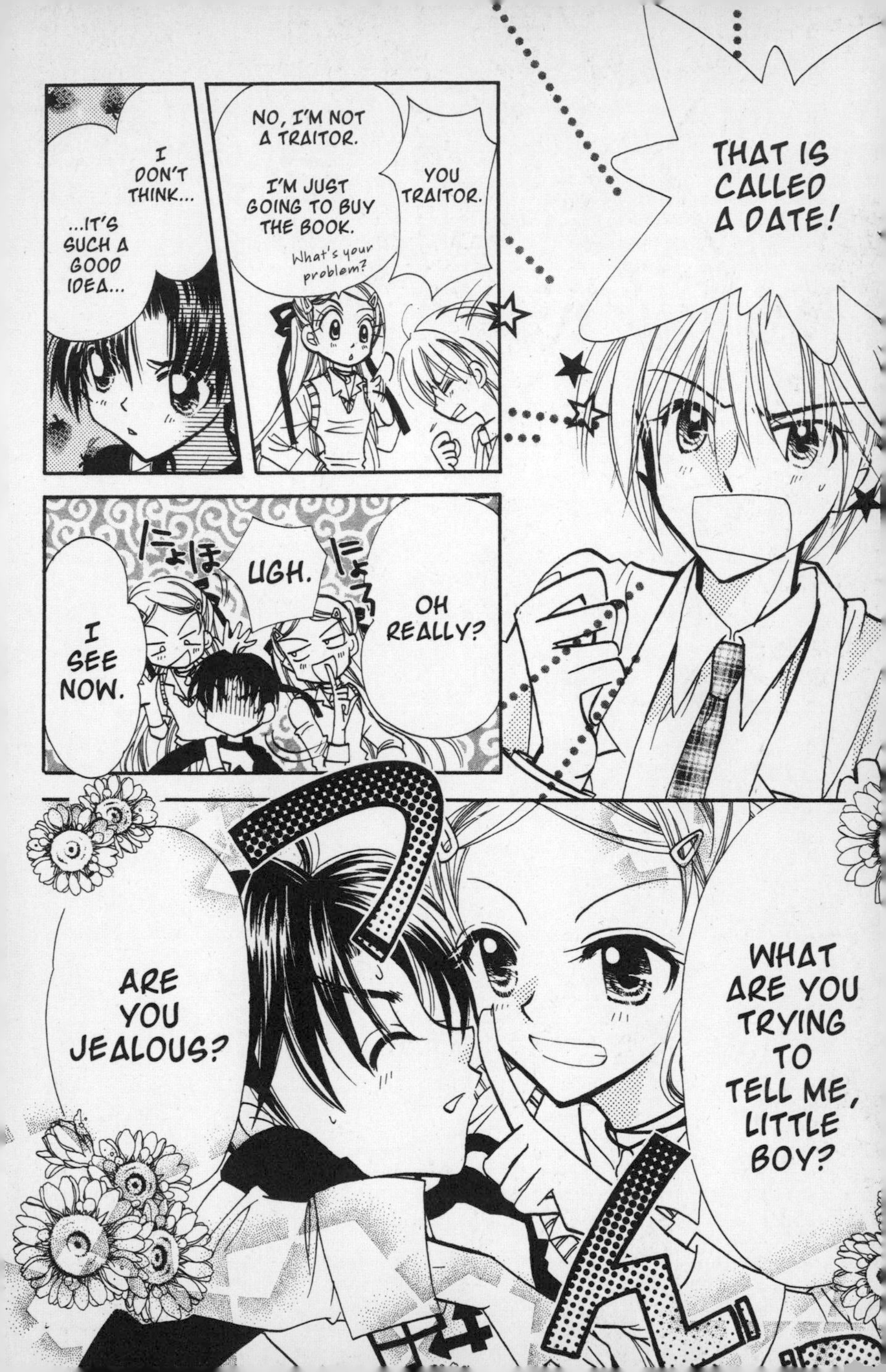
THAT IS CALLED A DATE!
YOU TRAITOR.
NO, I'M NOT A TRAITOR.
I'M JUST GOING TO BUY THE BOOK.
What's your problem?
I DON'T THINK...
...IT'S SUCH A GOOD IDEA...
OH REALLY?
にょろ
UGH.
にょほ
I SEE NOW.
WHAT ARE YOU TRYING TO TELL ME, LITTLE BOY?
ARE YOU JEALOUS?

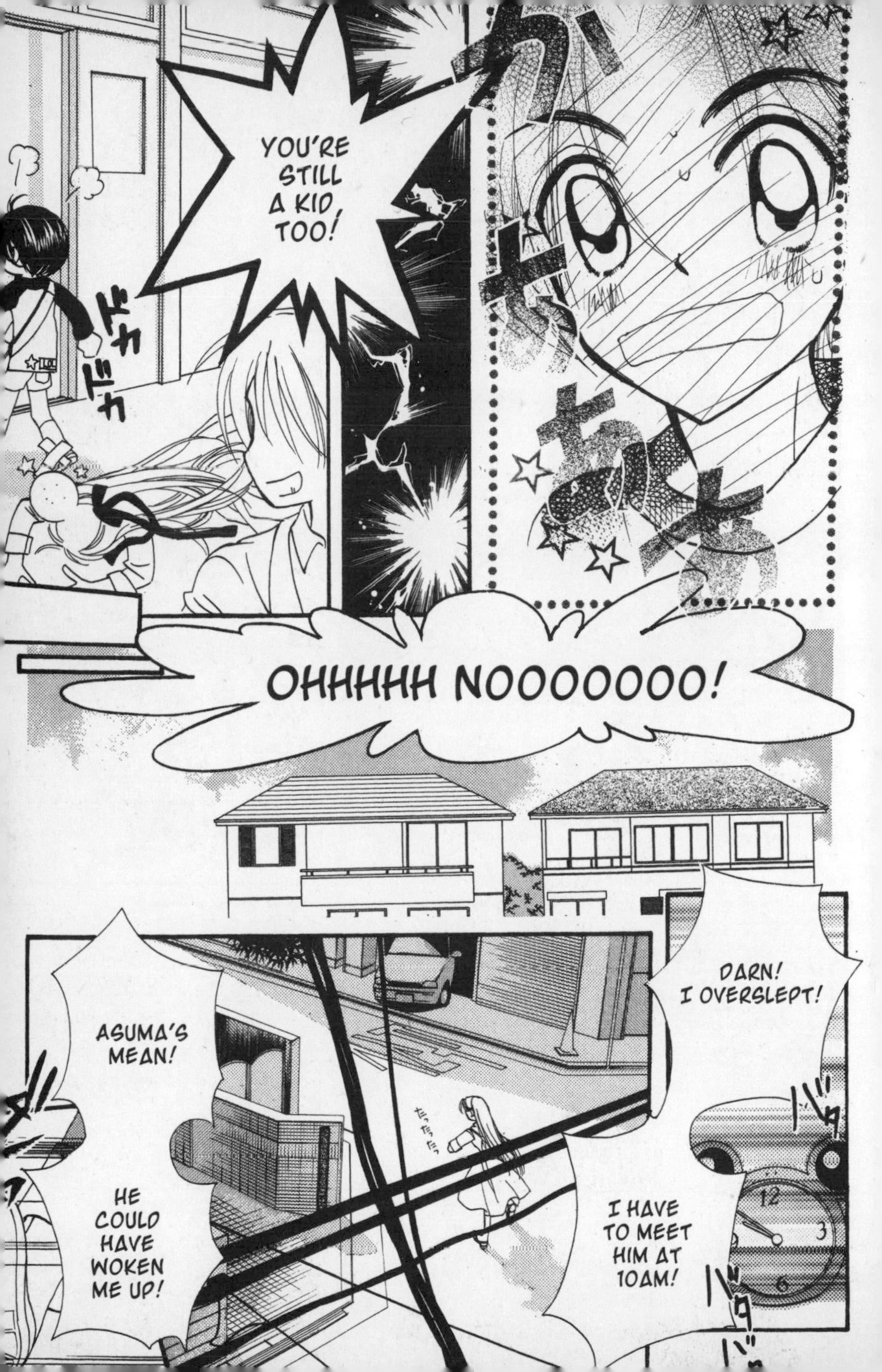
YOU'RE STILL A KID, TOO!
OHHHHH NOOOOOOO!
DARN! I OVERSLEPT!
I HAVE TO MEET HIM AT 10AM!
ASUMA'S MEAN!
HE COULD HAVE WOKEN ME UP!

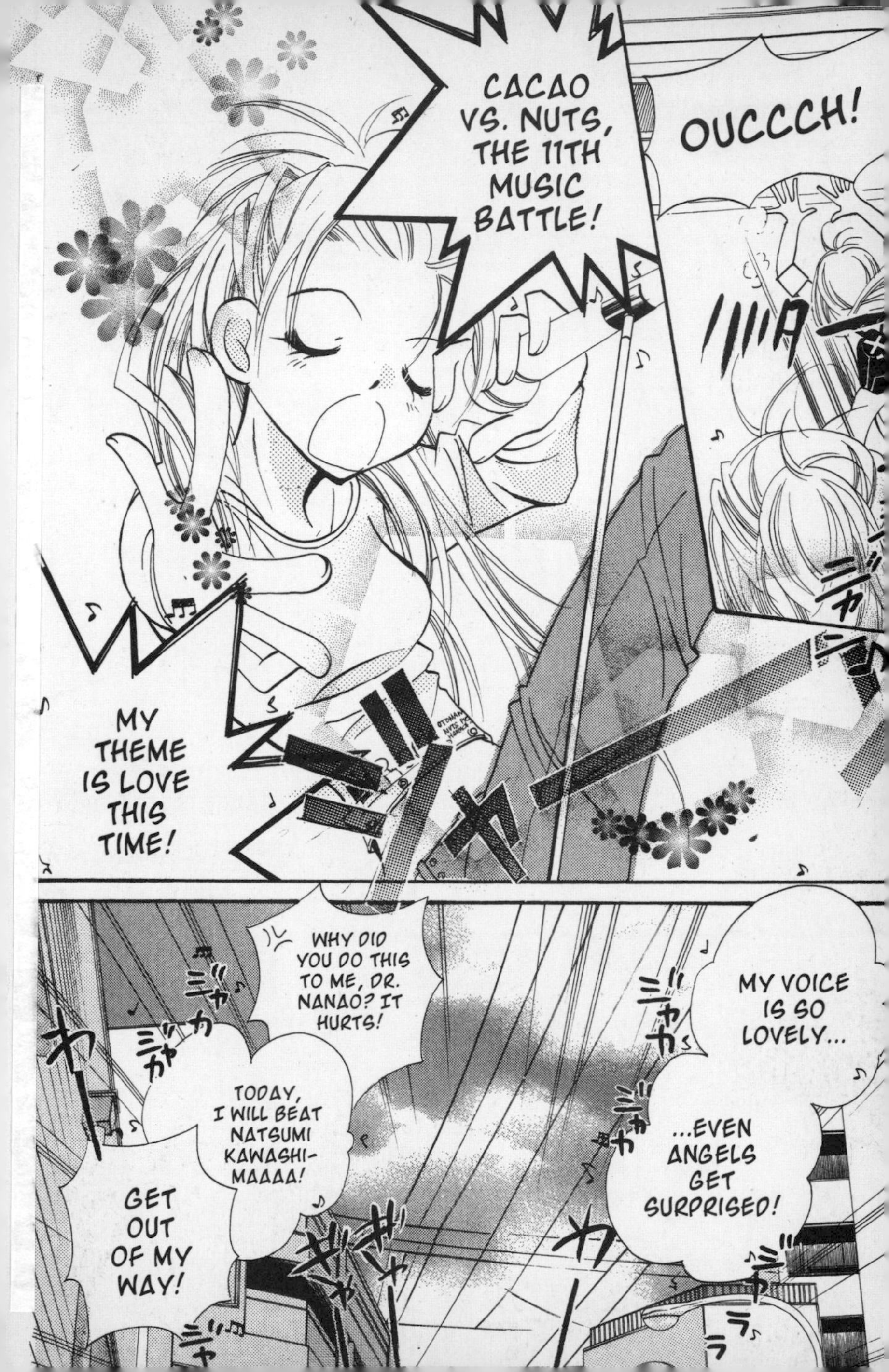
OUCCCH!
CACAO VS. NUTS, THE 11TH MUSIC BATTLE!
MY THEME IS LOVE THIS TIME!
MY VOICE IS SO LOVELY...
...EVEN ANGELS GET SURPRISED!
WHY DID YOU DO THIS TO ME, DR. NANAO? IT HURTS!
TODAY, I WILL BEAT NATSUMI KAWASHI-MAAAA!
GET OUT OF MY WAY!

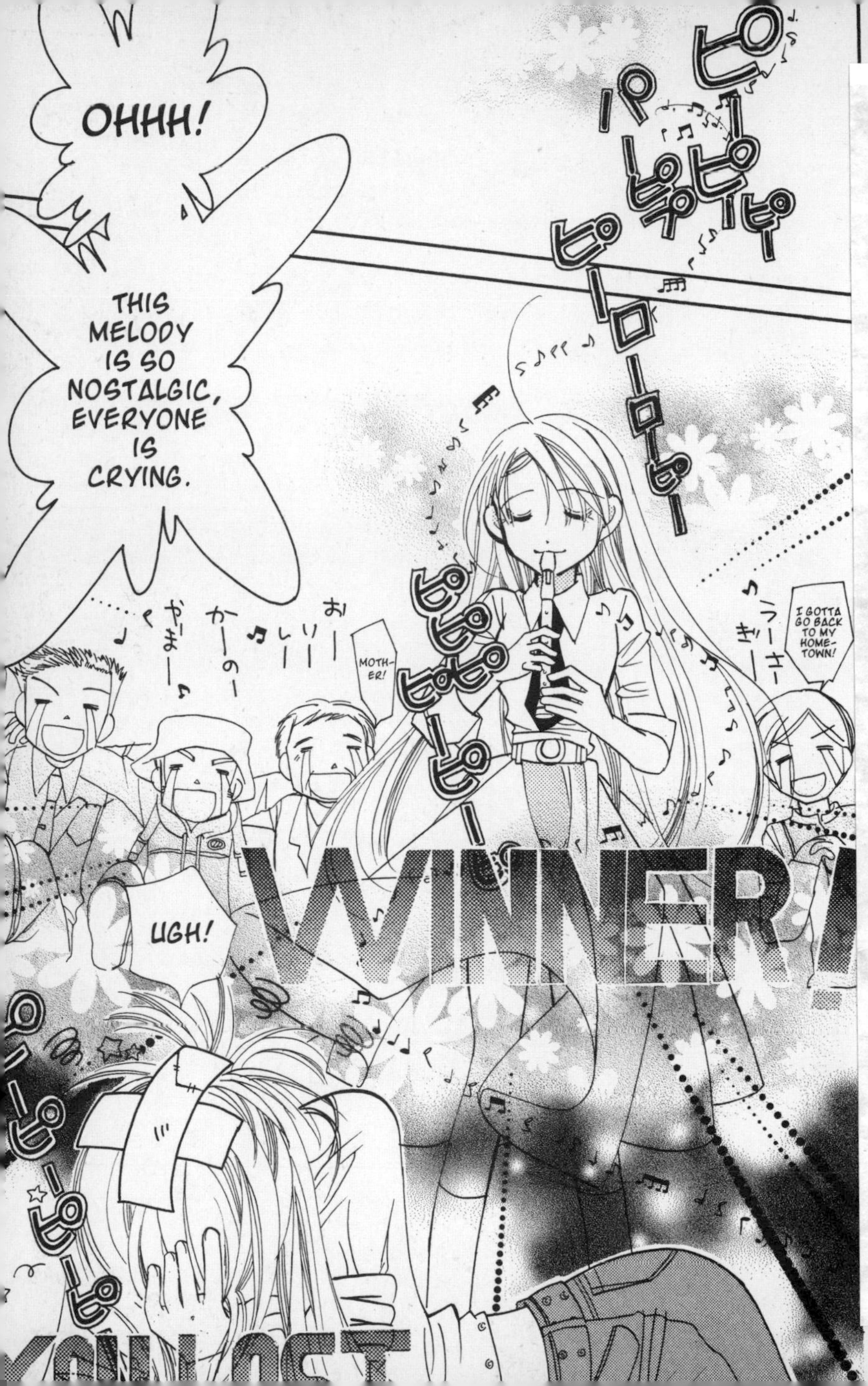
OHHH!
THIS MELODY IS SO NOSTALGIC, EVERYONE IS CRYING.
I GOTTA GO BACK TO MY HOME-TOWN!
MOTHER-ER!
WINNER!
UGH!
YOU LOST

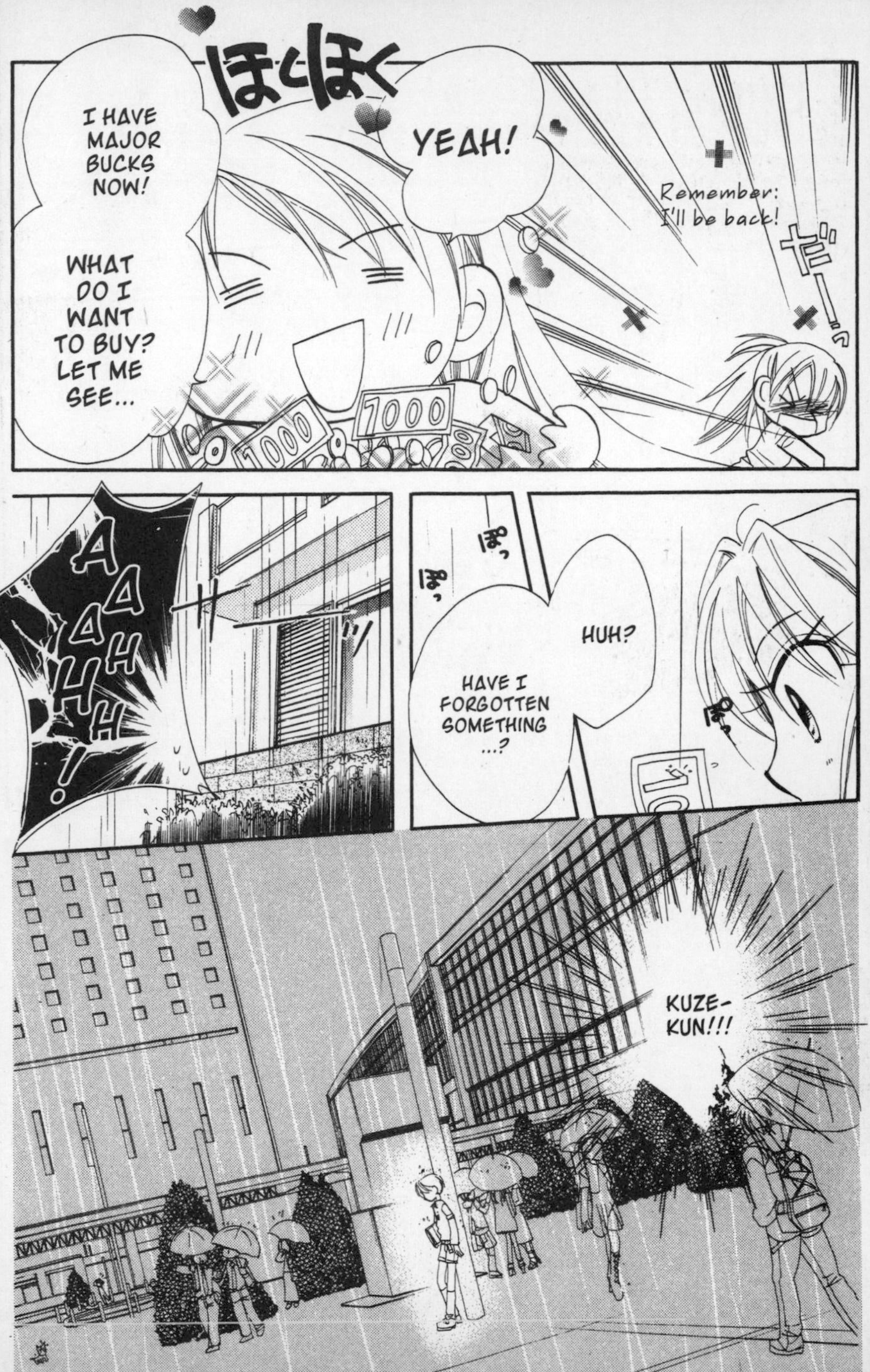

Remember: I'll be back!
だーっ
YEAH!
ほくほく
I HAVE MAJOR BUCKS NOW!
WHAT DO I WANT TO BUY? LET ME SEE...
ぽっ ぽっ
HUH?
HAVE I FORGOTTEN SOMETHING ...?
AAAHHH!
KUZE-KUN!!!

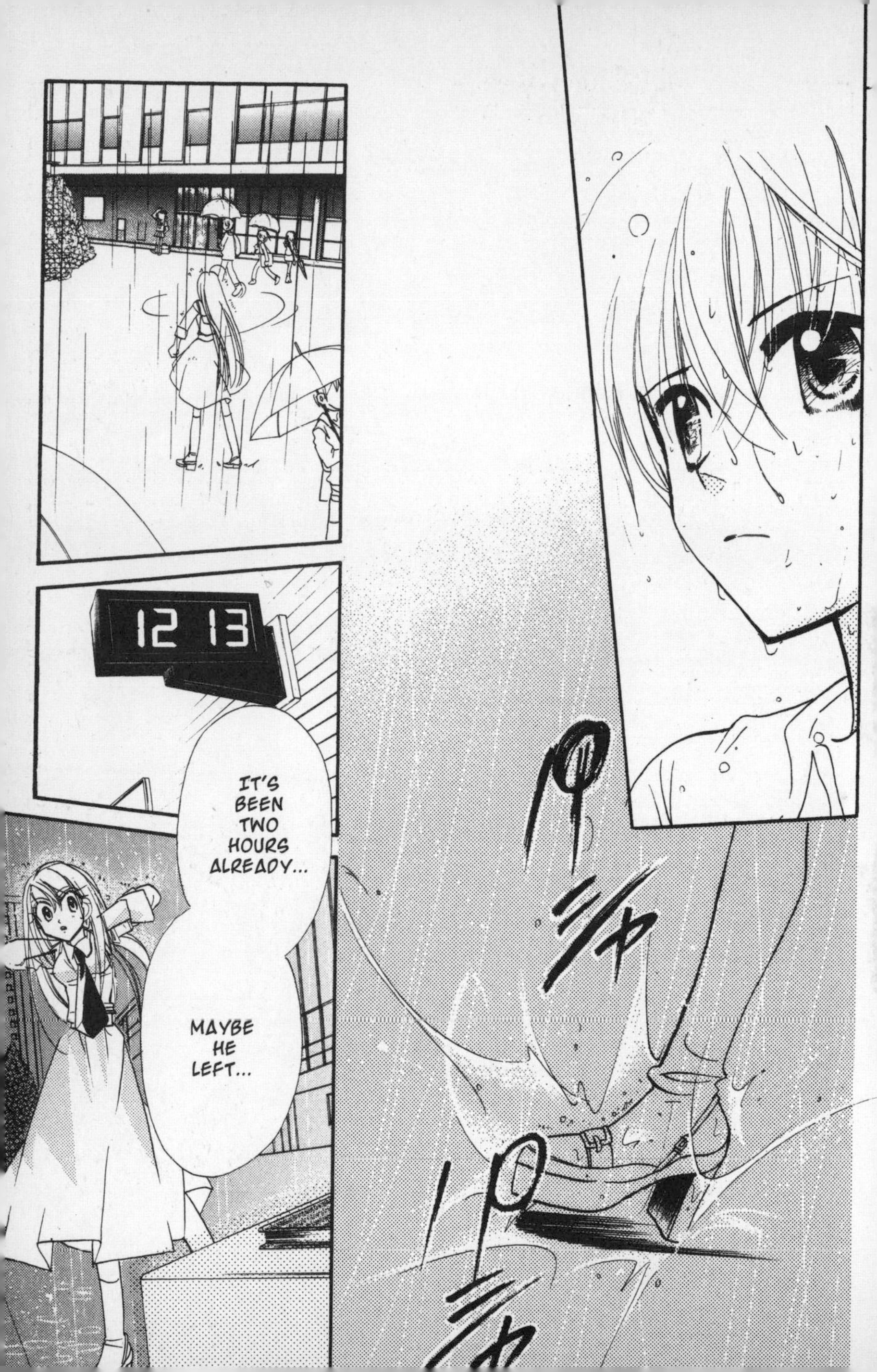
パシャ
パシャ
IT'S BEEN TWO HOURS ALREADY...
MAYBE HE LEFT...

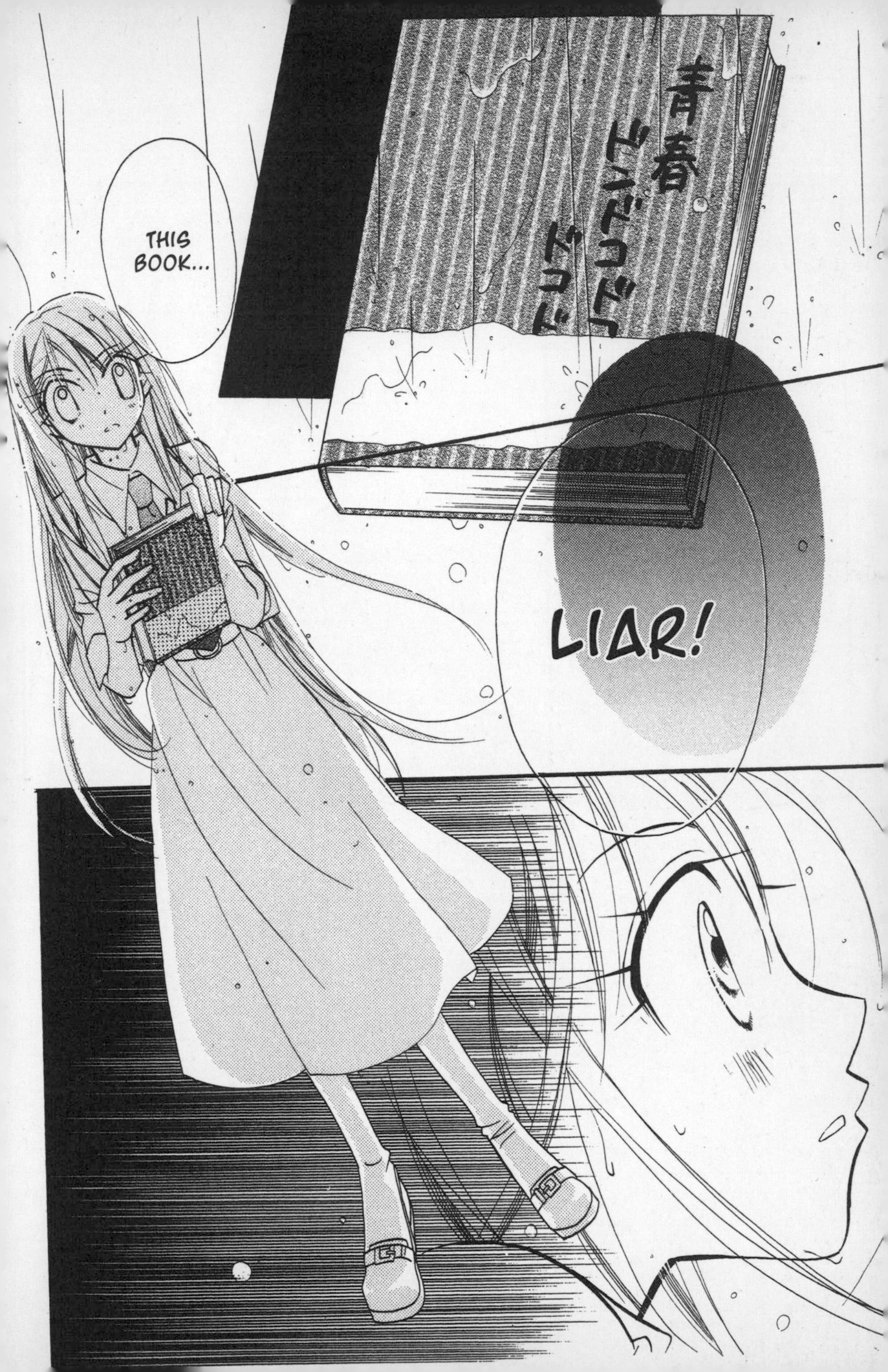
青春
ドンドコド
ドコド
THIS BOOK...
LIAR!

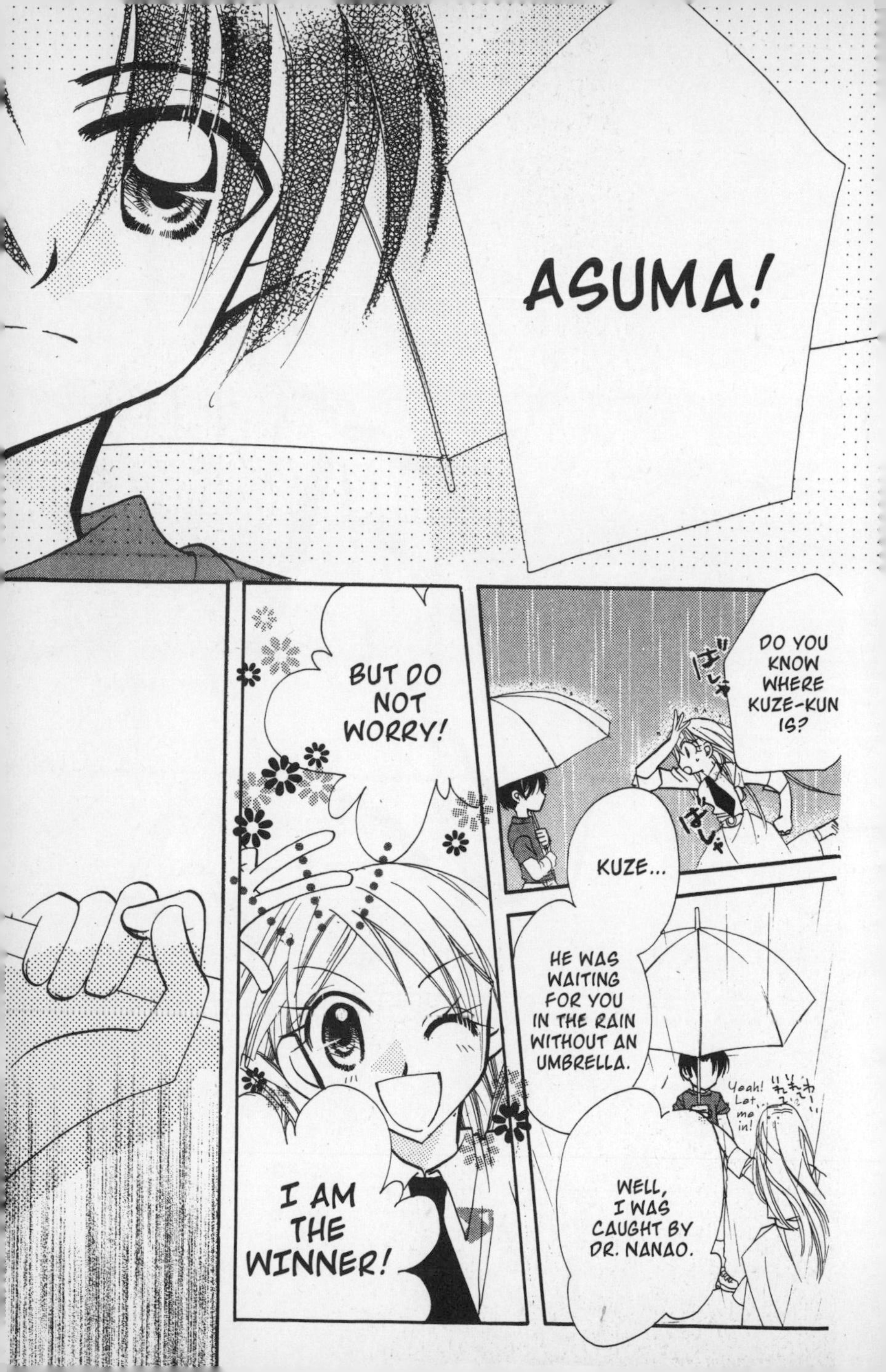
ASUMA!
DO YOU KNOW WHERE KUZE-KUN IS?
KUZE...
HE WAS WAITING FOR YOU IN THE RAIN WITHOUT AN UMBRELLA.
Yeah! Let me in!
WELL, I WAS CAUGHT BY DR. NANAO.
BUT DO NOT WORRY!
I AM THE WINNER!

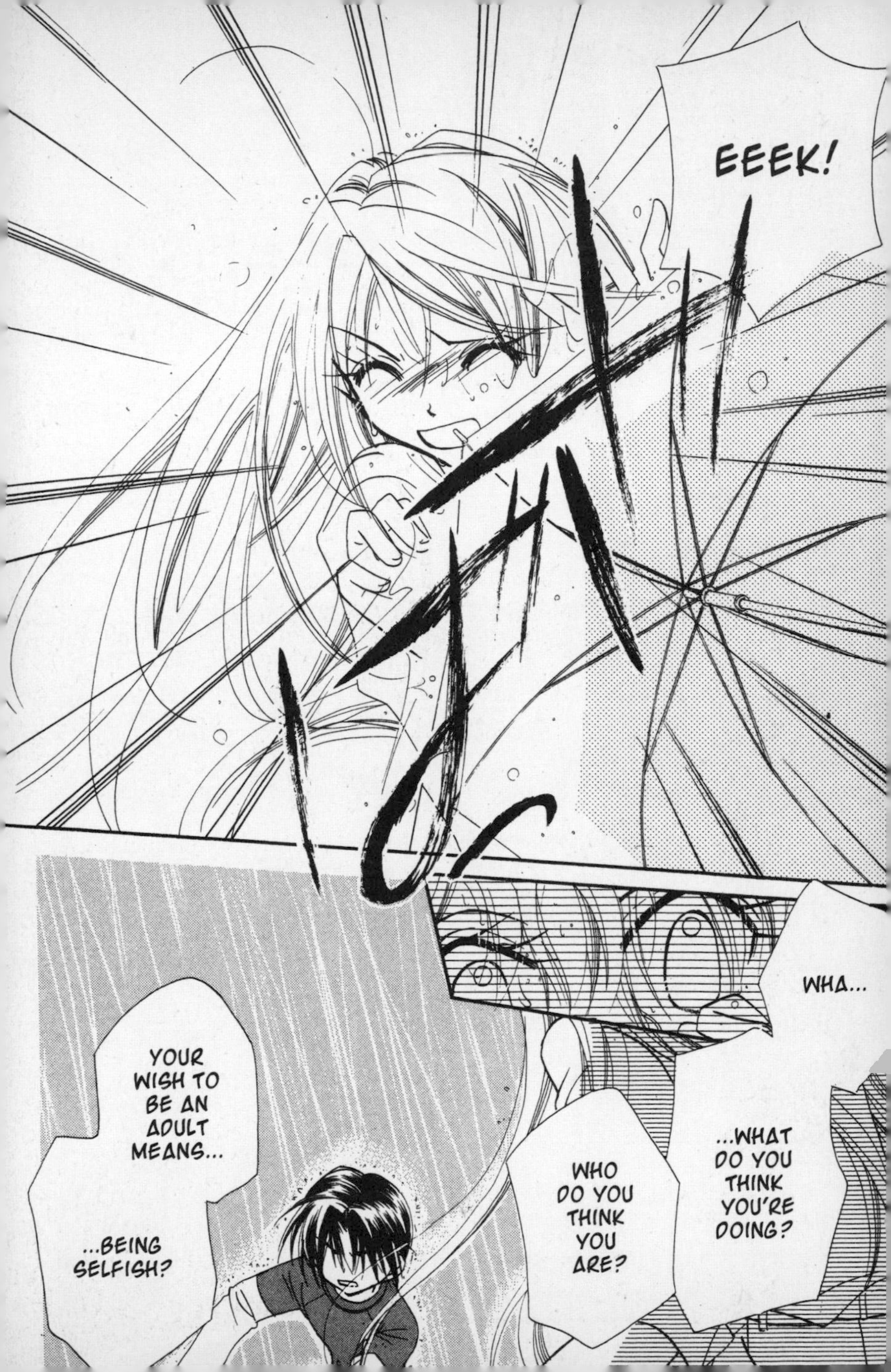
EEEK!
WHA...
...WHAT DO YOU THINK YOU'RE DOING?
WHO DO YOU THINK YOU ARE?
YOUR WISH TO BE AN ADULT MEANS...
...BEING SELFISH?

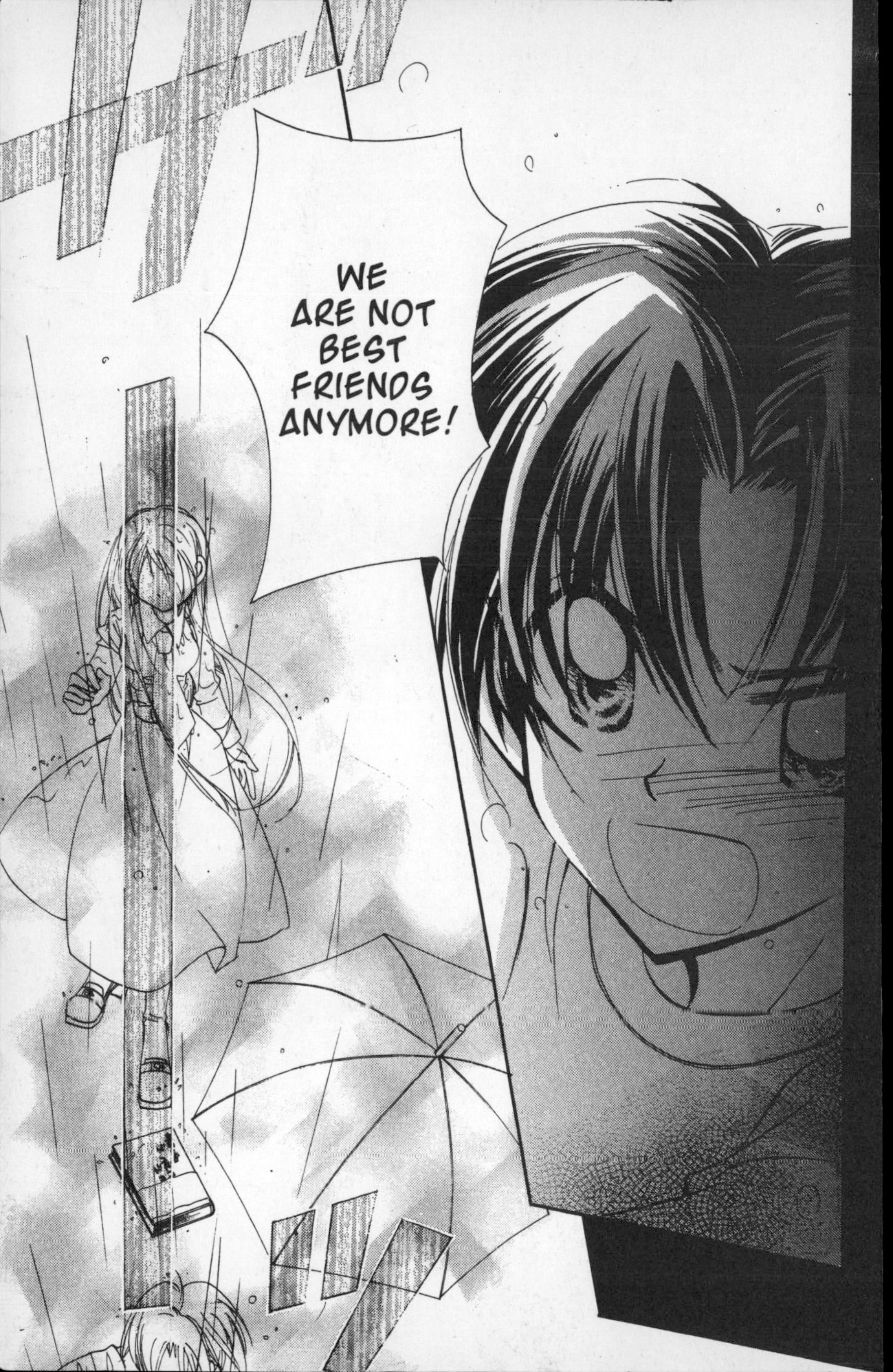
WE ARE NOT BEST FRIENDS ANYMORE!

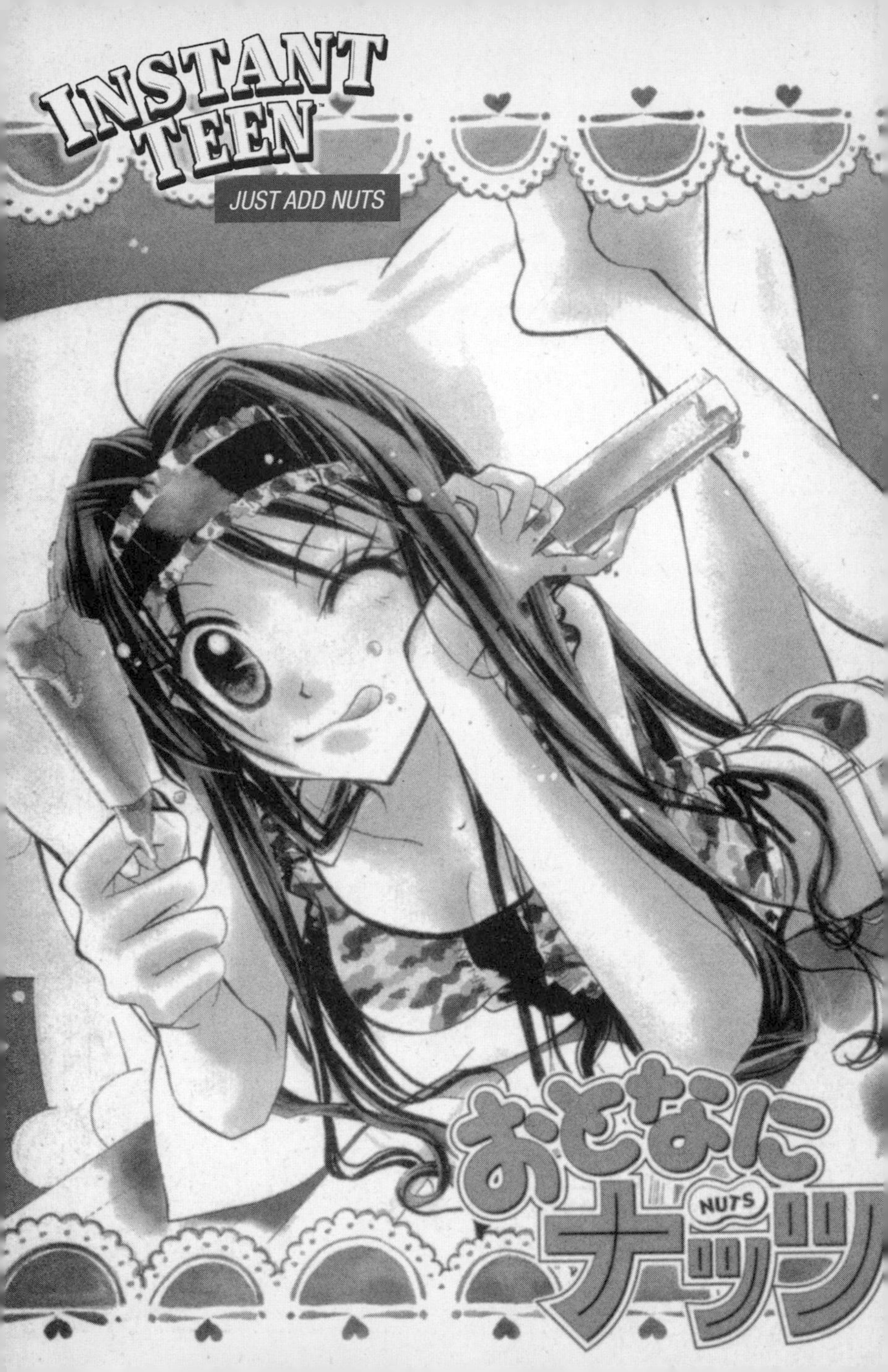
INSTANT TEEN™
JUST ADD NUTS
おとなにナッツ
NUTS

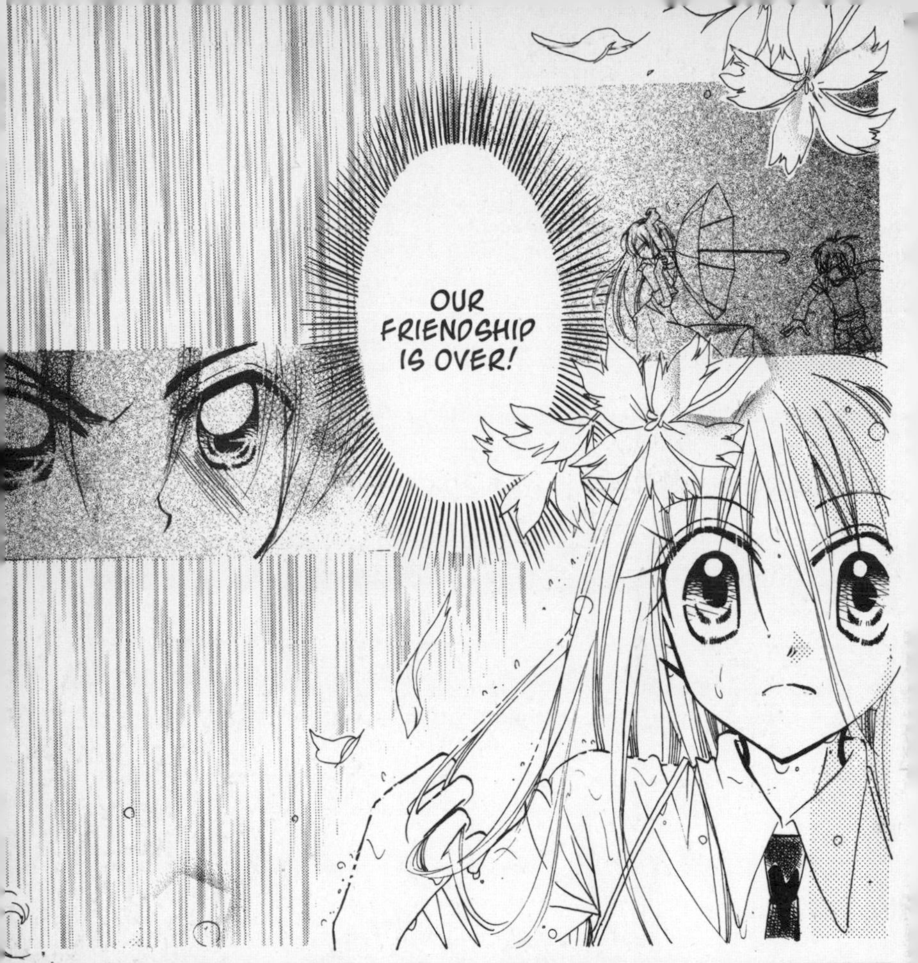
OUR FRIENDSHIP IS OVER!

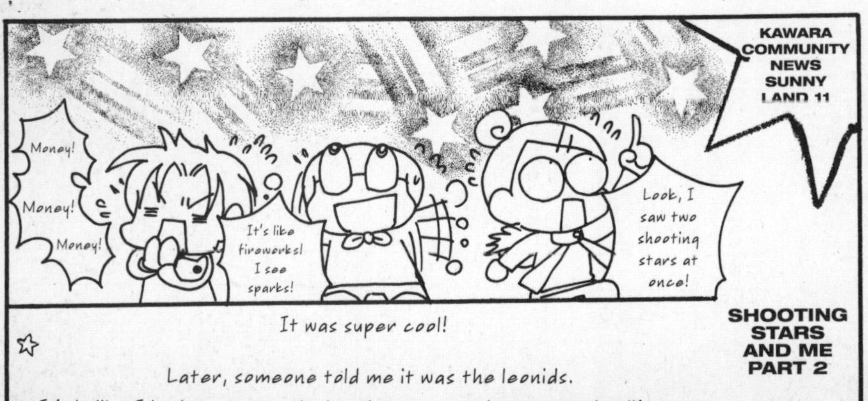
KAWARA COMMUNITY NEWS SUNNY LAND 11
SHOOTING STARS AND ME PART 2
Look, I saw two shooting stars at once!
It's like fireworks! I see sparks!
Money! Money! Money!
It was super cool!
Later, someone told me it was the leonids.
I felt like I had seen enough shooting stars to last my entire life.

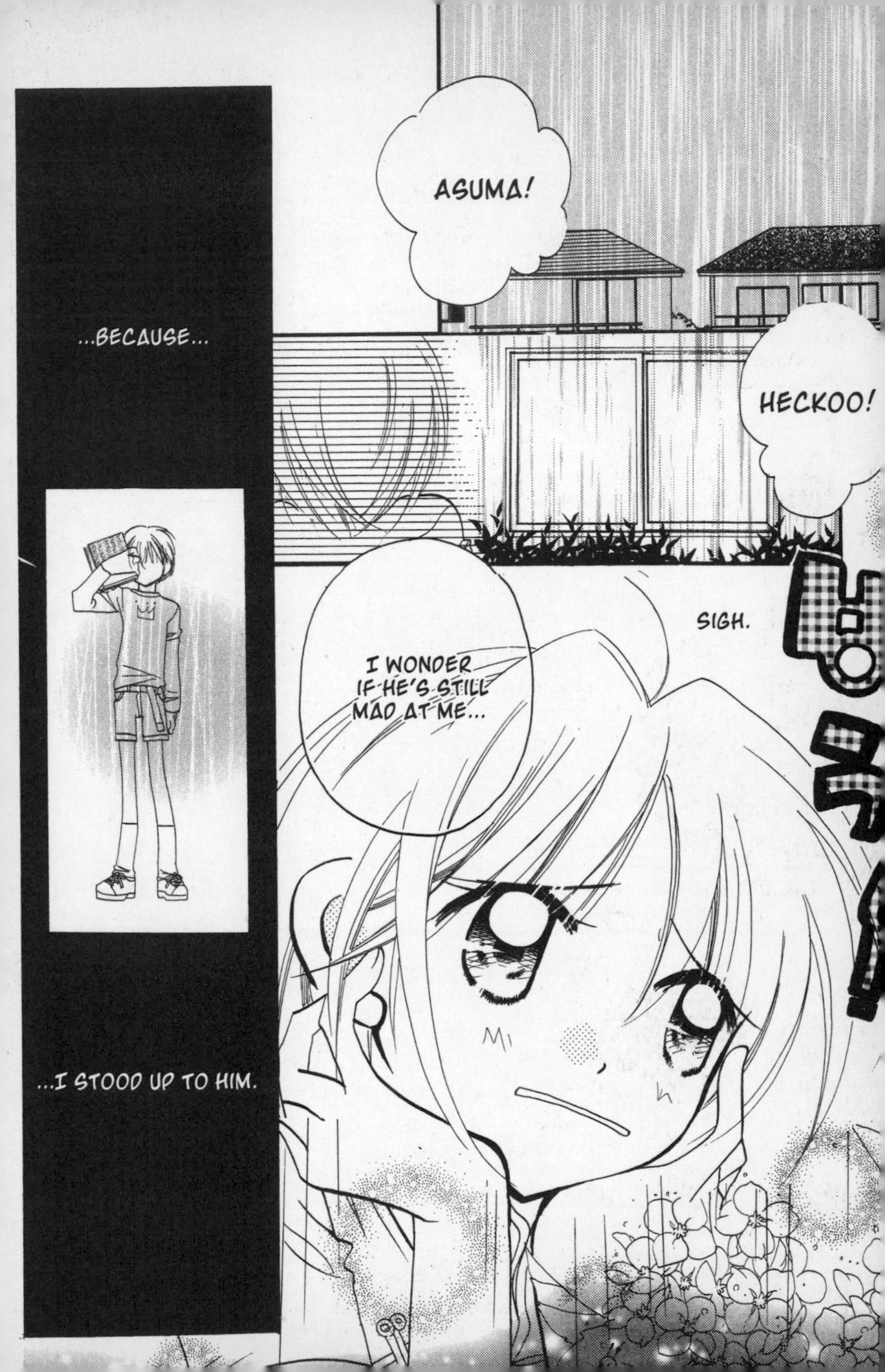
ASUMA!
HECKOO!
SIGH.
I WONDER IF HE'S STILL MAD AT ME...
...BECAUSE...
...I STOOD UP TO HIM.

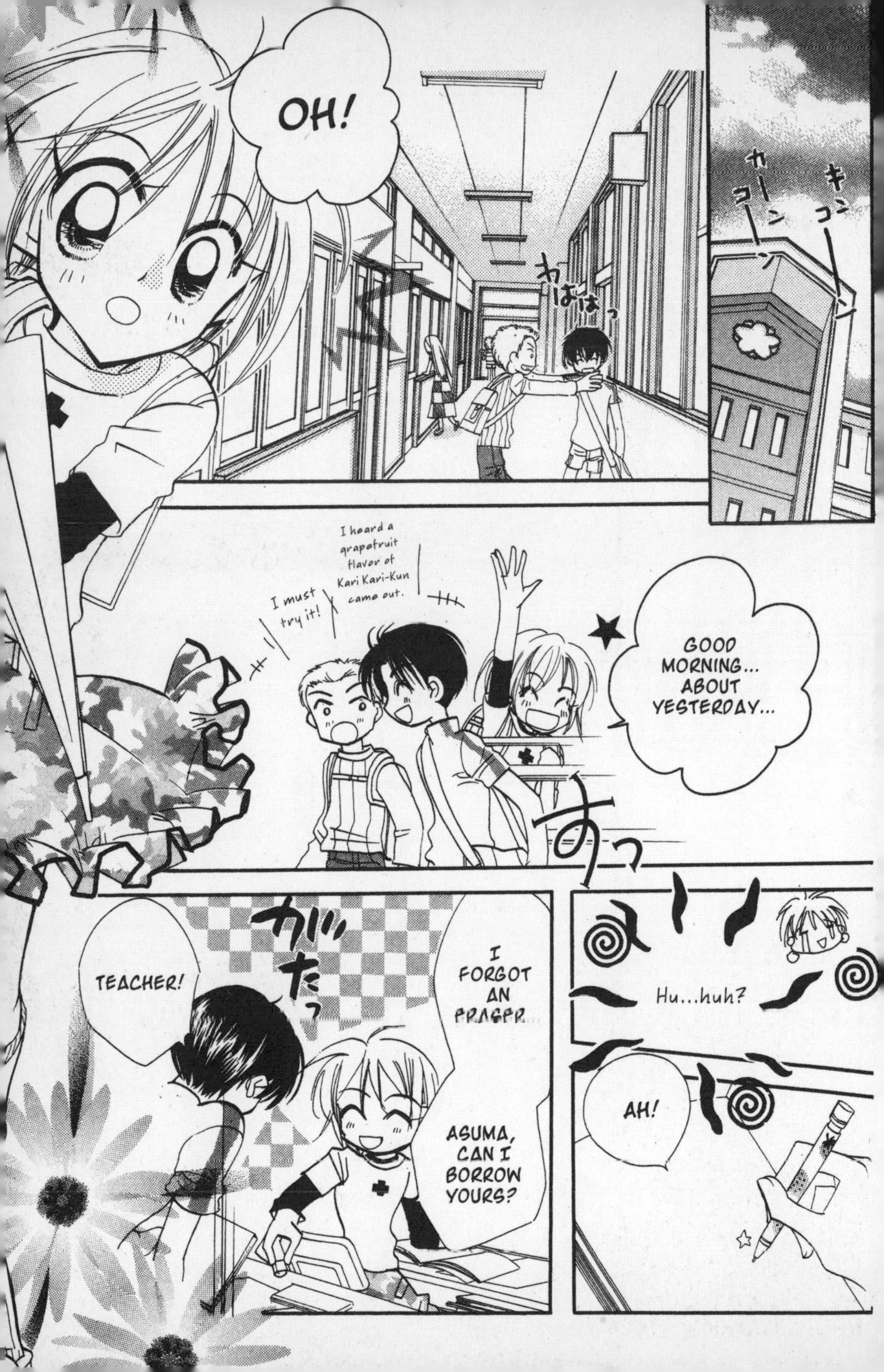
キーンコーン
カーンコーン
わははっ
OH!
I heard a grapefruit flavor of Kari Kari-Kun came out.
I must try it!
GOOD MORNING... ABOUT YESTERDAY...
あっ
Hu...huh?
AH!
I FORGOT AN ERASER...
がたっ
TEACHER!
ASUMA, CAN I BORROW YOURS?

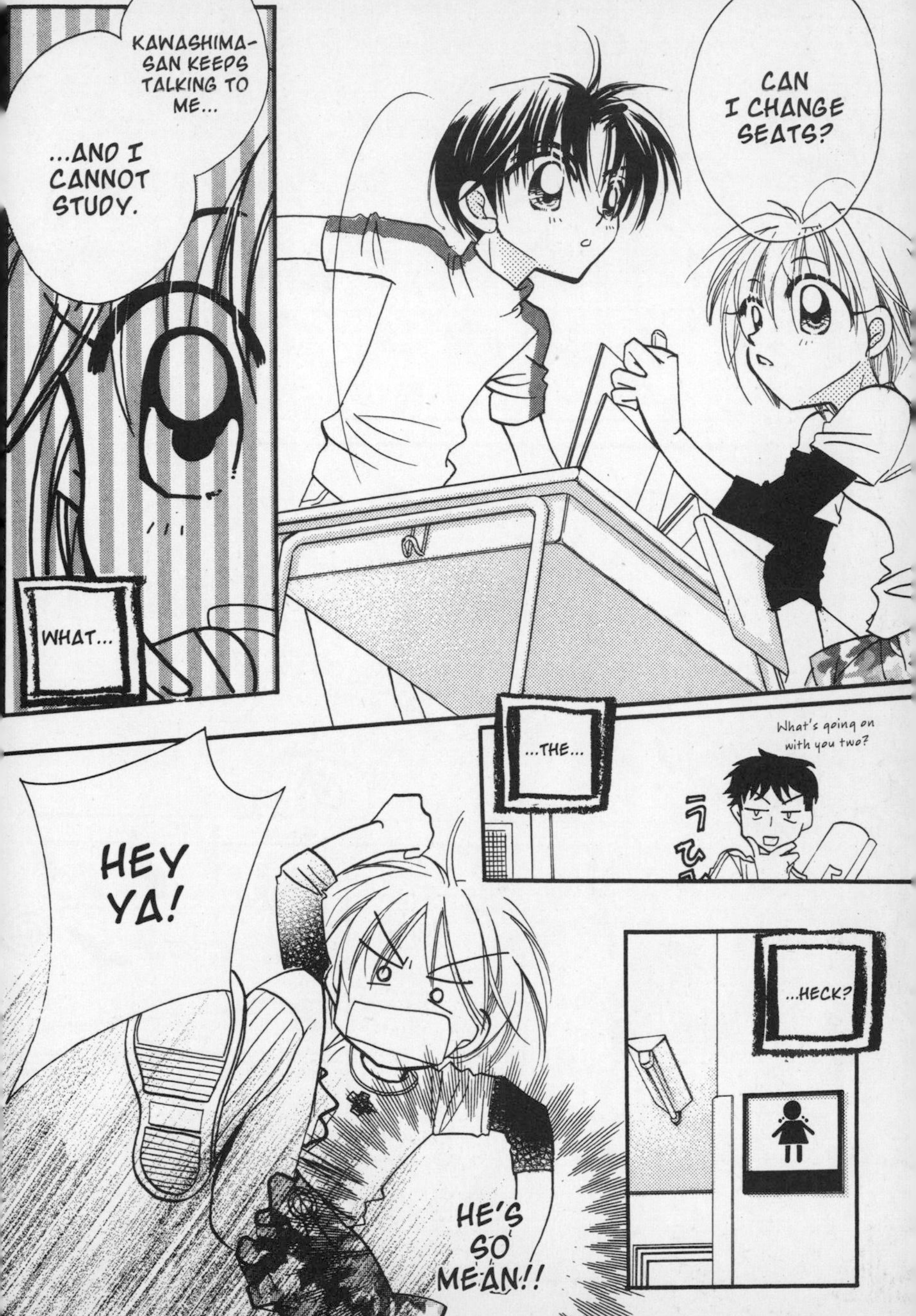
CAN I CHANGE SEATS?
KAWASHIMA-SAN KEEPS TALKING TO ME...
...AND I CANNOT STUDY.
WHAT...
...THE...
What's going on with you two?
...HECK?
HEY YA!
HE'S SO MEAN!!

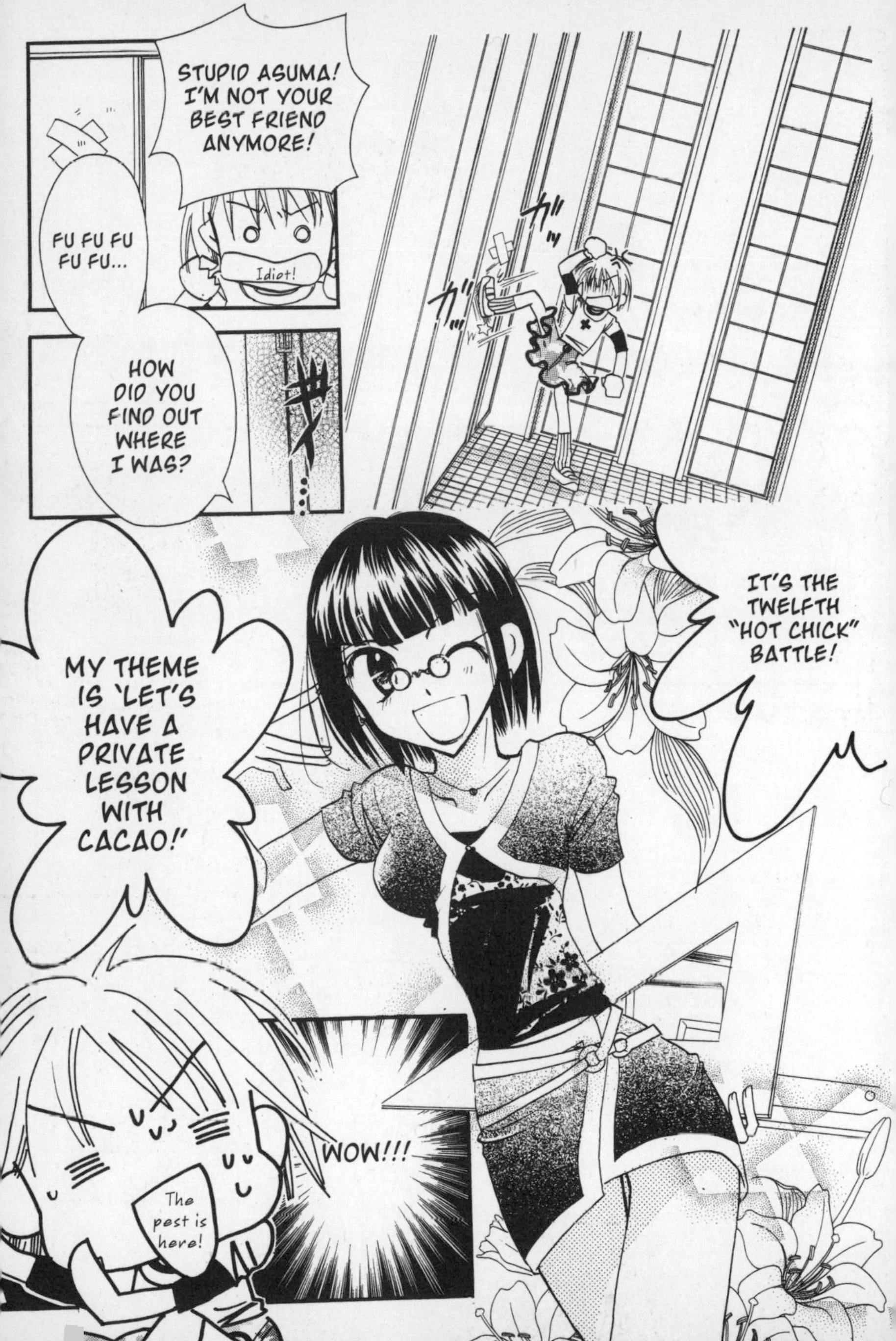
STUPID ASUMA! I'M NOT YOUR BEST FRIEND ANYMORE!
Idiot!
FU FU FU FU FU...
HOW DID YOU FIND OUT WHERE I WAS?
IT'S THE TWELFTH "HOT CHICK" BATTLE!
MY THEME IS 'LET'S HAVE A PRIVATE LESSON WITH CACAO!'
WOW!!!
The pest is here!

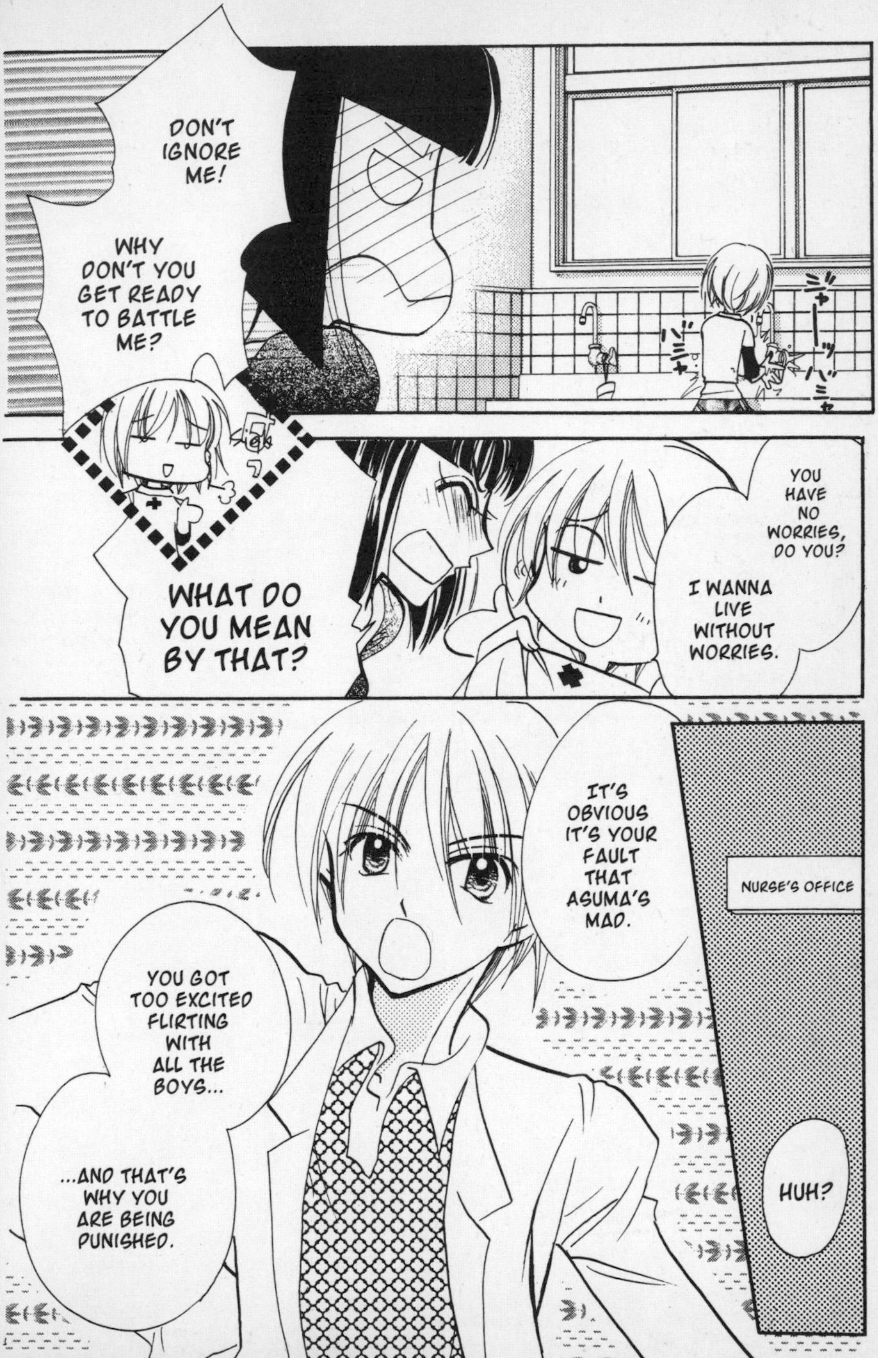
DON'T IGNORE ME!
WHY DON'T YOU GET READY TO BATTLE ME?
YOU HAVE NO WORRIES, DO YOU?
I WANNA LIVE WITHOUT WORRIES.
WHAT DO YOU MEAN BY THAT?
Sick
NURSE'S OFFICE
HUH?
IT'S OBVIOUS IT'S YOUR FAULT THAT ASUMA'S MAD.
YOU GOT TOO EXCITED FLIRTING WITH ALL THE BOYS...
...AND THAT'S WHY YOU ARE BEING PUNISHED.

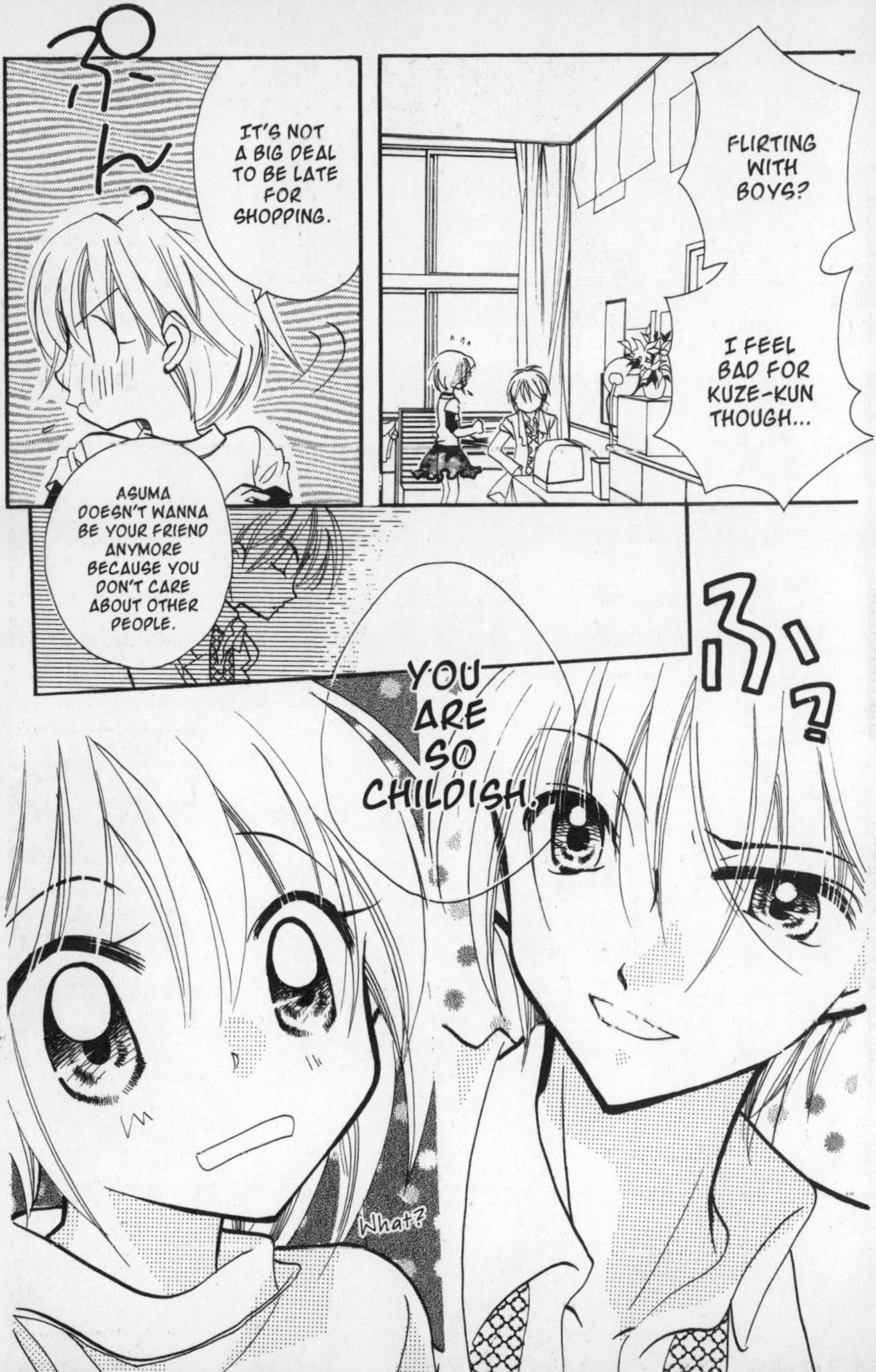
FLIRTING WITH BOYS?
I FEEL BAD FOR KUZE-KUN THOUGH...
ぷーん
IT'S NOT A BIG DEAL TO BE LATE FOR SHOPPING.
ASUMA DOESN'T WANNA BE YOUR FRIEND ANYMORE BECAUSE YOU DON'T CARE ABOUT OTHER PEOPLE.
ふ?
YOU ARE SO CHILDISH.
What?

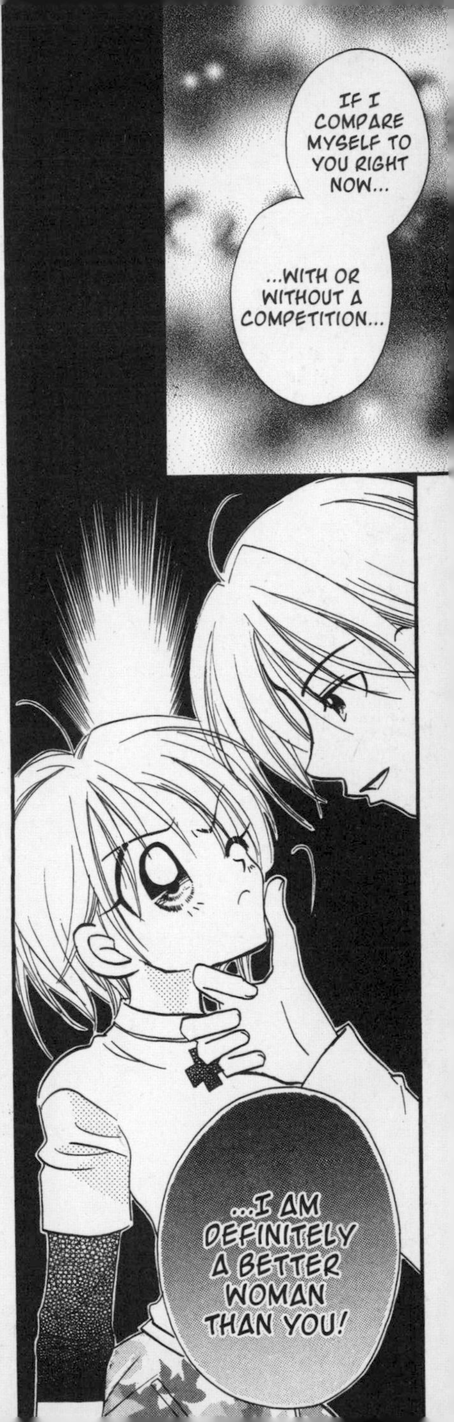
IF I COMPARE MYSELF TO YOU RIGHT NOW...
...WITH OR WITHOUT A COMPETITION...
...I AM DEFINITELY A BETTER WOMAN THAN YOU!

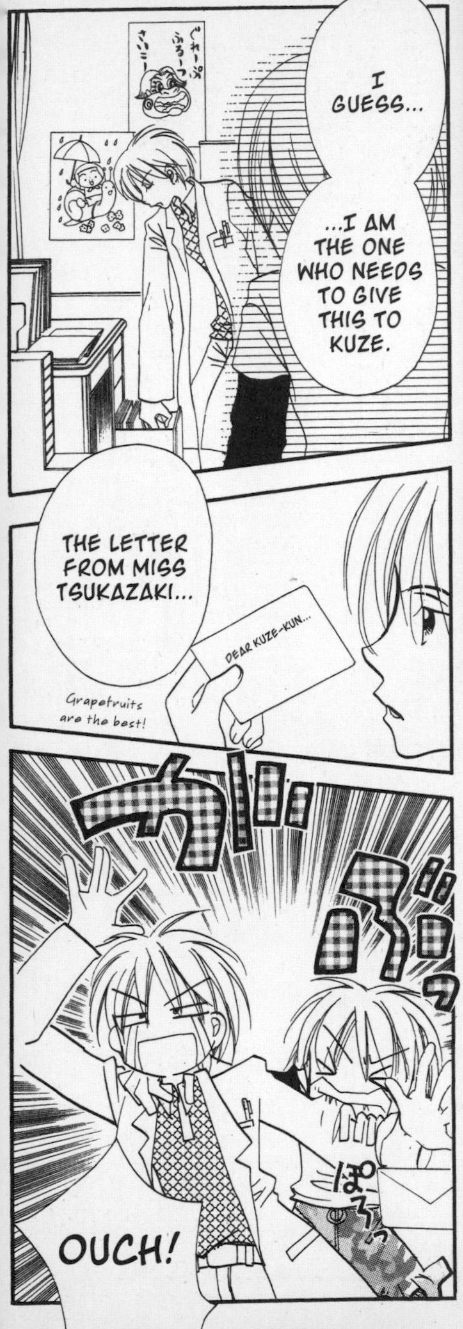
I GUESS...
...I AM THE ONE WHO NEEDS TO GIVE THIS TO KUZE.
ぐれーぷ ふるーつ さいこー
THE LETTER FROM MISS TSUKAZAKI...
DEAR KUZE-KUN...
Grapefruits are the best!
OUCH!

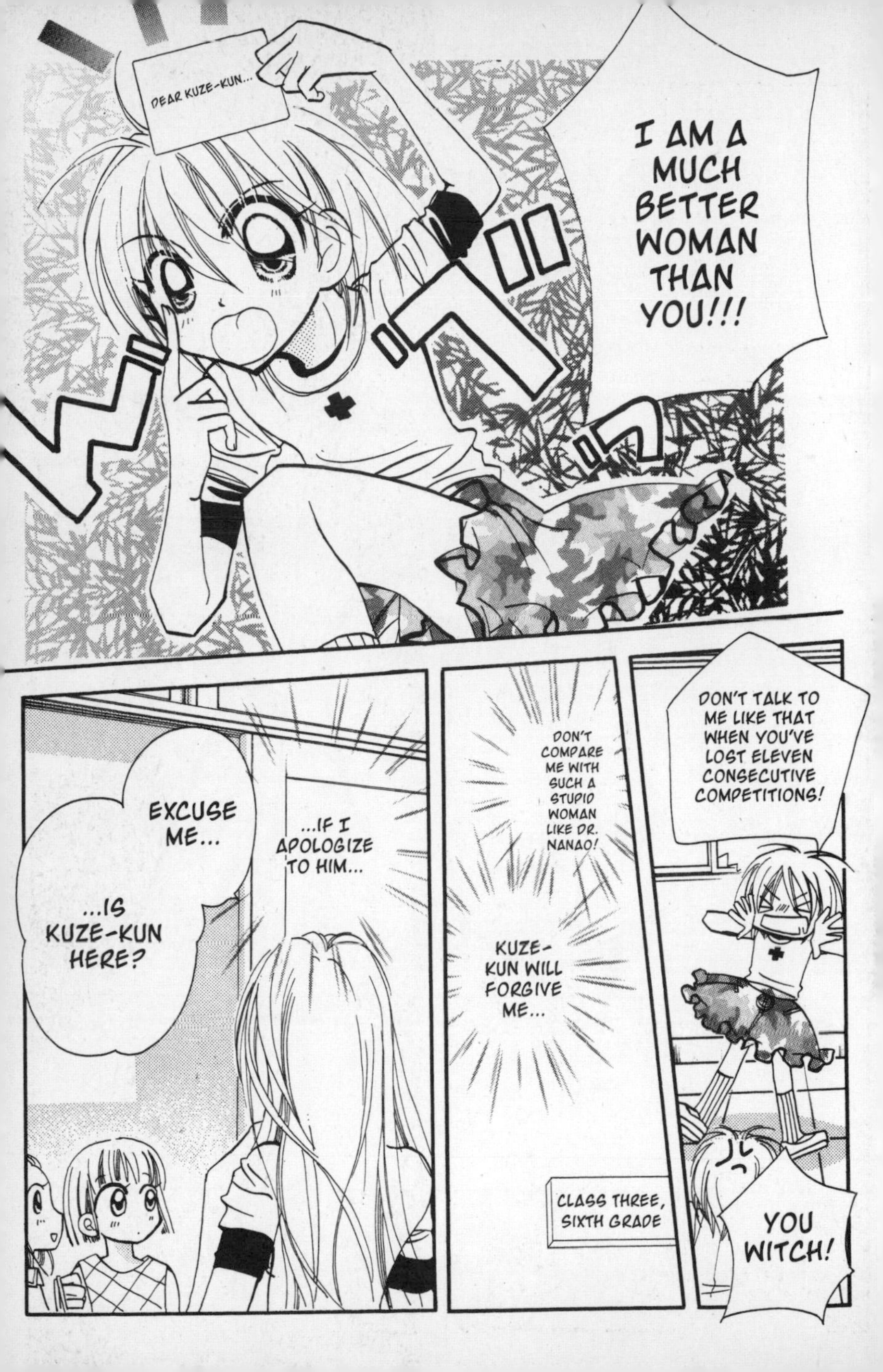
I AM A MUCH BETTER WOMAN THAN YOU!!!
DEAR KUZE-KUN...
DON'T TALK TO ME LIKE THAT WHEN YOU'VE LOST ELEVEN CONSECUTIVE COMPETITIONS!
YOU WITCH!
CLASS THREE, SIXTH GRADE
DON'T COMPARE ME WITH SUCH A STUPID WOMAN LIKE DR. NANAO!
KUZE-KUN WILL FORGIVE ME...
...IF I APOLOGIZE TO HIM...
EXCUSE ME...
...IS KUZE-KUN HERE?

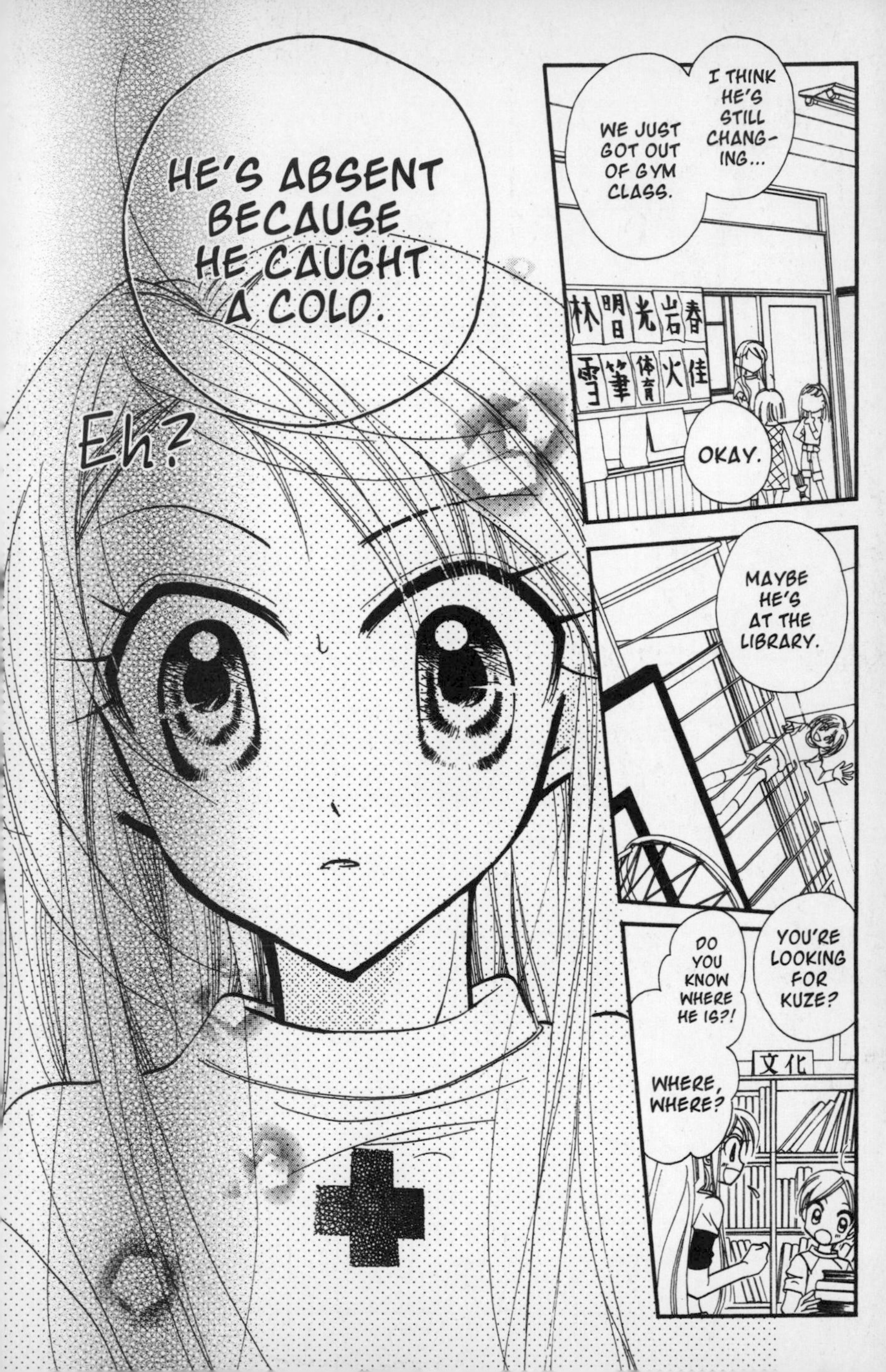
I THINK HE'S STILL CHANGING-ING...
WE JUST GOT OUT OF GYM CLASS.
春 岩 光 明日 林
佳 火 体育 筆 雪
OKAY.
MAYBE HE'S AT THE LIBRARY.
YOU'RE LOOKING FOR KUZE?
DO YOU KNOW WHERE HE IS?!
文化
WHERE, WHERE?
HE'S ABSENT BECAUSE HE CAUGHT A COLD.
Eh?

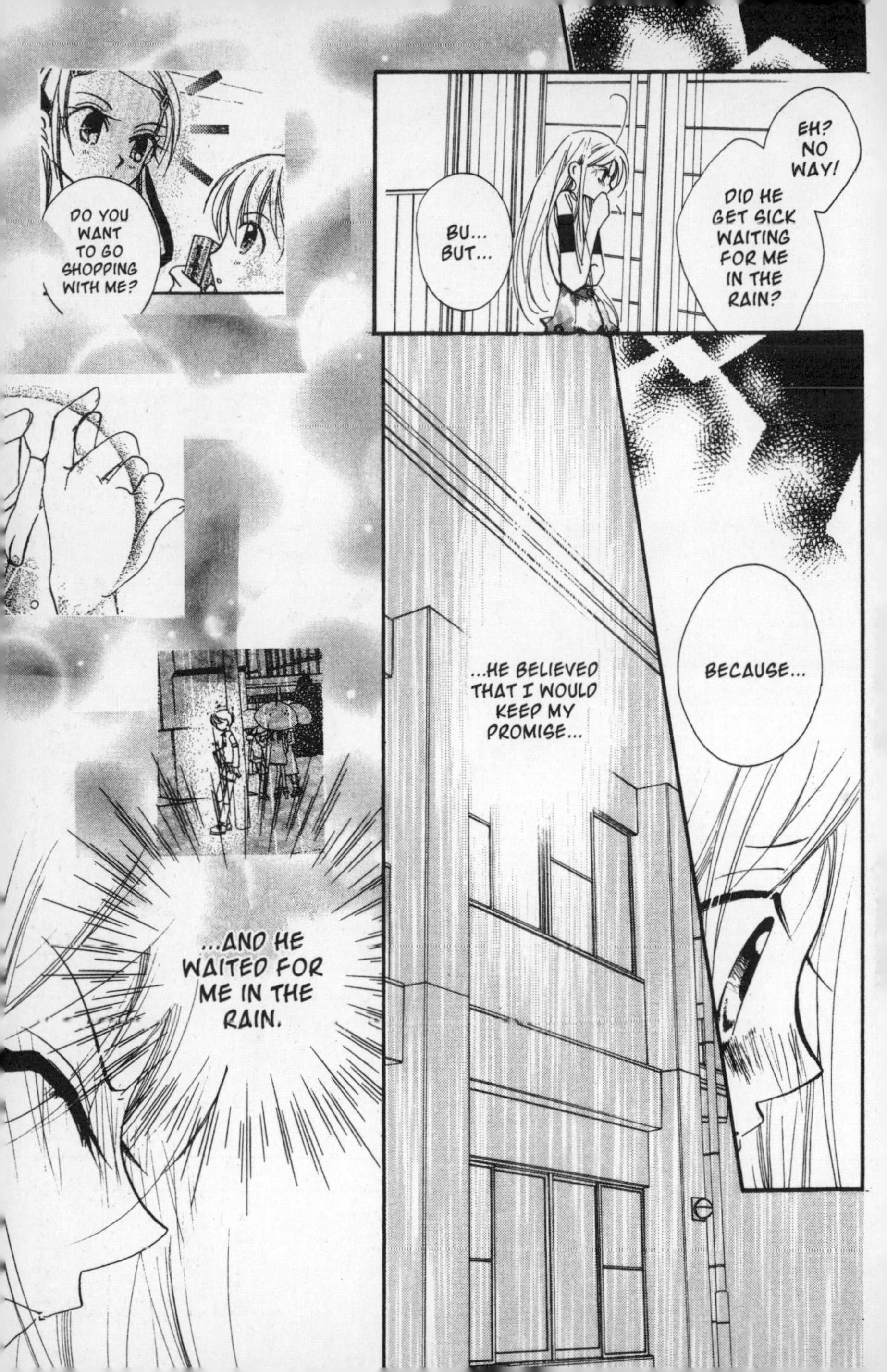
EH? NO WAY!
DID HE GET SICK WAITING FOR ME IN THE RAIN?
BU... BUT...
BECAUSE...
...HE BELIEVED THAT I WOULD KEEP MY PROMISE...
DO YOU WANT TO GO SHOPPING WITH ME?
...AND HE WAITED FOR ME IN THE RAIN.

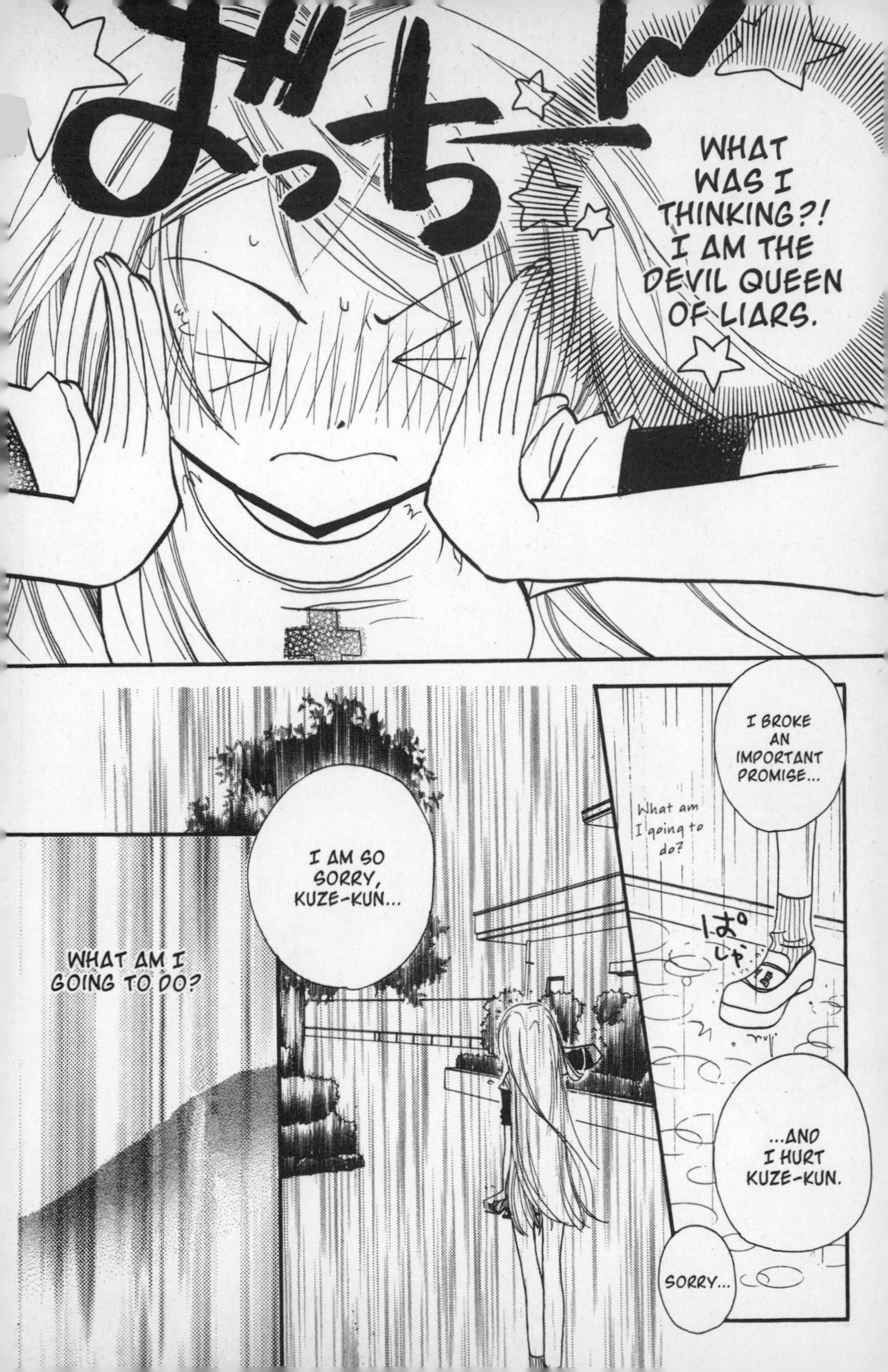
WHAT WAS I THINKING?! I AM THE DEVIL QUEEN OF LIARS.
I BROKE AN IMPORTANT PROMISE...
What am I going to do?
ぱしゃ
...AND I HURT KUZE-KUN.
SORRY...
I AM SO SORRY, KUZE-KUN...
WHAT AM I GOING TO DO?

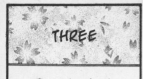

THREE

There is a book that I used as a resource for the book Kuze-kun is reading in the story.

In this book, the main character is hanging with his girlfriend at the beach and lining up jellyfish. His girlfriend says, "The jellyfish are like rice cakes!"

I read this book when I was in the twelfth grade in high school. I lived in the mountain countryside of Okayama-prefecture and didn't have any chance to see the ocean much. Even though I've never seen a jellyfish and I always dreamt of seeing one with my own eyes one of these days.

To be continued in Volume 4

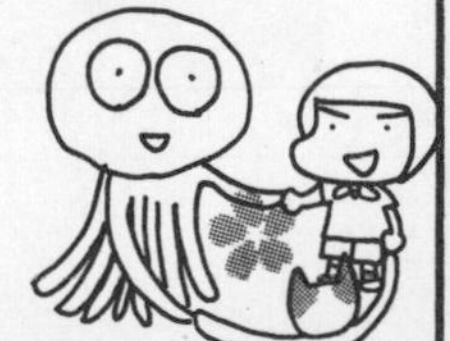

Jellyfish-Kun

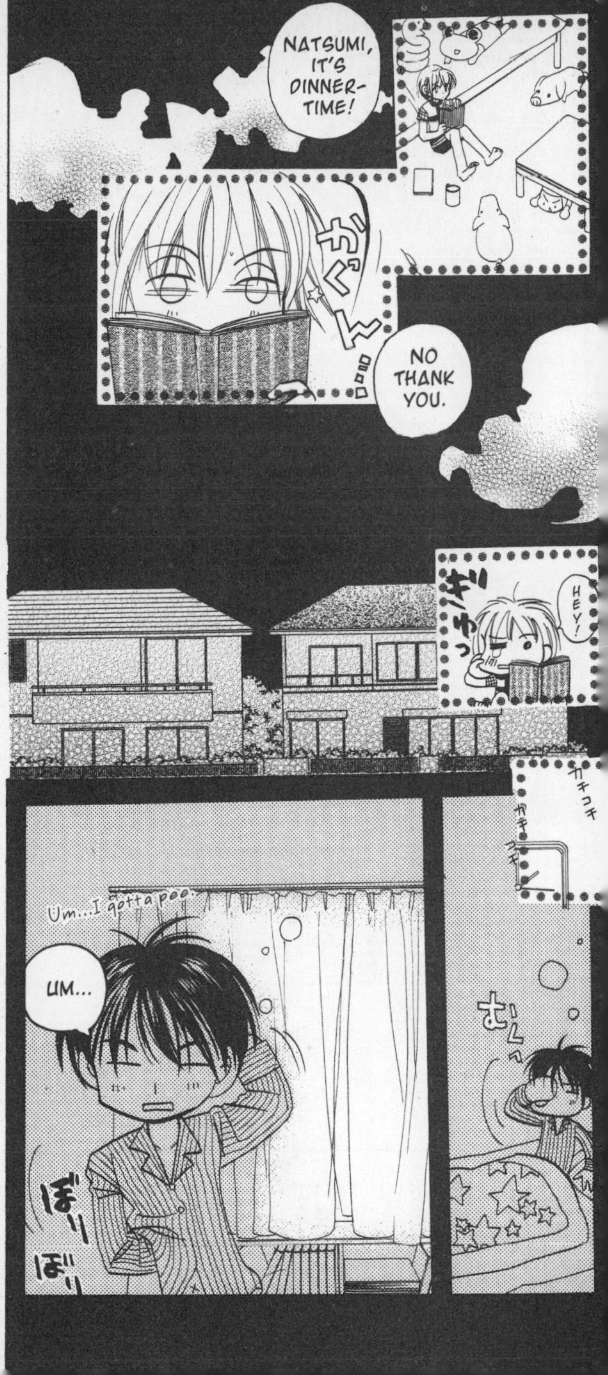
NATSUMI, IT'S DINNER-TIME!
NO THANK YOU.
HEY!
Um...I gotta pee.
UM...

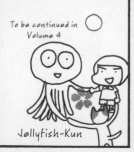

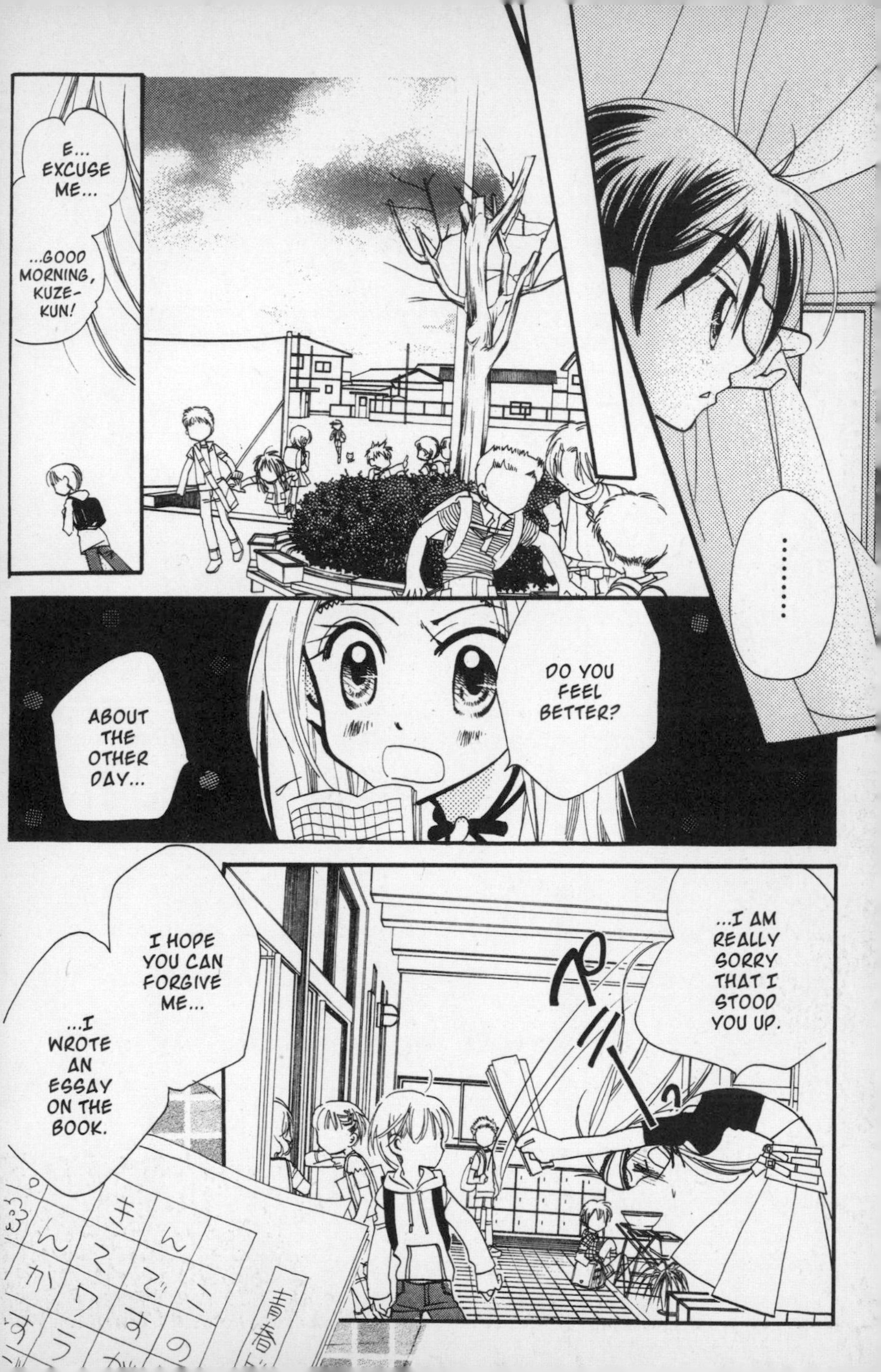
......
E... EXCUSE ME...
...GOOD MORNING, KUZE-KUN!
DO YOU FEEL BETTER?
ABOUT THE OTHER DAY...
...I AM REALLY SORRY THAT I STOOD YOU UP.
I HOPE YOU CAN FORGIVE ME...
...I WROTE AN ESSAY ON THE BOOK.

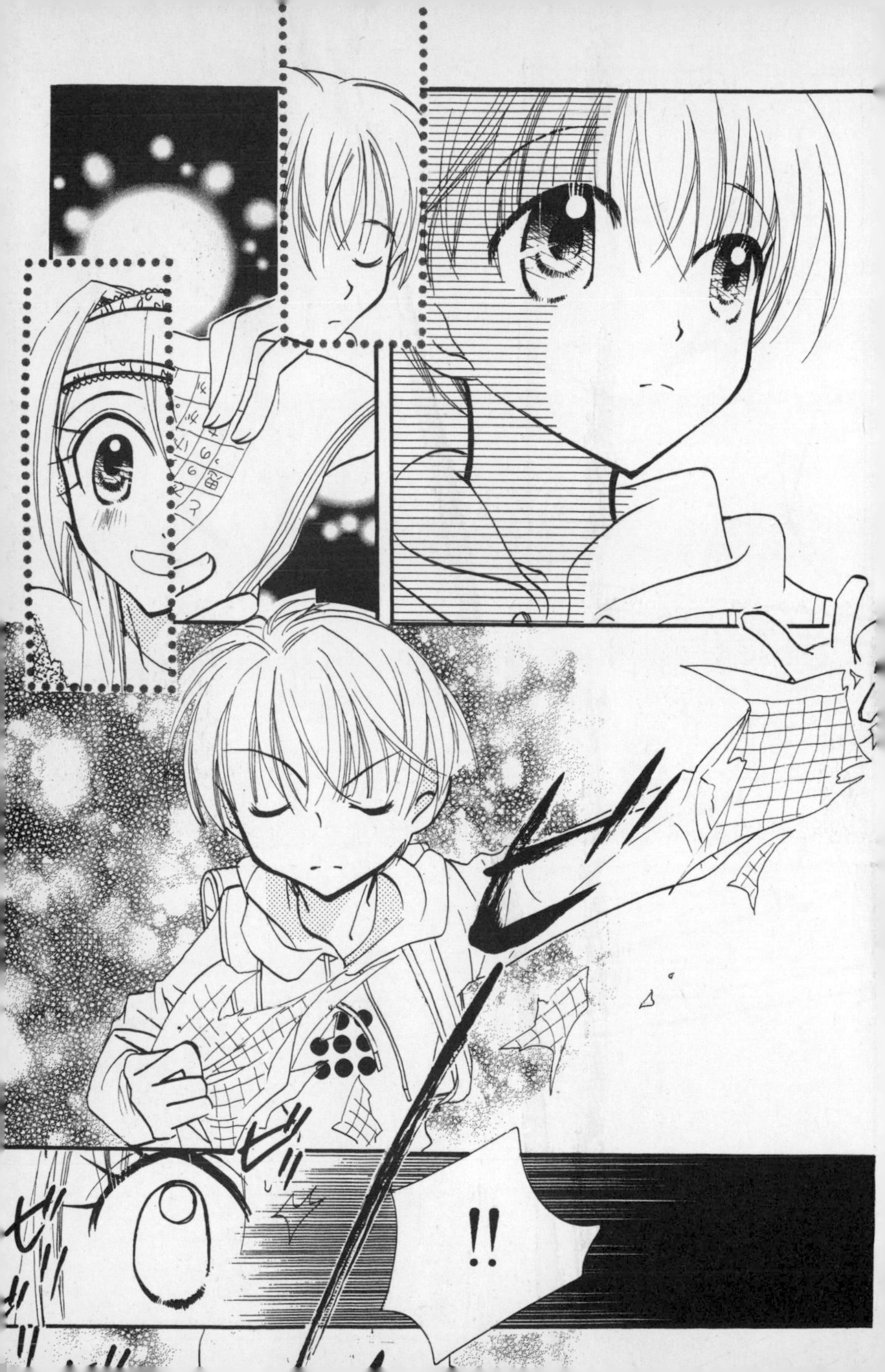
!!

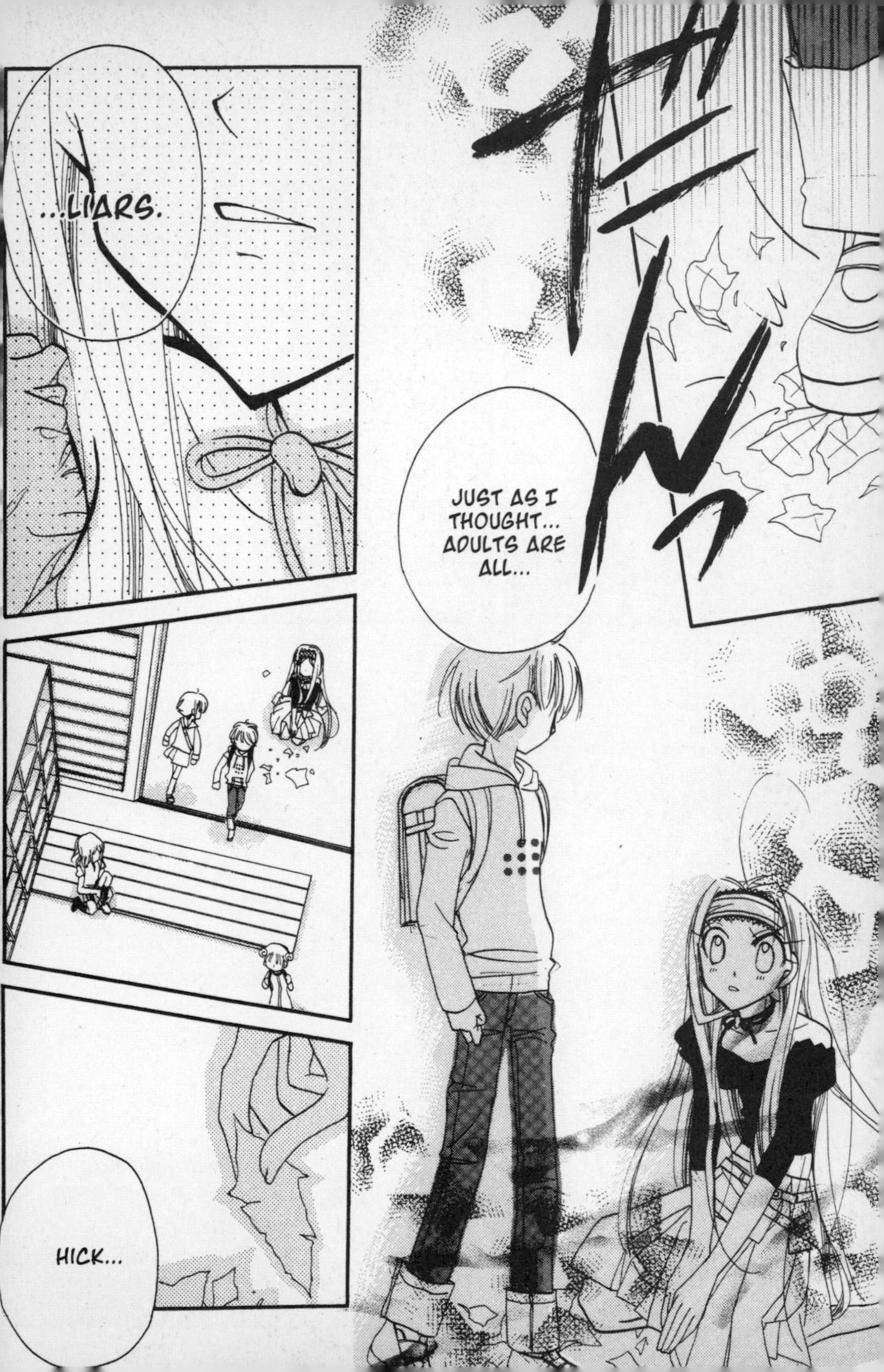

JUST AS I THOUGHT... ADULTS ARE ALL...
...LIARS.
HICK...

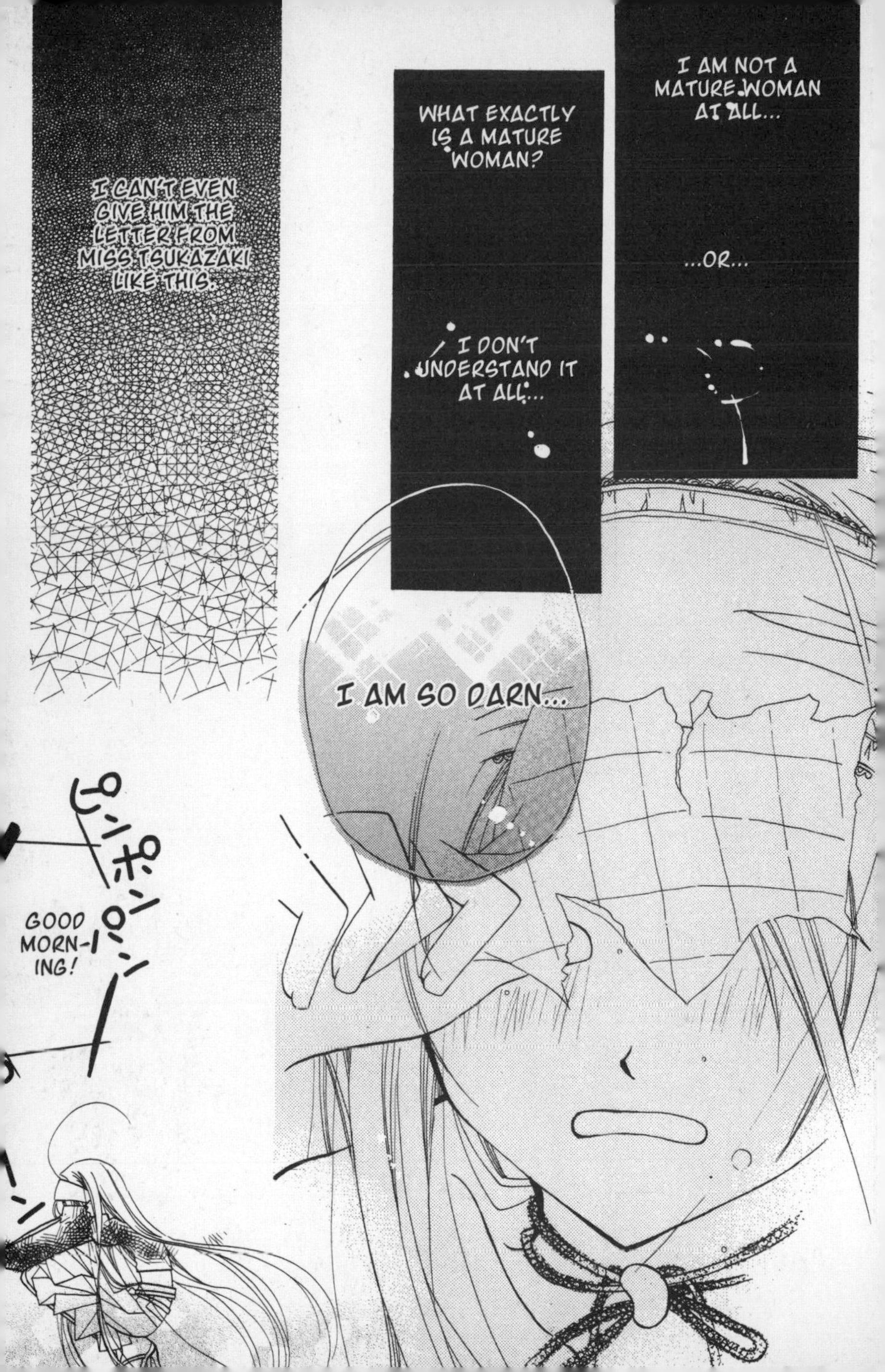
I AM NOT A MATURE WOMAN AT ALL...
...OR...
WHAT EXACTLY IS A MATURE WOMAN?
I DON'T UNDERSTAND IT AT ALL...
I CAN'T EVEN GIVE HIM THE LETTER FROM MISS TSUKAZAKI LIKE THIS.
I AM SO DARN...
GOOD MORN-ING!

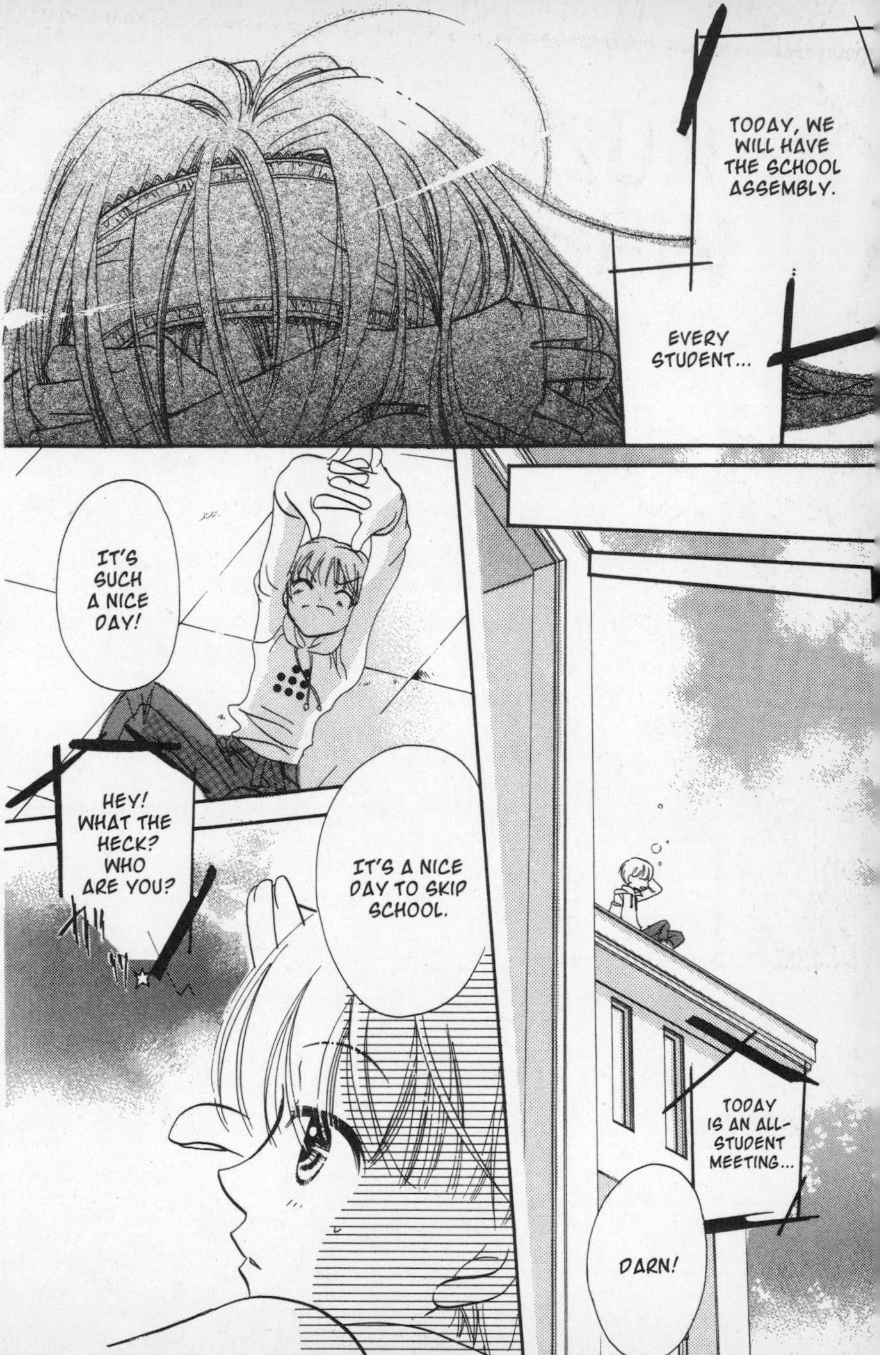
TODAY, WE WILL HAVE THE SCHOOL ASSEMBLY.
EVERY STUDENT...
TODAY IS AN ALL-STUDENT MEETING...
DARN!
IT'S SUCH A NICE DAY!
IT'S A NICE DAY TO SKIP SCHOOL.
HEY! WHAT THE HECK? WHO ARE YOU?

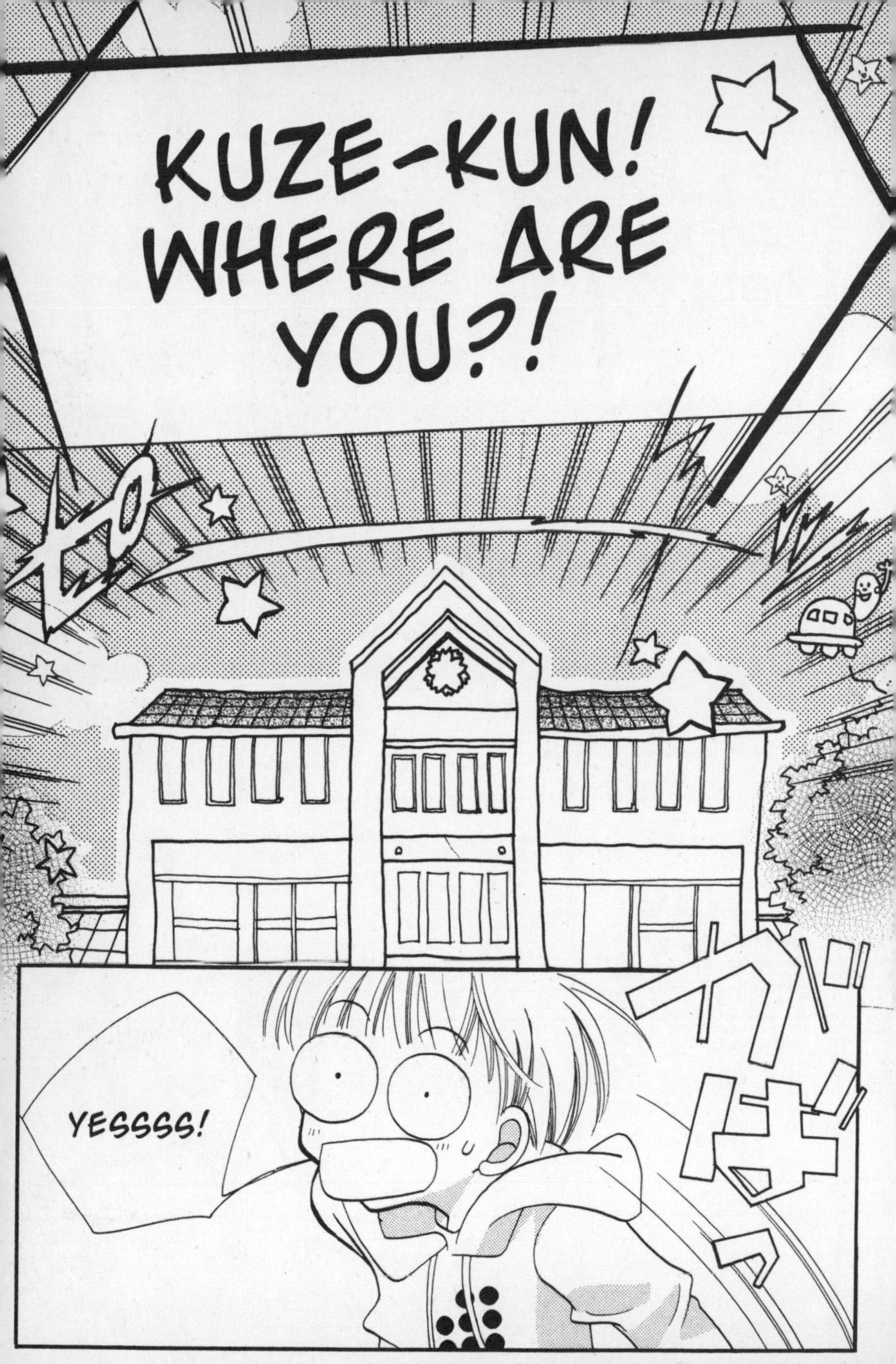
KUZE-KUN! WHERE ARE YOU?!
YESSSS!

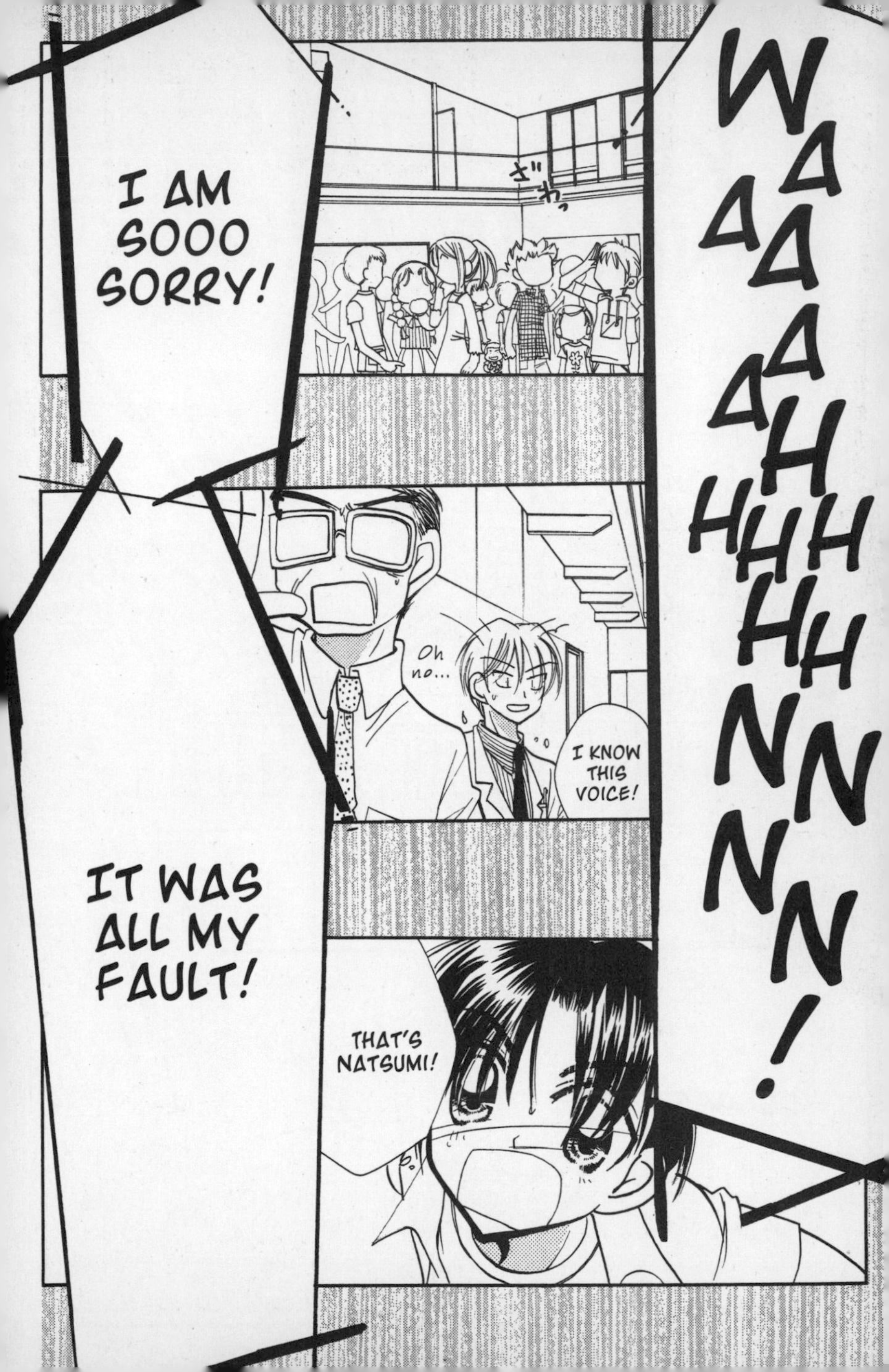
WAAAAAAHHHHHHHNNNNN!
ざわっ
I AM SOOO SORRY!
Oh no...
I KNOW THIS VOICE!
IT WAS ALL MY FAULT!
THAT'S NATSUMI!

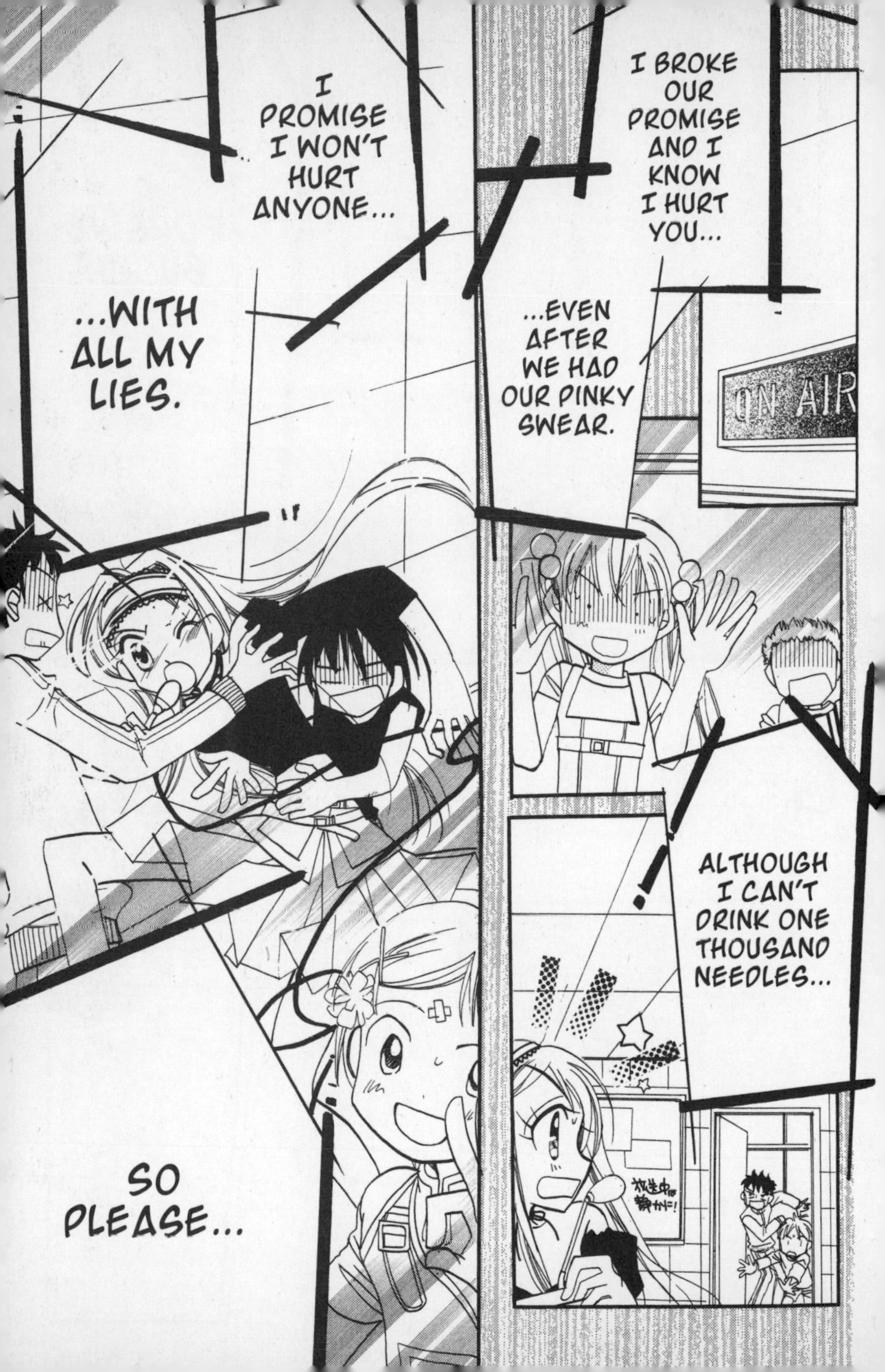
I BROKE OUR PROMISE AND I KNOW I HURT YOU...
...EVEN AFTER WE HAD OUR PINKY SWEAR.
ON AIR
ALTHOUGH I CAN'T DRINK ONE THOUSAND NEEDLES...
I PROMISE I WON'T HURT ANYONE...
...WITH ALL MY LIES.
SO PLEASE...

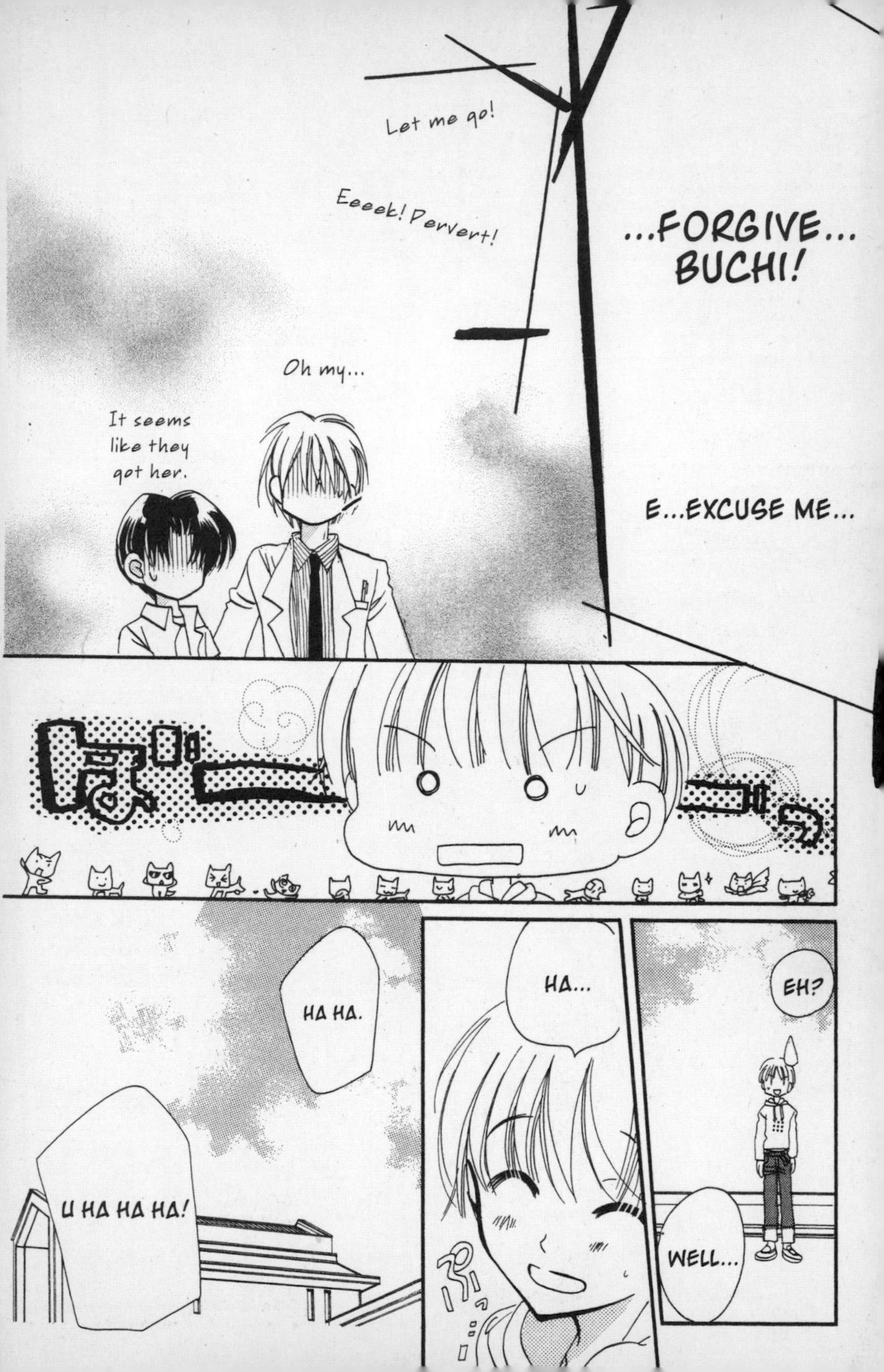
...FORGIVE... BUCHI!
Let me go!
Eeeek! Pervert!
E...EXCUSE ME...
Oh my...
It seems like they got her.
EH?
WELL...
HA...
HA HA.
U HA HA HA!

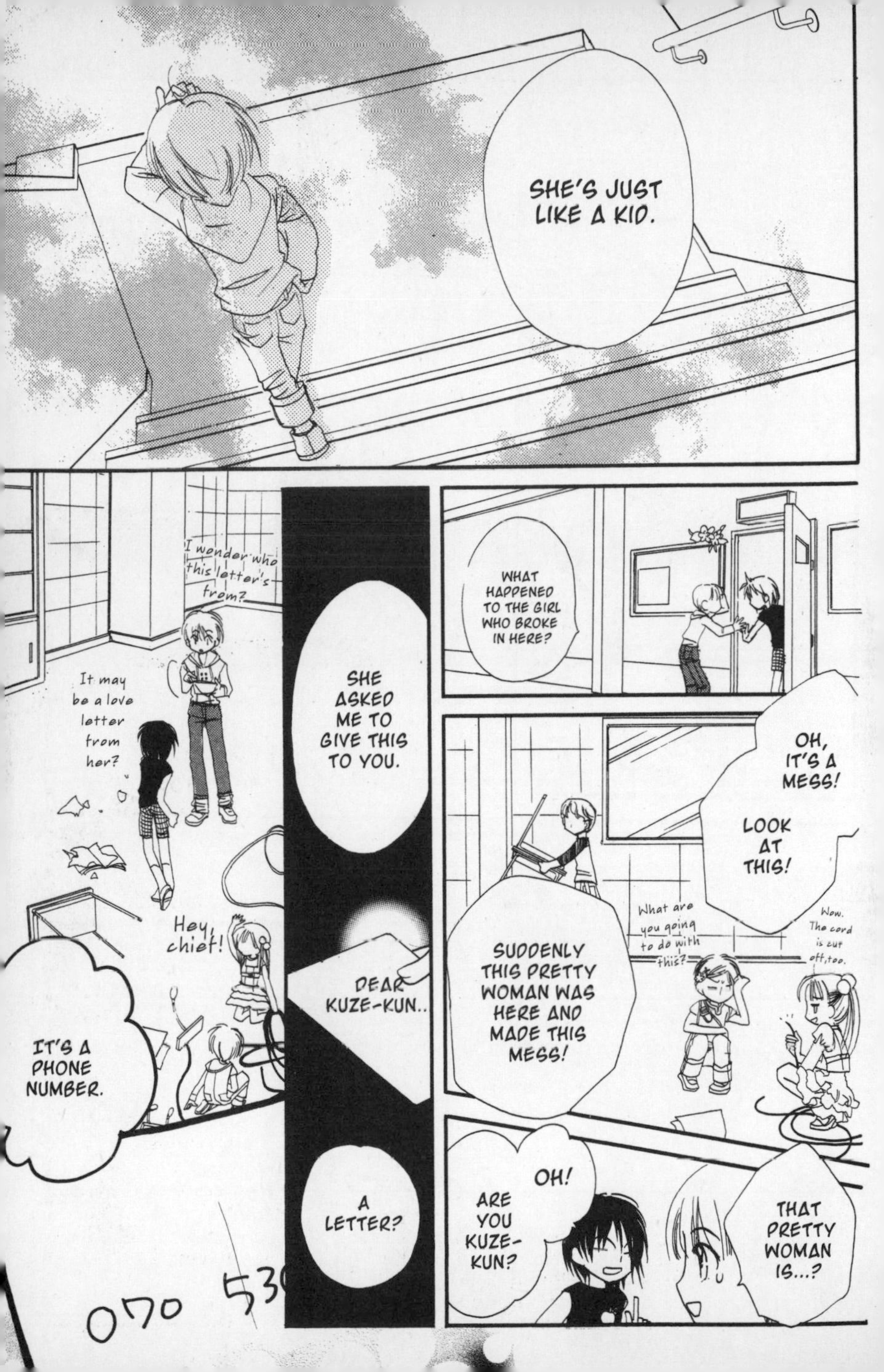

SHE'S JUST LIKE A KID.
WHAT HAPPENED TO THE GIRL WHO BROKE IN HERE?
OH, IT'S A MESS!
LOOK AT THIS!
Wow. The cord is cut off, too.
What are you going to do with this?
SUDDENLY THIS PRETTY WOMAN WAS HERE AND MADE THIS MESS!
THAT PRETTY WOMAN IS...?
OH!
ARE YOU KUZE-KUN?
SHE ASKED ME TO GIVE THIS TO YOU.
DEAR KUZE-KUN..
A LETTER?
I wonder who this letter's from?
It may be a love letter from her?
Hey, chief!
IT'S A PHONE NUMBER.
070 53

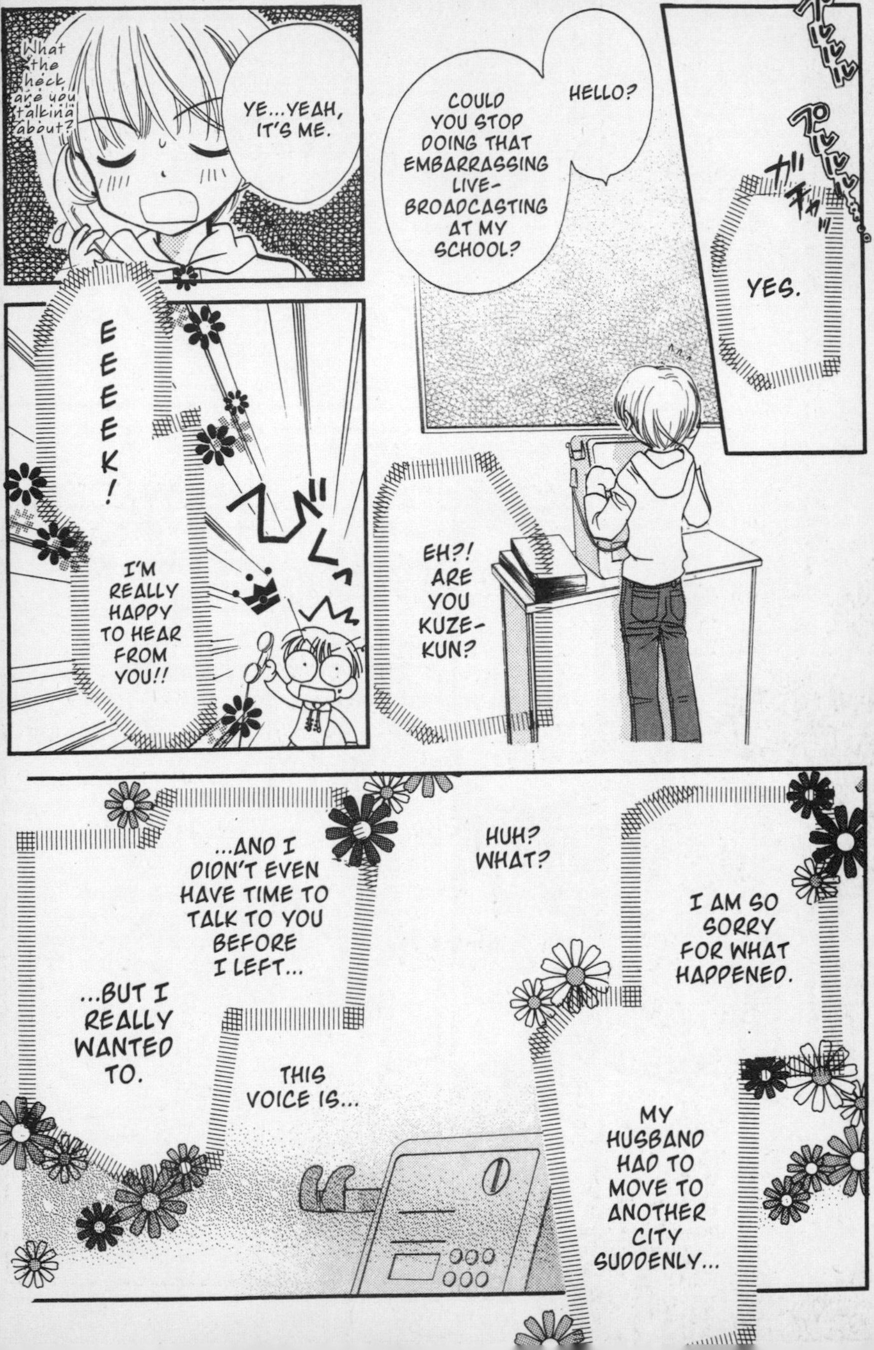
YES.
HELLO?
COULD YOU STOP DOING THAT EMBARRASSING LIVE-BROADCASTING AT MY SCHOOL?
EH?! ARE YOU KUZE-KUN?
YE...YEAH, IT'S ME.
What the heck are you talking about?
EEEEK!
I'M REALLY HAPPY TO HEAR FROM YOU!!
I AM SO SORRY FOR WHAT HAPPENED.
MY HUSBAND HAD TO MOVE TO ANOTHER CITY SUDDENLY...
HUH? WHAT?
...AND I DIDN'T EVEN HAVE TIME TO TALK TO YOU BEFORE I LEFT...
...BUT I REALLY WANTED TO.
THIS VOICE IS...

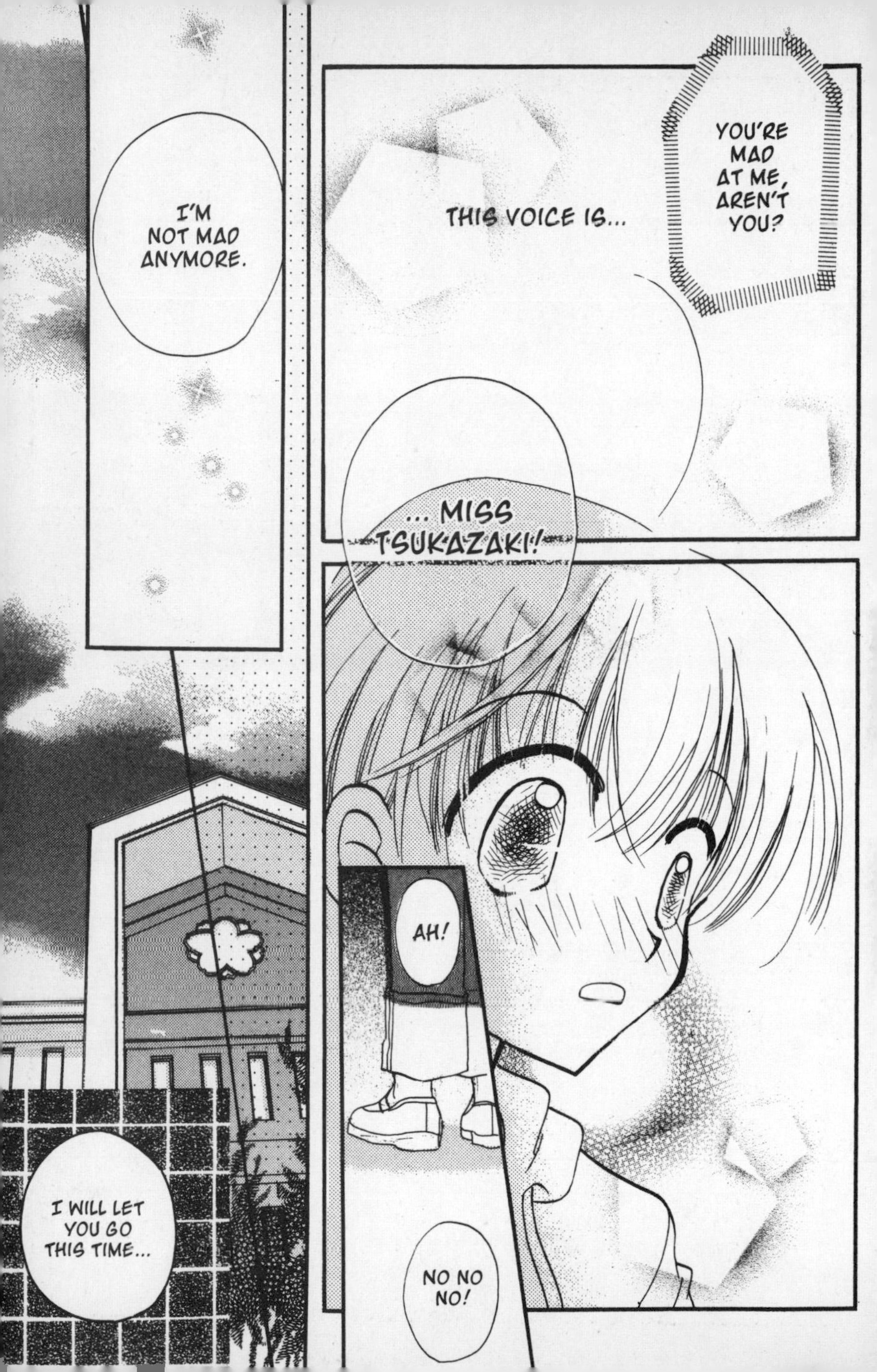
YOU'RE MAD AT ME, AREN'T YOU?
THIS VOICE IS...
... MISS TSUKAZAKI!
AH!
NO NO NO!
I'M NOT MAD ANYMORE.
I WILL LET YOU GO THIS TIME...

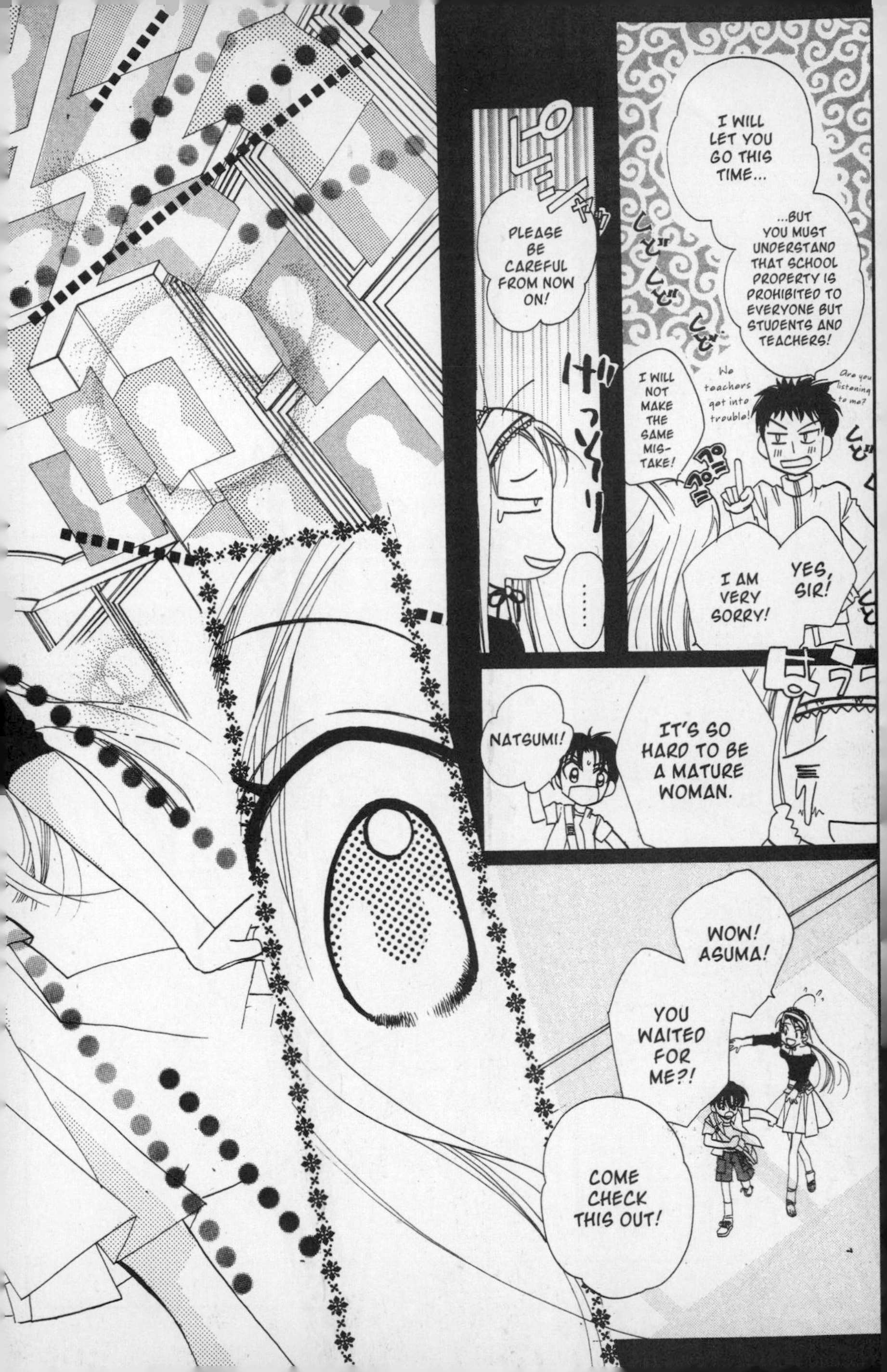
I WILL LET YOU GO THIS TIME...
...BUT YOU MUST UNDERSTAND THAT SCHOOL PROPERTY IS PROHIBITED TO EVERYONE BUT STUDENTS AND TEACHERS!
Are you listening to me?
We teachers got into trouble!
I WILL NOT MAKE THE SAME MIS-TAKE!
YES, SIR!
I AM VERY SORRY!
PLEASE BE CAREFUL FROM NOW ON!
......
IT'S SO HARD TO BE A MATURE WOMAN.
NATSUMI!
WOW! ASUMA!
YOU WAITED FOR ME?!
COME CHECK THIS OUT!

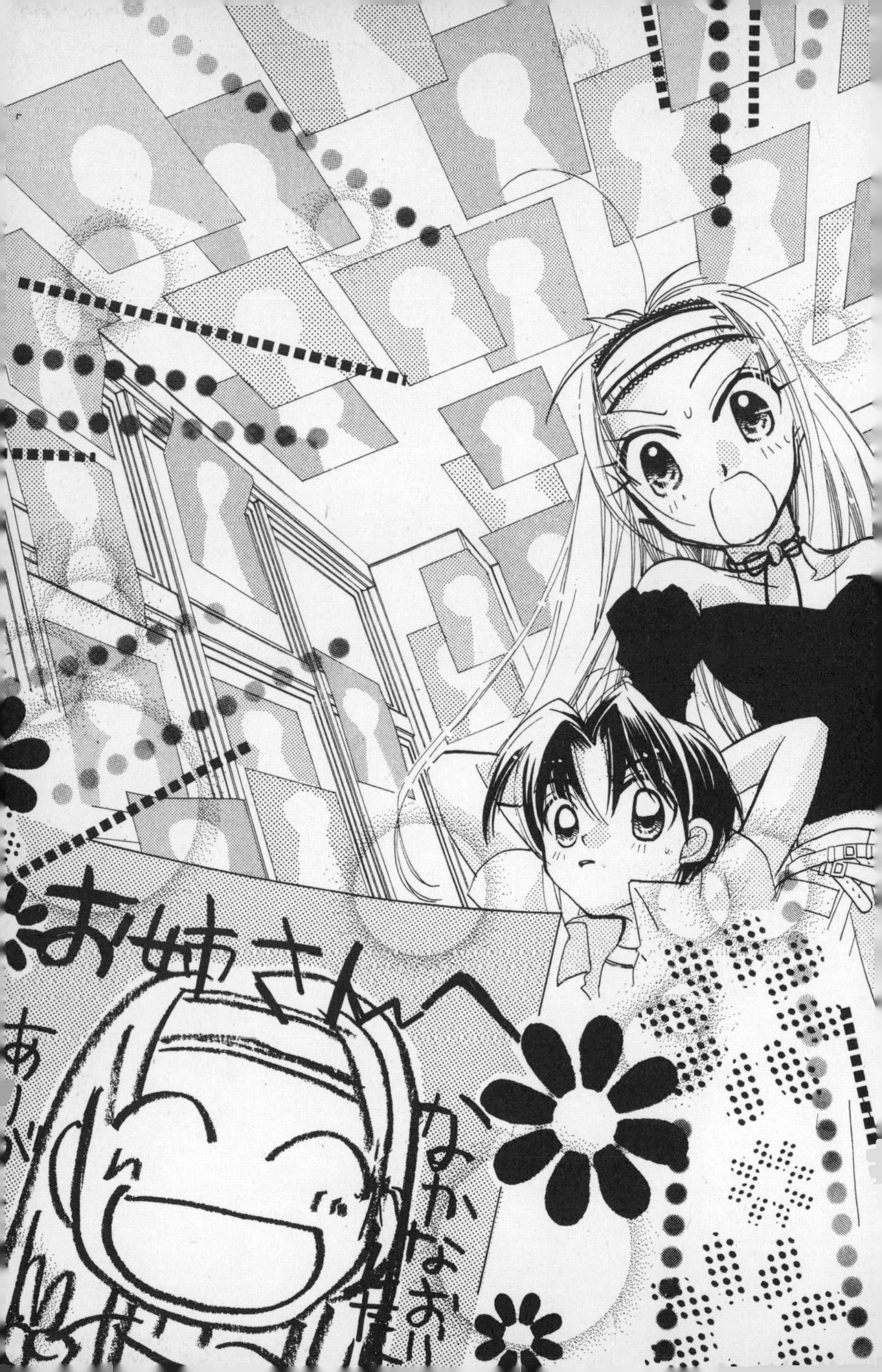
お姉さんへ

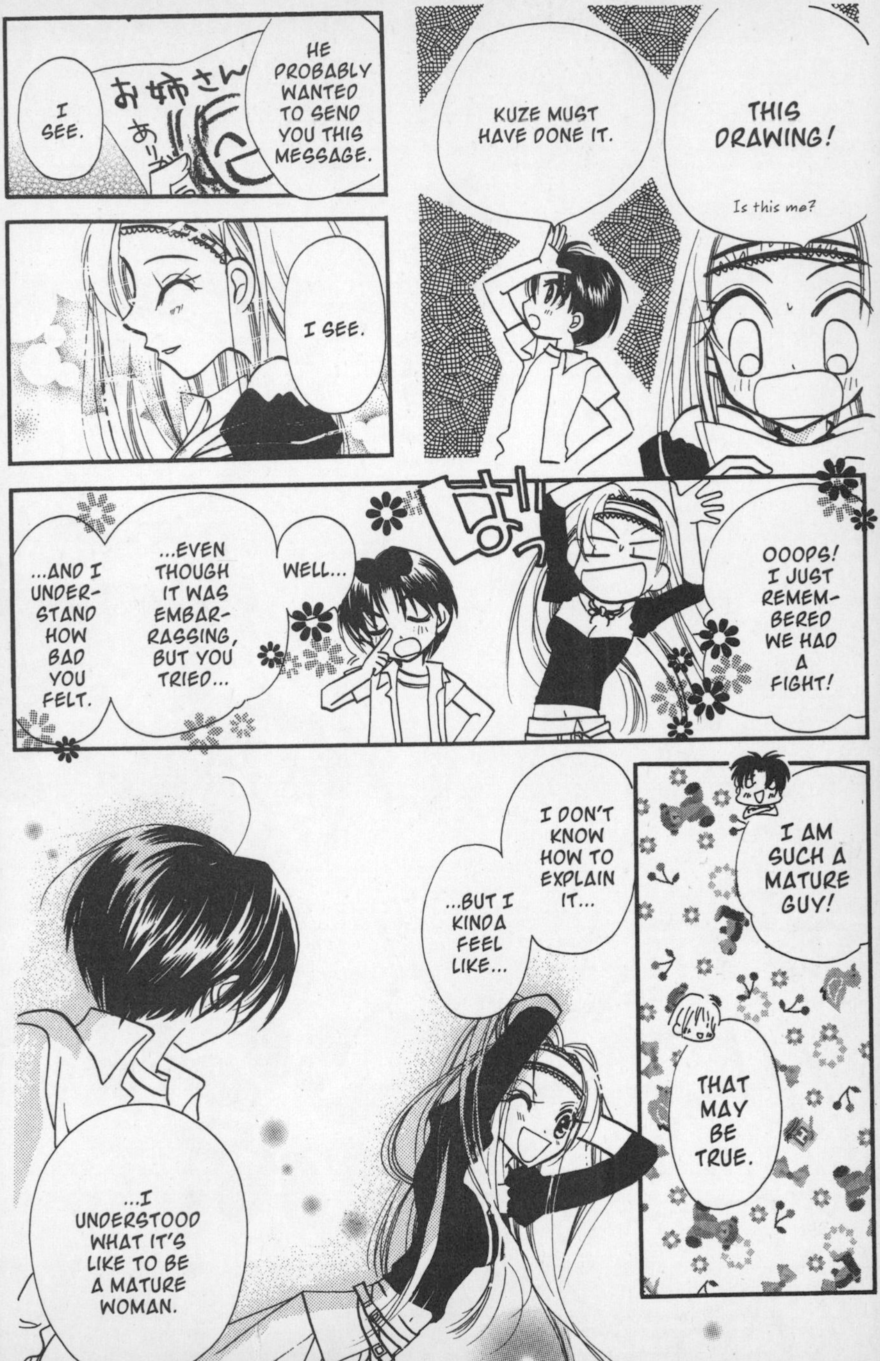
THIS DRAWING!
Is this me?
KUZE MUST HAVE DONE IT.
HE PROBABLY WANTED TO SEND YOU THIS MESSAGE.
お姉さん あり
I SEE.
I SEE.
OOOPS! I JUST REMEMBERED WE HAD A FIGHT!
はっ
WELL...
...EVEN THOUGH IT WAS EMBARRASSING, BUT YOU TRIED...
...AND I UNDERSTAND HOW BAD YOU FELT.
I AM SUCH A MATURE GUY!
THAT MAY BE TRUE.
I DON'T KNOW HOW TO EXPLAIN IT...
...BUT I KINDA FEEL LIKE...
...I UNDERSTOOD WHAT IT'S LIKE TO BE A MATURE WOMAN.

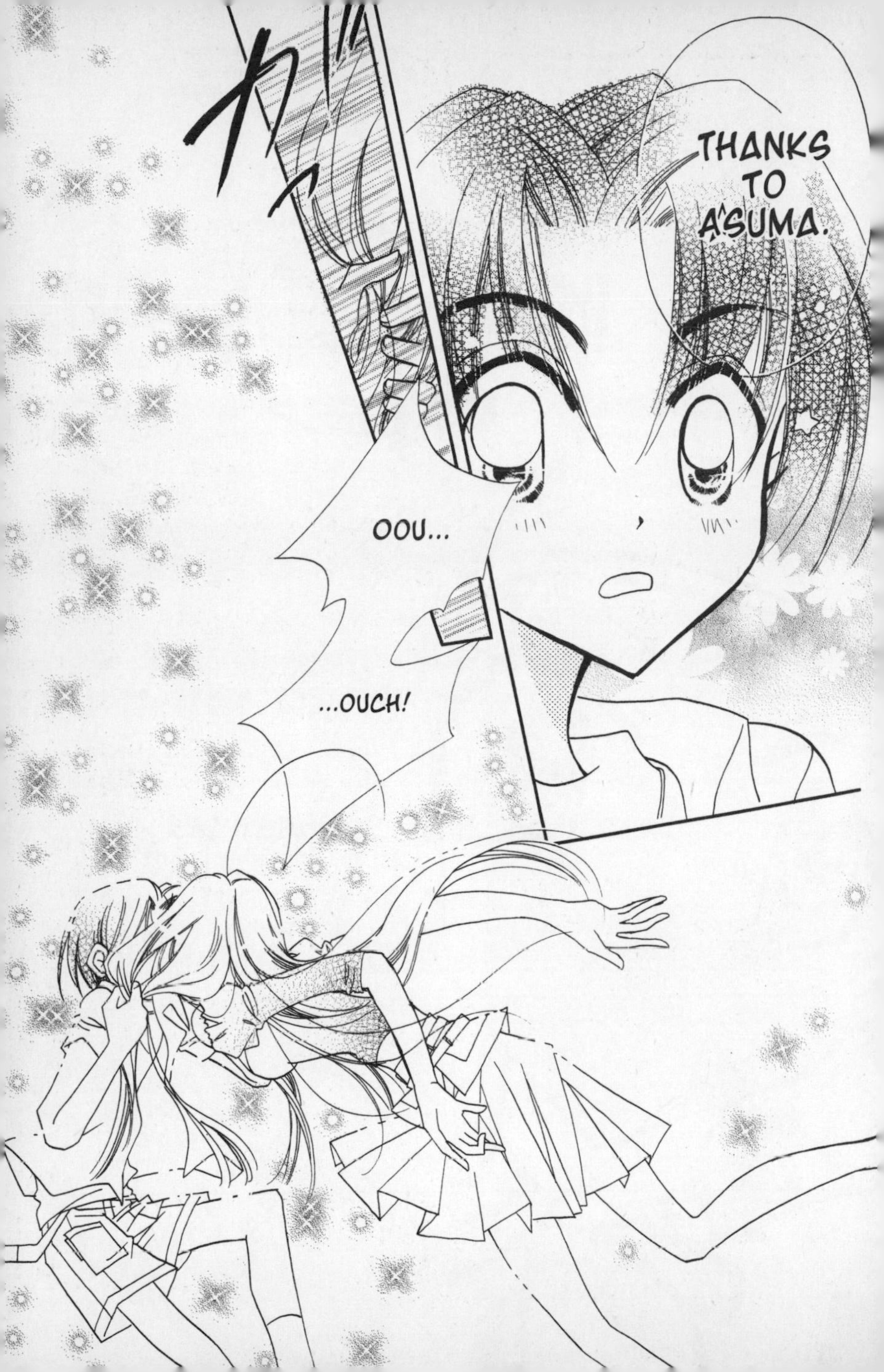
THANKS TO ASUMA.
ガッ
OOU...
...OUCH!

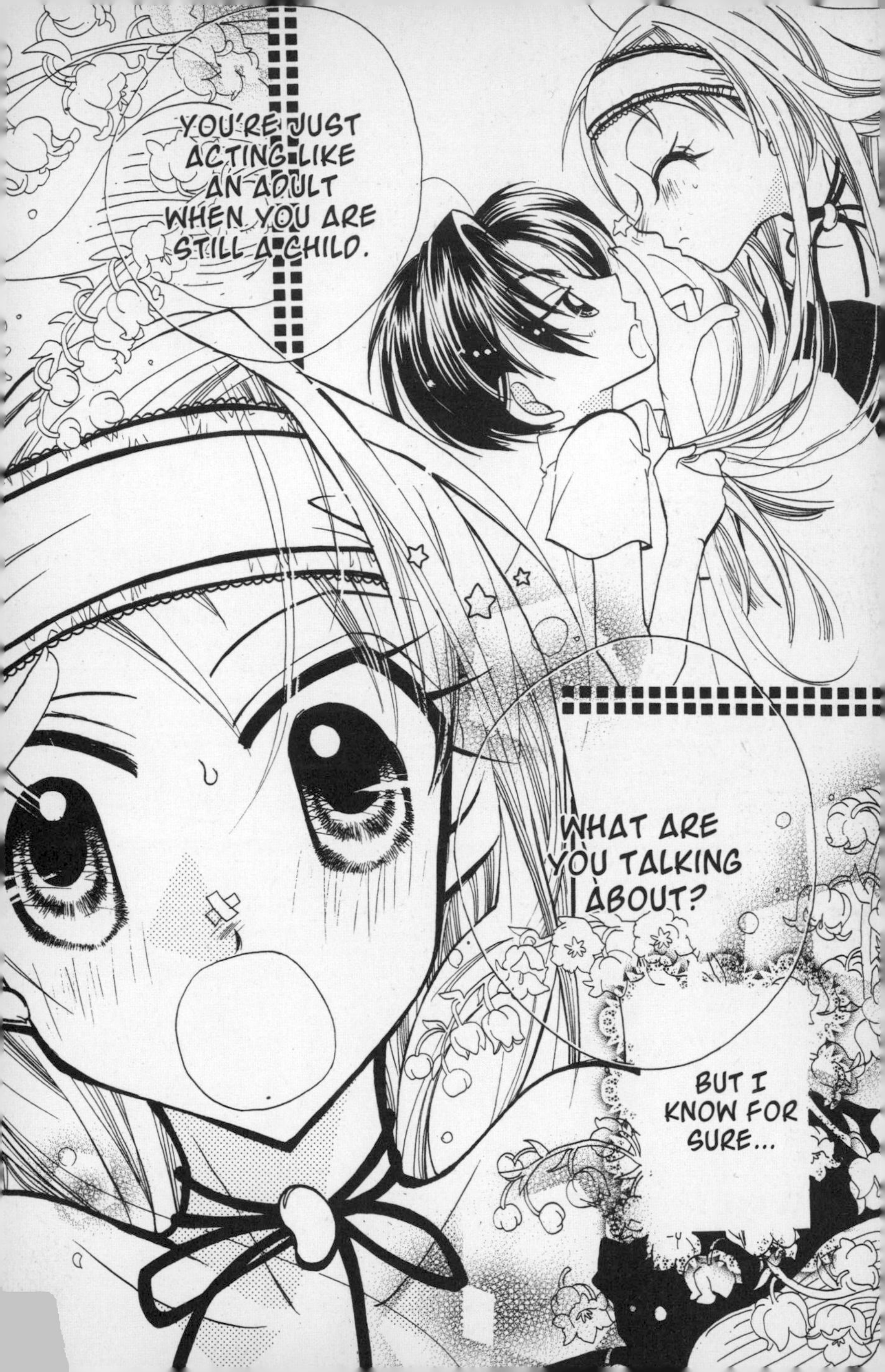
YOU'RE JUST ACTING LIKE AN ADULT WHEN YOU ARE STILL A CHILD.
WHAT ARE YOU TALKING ABOUT?
BUT I KNOW FOR SURE...

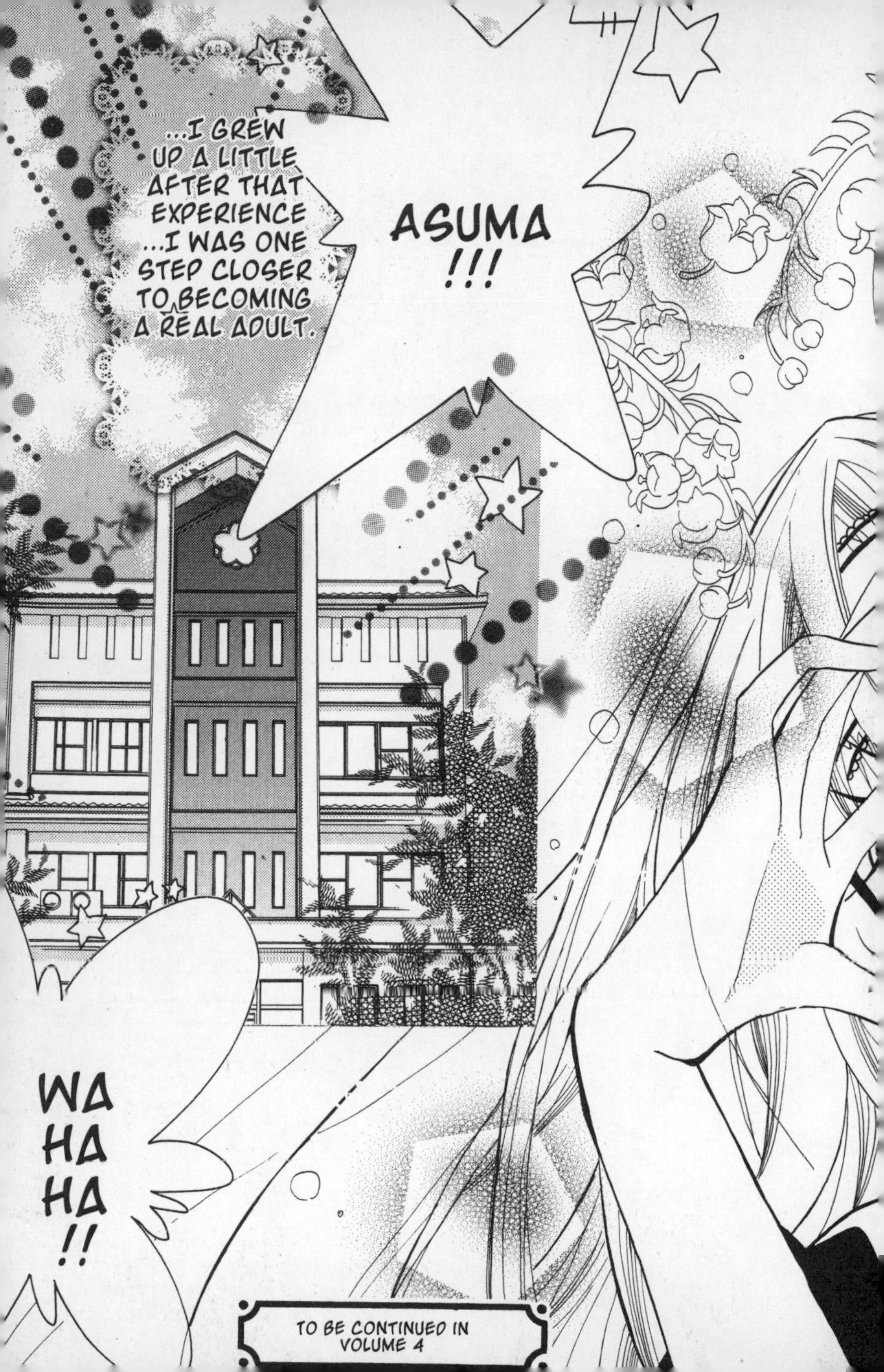
ASUMA !!!
...I GREW UP A LITTLE AFTER THAT EXPERIENCE ...I WAS ONE STEP CLOSER TO BECOMING A REAL ADULT.
WA HA HA !!
TO BE CONTINUED IN VOLUME 4

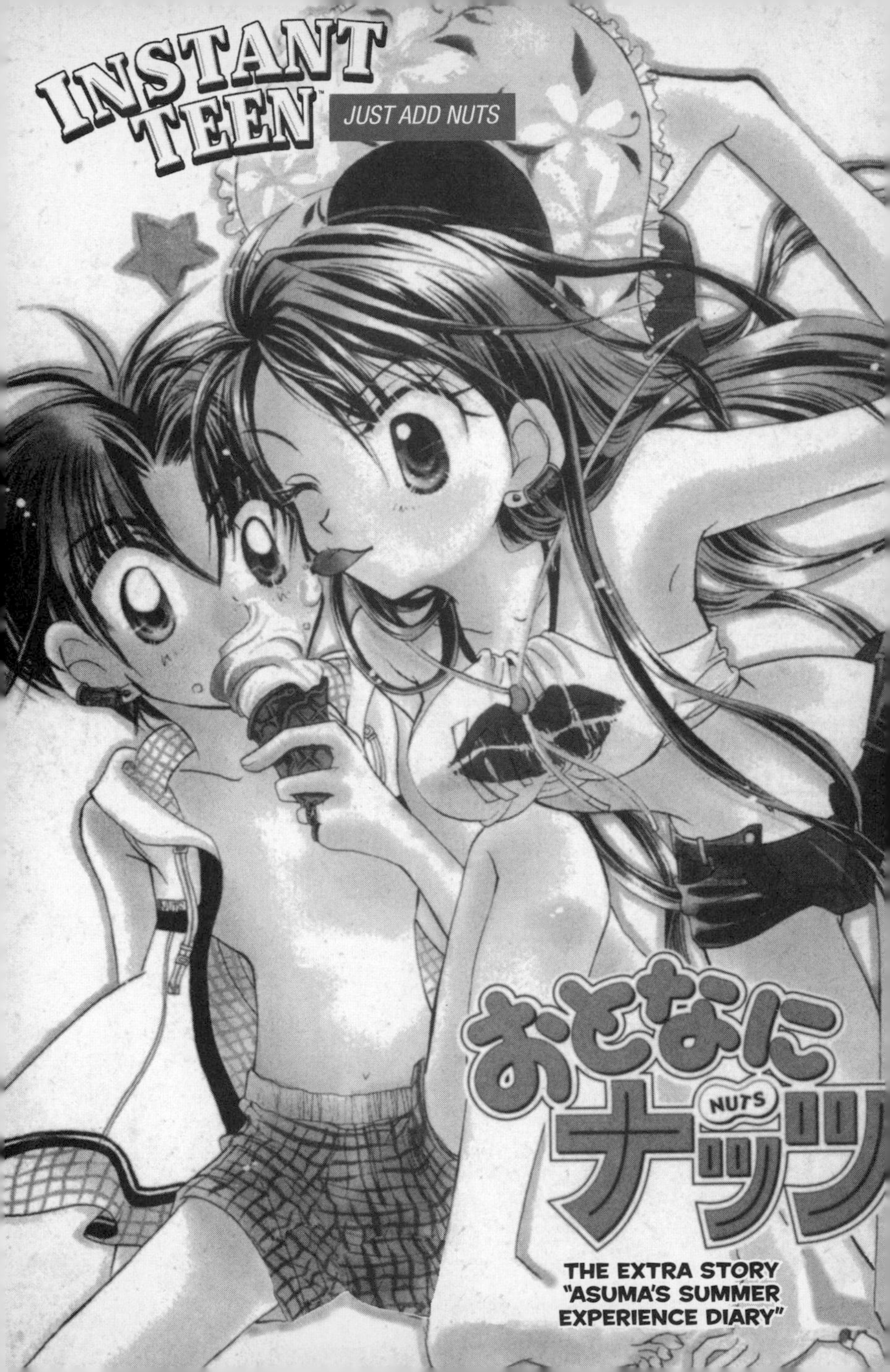
INSTANT TEEN™
JUST ADD NUTS
おとなにナッツ
NUTS
THE EXTRA STORY "ASUMA'S SUMMER EXPERIENCE DIARY"

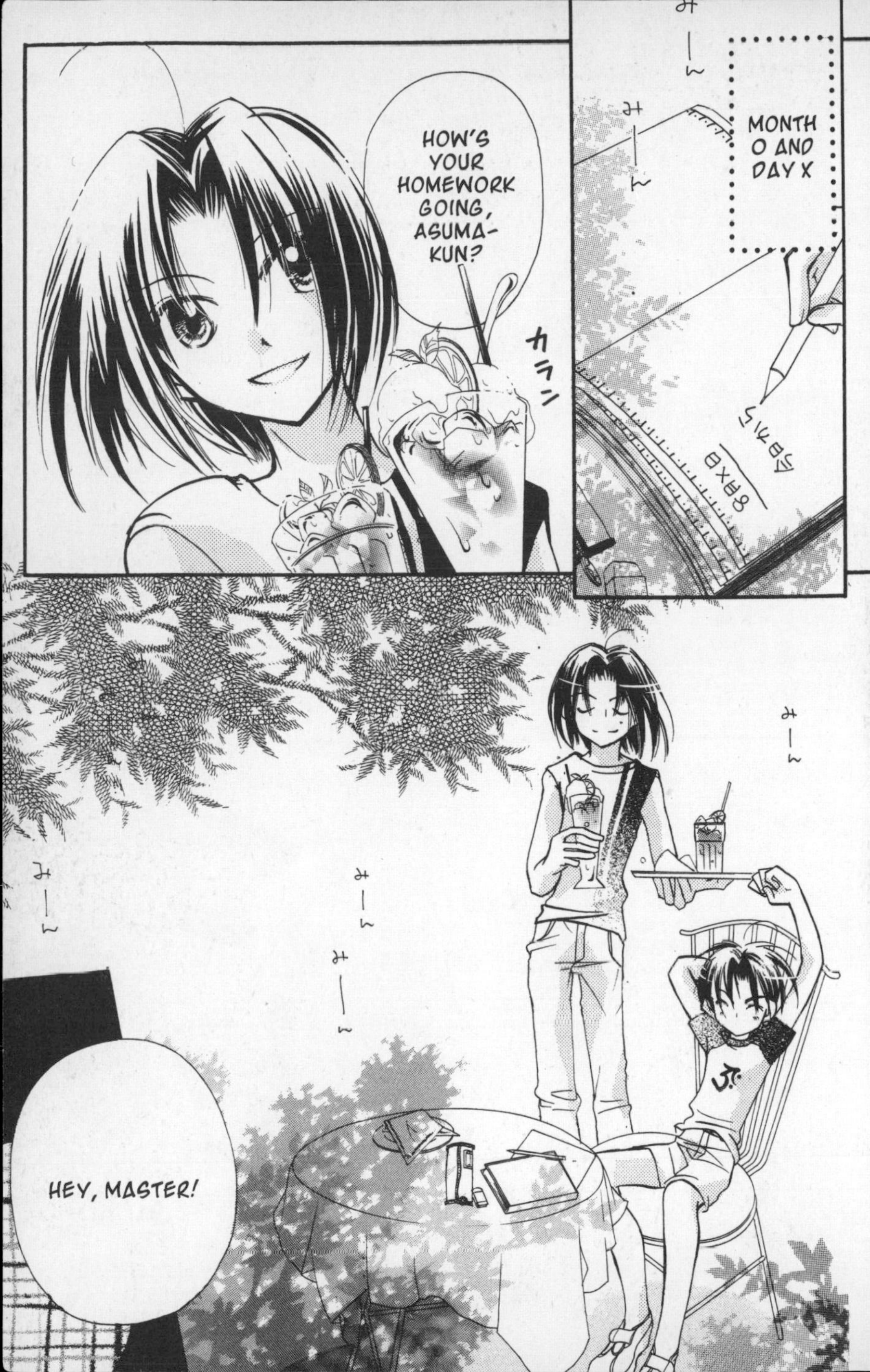

みーーん
みーーん
MONTH O AND DAY X
HOW'S YOUR HOMEWORK GOING, ASUMA-KUN?
カラン
みーん
みーん
みーーん
みーーん
HEY, MASTER!

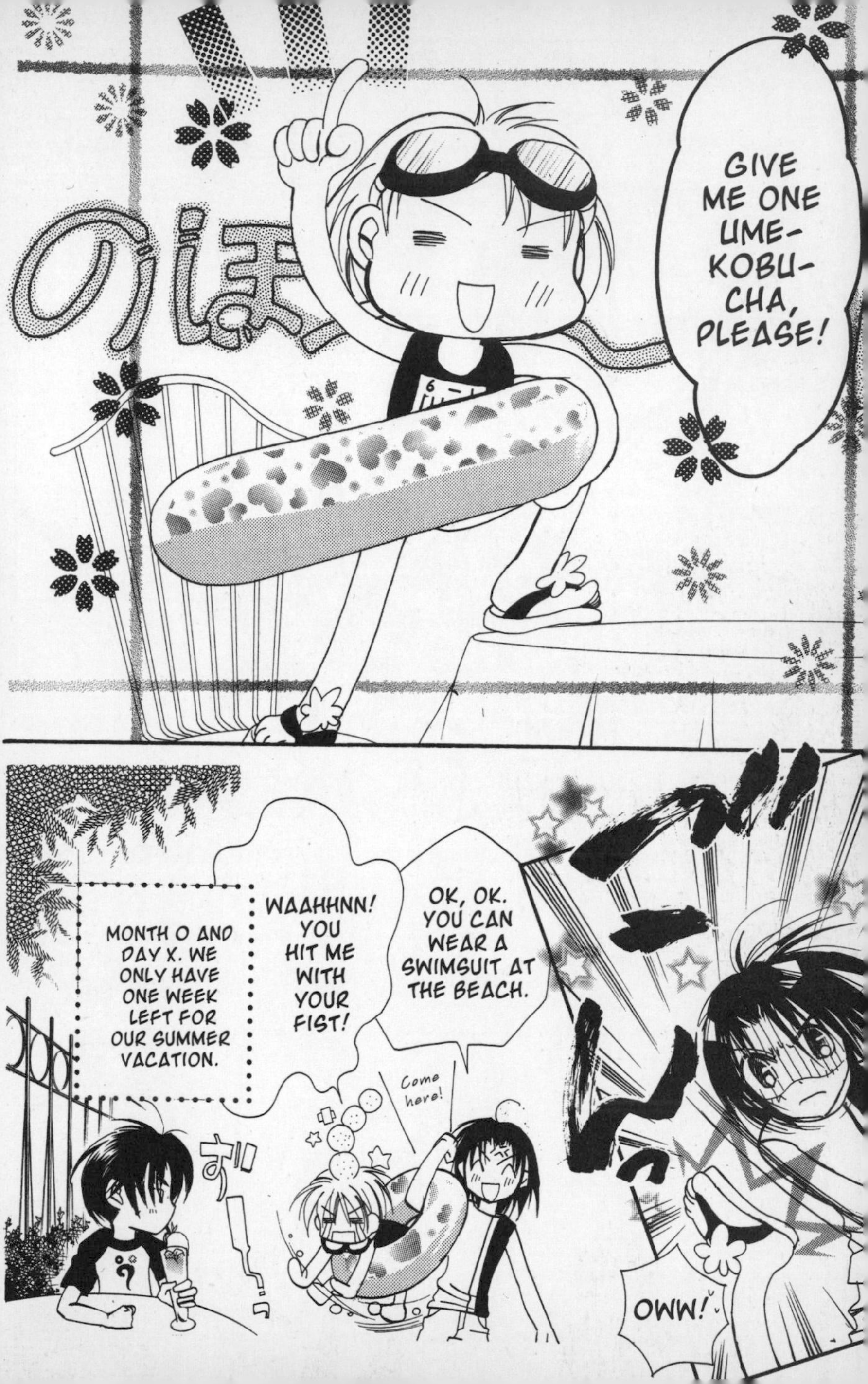
GIVE ME ONE UME-KOBUCHA, PLEASE!
OWW!
OK, OK. YOU CAN WEAR A SWIMSUIT AT THE BEACH.
Come here!
WAAHHNN! YOU HIT ME WITH YOUR FIST!
MONTH O AND DAY X. WE ONLY HAVE ONE WEEK LEFT FOR OUR SUMMER VACATION.

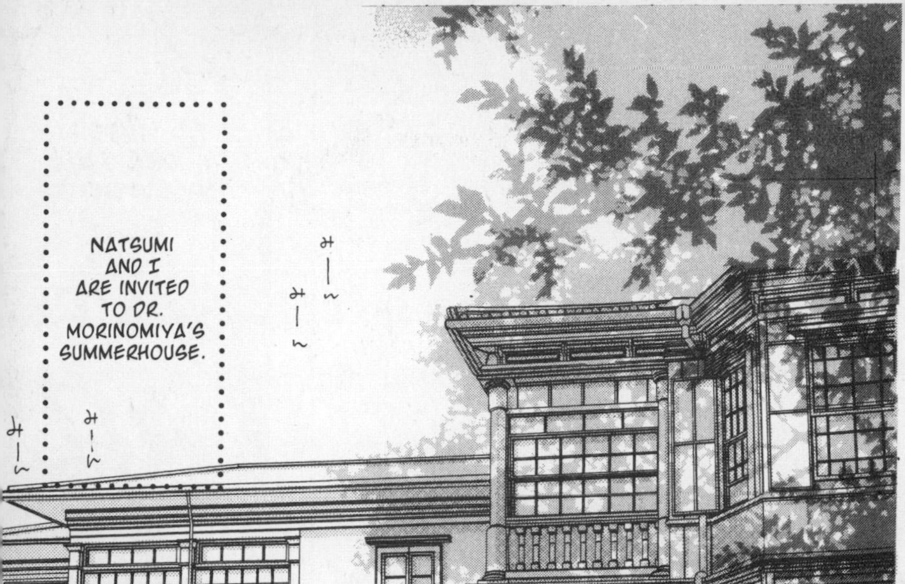
NATSUMI AND I ARE INVITED TO DR. MORINOMIYA'S SUMMERHOUSE.
みーん
みーん
みーん
みーん

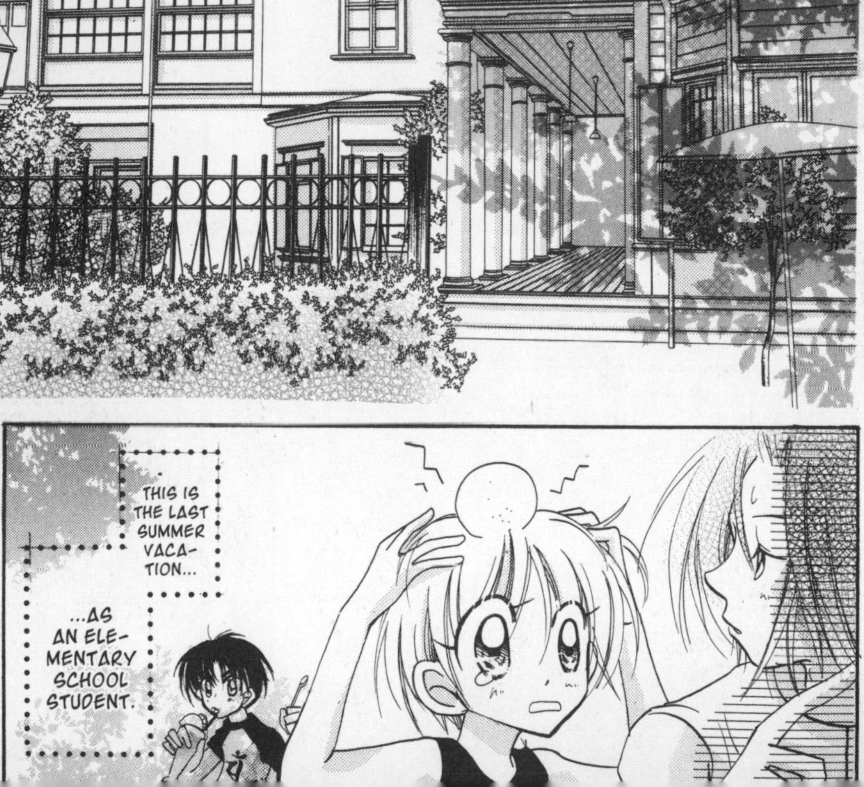
THIS IS THE LAST SUMMER VACATION...
...AS AN ELEMENTARY SCHOOL STUDENT.

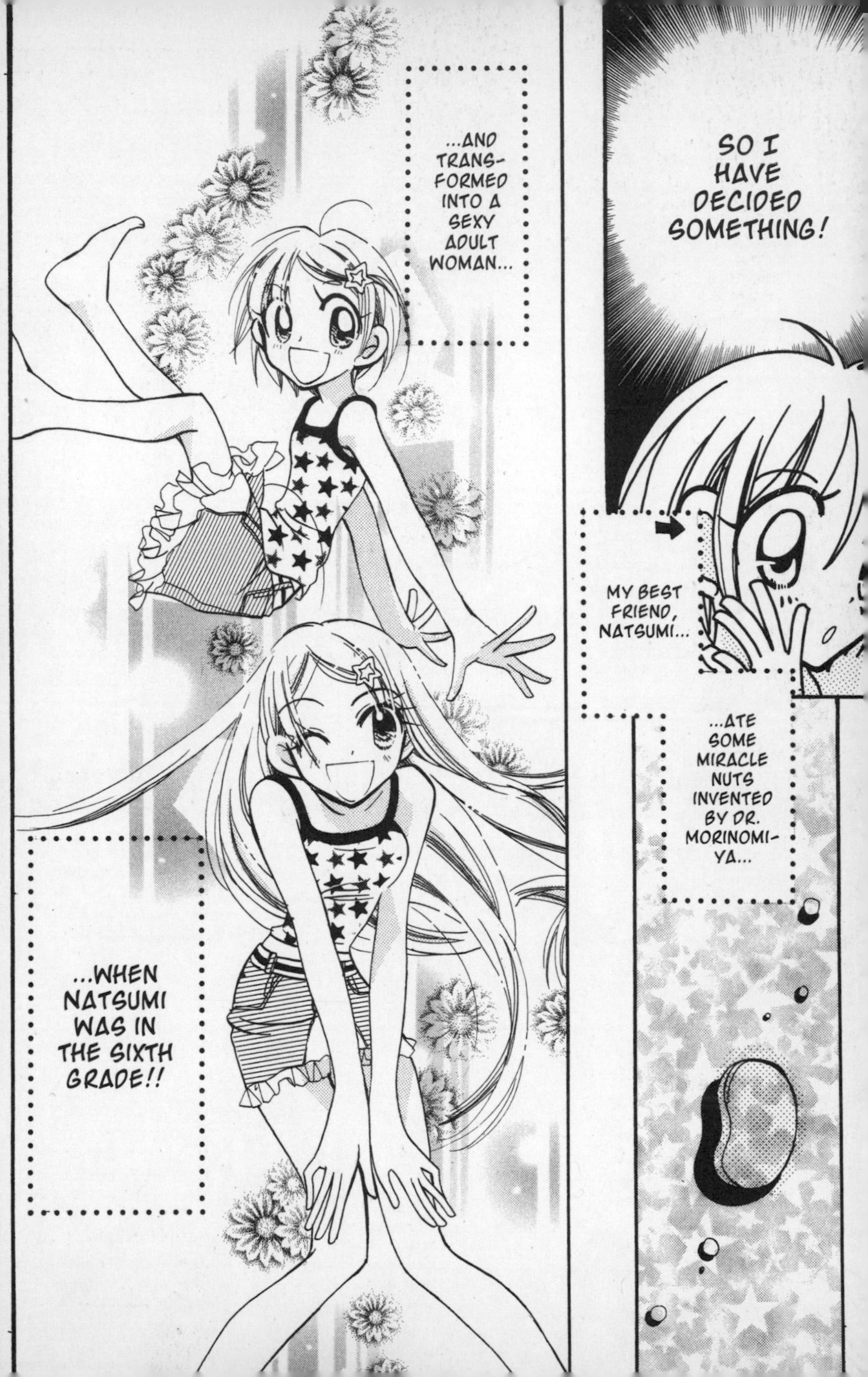
SO I HAVE DECIDED SOMETHING!
MY BEST FRIEND, NATSUMI...
...ATE SOME MIRACLE NUTS INVENTED BY DR. MORINOMIYA...
...AND TRANS-FORMED INTO A SEXY ADULT WOMAN...
...WHEN NATSUMI WAS IN THE SIXTH GRADE!!

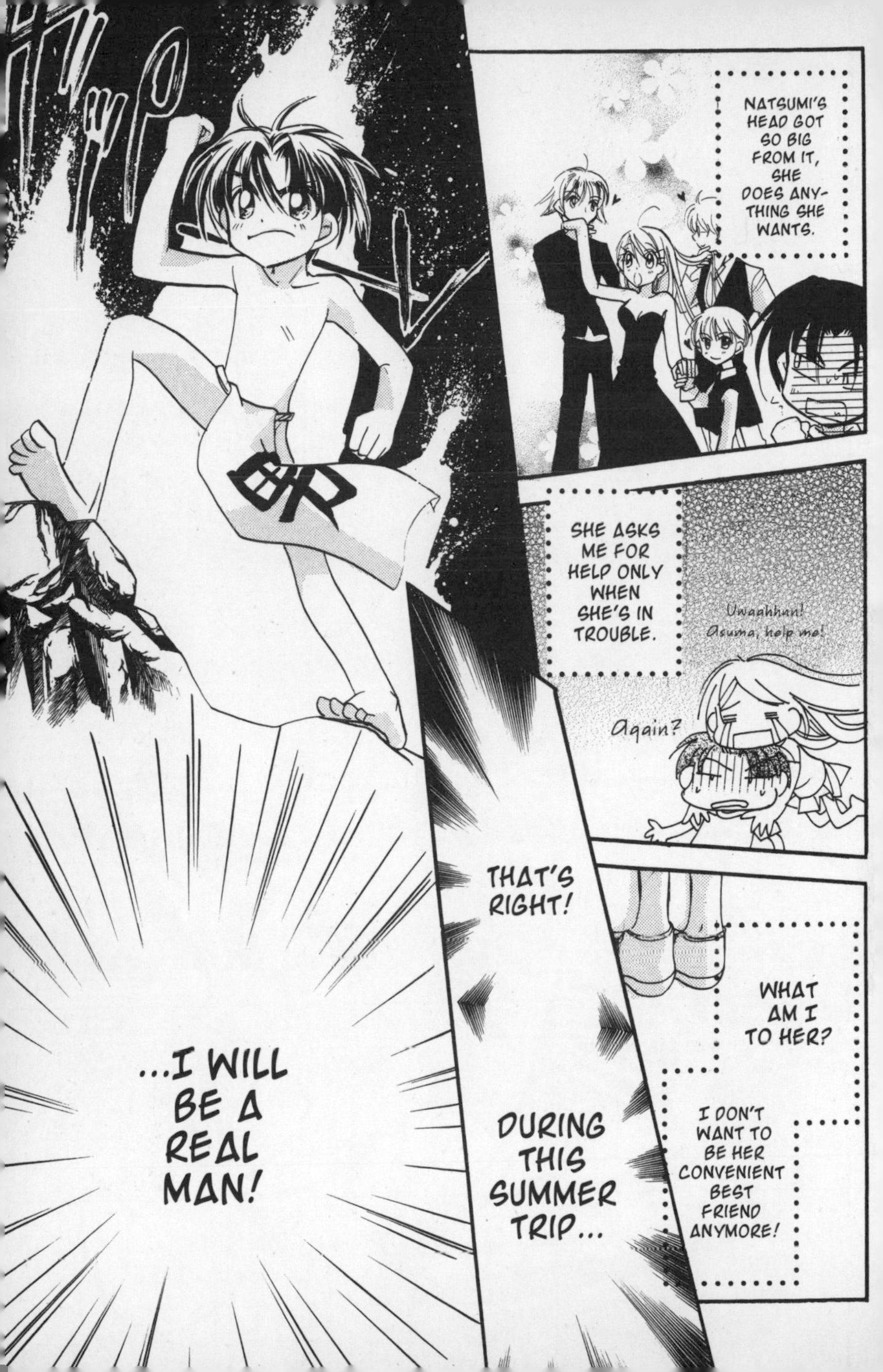
NATSUMI'S HEAD GOT SO BIG FROM IT, SHE DOES ANY-THING SHE WANTS.
SHE ASKS ME FOR HELP ONLY WHEN SHE'S IN TROUBLE.
Uwaahhan! Asuma, help me!
Again?
WHAT AM I TO HER?
I DON'T WANT TO BE HER CONVENIENT BEST FRIEND ANYMORE!
THAT'S RIGHT!
DURING THIS SUMMER TRIP...
...I WILL BE A REAL MAN!

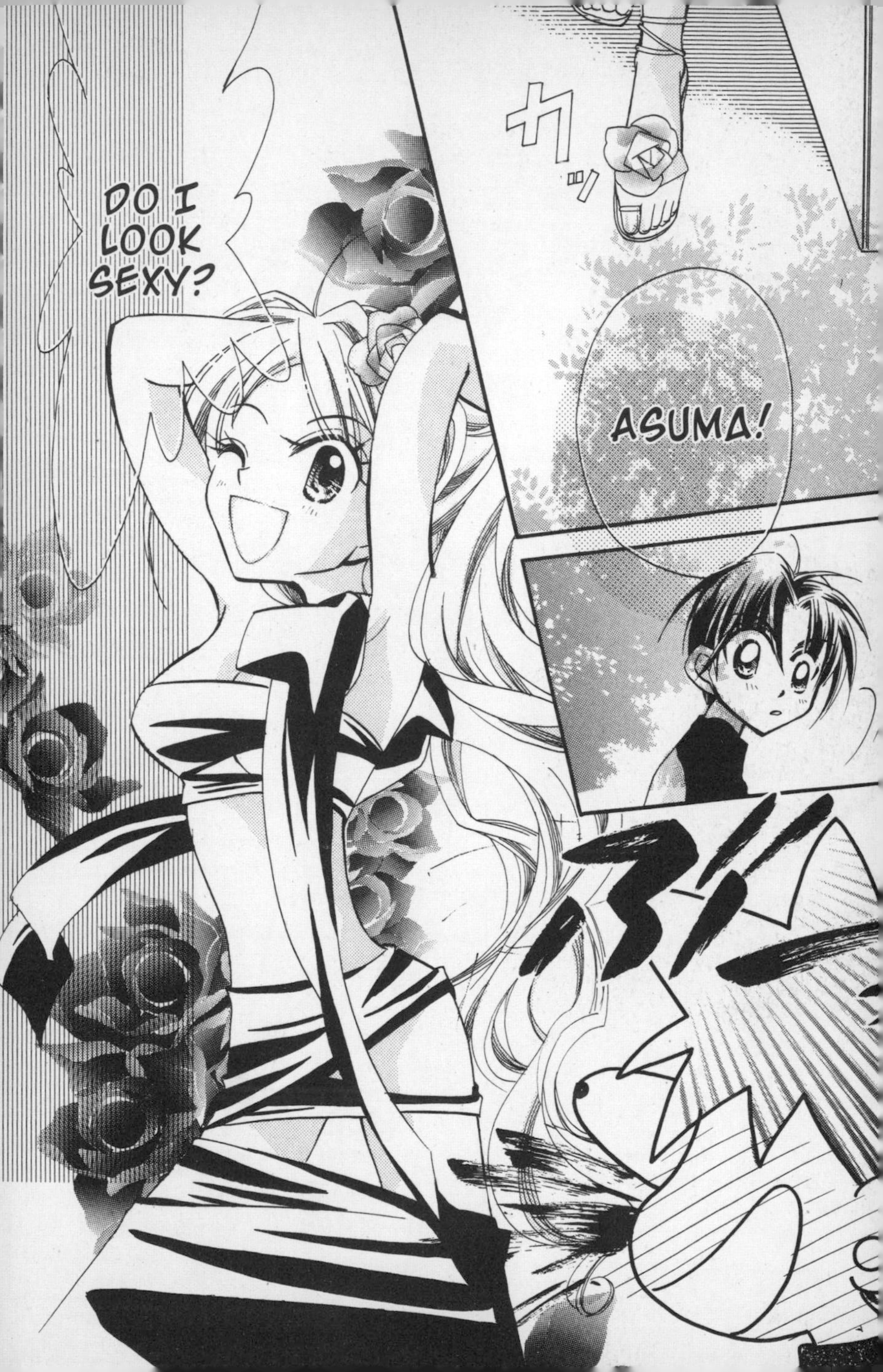

カッ
ASUMA!
DO I LOOK SEXY?

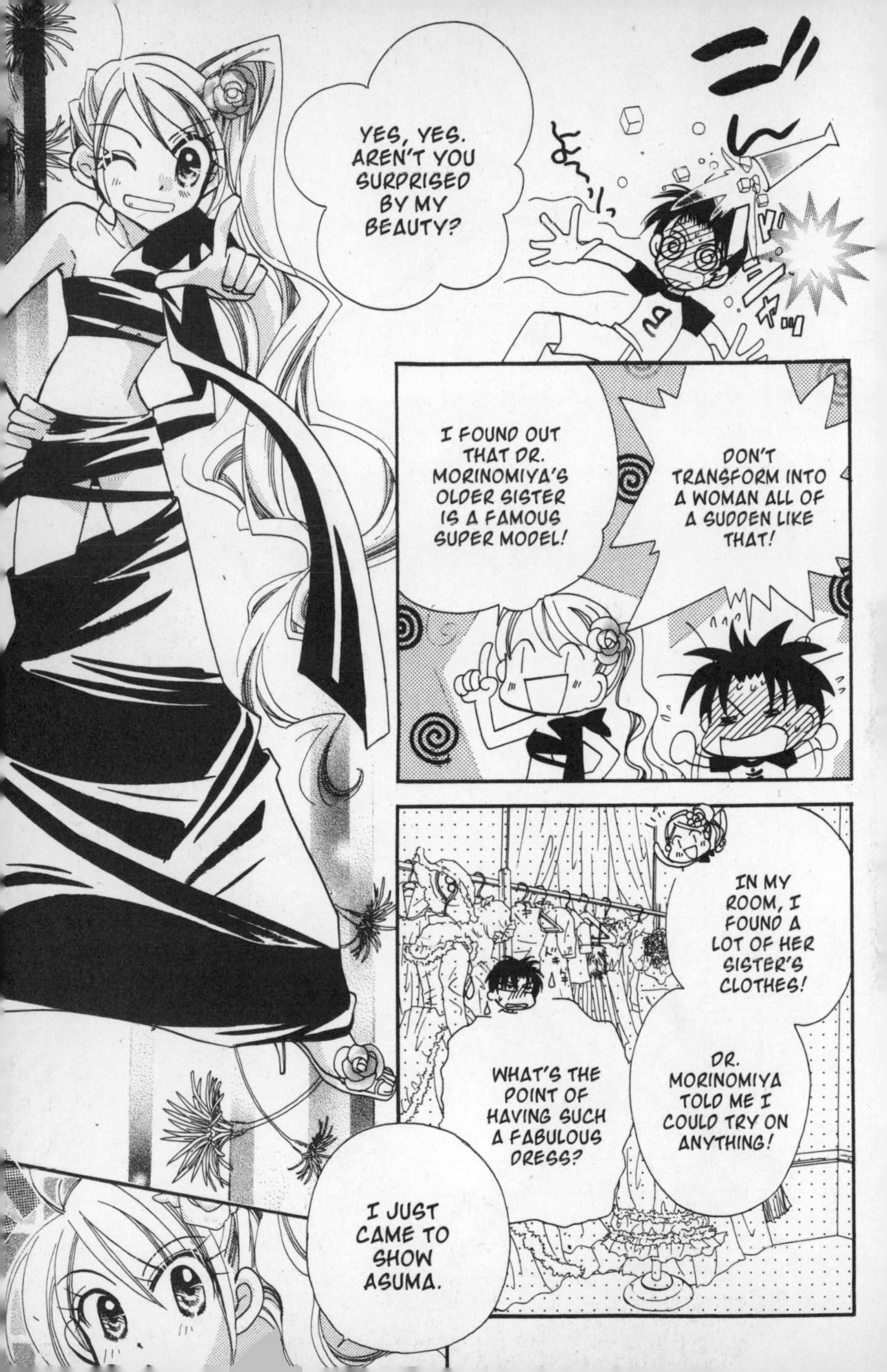
DON'T TRANSFORM INTO A WOMAN ALL OF A SUDDEN LIKE THAT!
I FOUND OUT THAT DR. MORINOMIYA'S OLDER SISTER IS A FAMOUS SUPER MODEL!
IN MY ROOM, I FOUND A LOT OF HER SISTER'S CLOTHES!
DR. MORINOMIYA TOLD ME I COULD TRY ON ANYTHING!
WHAT'S THE POINT OF HAVING SUCH A FABULOUS DRESS?
YES, YES. AREN'T YOU SURPRISED BY MY BEAUTY?
I JUST CAME TO SHOW ASUMA.

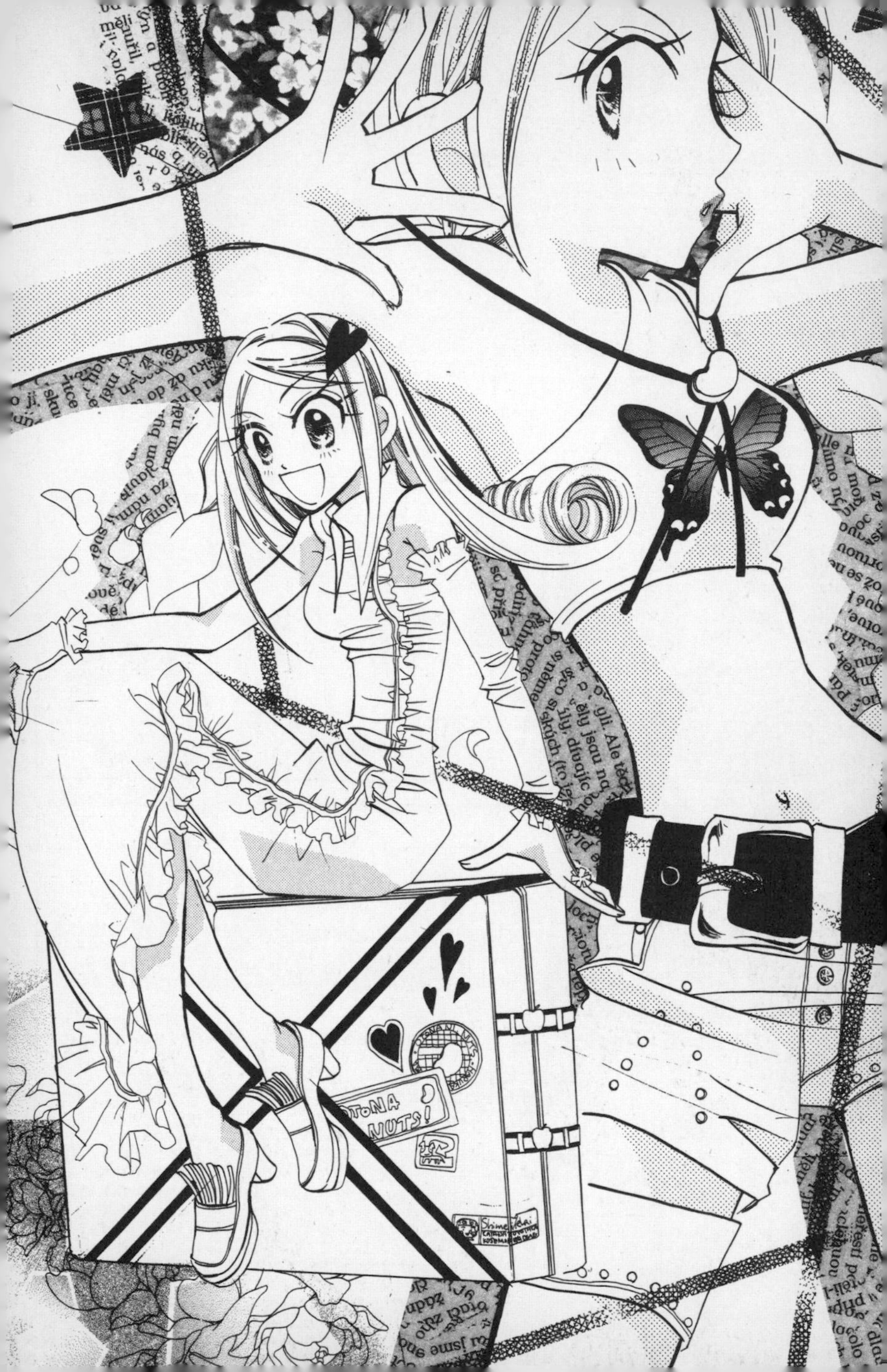
OTONA NUTS!

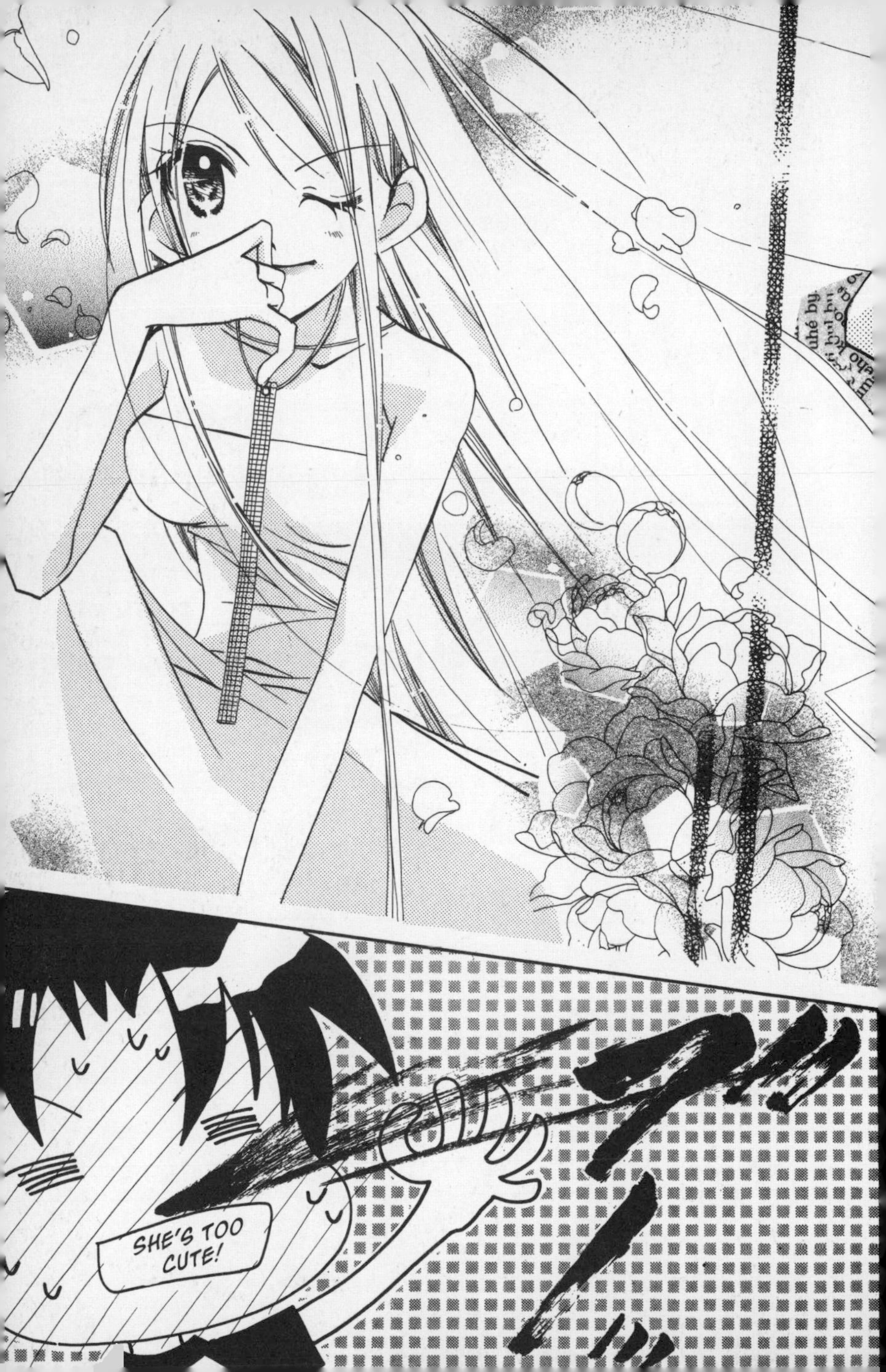
SHE'S TOO CUTE!

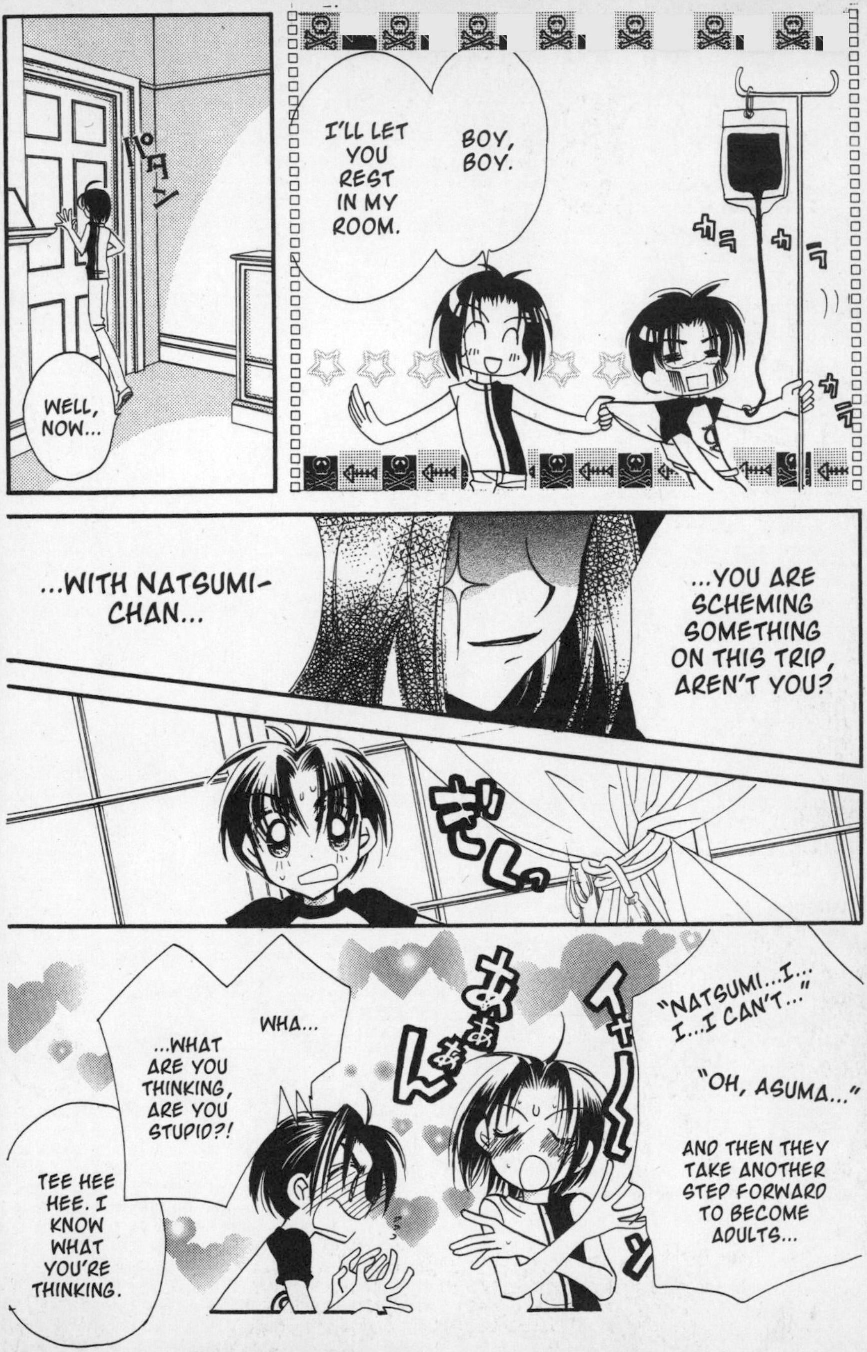
BOY, BOY.
I'LL LET YOU REST IN MY ROOM.
WELL, NOW...
...YOU ARE SCHEMING SOMETHING ON THIS TRIP, AREN'T YOU?
...WITH NATSUMI-CHAN...
"NATSUMI...I... I...I CAN'T..."
"OH, ASUMA..."
AND THEN THEY TAKE ANOTHER STEP FORWARD TO BECOME ADULTS...
WHA...
...WHAT ARE YOU THINKING, ARE YOU STUPID?!
TEE HEE HEE. I KNOW WHAT YOU'RE THINKING.

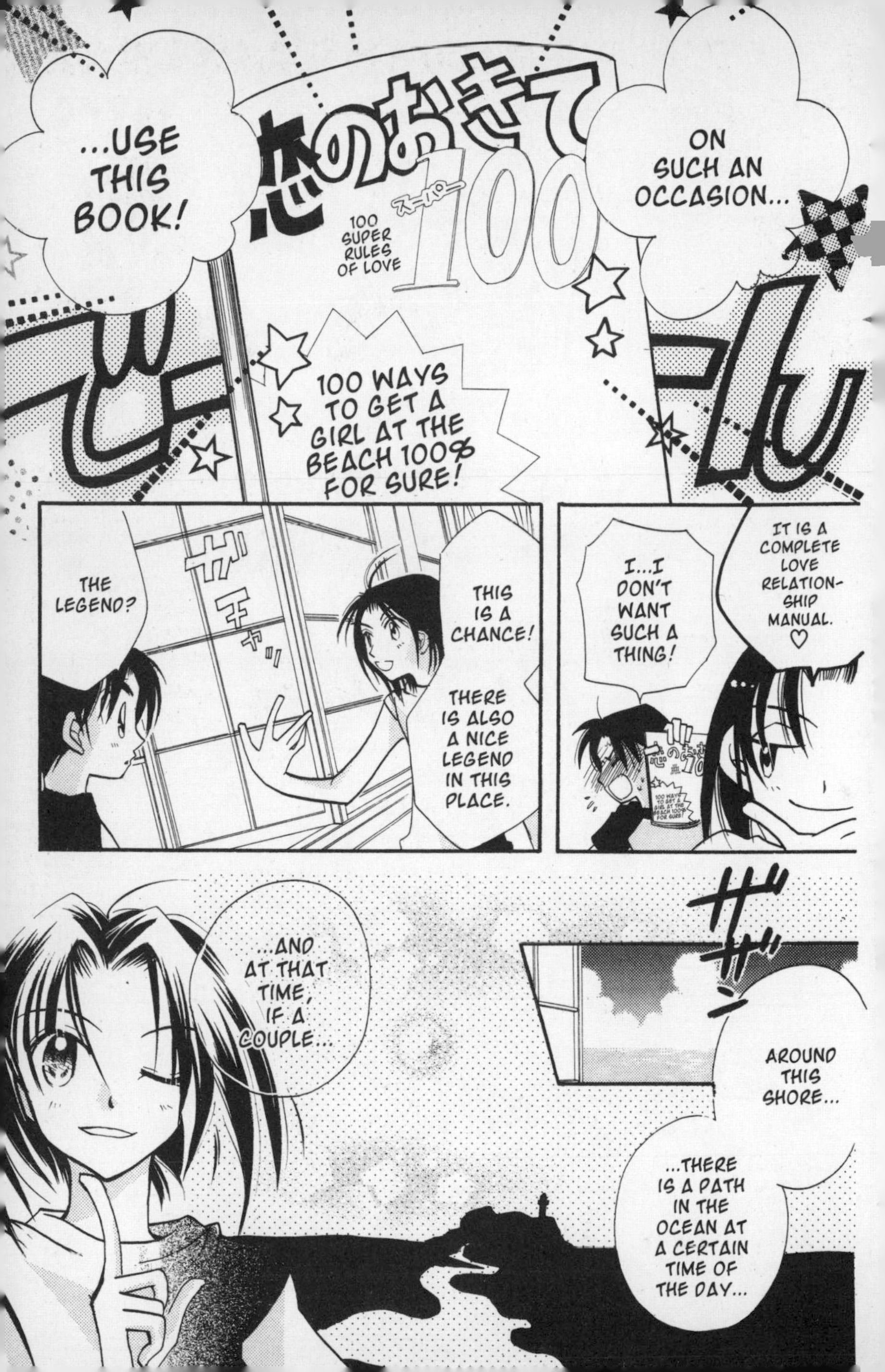
ON SUCH AN OCCASION...
...USE THIS BOOK!
恋のおきて
スーパー
100
100 SUPER RULES OF LOVE
でーん
100 WAYS TO GET A GIRL AT THE BEACH 100% FOR SURE!
IT IS A COMPLETE LOVE RELATIONSHIP MANUAL. ♡
I...I DON'T WANT SUCH A THING!
ガチャッ
THIS IS A CHANCE!
THERE IS ALSO A NICE LEGEND IN THIS PLACE.
THE LEGEND?
ザザー
AROUND THIS SHORE...
...THERE IS A PATH IN THE OCEAN AT A CERTAIN TIME OF THE DAY...
...AND AT THAT TIME, IF A COUPLE...

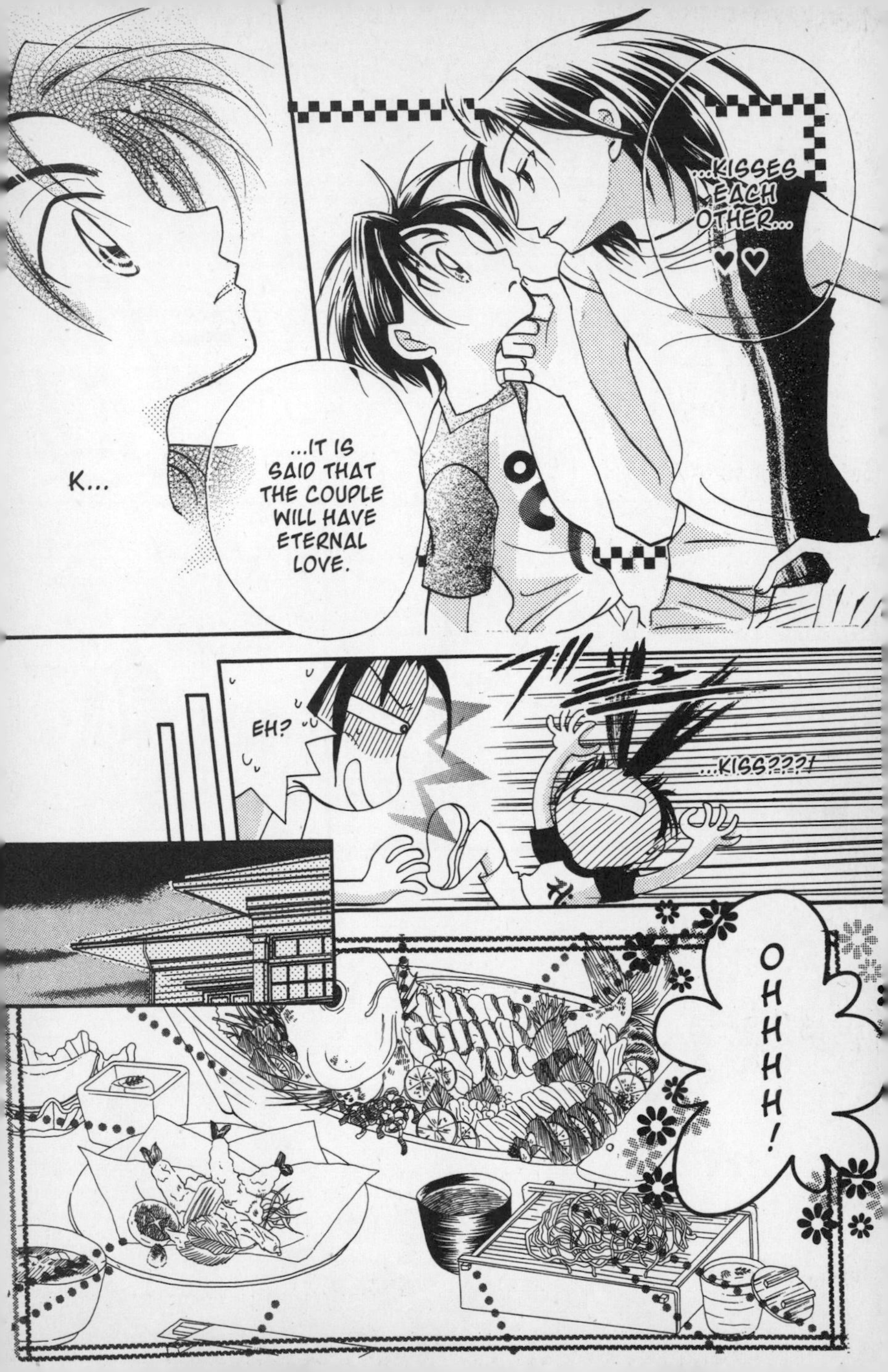
...KISSES EACH OTHER... ♥♡
...IT IS SAID THAT THE COUPLE WILL HAVE ETERNAL LOVE.
K...
...KISS???!
EH?
OHHHH!

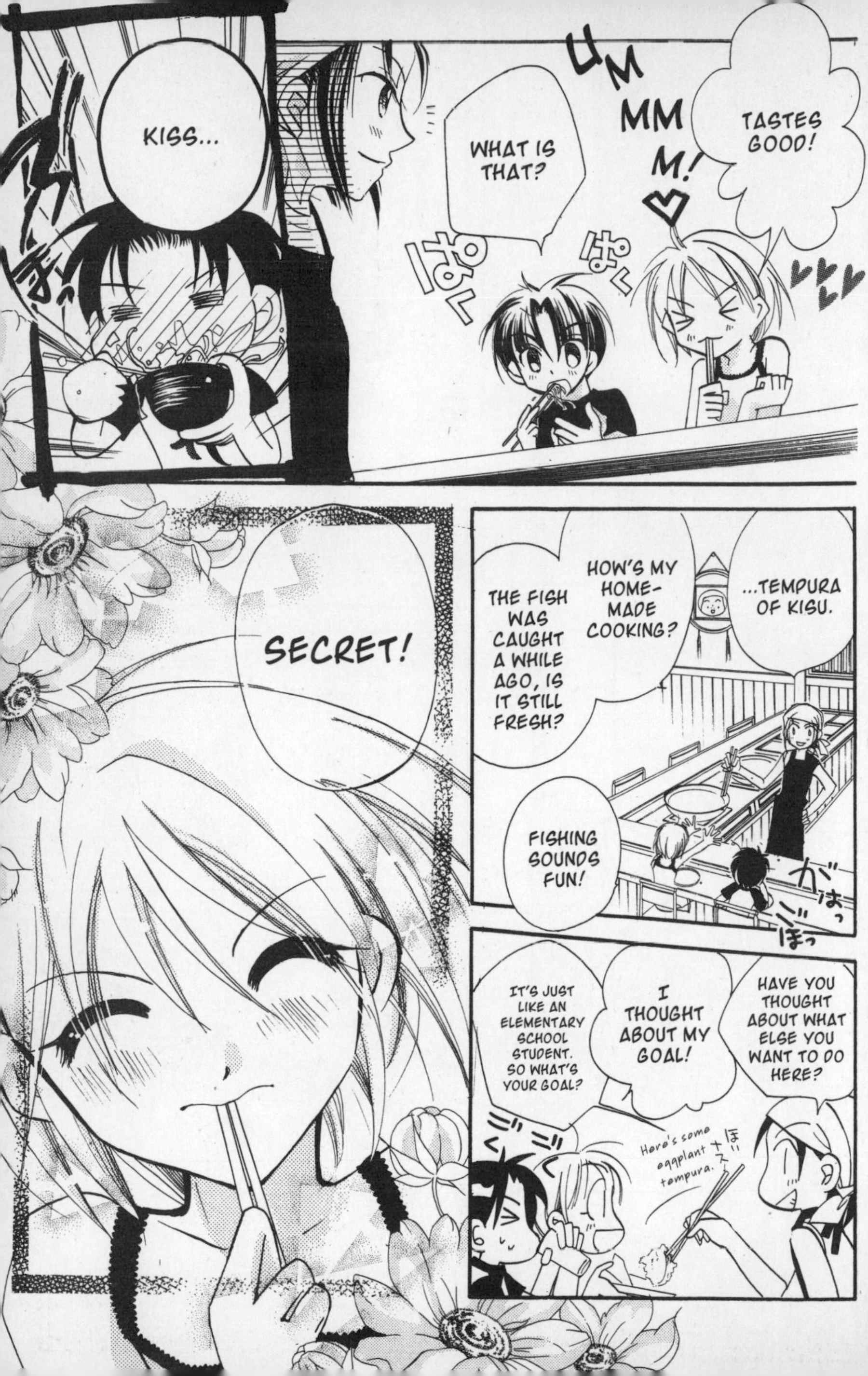
TASTES GOOD!
UMMMMM!
WHAT IS THAT?
ぱく
ぱく
KISS...
...TEMPURA OF KISU.
HOW'S MY HOME-MADE COOKING?
THE FISH WAS CAUGHT A WHILE AGO, IS IT STILL FRESH?
FISHING SOUNDS FUN!
がはっ
ごほっ
HAVE YOU THOUGHT ABOUT WHAT ELSE YOU WANT TO DO HERE?
I THOUGHT ABOUT MY GOAL!
IT'S JUST LIKE AN ELEMENTARY SCHOOL STUDENT. SO WHAT'S YOUR GOAL?
ほい
ナス
Here's some eggplant tempura.
SECRET!

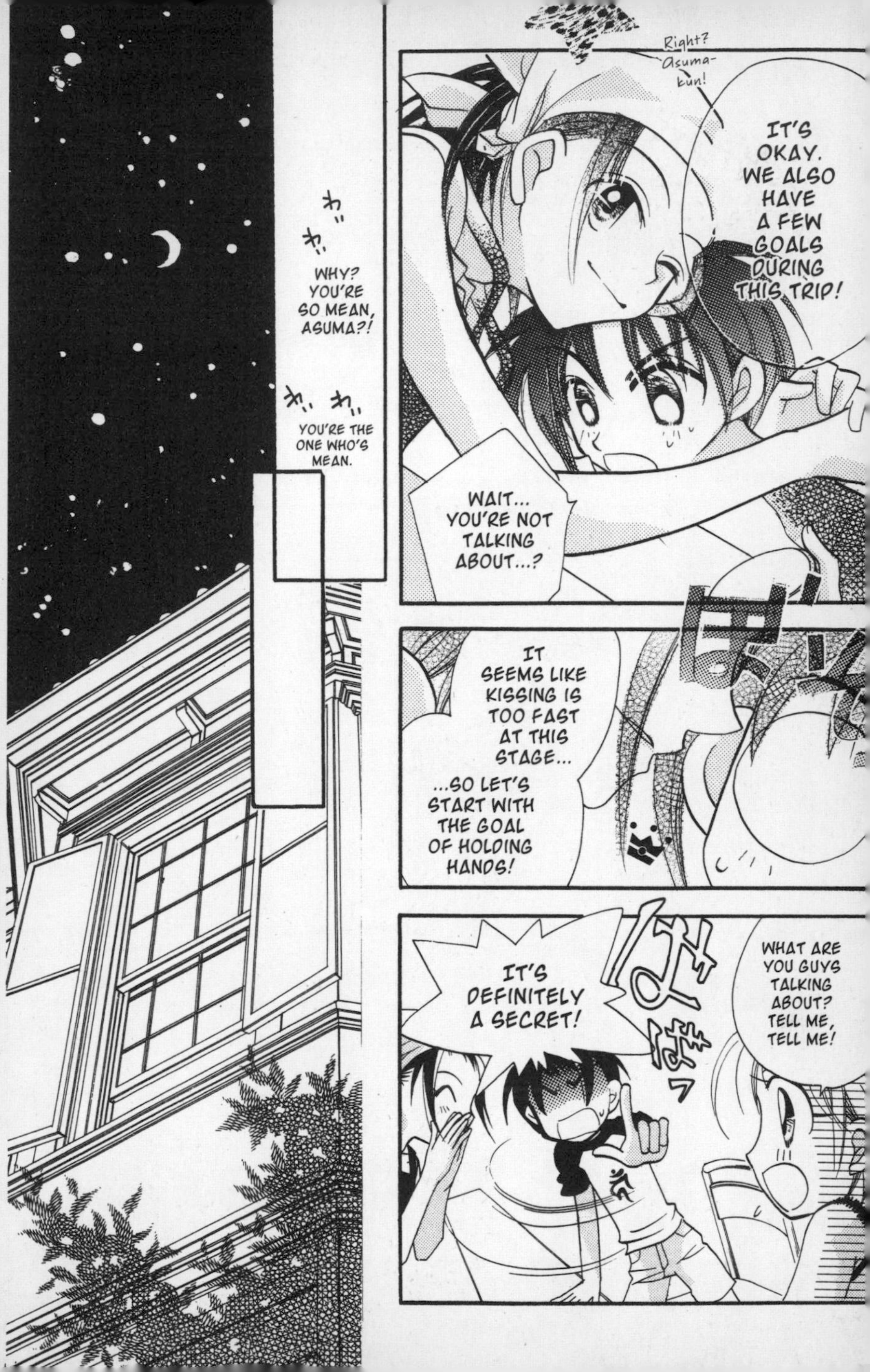
IT'S OKAY. WE ALSO HAVE A FEW GOALS DURING THIS TRIP!
Right? Asuma-kun!
WAIT... YOU'RE NOT TALKING ABOUT...?
IT SEEMS LIKE KISSING IS TOO FAST AT THIS STAGE...
...SO LET'S START WITH THE GOAL OF HOLDING HANDS!
WHAT ARE YOU GUYS TALKING ABOUT? TELL ME, TELL ME!
IT'S DEFINITELY A SECRET!
WHY? YOU'RE SO MEAN, ASUMA?!
YOU'RE THE ONE WHO'S MEAN.

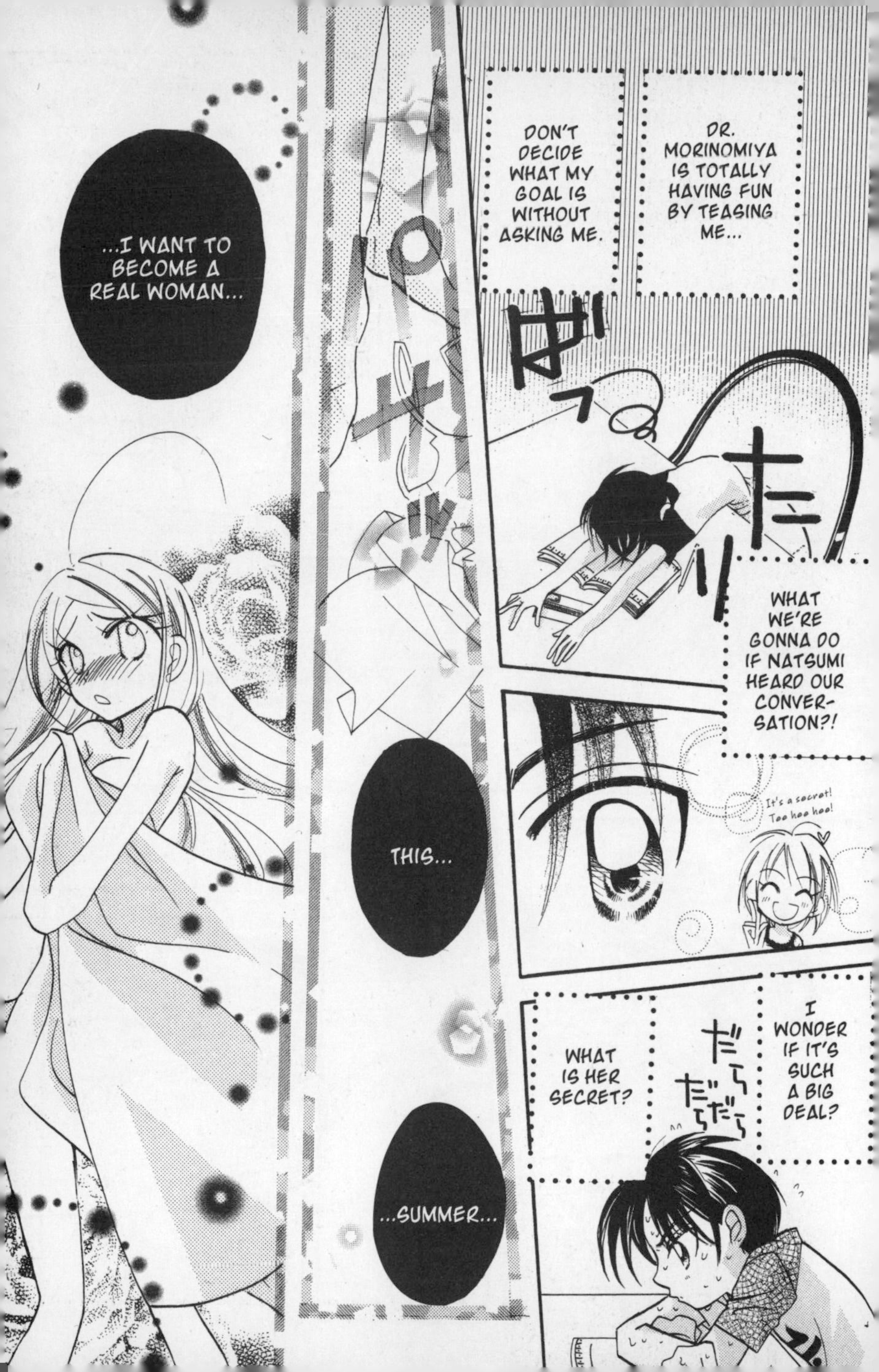
DR. MORINOMIYA IS TOTALLY HAVING FUN BY TEASING ME...
DON'T DECIDE WHAT MY GOAL IS WITHOUT ASKING ME.
WHAT WE'RE GONNA DO IF NATSUMI HEARD OUR CONVERSATION?!
It's a secret! Tee hee hee!
I WONDER IF IT'S SUCH A BIG DEAL?
WHAT IS HER SECRET?
THIS...
...SUMMER...
...I WANT TO BECOME A REAL WOMAN...

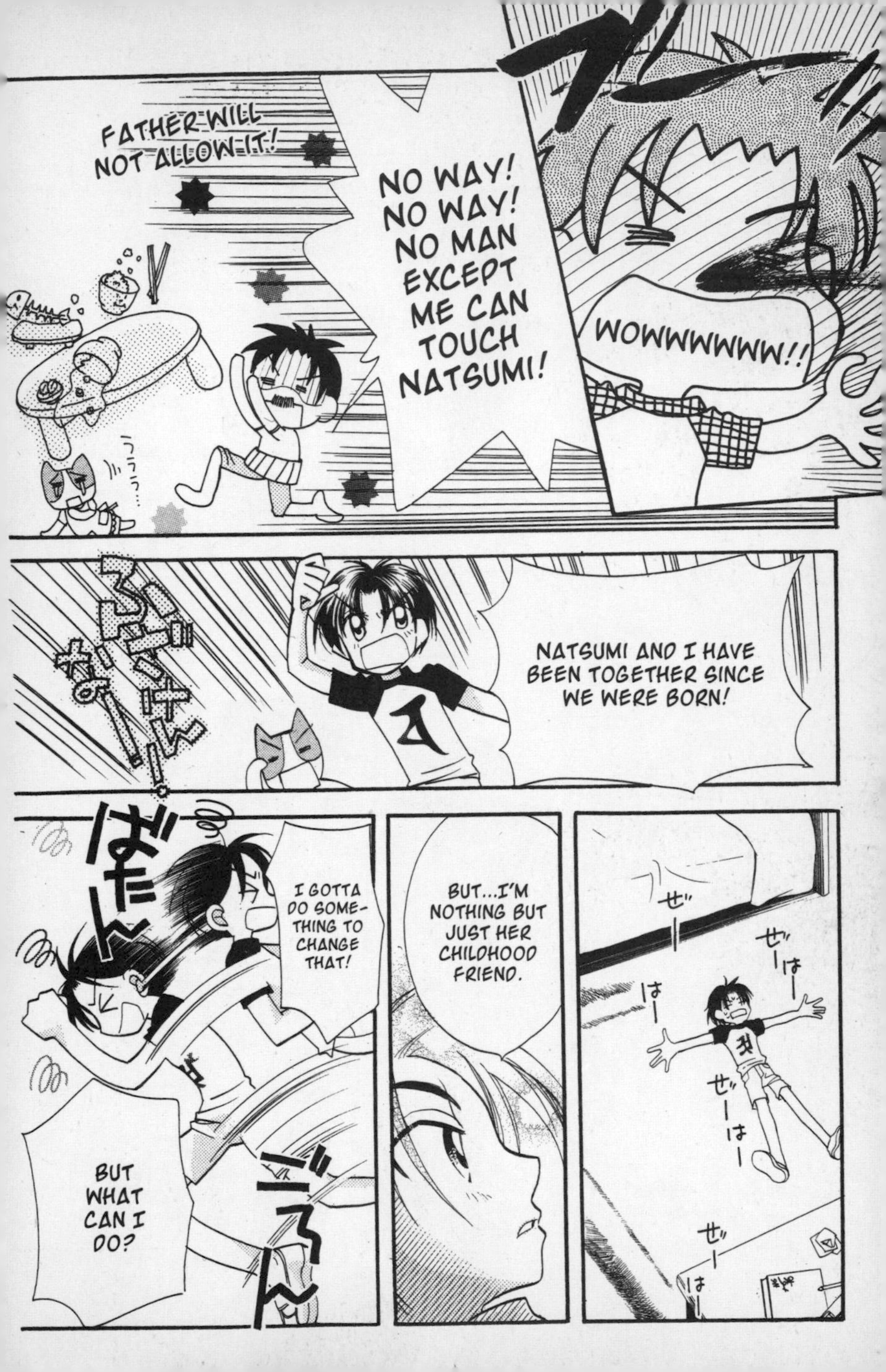
WOWWWWWW!!
NO WAY! NO WAY! NO MAN EXCEPT ME CAN TOUCH NATSUMI!
FATHER WILL NOT ALLOW IT!
NATSUMI AND I HAVE BEEN TOGETHER SINCE WE WERE BORN!
ぜーはー
BUT...I'M NOTHING BUT JUST HER CHILDHOOD FRIEND.
I GOTTA DO SOMETHING TO CHANGE THAT!
ばたん
BUT WHAT CAN I DO?

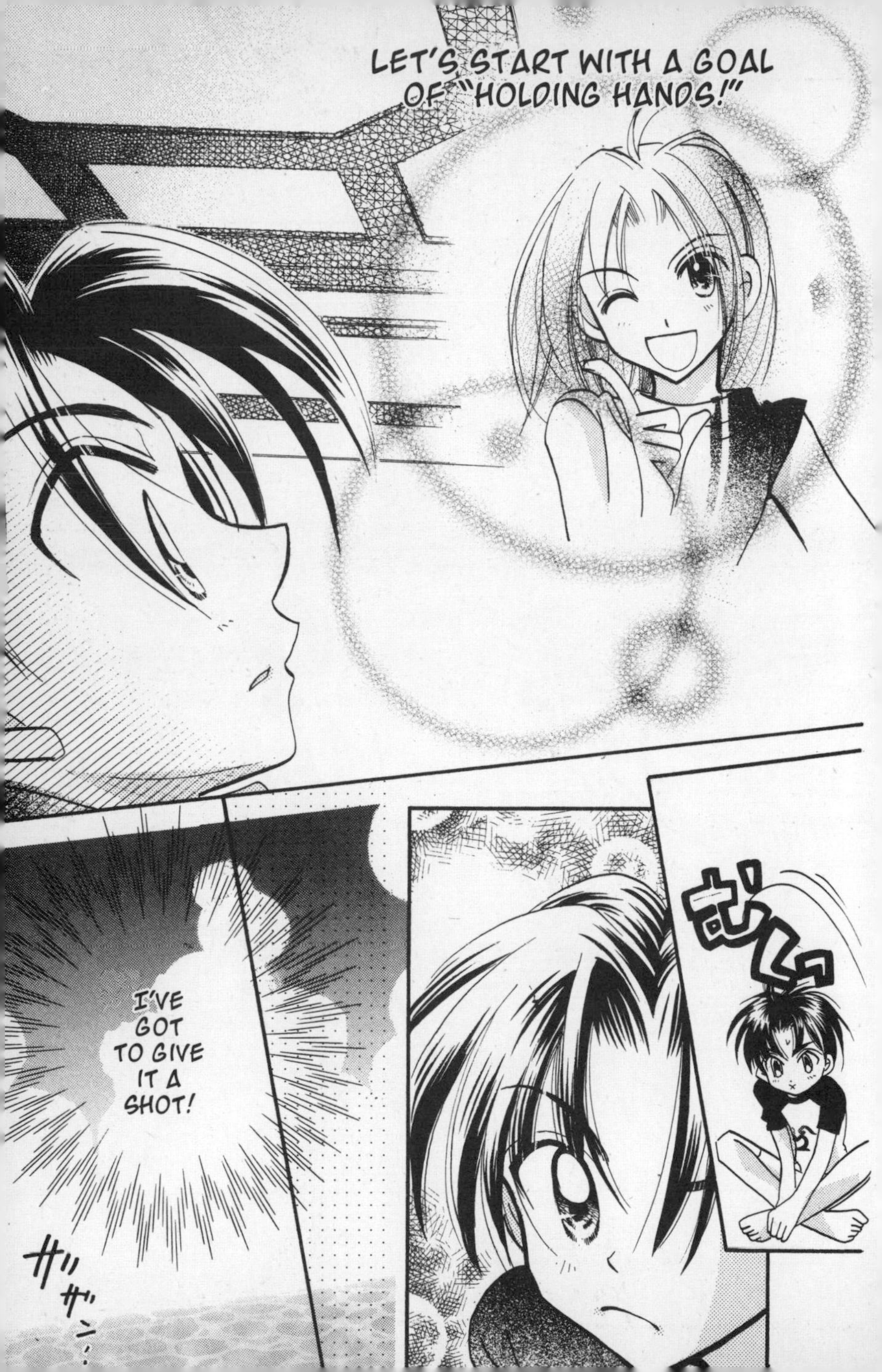
LET'S START WITH A GOAL OF "HOLDING HANDS!"
むん
I'VE GOT TO GIVE IT A SHOT!
ザザン

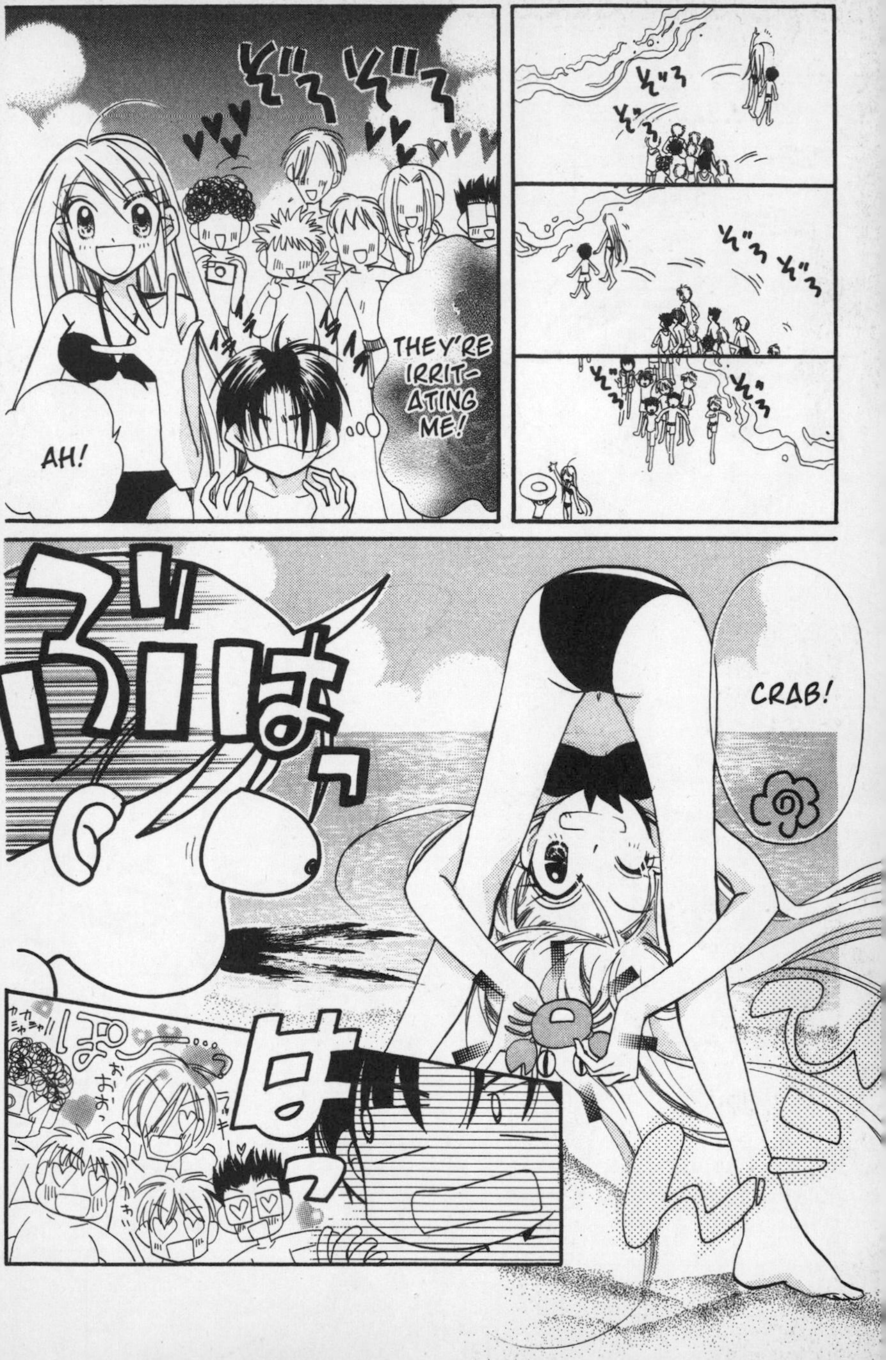
ぞろぞろ
THEY'RE IRRIT-ATING ME!
AH!
CRAB!

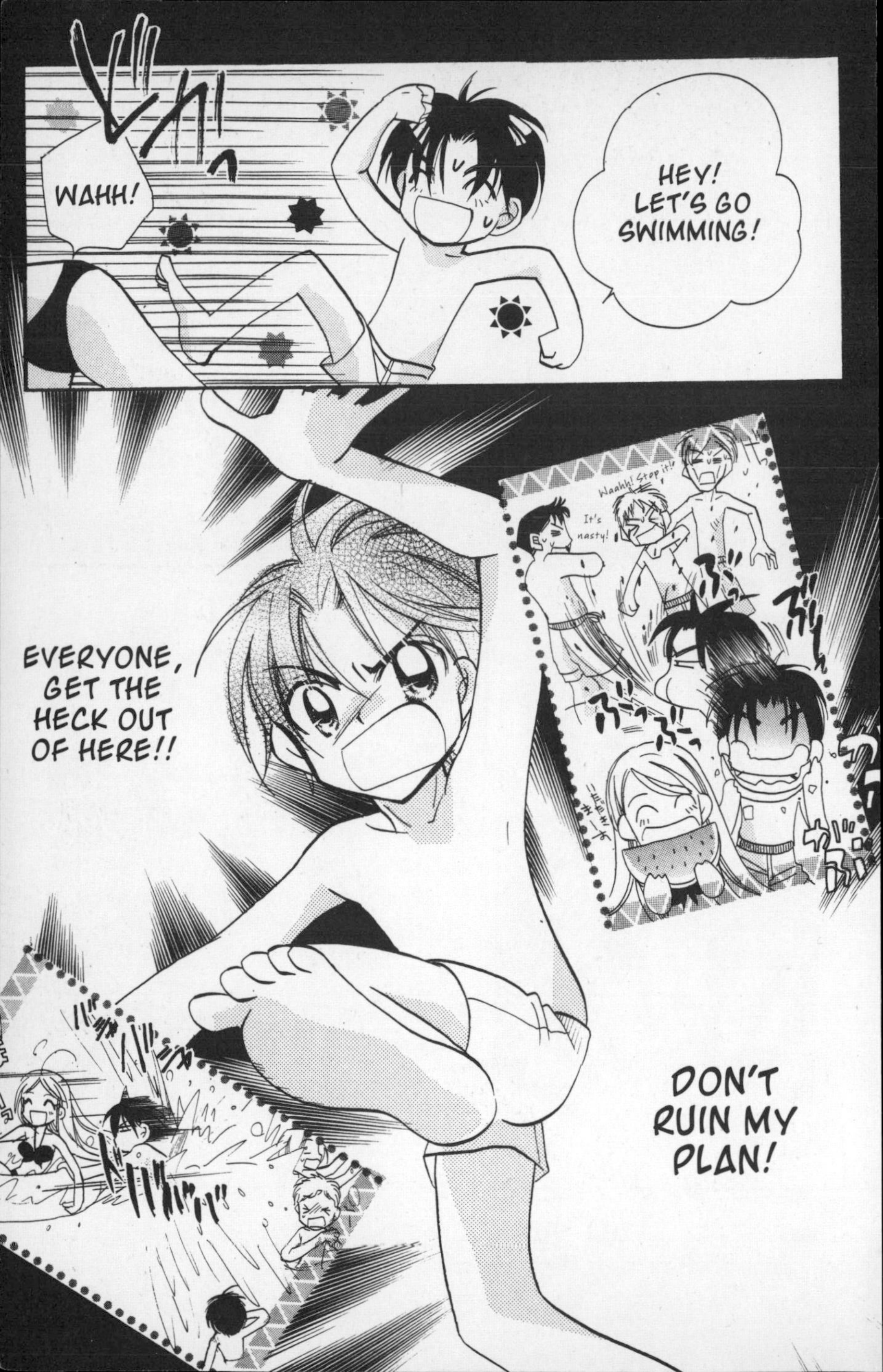
HEY! LET'S GO SWIMMING!
WAHH!
Waahh! Stop it!
It's nasty!
EVERYONE, GET THE HECK OUT OF HERE!!
DON'T RUIN MY PLAN!

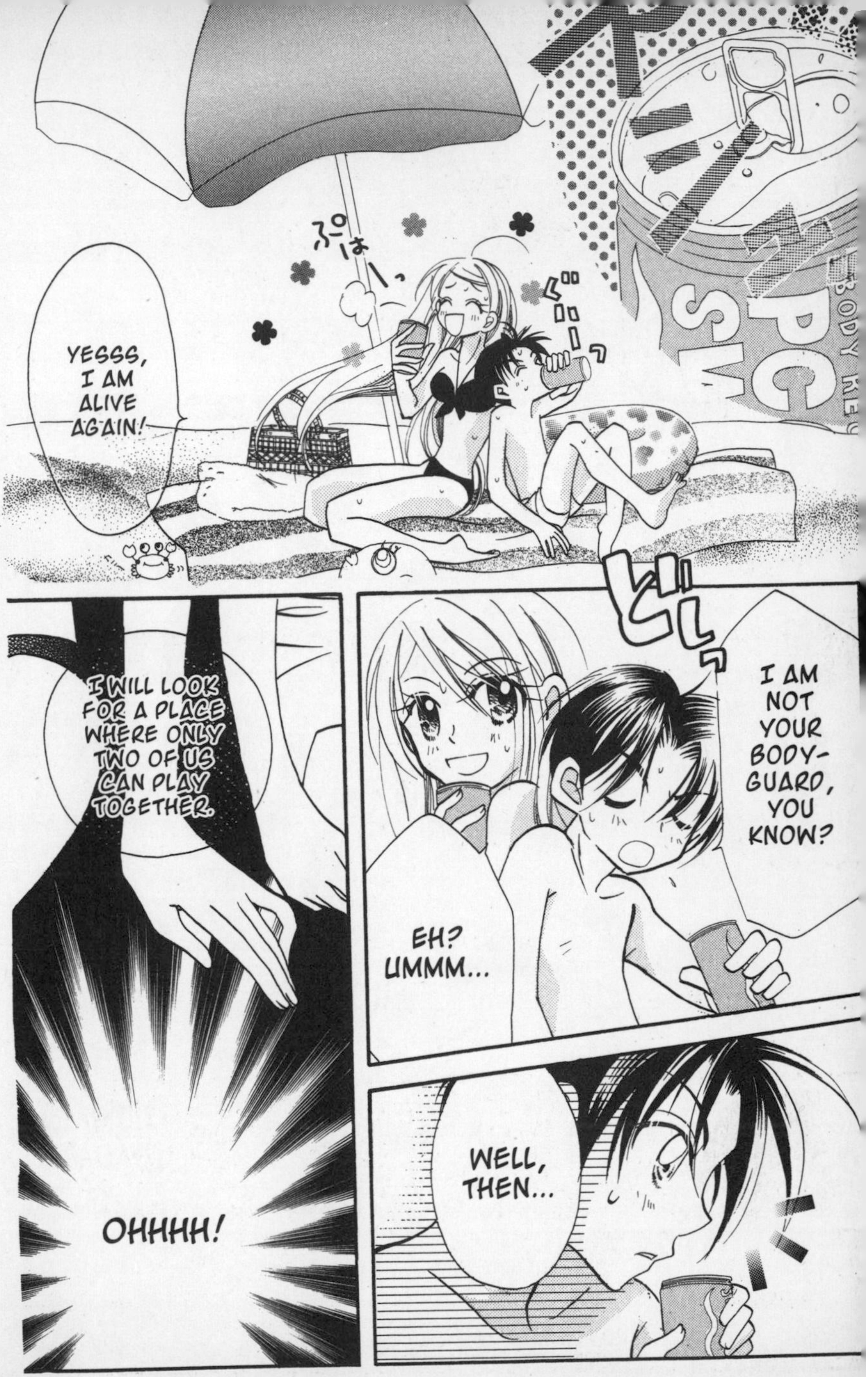
ぷはーっ
YESSS, I AM ALIVE AGAIN!
I AM NOT YOUR BODY-GUARD, YOU KNOW?
EH? UMMM...
WELL, THEN...
I WILL LOOK FOR A PLACE WHERE ONLY TWO OF US CAN PLAY TOGETHER.
OHHHH!

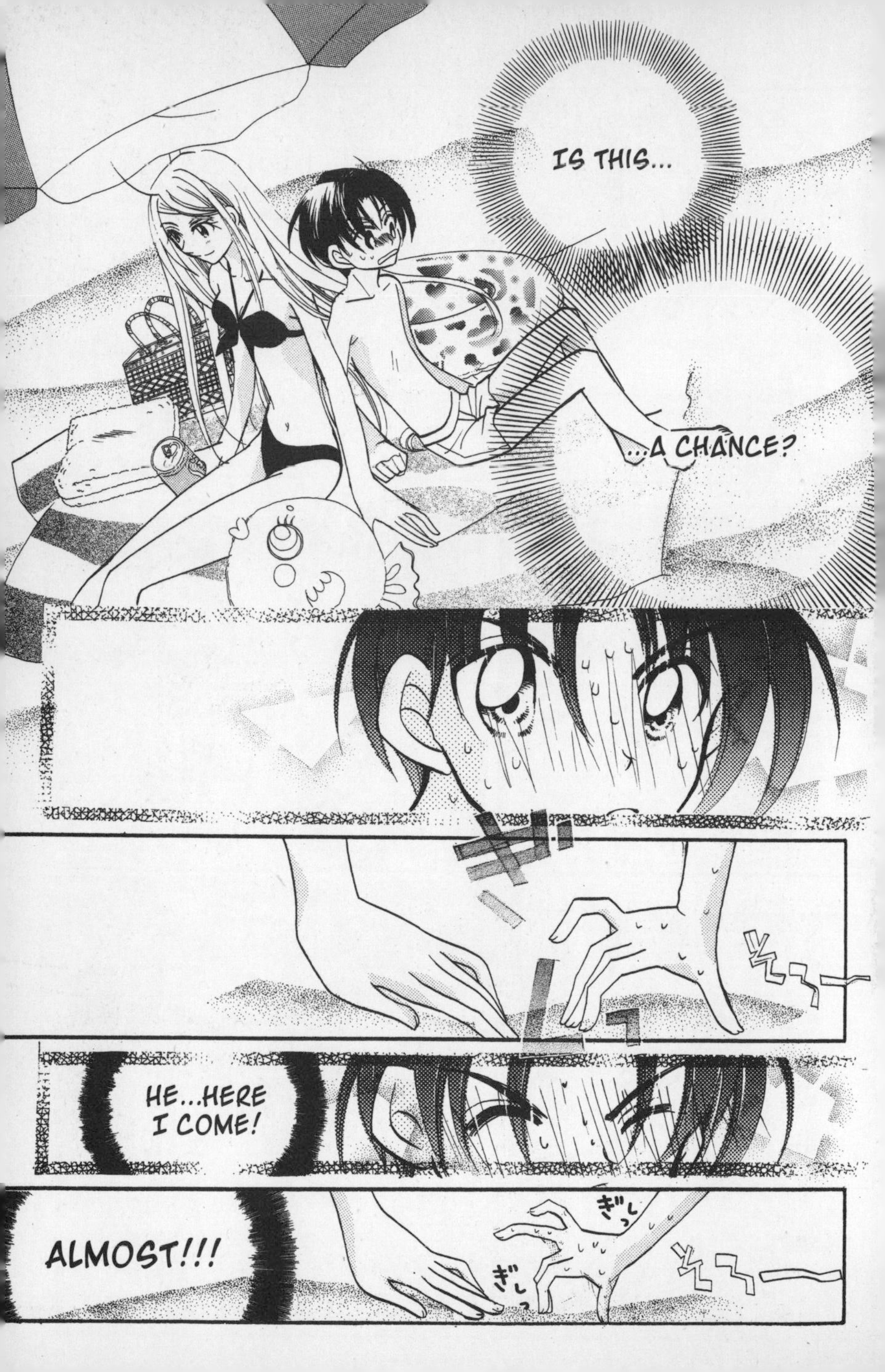
IS THIS...
...A CHANCE?
HE...HERE I COME!
ALMOST!!!

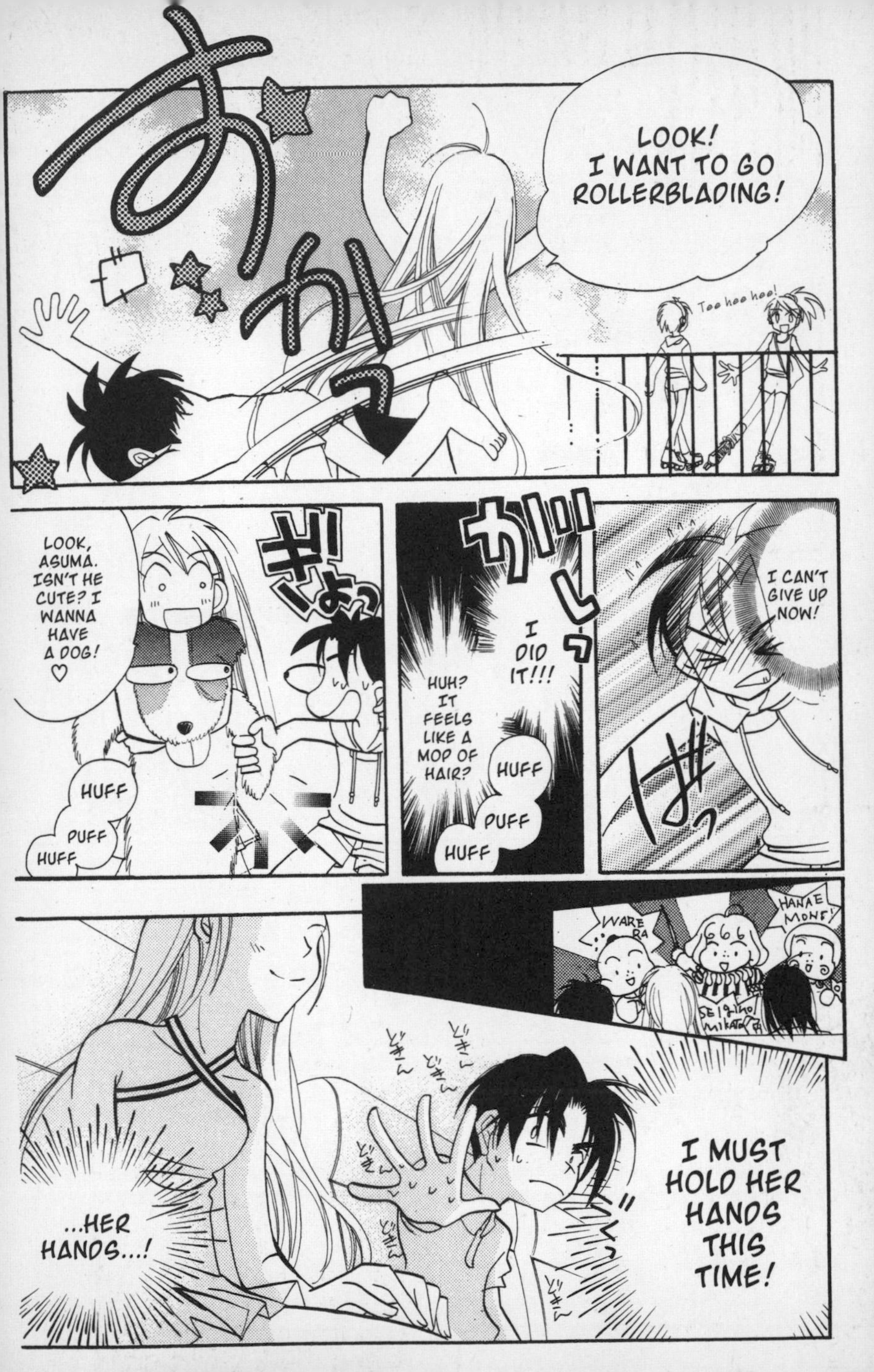
LOOK! I WANT TO GO ROLLERBLADING!
Tee hee hee!
I CAN'T GIVE UP NOW!
I DID IT!!!
HUH? IT FEELS LIKE A MOP OF HAIR?
HUFF
PUFF
HUFF
LOOK, ASUMA. ISN'T HE CUTE? I WANNA HAVE A DOG! ♡
HUFF
PUFF
HUFF
HANAE MONE!
WARE RA
I MUST HOLD HER HANDS THIS TIME!
...HER HANDS...!

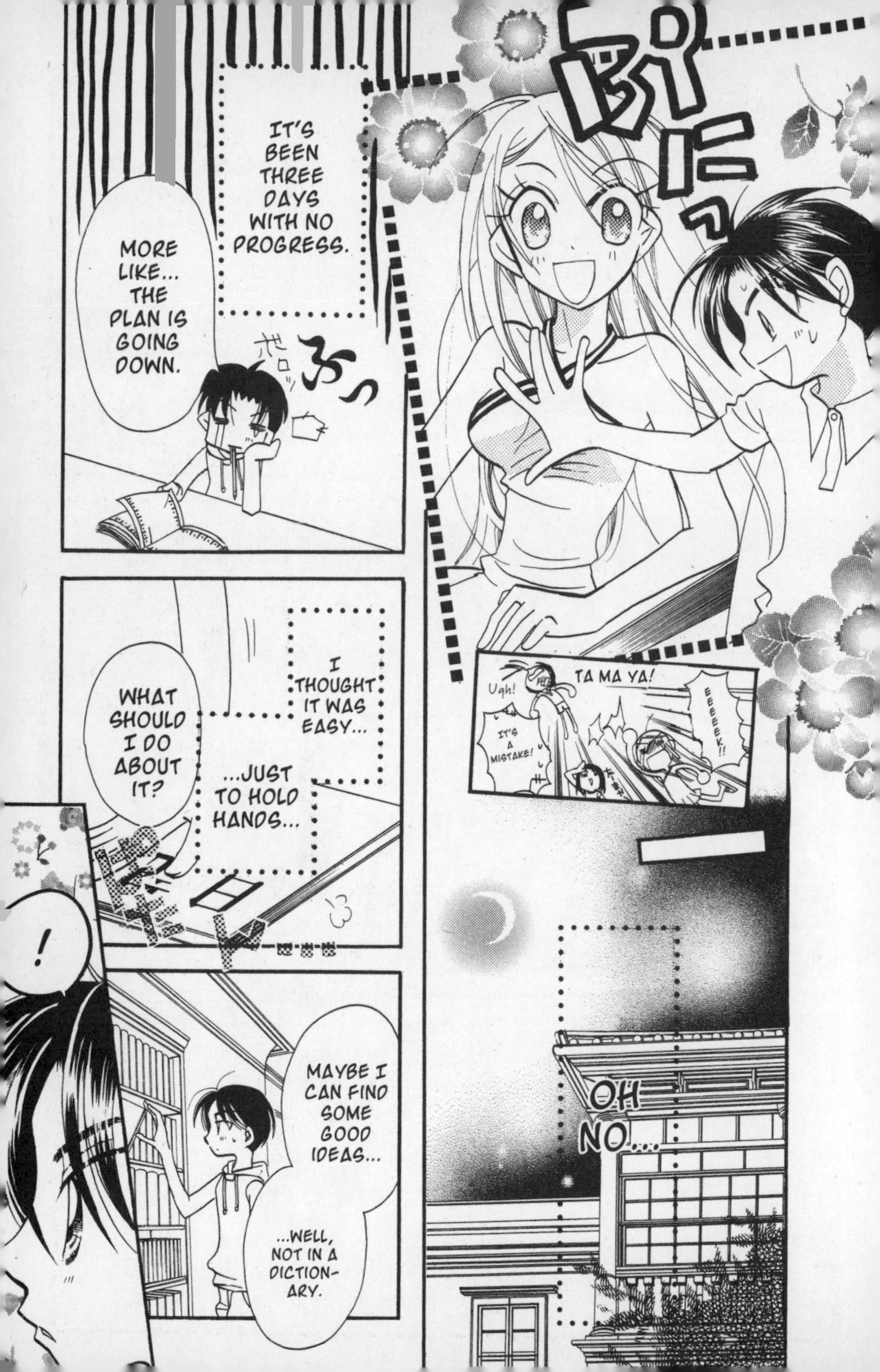
TA MA YA!
EEEEEK!!
Ugh!
IT'S A MISTAKE!
OH NO...
IT'S BEEN THREE DAYS WITH NO PROGRESS.
MORE LIKE... THE PLAN IS GOING DOWN.
I THOUGHT IT WAS EASY...
...JUST TO HOLD HANDS...
WHAT SHOULD I DO ABOUT IT?
!
MAYBE I CAN FIND SOME GOOD IDEAS...
...WELL, NOT IN A DICTIONARY.

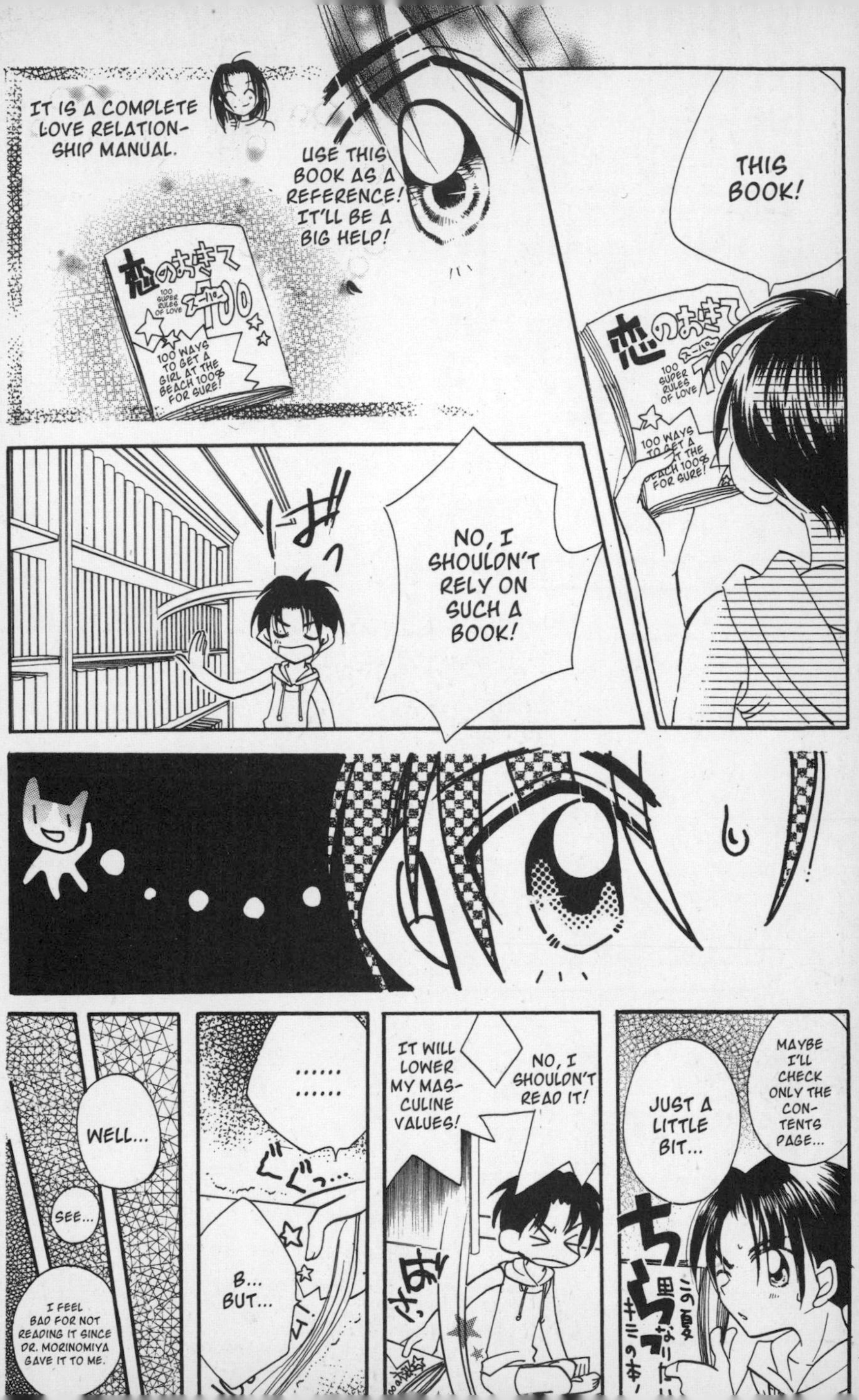
THIS BOOK!
恋のおきて スーパー 100
100 SUPER RULES OF LOVE
100 WAYS TO GET A GIRL AT THE BEACH 100% FOR SURE!
USE THIS BOOK AS A REFERENCE! IT'LL BE A BIG HELP!
IT IS A COMPLETE LOVE RELATIONSHIP MANUAL.
恋のおきて スーパー 100
100 SUPER RULES OF LOVE
100 WAYS TO GET A GIRL AT THE BEACH 100% FOR SURE!
NO, I SHOULDN'T RELY ON SUCH A BOOK!
MAYBE I'LL CHECK ONLY THE CONTENTS PAGE...
JUST A LITTLE BIT...
NO, I SHOULDN'T READ IT!
IT WILL LOWER MY MASCULINE VALUES!
......
......
B... BUT...
WELL...
SEE...
I FEEL BAD FOR NOT READING IT SINCE DR. MORINOMIYA GAVE IT TO ME.

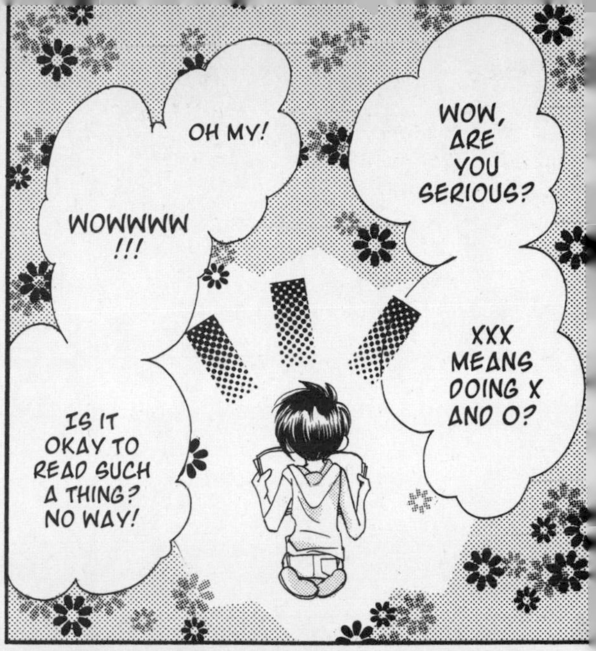
WOW, ARE YOU SERIOUS?
XXX MEANS DOING X AND O?
OH MY!
WOWWWW !!!
IS IT OKAY TO READ SUCH A THING? NO WAY!

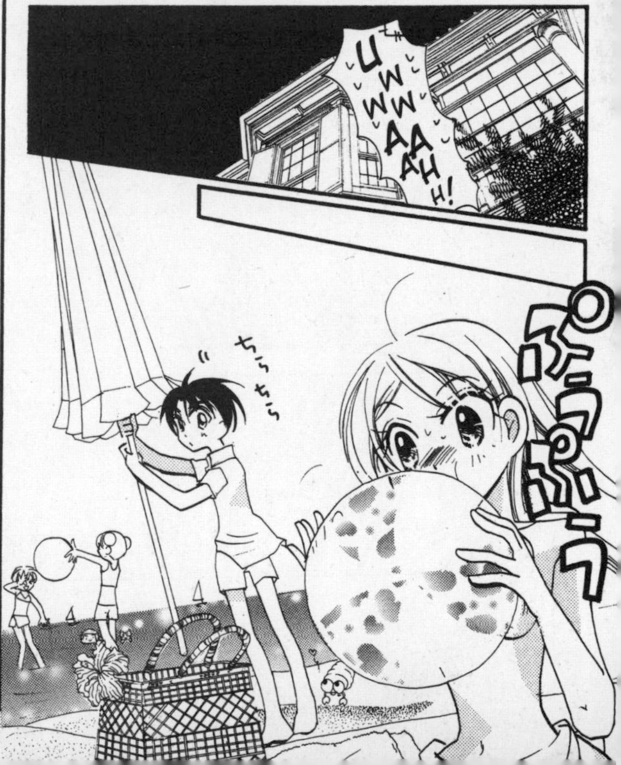
UWWWWAAAH!

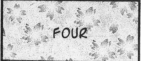

FOUR

CONTINUATION OF SAN (THREE)

After reading the book, I believe that jellyfish is just like a MOCHI (rice-cake). And I still dream of lining up the jellyfish at the beach someday! But my friend recently said to me, "Jellyfish will sting you, so you can't really touch them"

Is this true? Does anyone know the truth? Are you serious?!

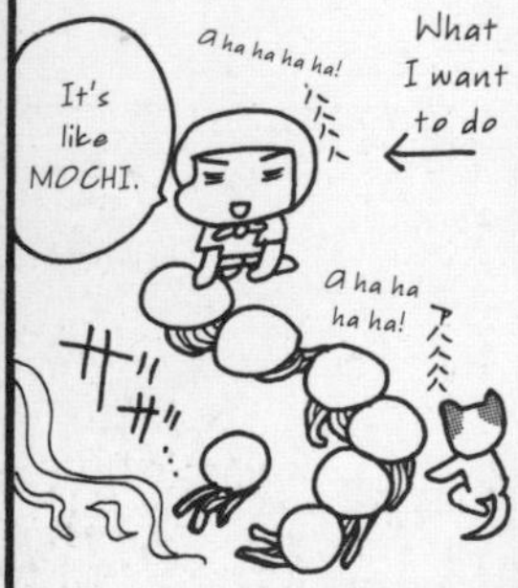
What I want to do
It's like MOCHI.
a ha ha ha ha!
a ha ha ha ha!

How about the people who live around the beach? Have you ever lined up jellyfish at the beach?

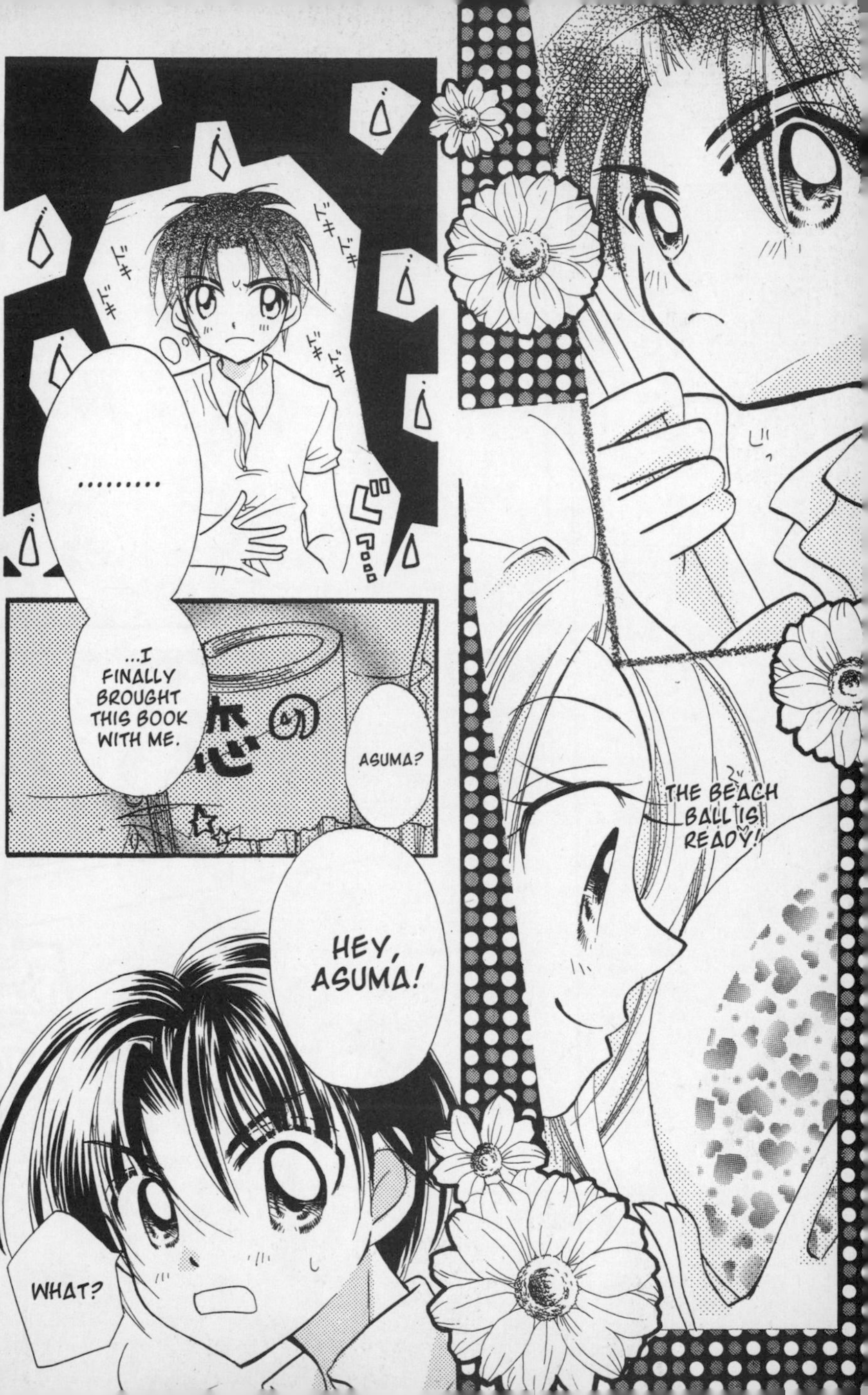
THE BEACH BALL IS READY!
ドキドキ
ドキドキ
ドキドキ
....
...I FINALLY BROUGHT THIS BOOK WITH ME.
恋の
ASUMA?
HEY, ASUMA!
WHAT?

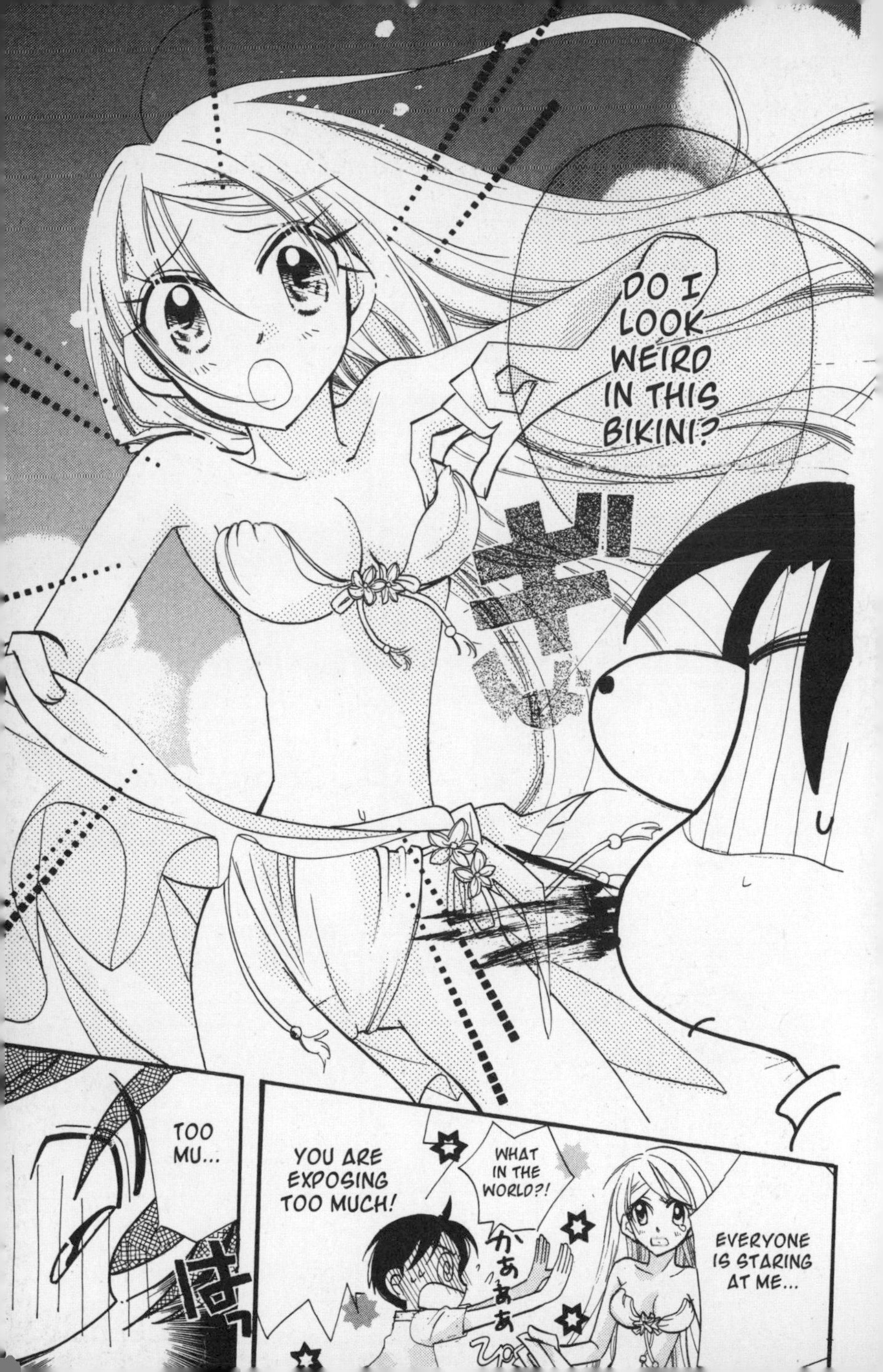
DO I LOOK WEIRD IN THIS BIKINI?
EVERYONE IS STARING AT ME...
WHAT IN THE WORLD?!
かあああ
YOU ARE EXPOSING TOO MUCH!
TOO MU...

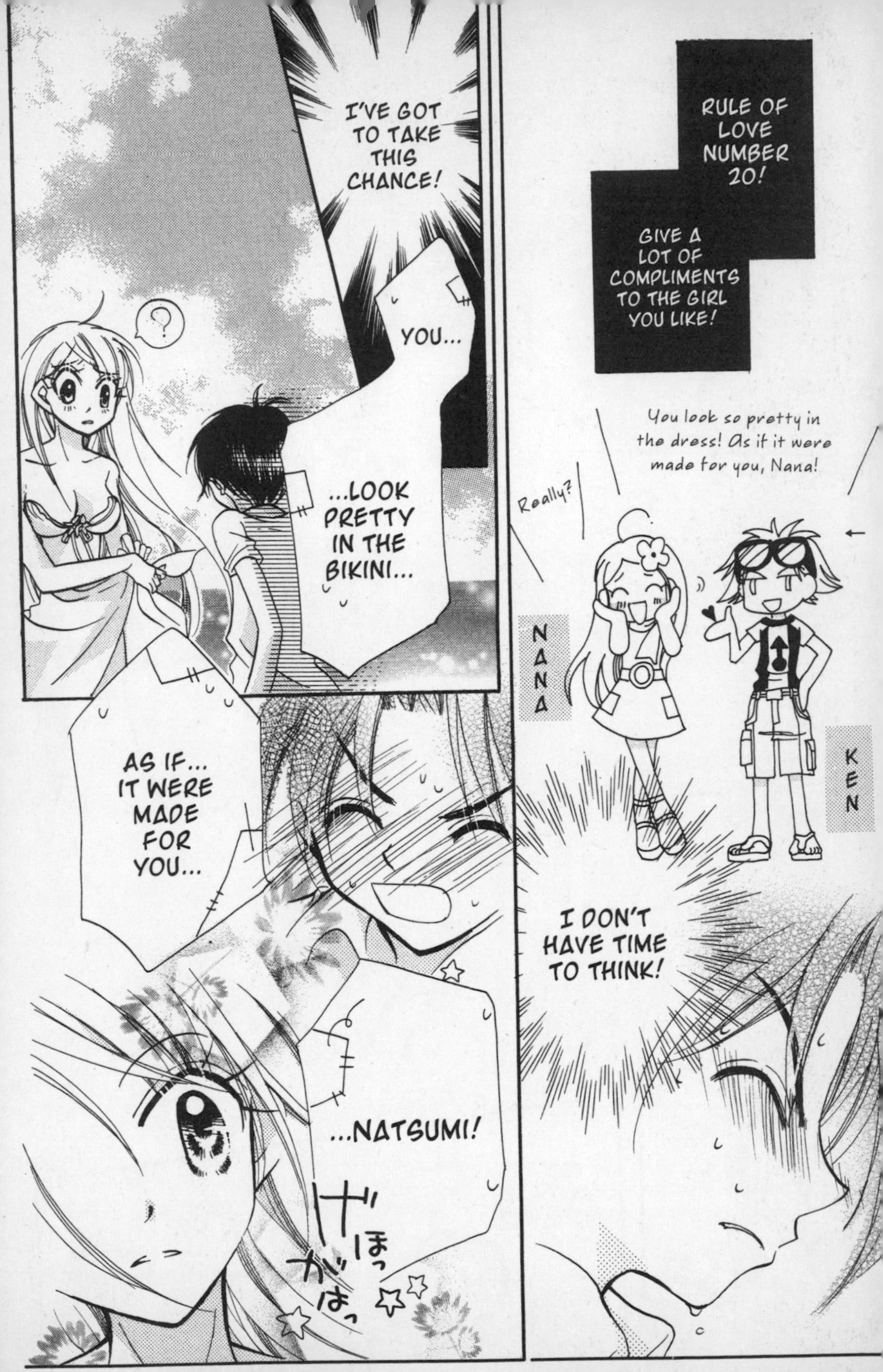
RULE OF LOVE NUMBER 20!
GIVE A LOT OF COMPLIMENTS TO THE GIRL YOU LIKE!
You look so pretty in the dress! As if it were made for you, Nana!
Really?
NANA
KEN
I DON'T HAVE TIME TO THINK!
I'VE GOT TO TAKE THIS CHANCE!
YOU...
...LOOK PRETTY IN THE BIKINI...
AS IF... IT WERE MADE FOR YOU...
...NATSUMI!
ザほっ
ガはっ

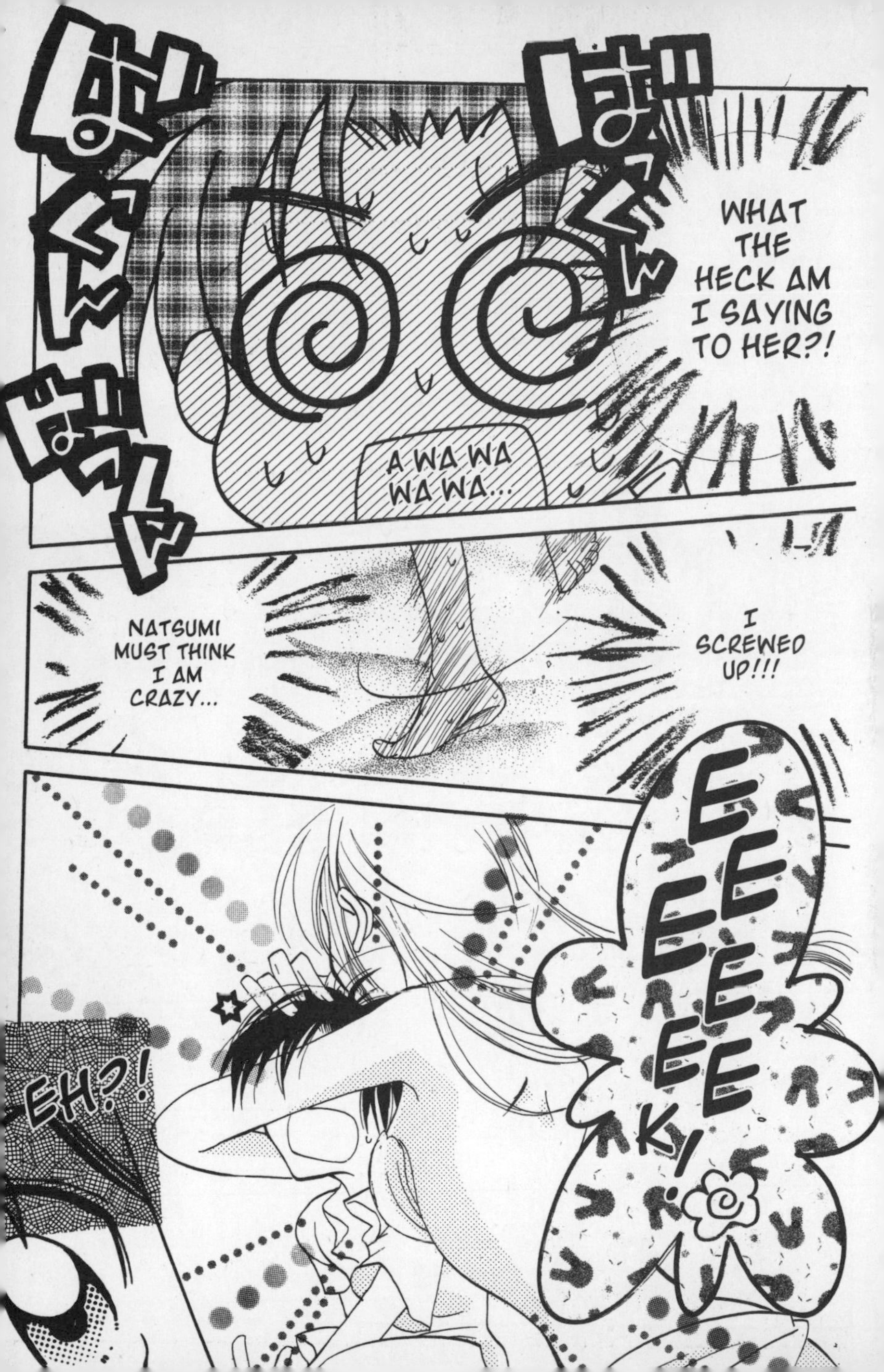
WHAT THE HECK AM I SAYING TO HER?!
A WA WA WA WA...
I SCREWED UP!!!
NATSUMI MUST THINK I AM CRAZY...
EEEEEEEEEK!
EH?!

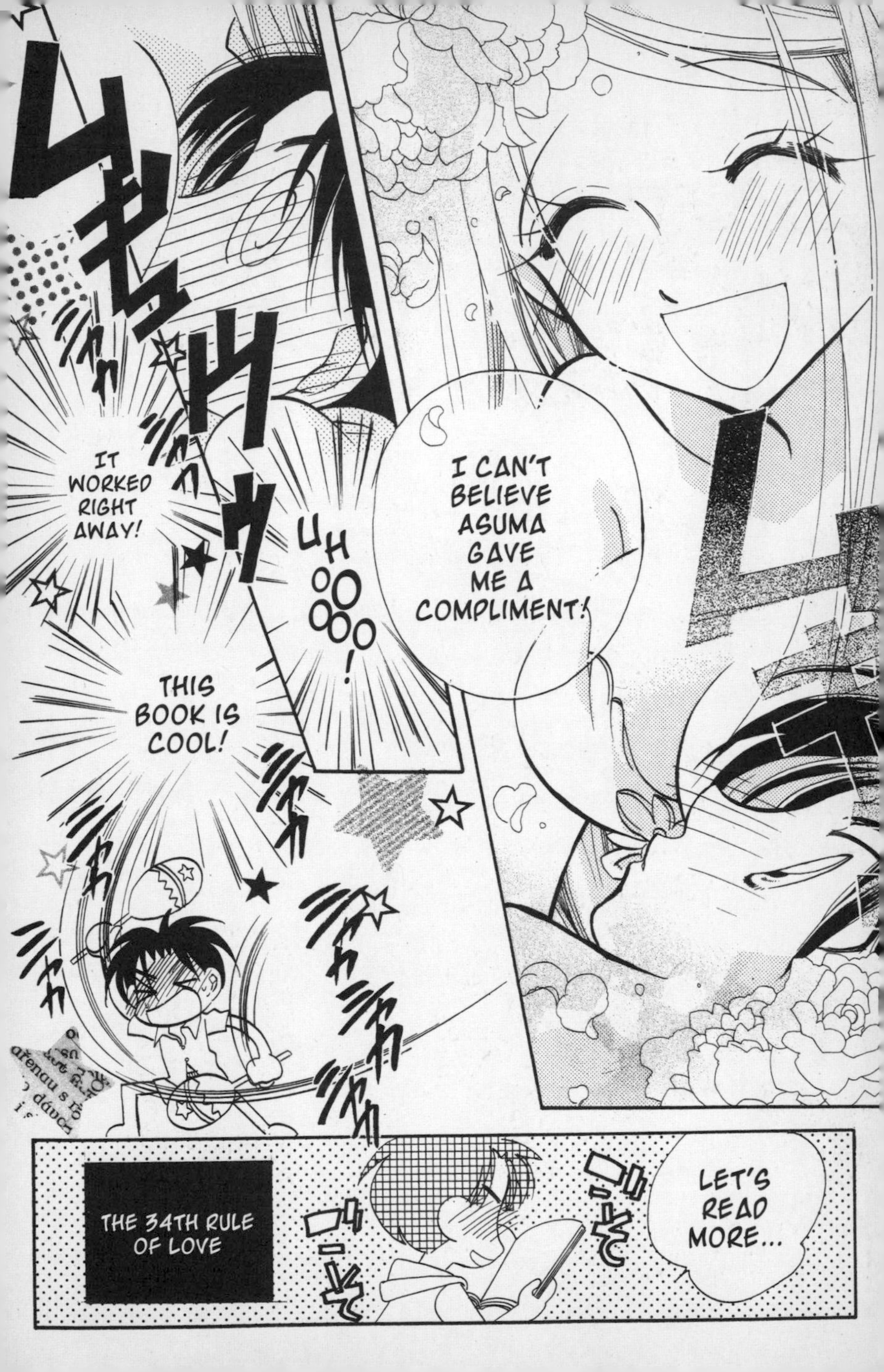
I CAN'T BELIEVE ASUMA GAVE ME A COMPLIMENT!
UHOOOOOO!
IT WORKED RIGHT AWAY!
THIS BOOK IS COOL!
LET'S READ MORE...
THE 34TH RULE OF LOVE

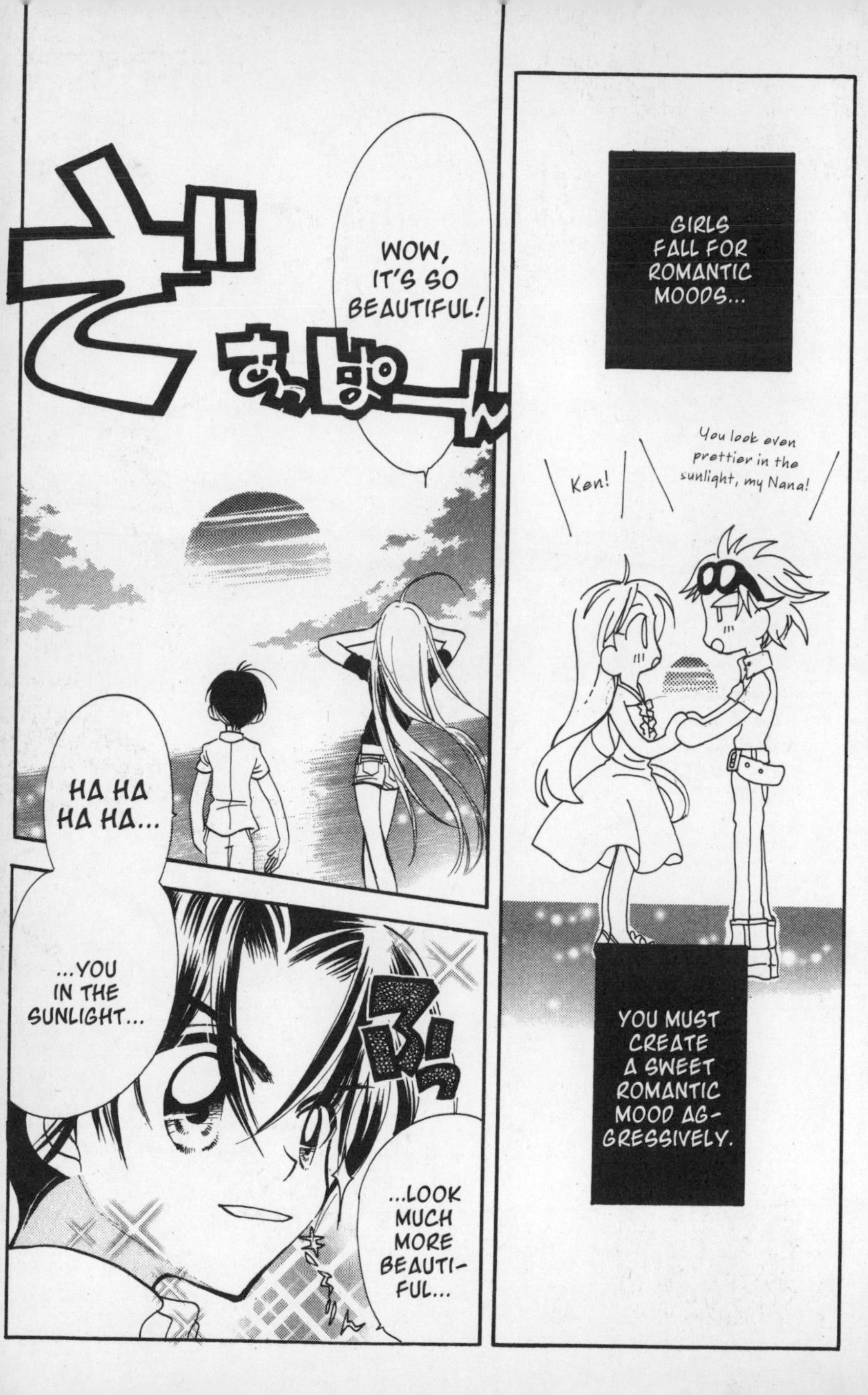
GIRLS FALL FOR ROMANTIC MOODS...
You look even prettier in the sunlight, my Nana!
Ken!
YOU MUST CREATE A SWEET ROMANTIC MOOD AG-GRESSIVELY.
WOW, IT'S SO BEAUTIFUL!
HA HA HA HA...
...YOU IN THE SUNLIGHT...
...LOOK MUCH MORE BEAUTI-FUL...

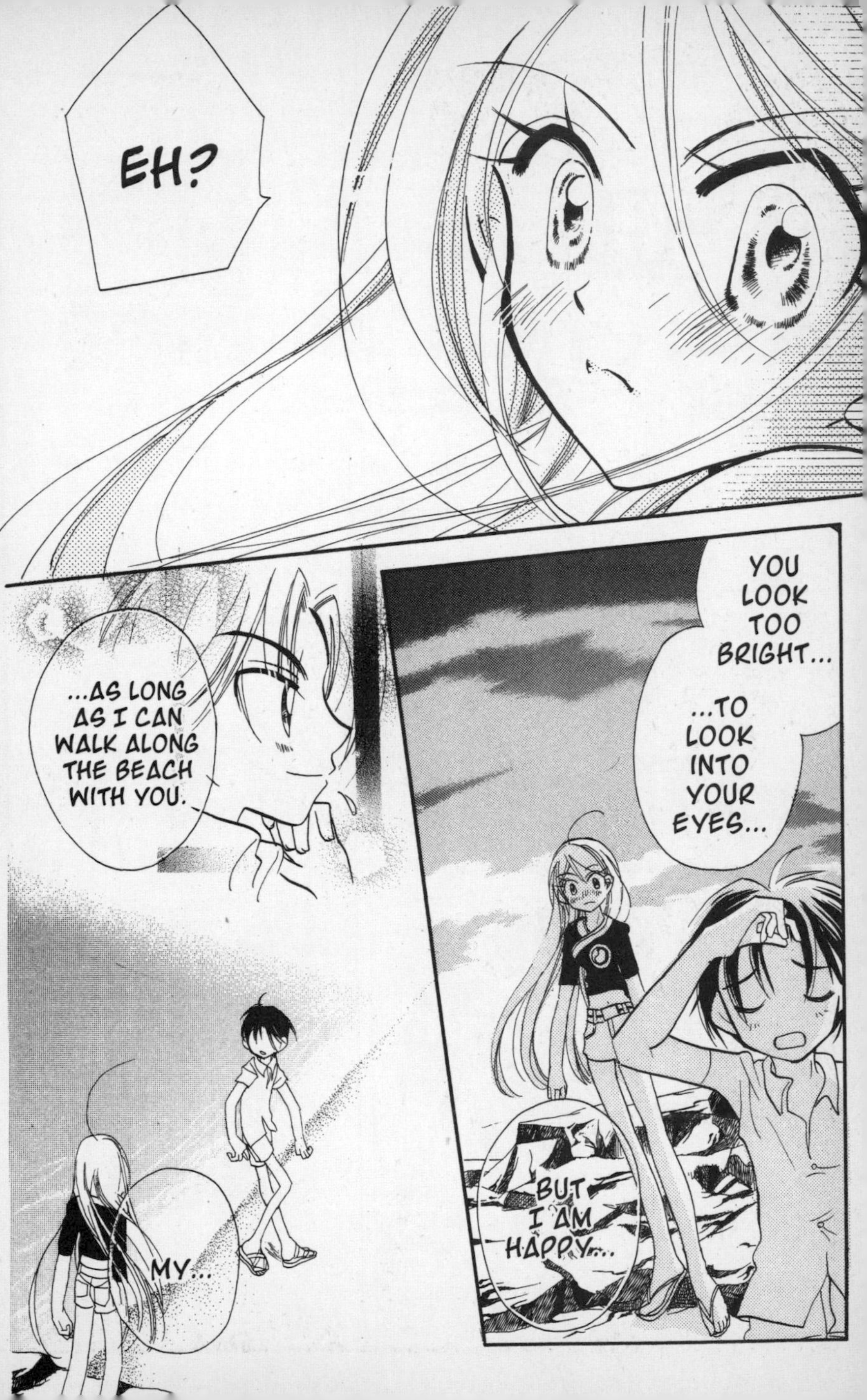
EH?
YOU LOOK TOO BRIGHT...
...TO LOOK INTO YOUR EYES...
BUT I AM HAPPY...
...AS LONG AS I CAN WALK ALONG THE BEACH WITH YOU.
MY...

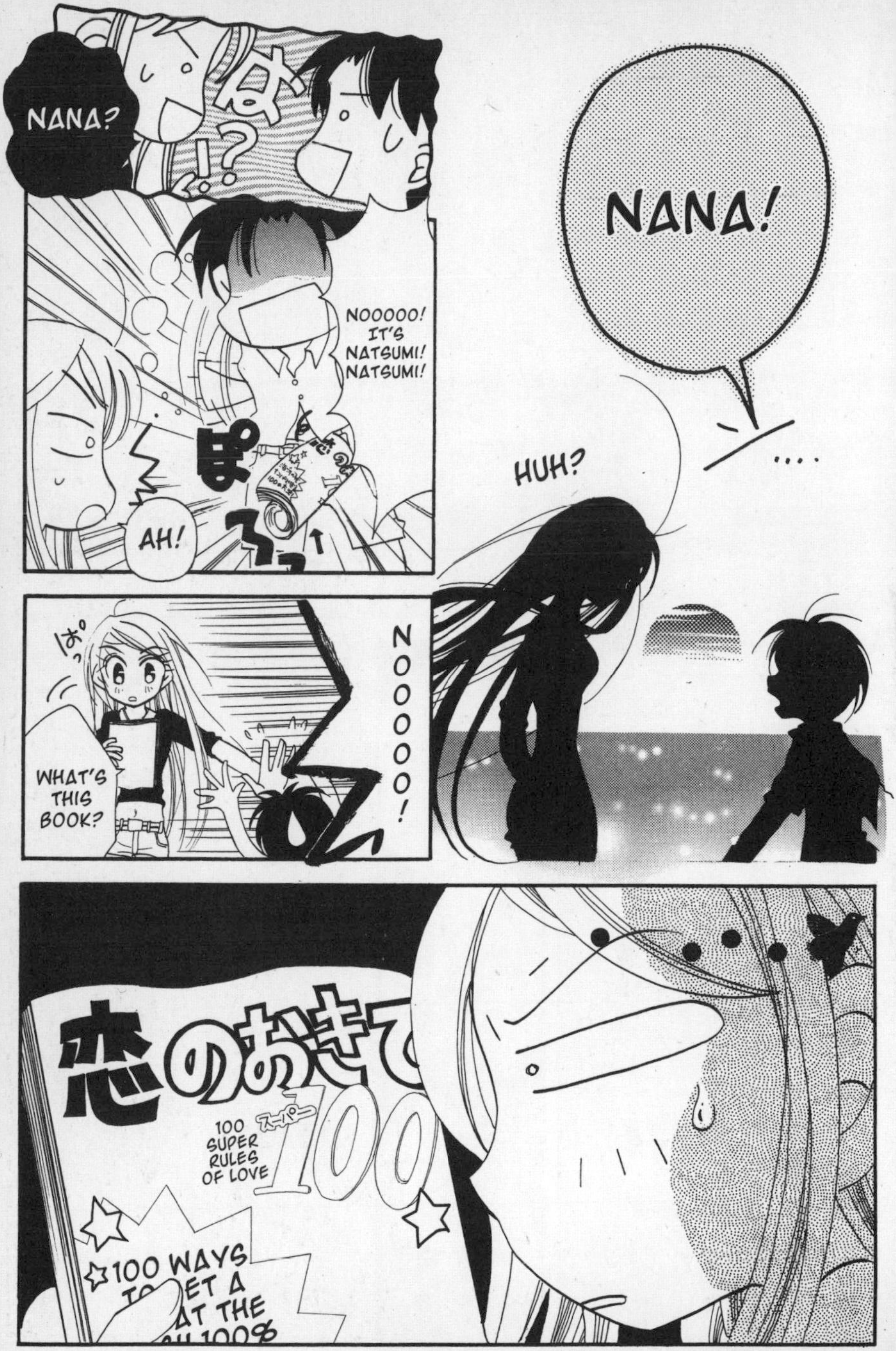
NANA!
...
HUH?
NANA?
NOOOOO! IT'S NATSUMI! NATSUMI!
AH!
NOOOOOO!
WHAT'S THIS BOOK?
恋のおきて
スーパー
100
100 SUPER RULES OF LOVE
☆100 WAYS
ET A
AT THE
100%

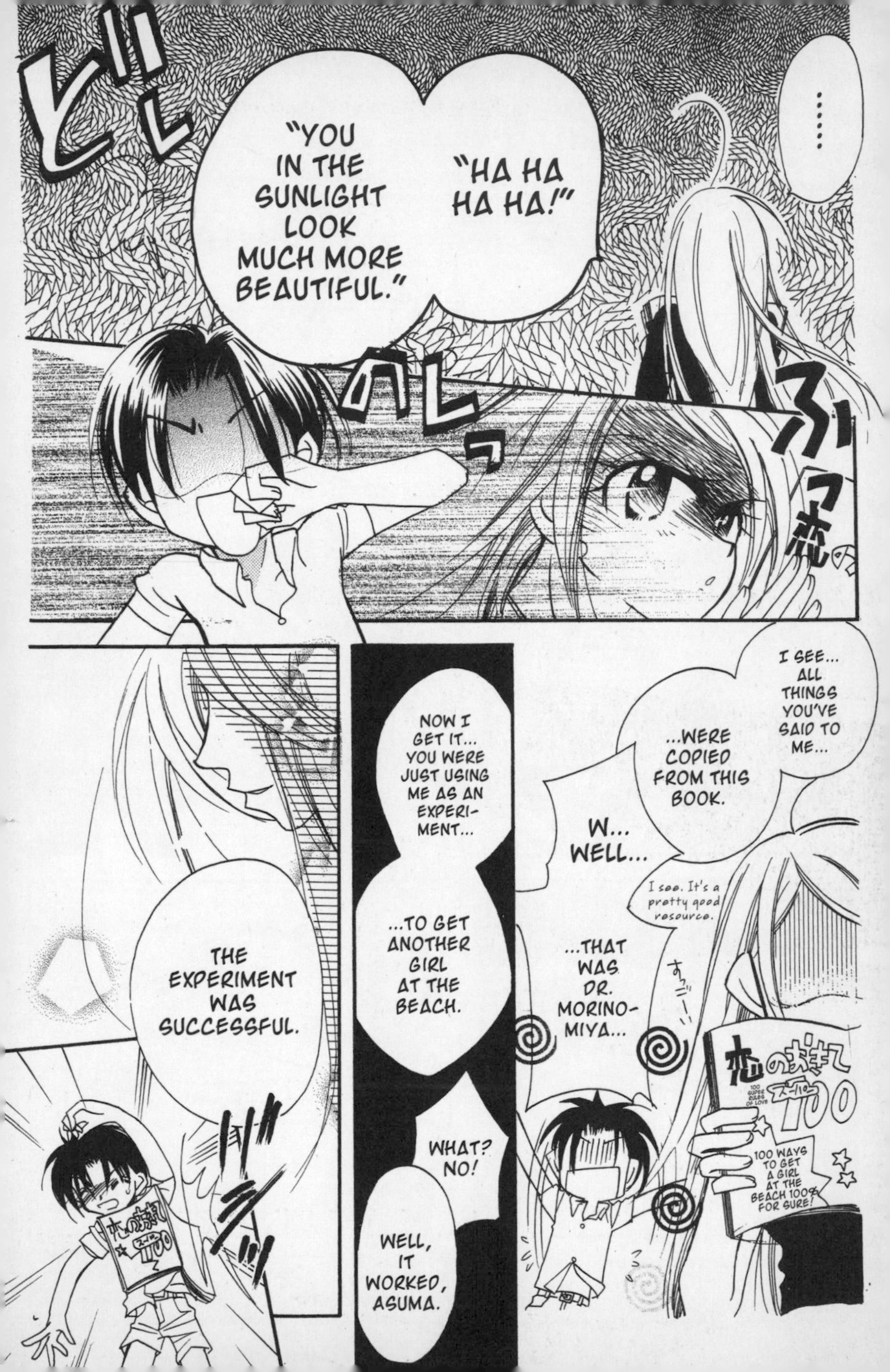
……
"YOU IN THE SUNLIGHT LOOK MUCH MORE BEAUTIFUL."
"HA HA HA HA!"
I SEE... ALL THINGS YOU'VE SAID TO ME...
...WERE COPIED FROM THIS BOOK.
W... WELL...
I see. It's a pretty good resource.
...THAT WAS DR. MORINO-MIYA...
100 SUPER RULES OF LOVE
100
100 WAYS TO GET A GIRL AT THE BEACH 100% FOR SURE!
NOW I GET IT... YOU WERE JUST USING ME AS AN EXPERIMENT...
...TO GET ANOTHER GIRL AT THE BEACH.
WHAT? NO!
WELL, IT WORKED, ASUMA.
THE EXPERIMENT WAS SUCCESSFUL.

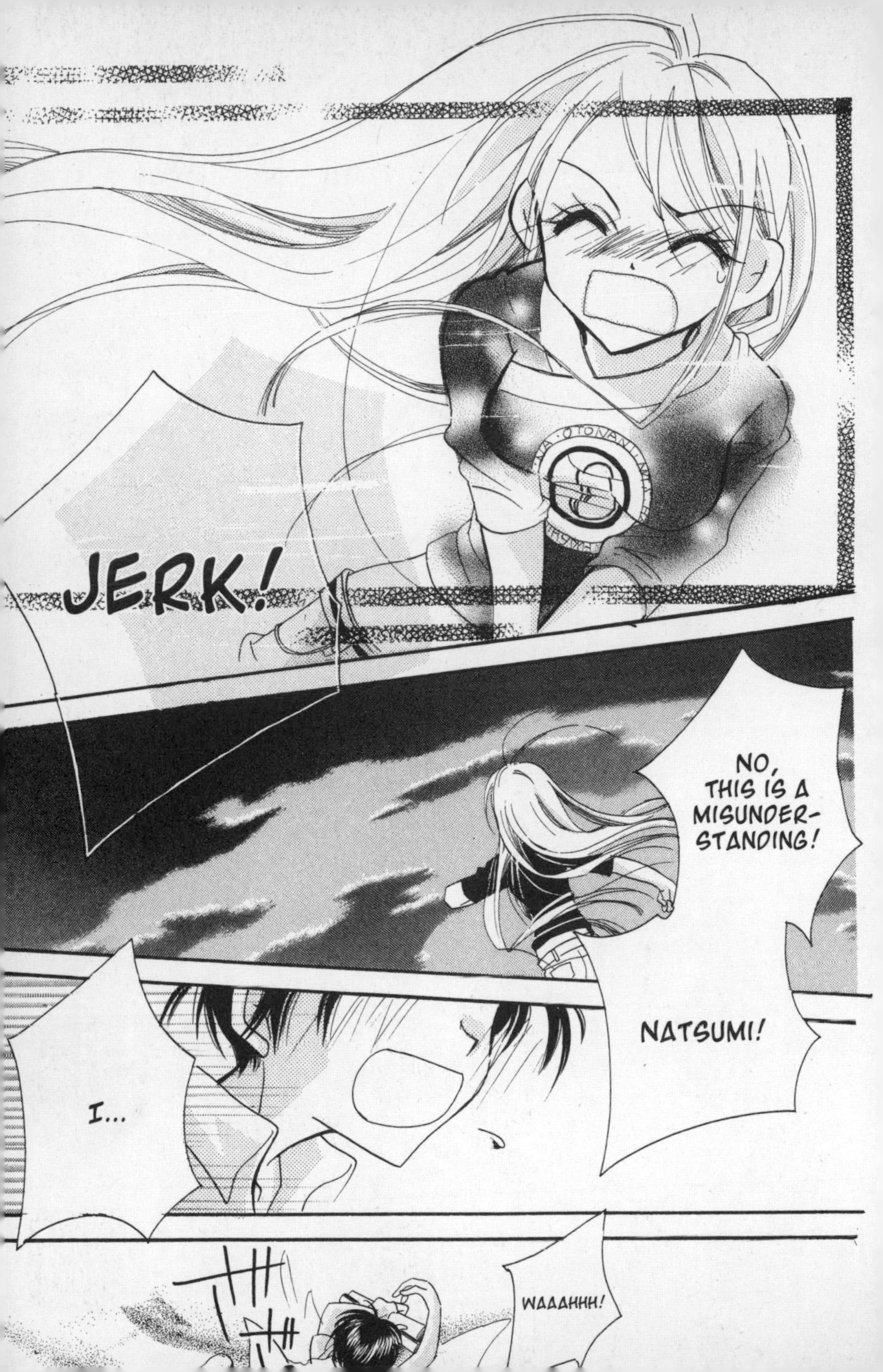
JERK!
NO, THIS IS A MISUNDER-STANDING!
NATSUMI!
I...
WAAAHHH!

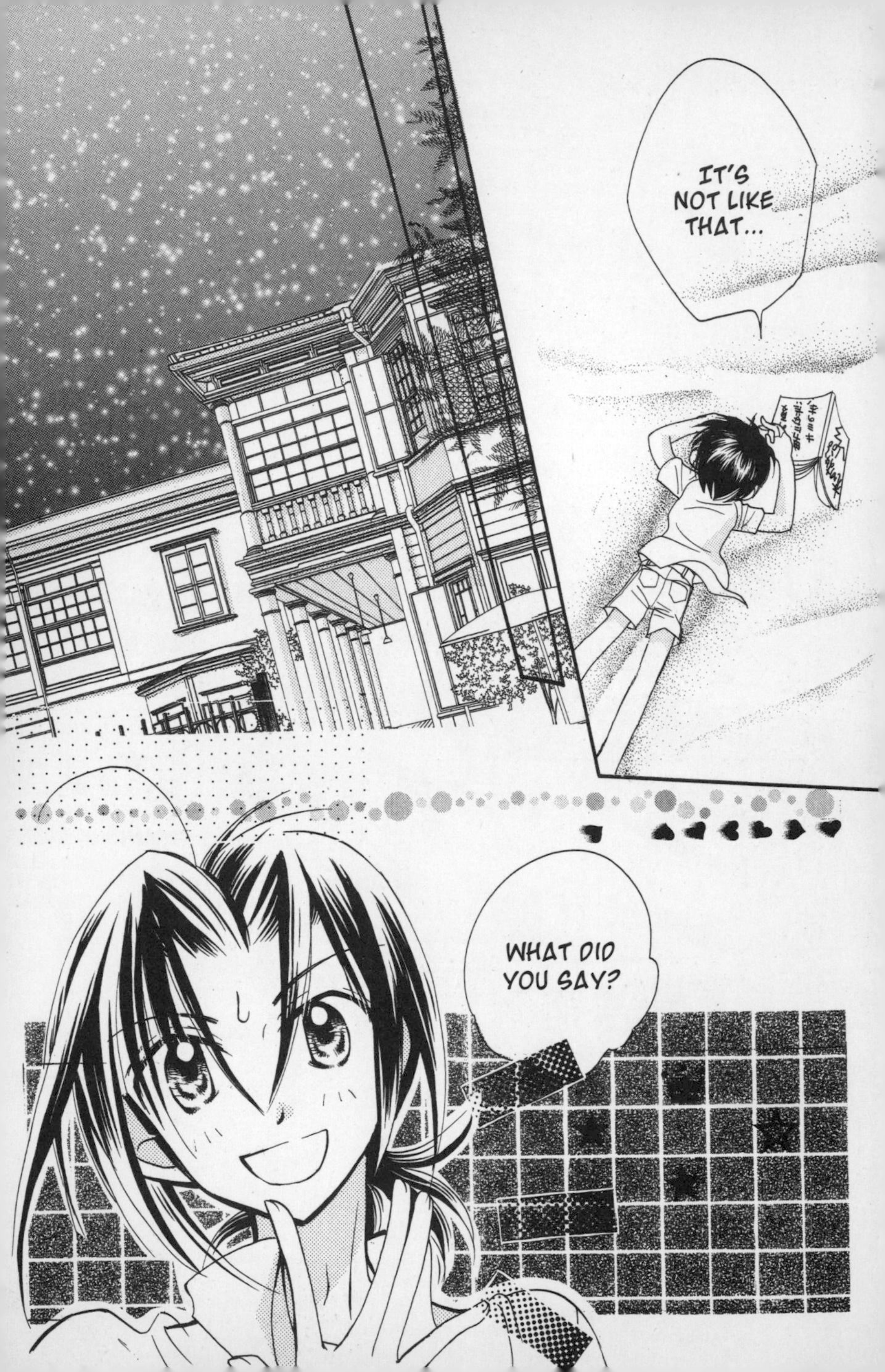
IT'S NOT LIKE THAT...
WHAT DID YOU SAY?

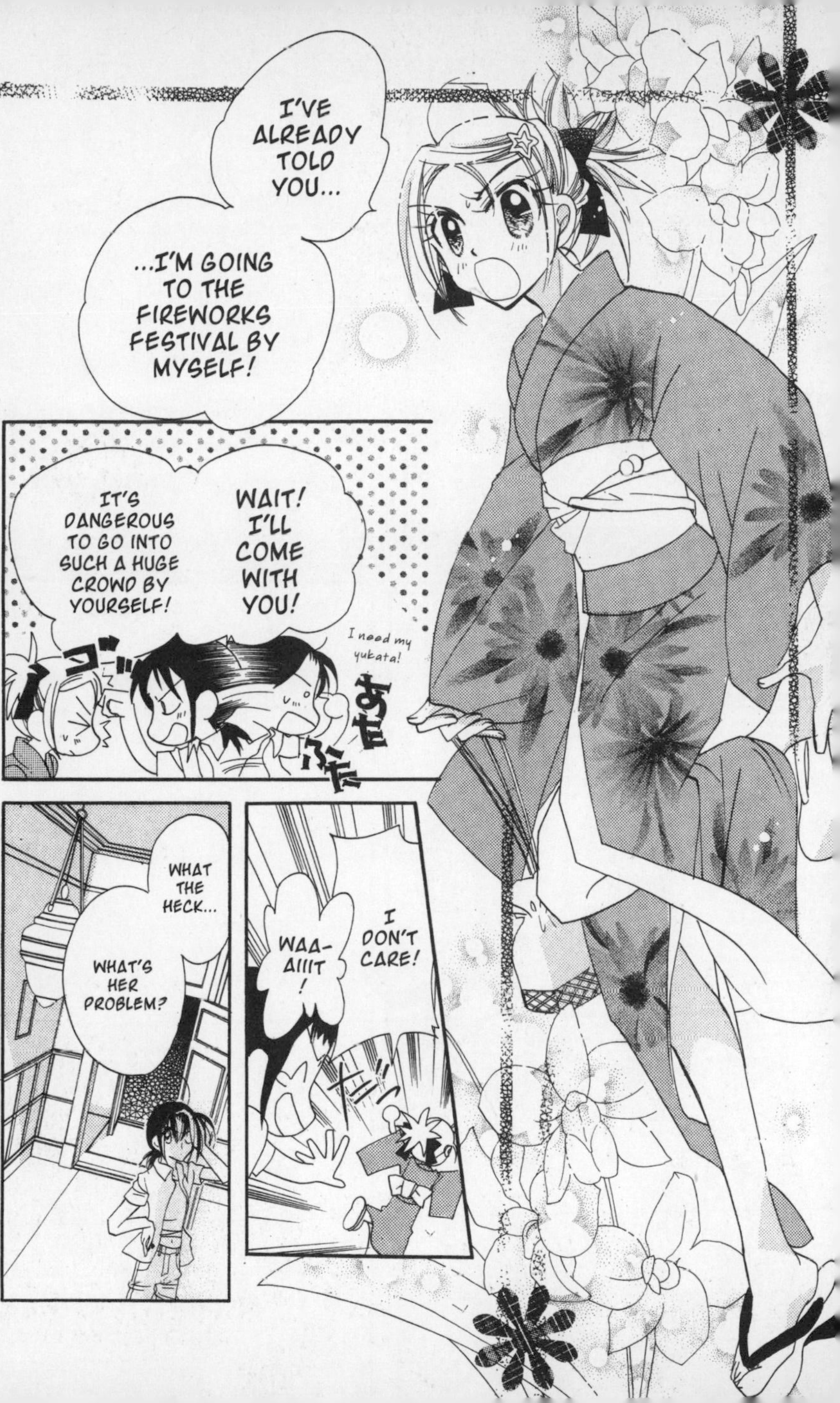
I'VE ALREADY TOLD YOU...
...I'M GOING TO THE FIREWORKS FESTIVAL BY MYSELF!
WAIT! I'LL COME WITH YOU!
IT'S DANGEROUS TO GO INTO SUCH A HUGE CROWD BY YOURSELF!
I need my yukata!
I DON'T CARE!
WAA-AIIIT!
WHAT THE HECK...
WHAT'S HER PROBLEM?

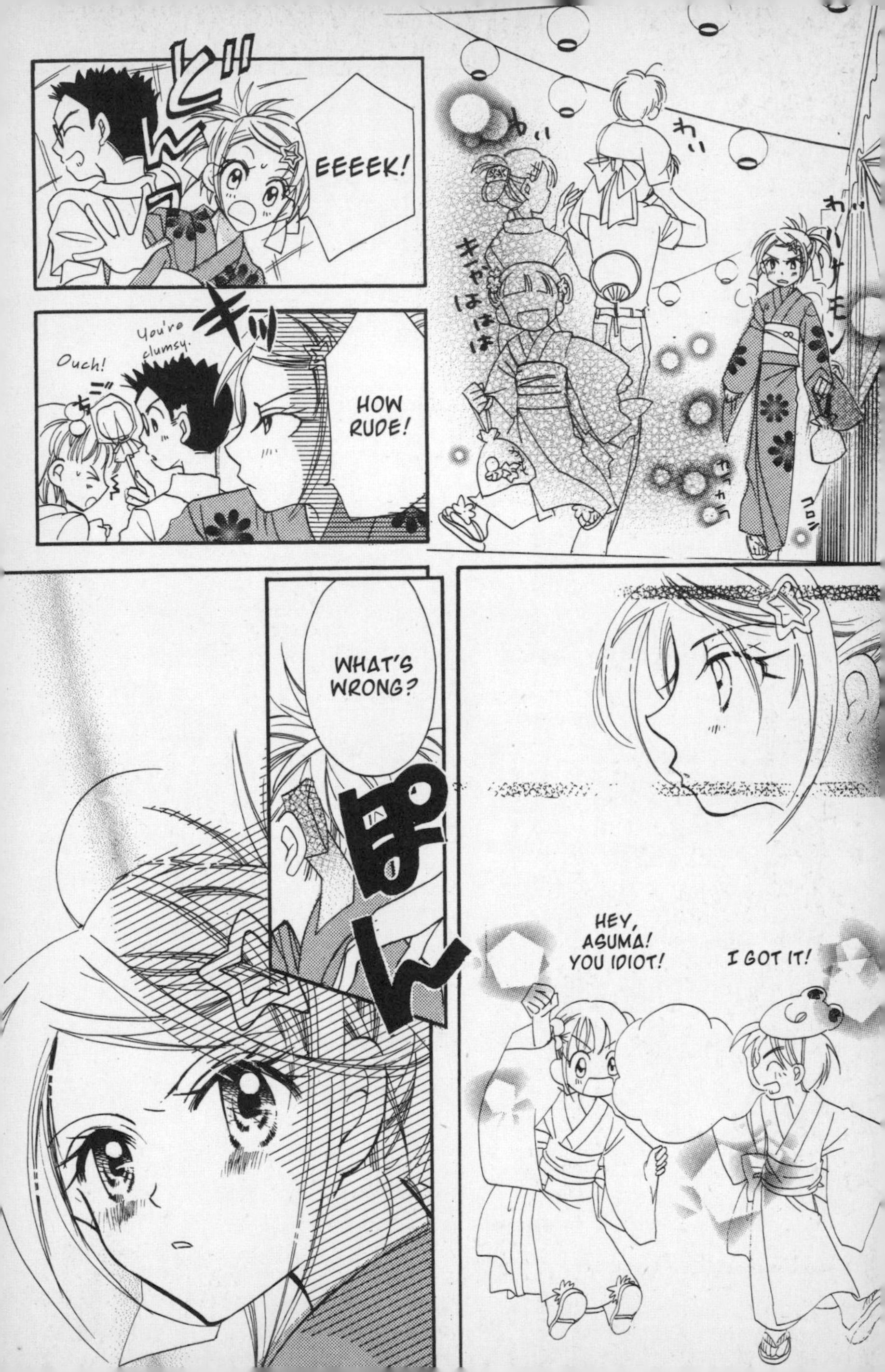
EEEEK!
HOW RUDE!
You're clumsy.
Ouch!
I GOT IT!
HEY, ASUMA! YOU IDIOT!
WHAT'S WRONG?

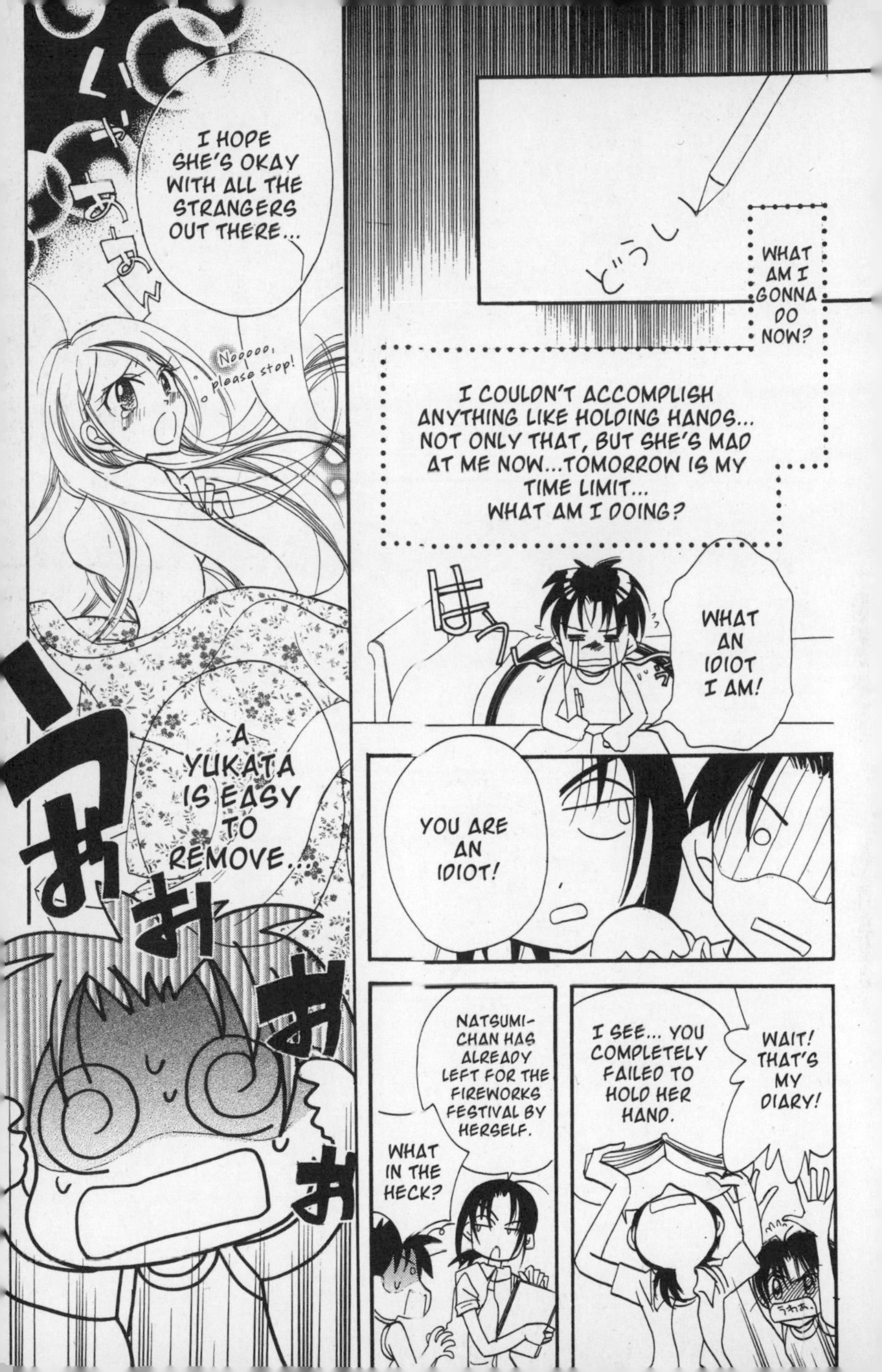
どうし
WHAT AM I GONNA DO NOW?
I COULDN'T ACCOMPLISH ANYTHING LIKE HOLDING HANDS... NOT ONLY THAT, BUT SHE'S MAD AT ME NOW...TOMORROW IS MY TIME LIMIT... WHAT AM I DOING?
WHAT AN IDIOT I AM!
YOU ARE AN IDIOT!
WAIT! THAT'S MY DIARY!
I SEE... YOU COMPLETELY FAILED TO HOLD HER HAND.
NATSUMI-CHAN HAS ALREADY LEFT FOR THE FIREWORKS FESTIVAL BY HERSELF.
WHAT IN THE HECK?
I HOPE SHE'S OKAY WITH ALL THE STRANGERS OUT THERE...
Nooooo, please stop!
A YUKATA IS EASY TO REMOVE...

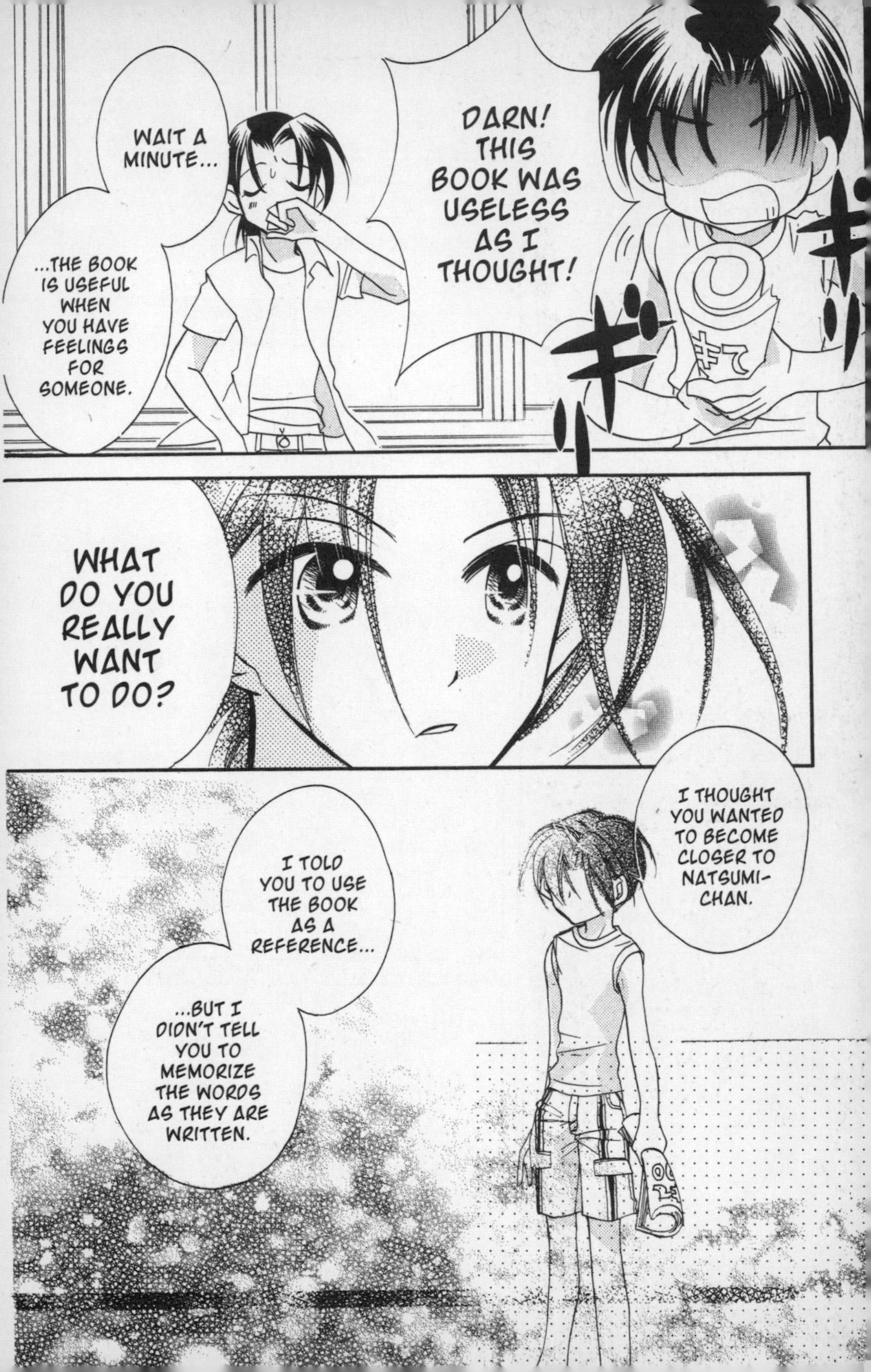
DARN! THIS BOOK WAS USELESS AS I THOUGHT!
ギリ
ギリ
WAIT A MINUTE...
...THE BOOK IS USEFUL WHEN YOU HAVE FEELINGS FOR SOMEONE.
WHAT DO YOU REALLY WANT TO DO?
I THOUGHT YOU WANTED TO BECOME CLOSER TO NATSUMI-CHAN.
I TOLD YOU TO USE THE BOOK AS A REFERENCE...
...BUT I DIDN'T TELL YOU TO MEMORIZE THE WORDS AS THEY ARE WRITTEN.

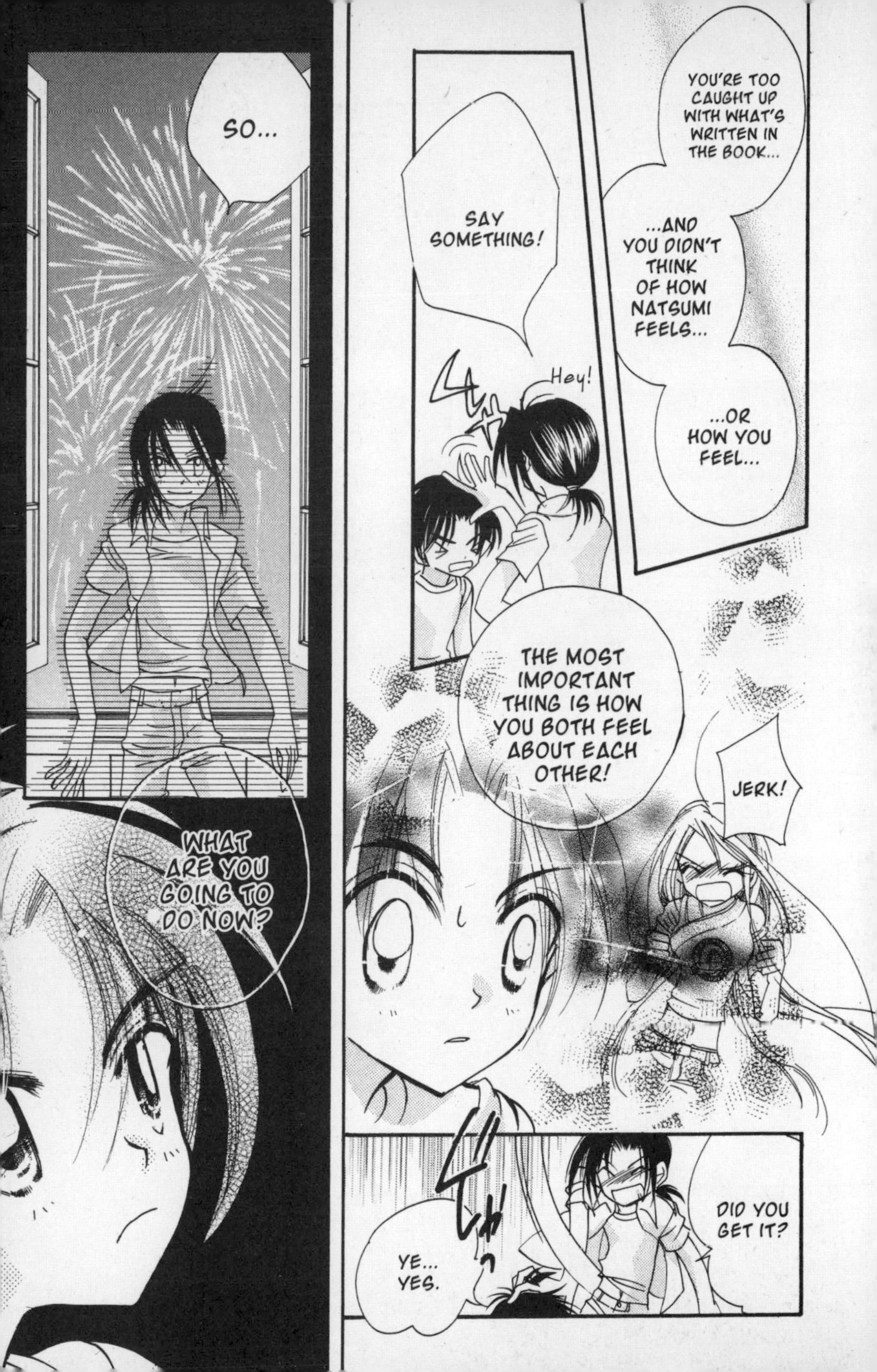
YOU'RE TOO CAUGHT UP WITH WHAT'S WRITTEN IN THE BOOK...
...AND YOU DIDN'T THINK OF HOW NATSUMI FEELS...
...OR HOW YOU FEEL...
SAY SOMETHING!
Hey!
THE MOST IMPORTANT THING IS HOW YOU BOTH FEEL ABOUT EACH OTHER!
JERK!
DID YOU GET IT?
YE... YES.
SO...
WHAT ARE YOU GOING TO DO NOW?

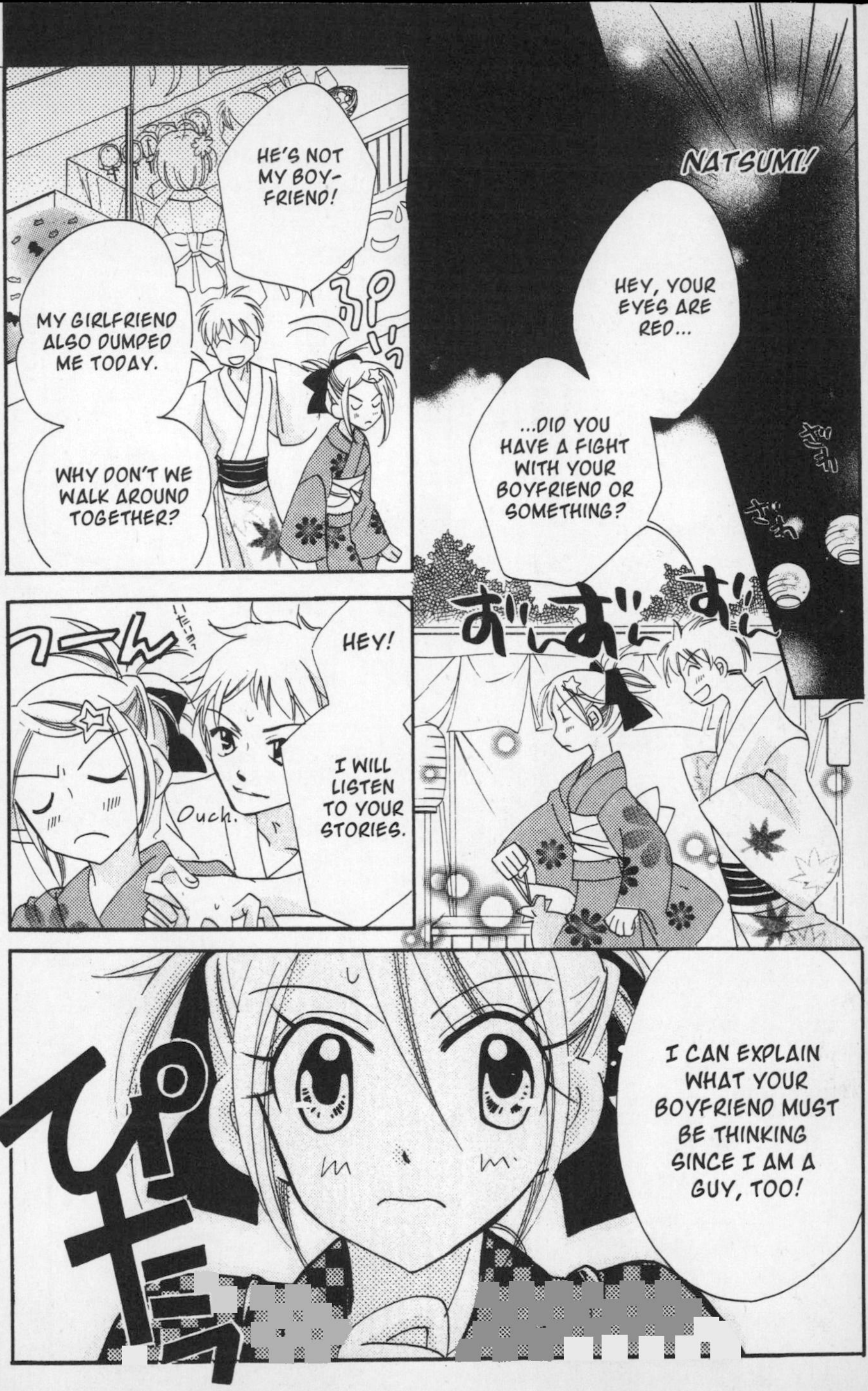
NATSUMI!
HEY, YOUR EYES ARE RED...
...DID YOU HAVE A FIGHT WITH YOUR BOYFRIEND OR SOMETHING?
HE'S NOT MY BOY-FRIEND!
MY GIRLFRIEND ALSO DUMPED ME TODAY.
WHY DON'T WE WALK AROUND TOGETHER?
HEY!
I WILL LISTEN TO YOUR STORIES.
Ouch.
I CAN EXPLAIN WHAT YOUR BOYFRIEND MUST BE THINKING SINCE I AM A GUY, TOO!

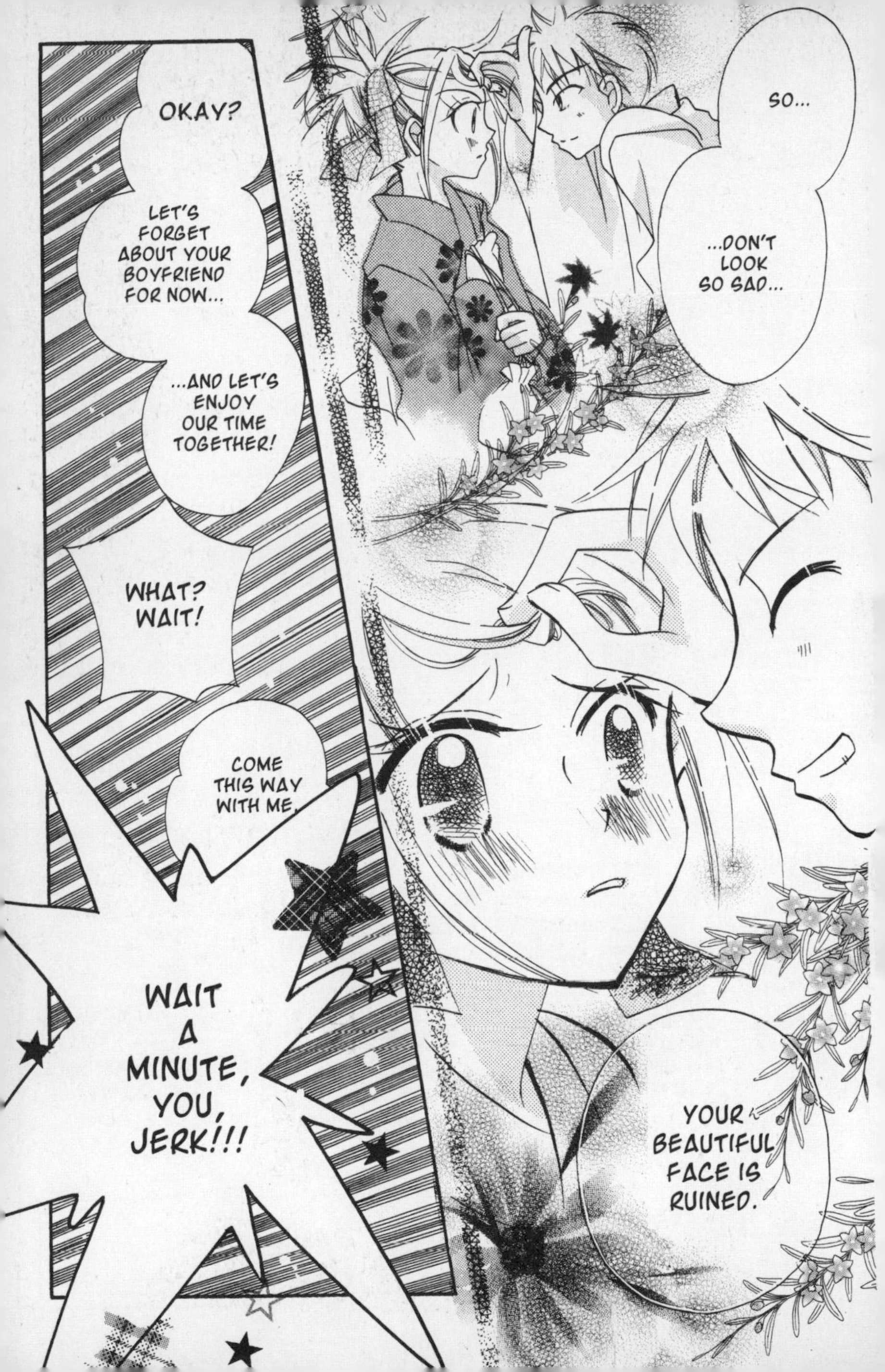
SO...
...DON'T LOOK SO SAD...
YOUR BEAUTIFUL FACE IS RUINED.
OKAY?
LET'S FORGET ABOUT YOUR BOYFRIEND FOR NOW...
...AND LET'S ENJOY OUR TIME TOGETHER!
WHAT? WAIT!
COME THIS WAY WITH ME.
WAIT A MINUTE, YOU, JERK!!!

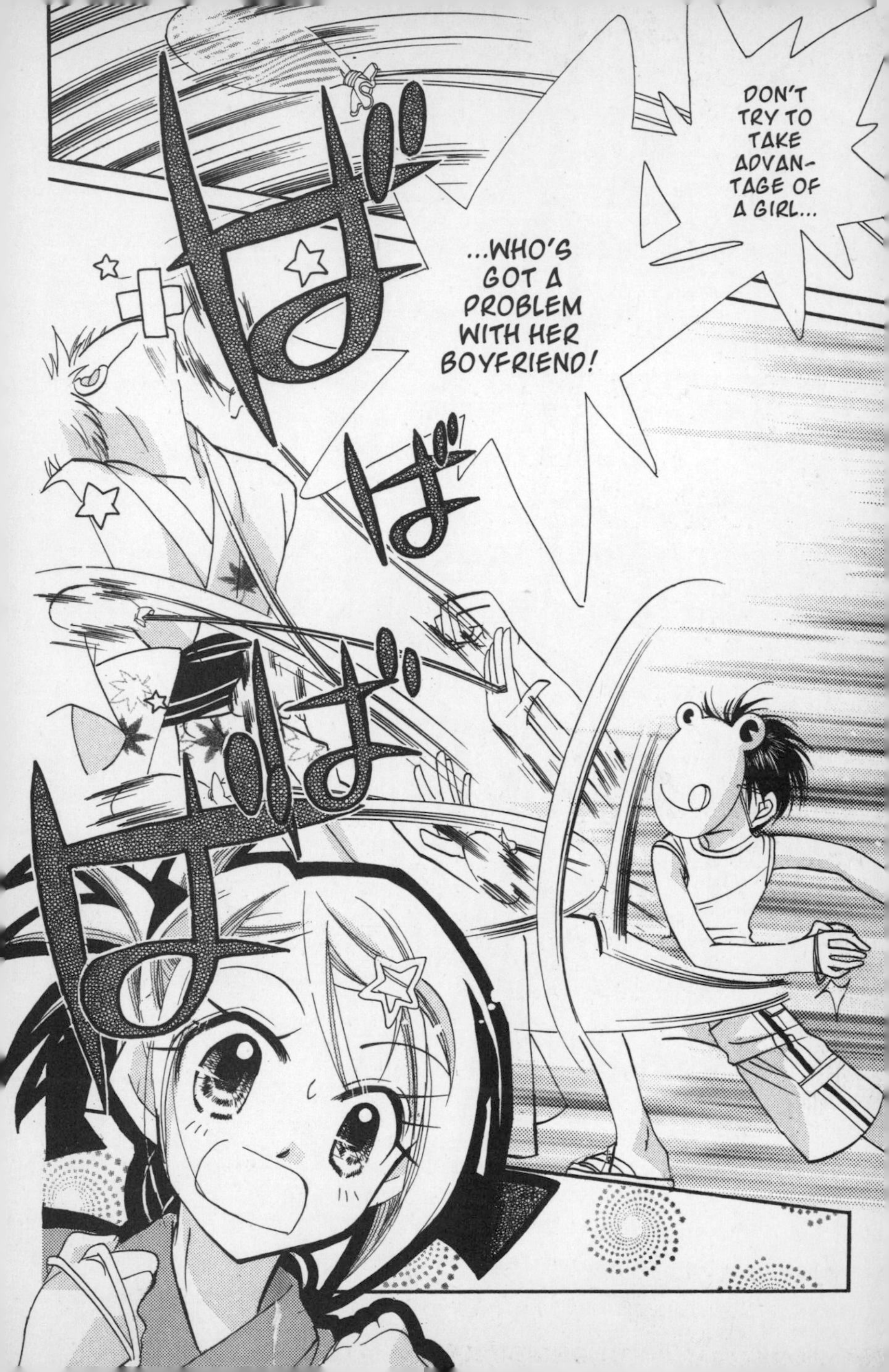
DON'T TRY TO TAKE ADVAN-TAGE OF A GIRL...
...WHO'S GOT A PROBLEM WITH HER BOYFRIEND!
ばばばば

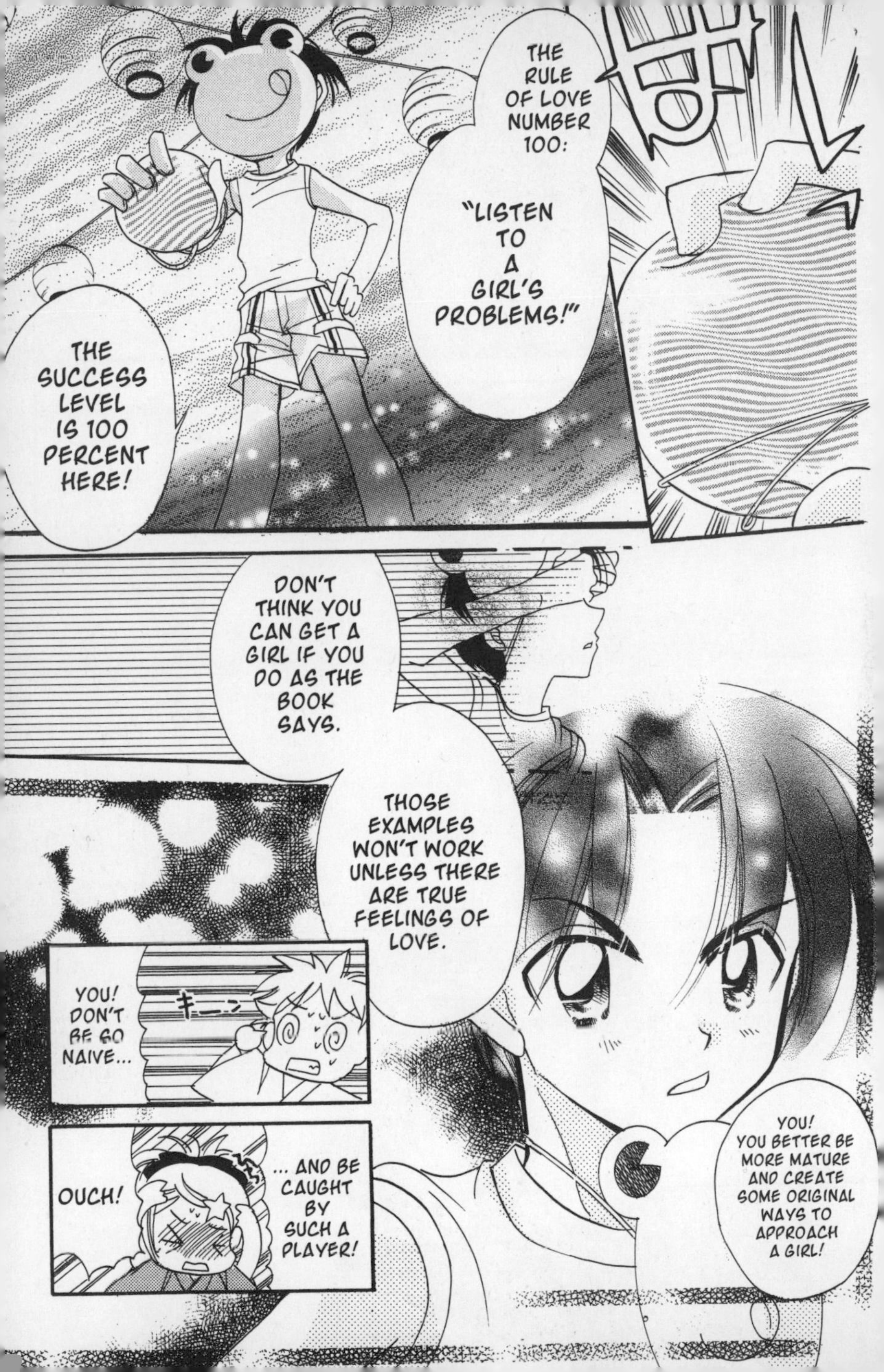
THE RULE OF LOVE NUMBER 100:
"LISTEN TO A GIRL'S PROBLEMS!"
THE SUCCESS LEVEL IS 100 PERCENT HERE!
DON'T THINK YOU CAN GET A GIRL IF YOU DO AS THE BOOK SAYS.
THOSE EXAMPLES WON'T WORK UNLESS THERE ARE TRUE FEELINGS OF LOVE.
YOU! YOU BETTER BE MORE MATURE AND CREATE SOME ORIGINAL WAYS TO APPROACH A GIRL!
YOU! DON'T BE SO NAIVE...
キーン
... AND BE CAUGHT BY SUCH A PLAYER!
OUCH!

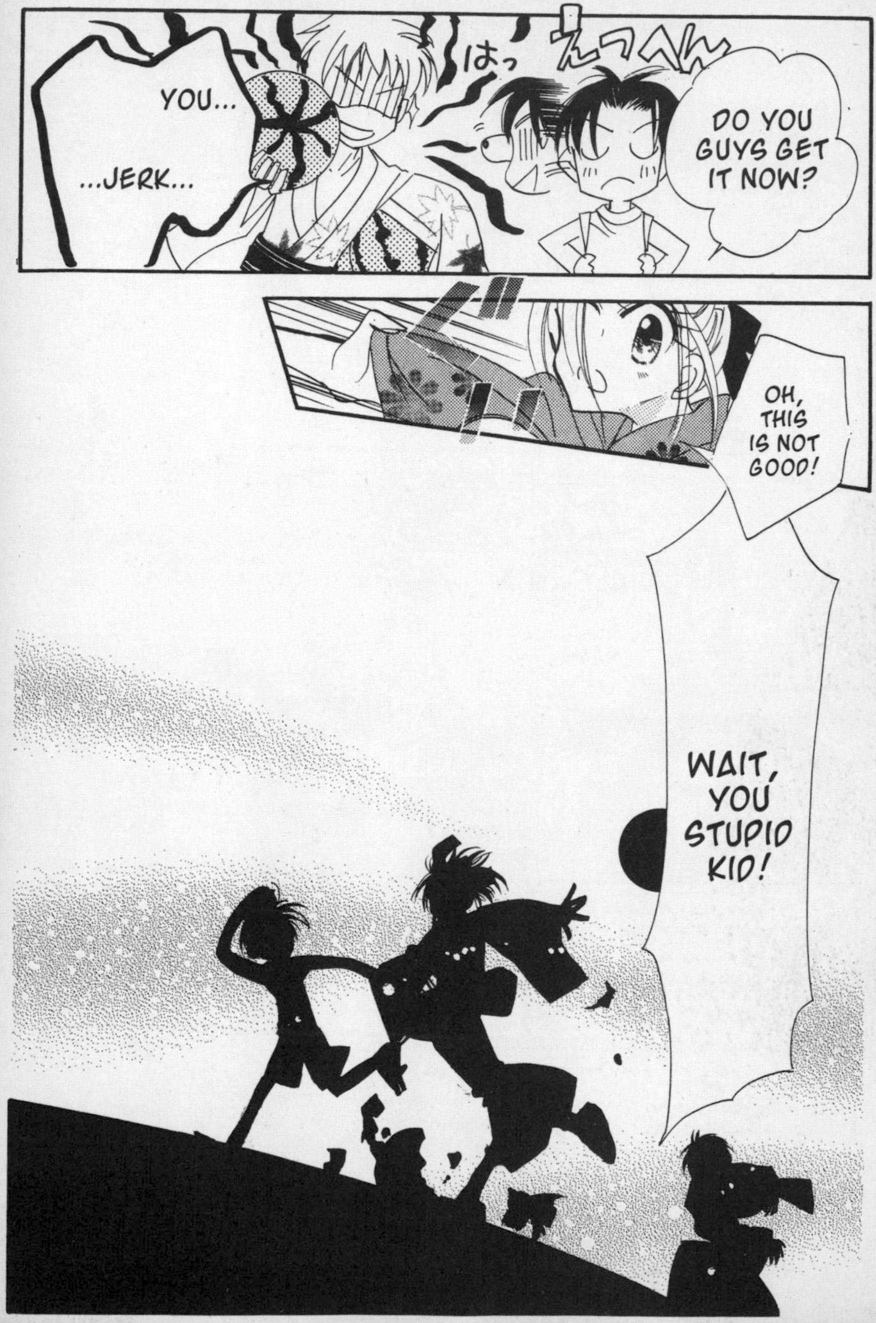
DO YOU GUYS GET IT NOW?
えっへん
はっ
YOU...
...JERK...
OH, THIS IS NOT GOOD!
WAIT, YOU STUPID KID!

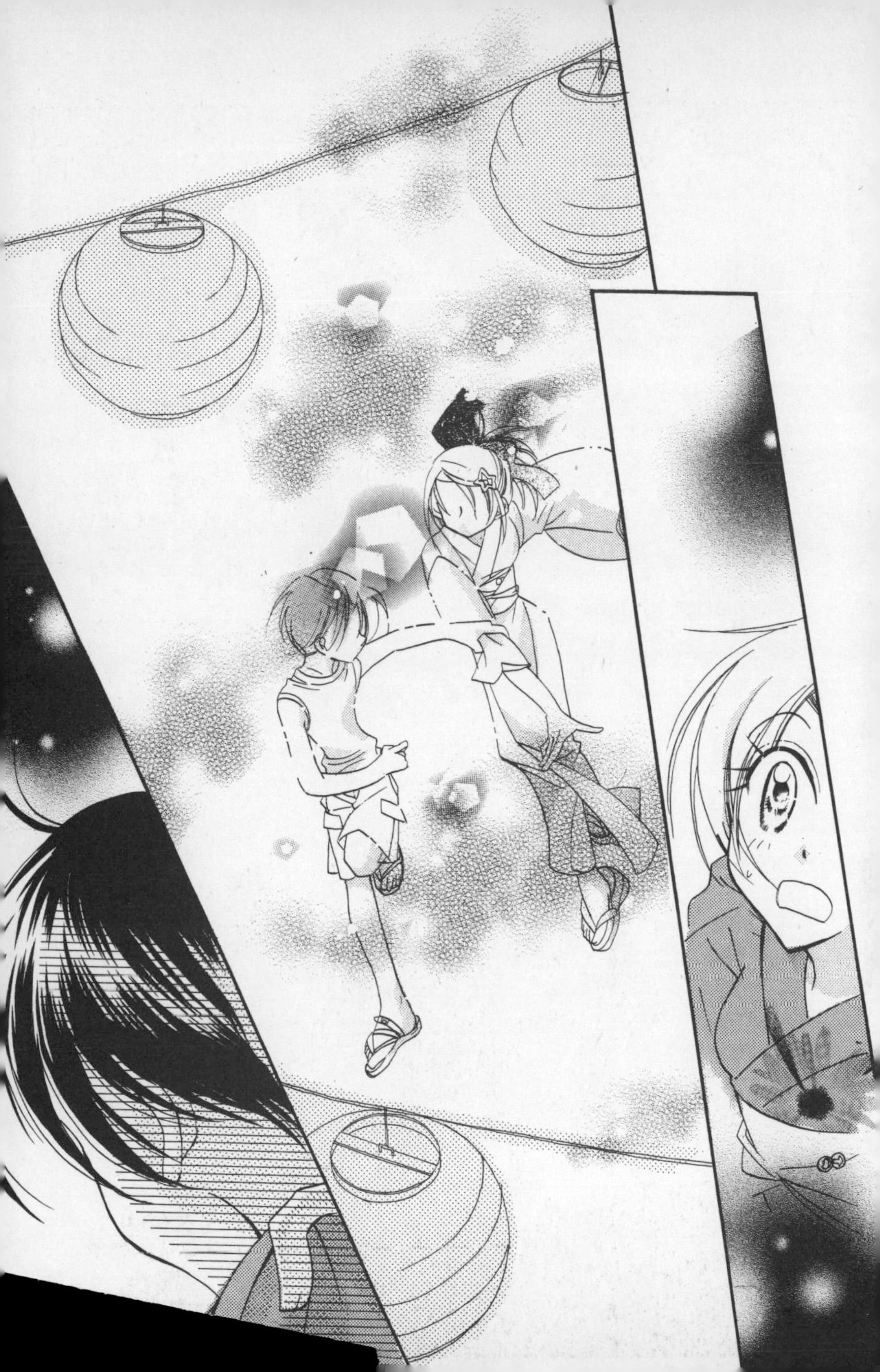

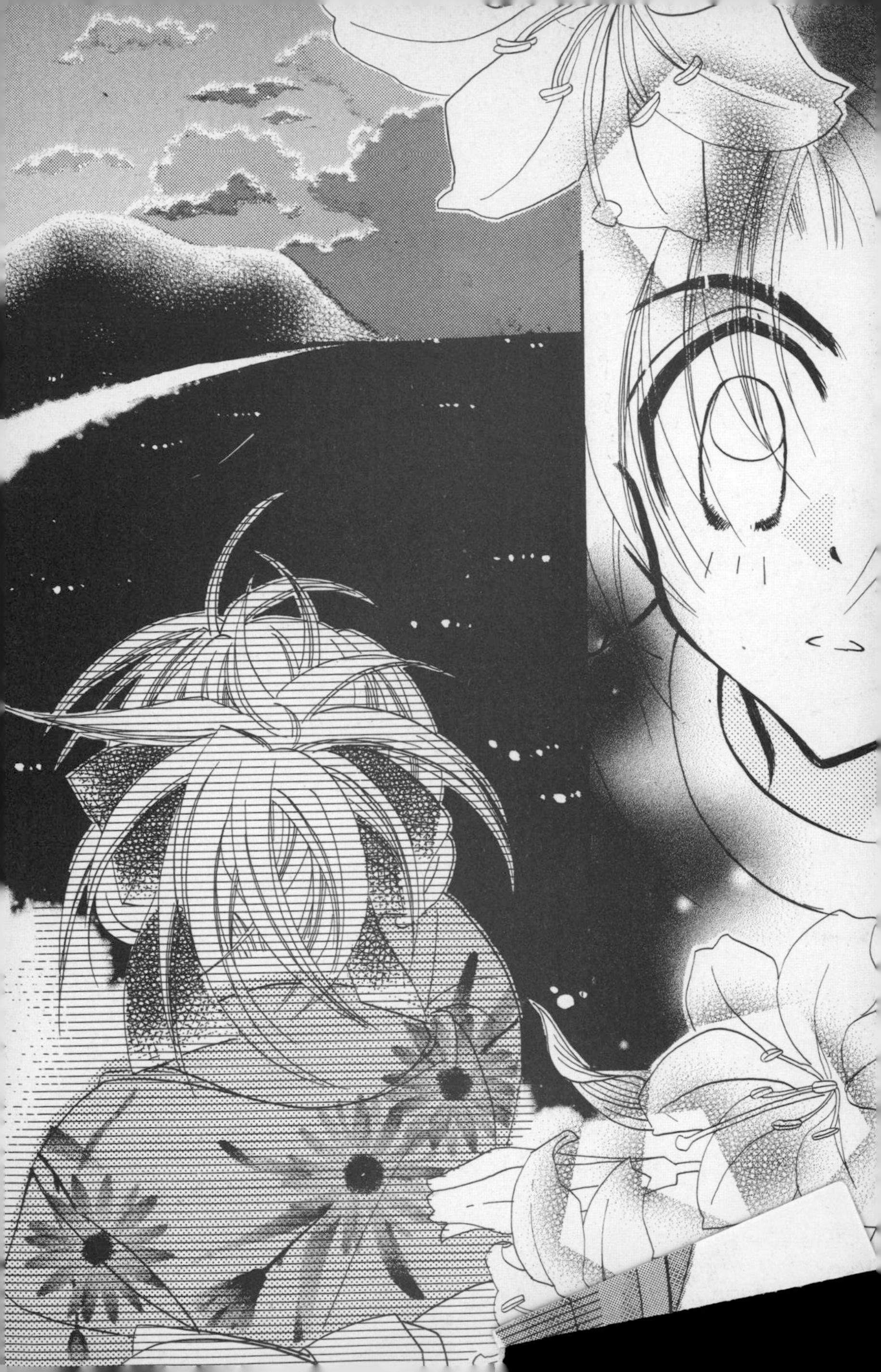

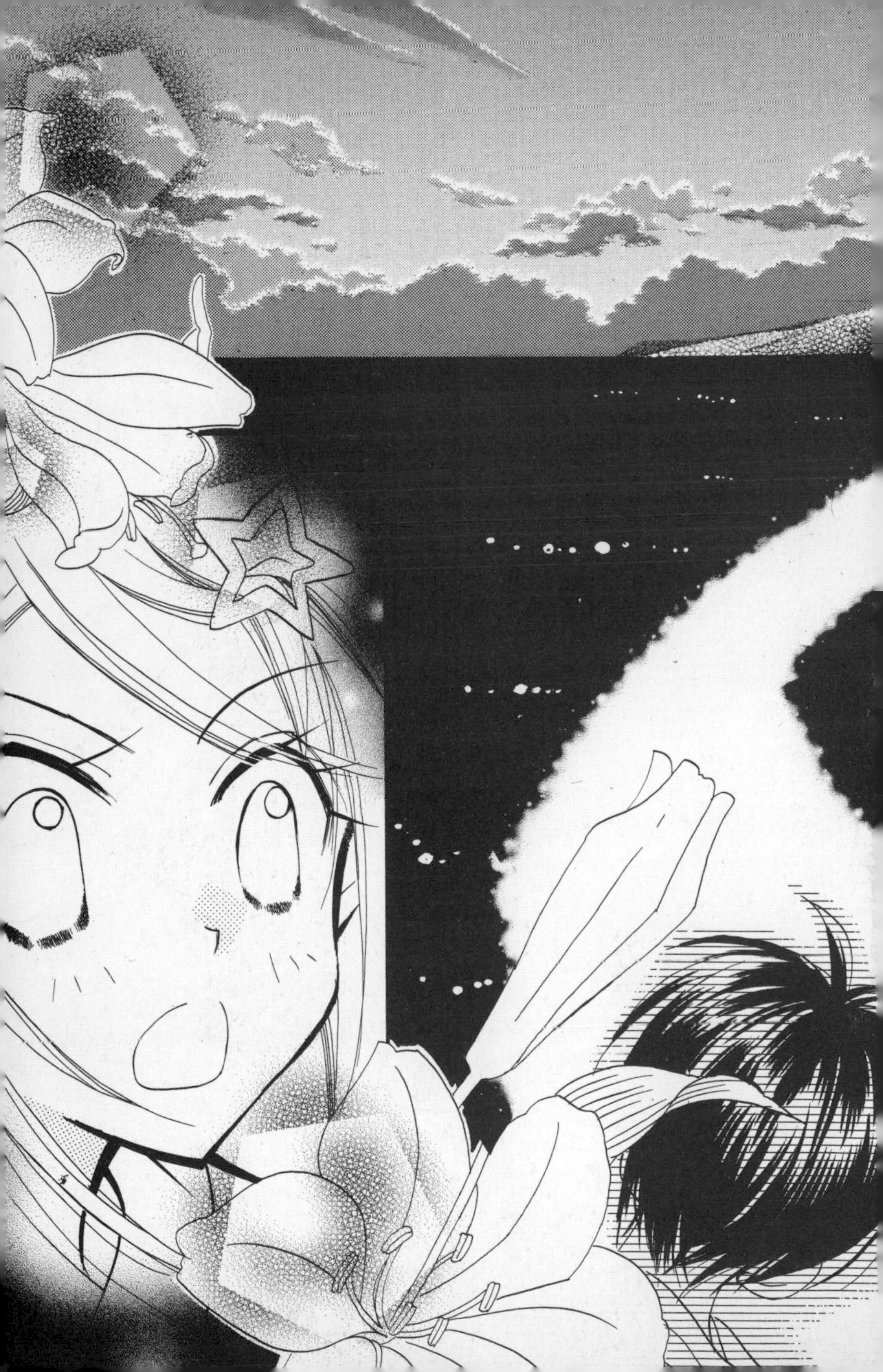

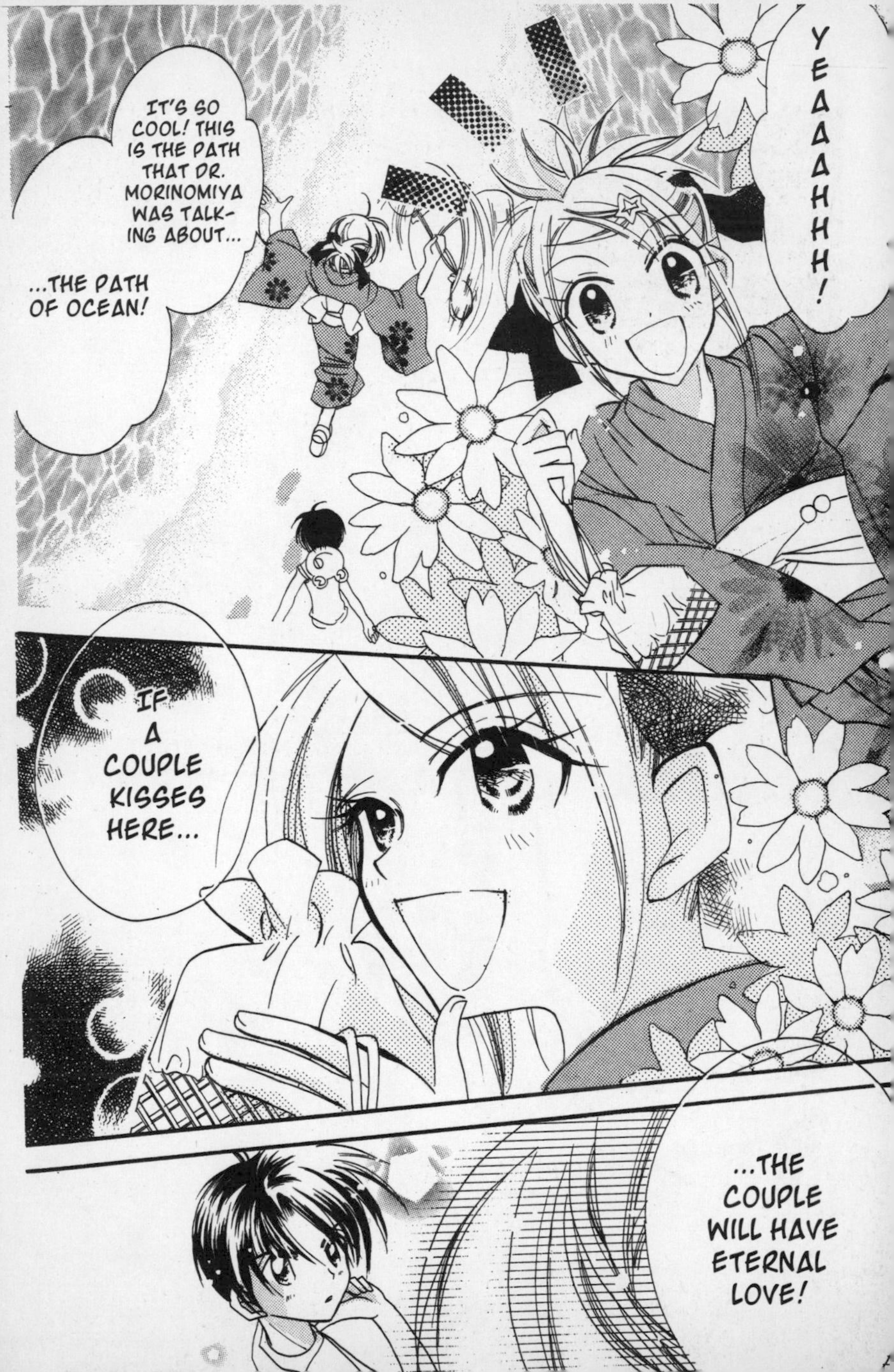
YEAAAAHHHH!
IT'S SO COOL! THIS IS THE PATH THAT DR. MORINOMIYA WAS TALKING ABOUT...
...THE PATH OF OCEAN!
IF A COUPLE KISSES HERE...
...THE COUPLE WILL HAVE ETERNAL LOVE!

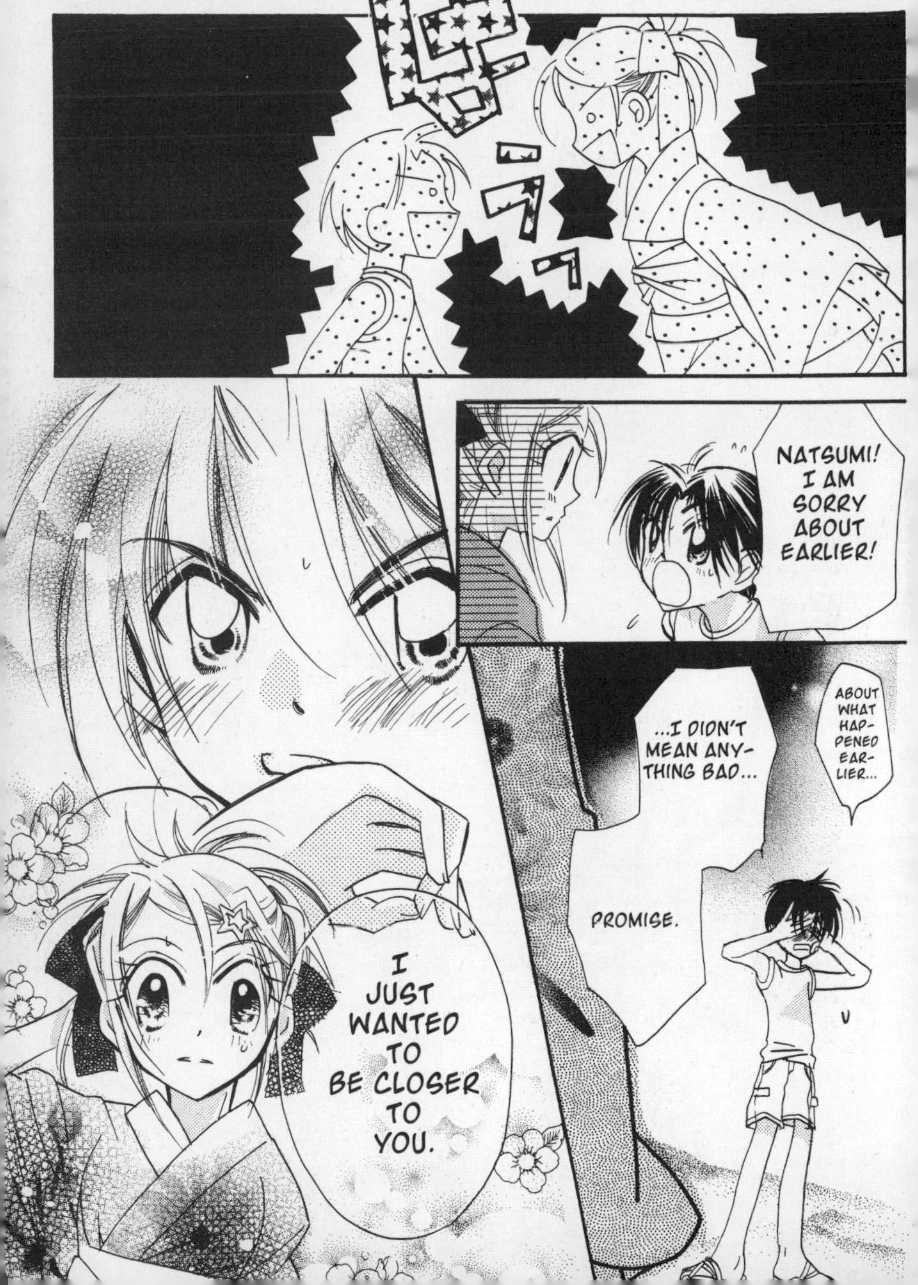
NATSUMI! I AM SORRY ABOUT EARLIER!
ABOUT WHAT HAP-PENED EAR-LIER...
...I DIDN'T MEAN ANY-THING BAD...
PROMISE.
I JUST WANTED TO BE CLOSER TO YOU.

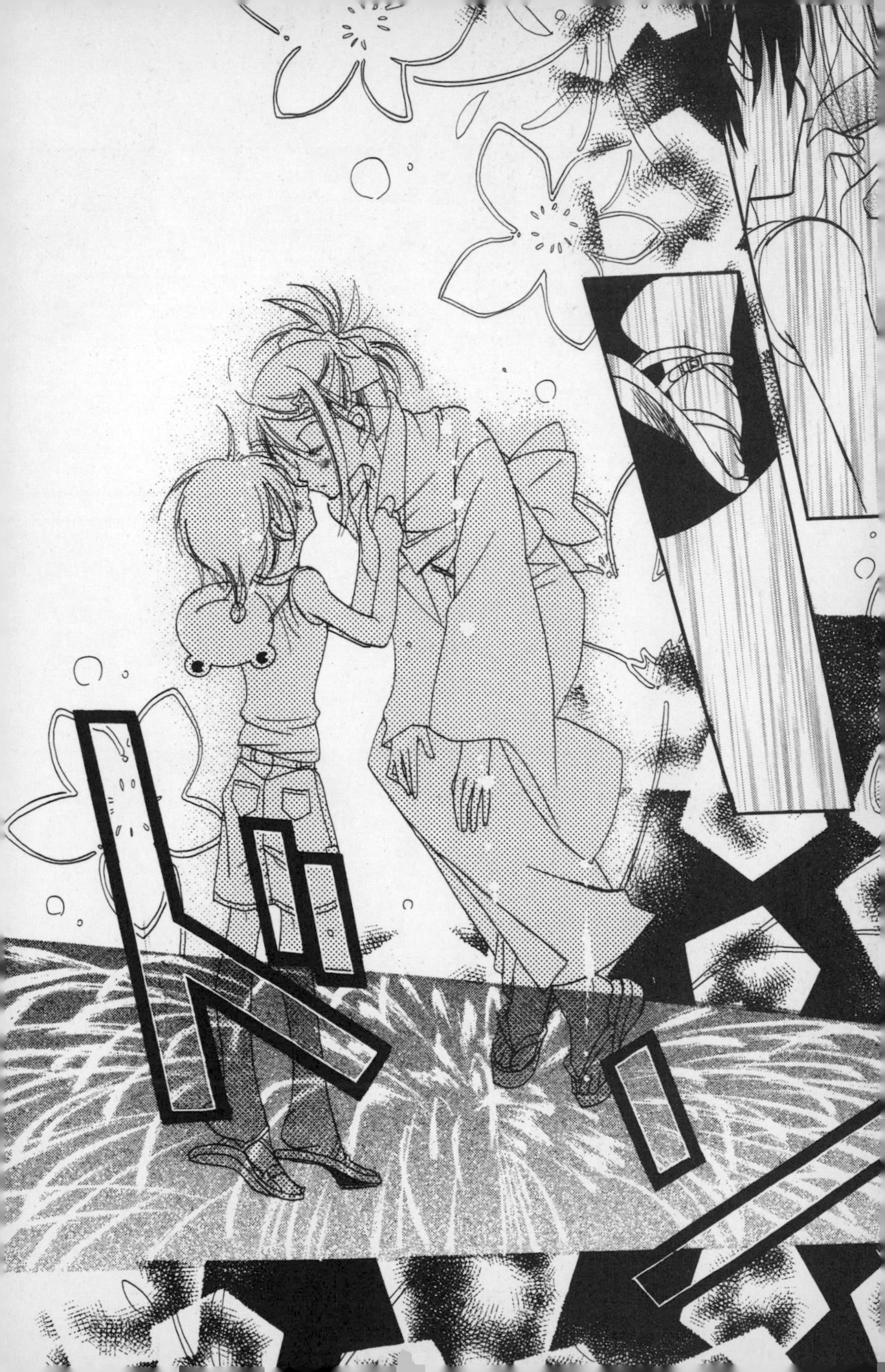

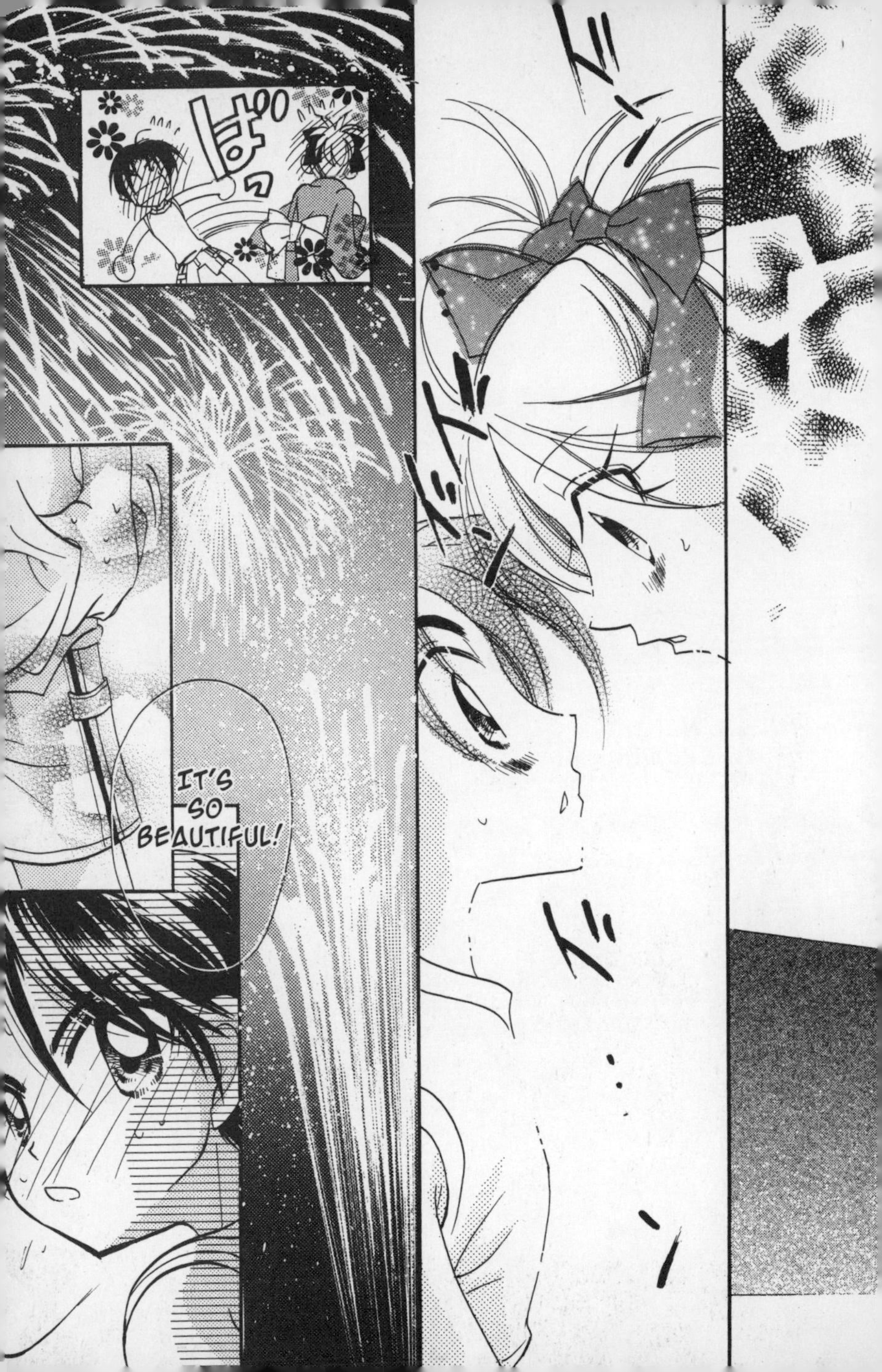
ぼっ
IT'S SO BEAUTIFUL!

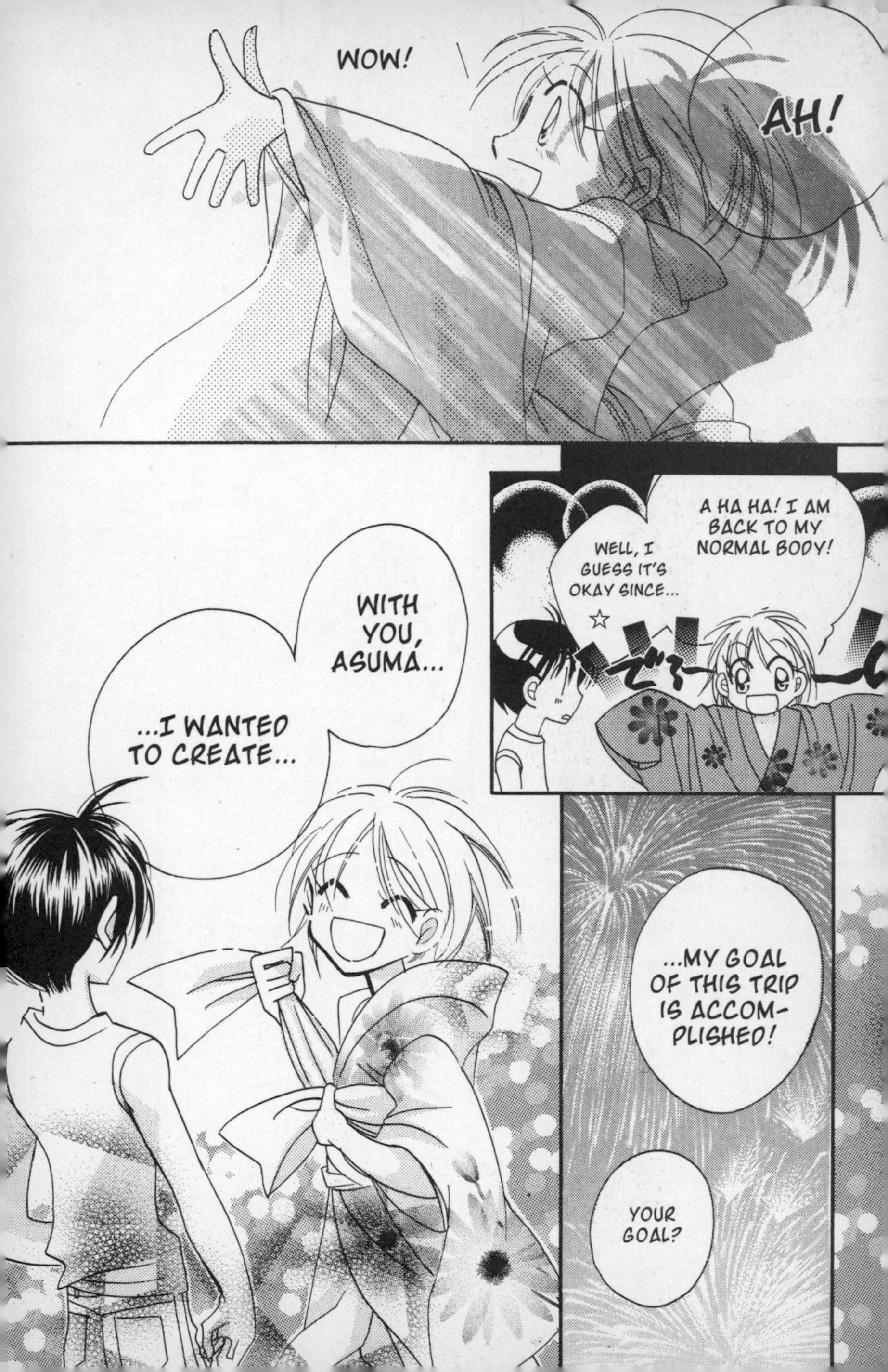
AH!
WOW!
A HA HA! I AM BACK TO MY NORMAL BODY!
WELL, I GUESS IT'S OKAY SINCE...
...MY GOAL OF THIS TRIP IS ACCOM-PLISHED!
YOUR GOAL?
WITH YOU, ASUMA...
...I WANTED TO CREATE...

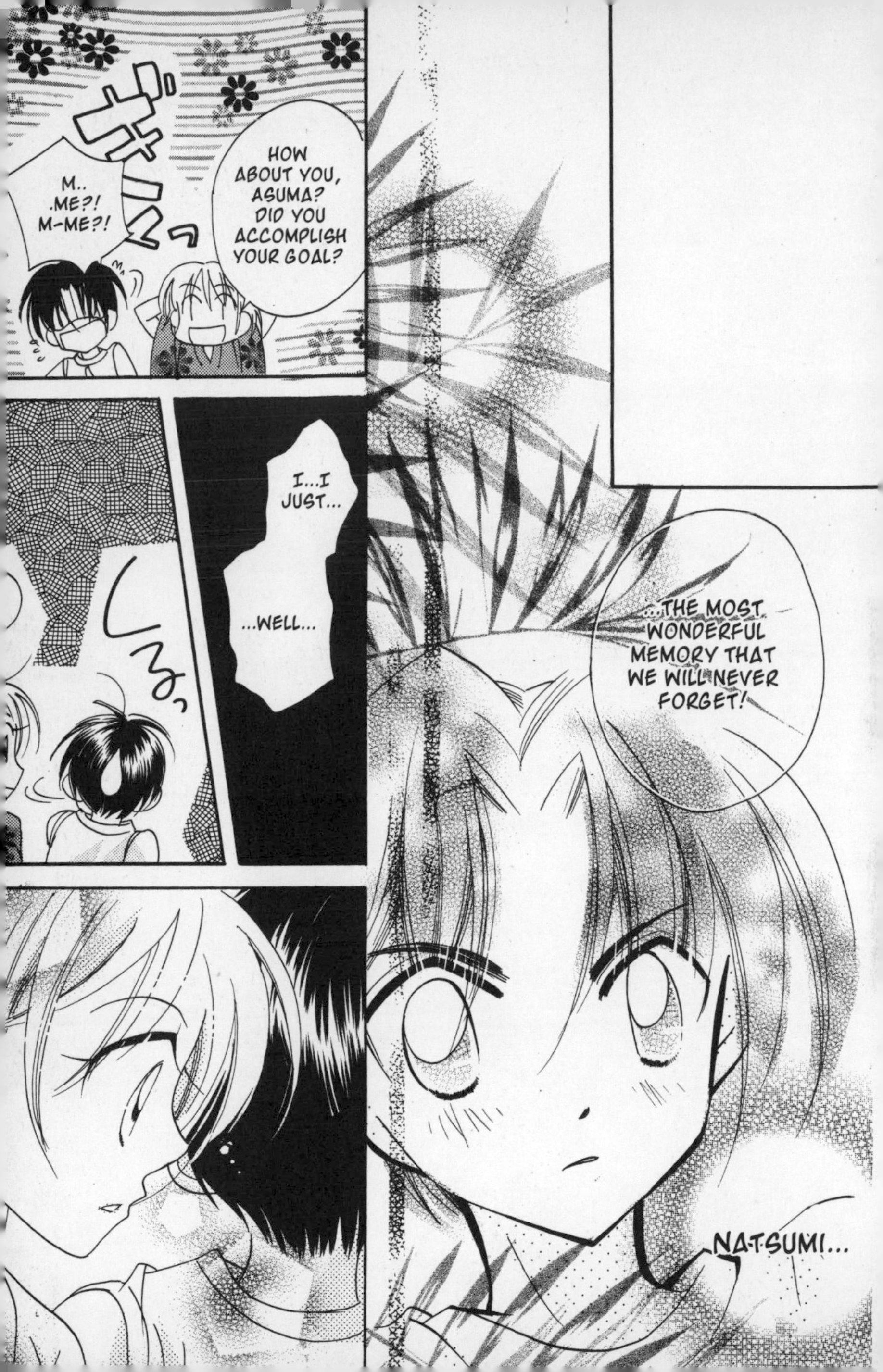
HOW ABOUT YOU, ASUMA? DID YOU ACCOMPLISH YOUR GOAL?
M.. .ME?! M-ME?!
I...I JUST...
...WELL...
...THE MOST WONDERFUL MEMORY THAT WE WILL NEVER FORGET!
NATSUMI...

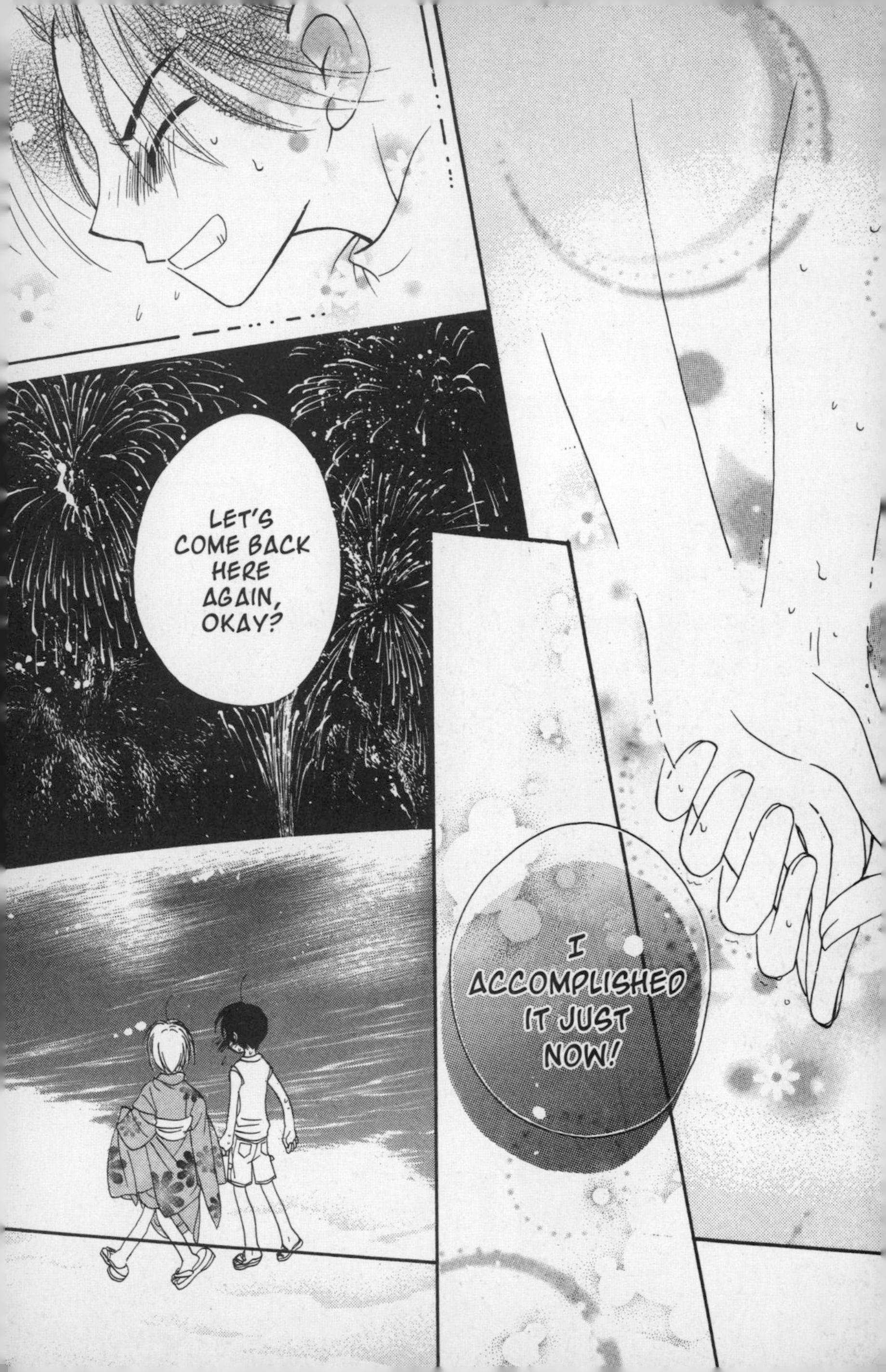
I ACCOMPLISHED IT JUST NOW!
LET'S COME BACK HERE AGAIN, OKAY?

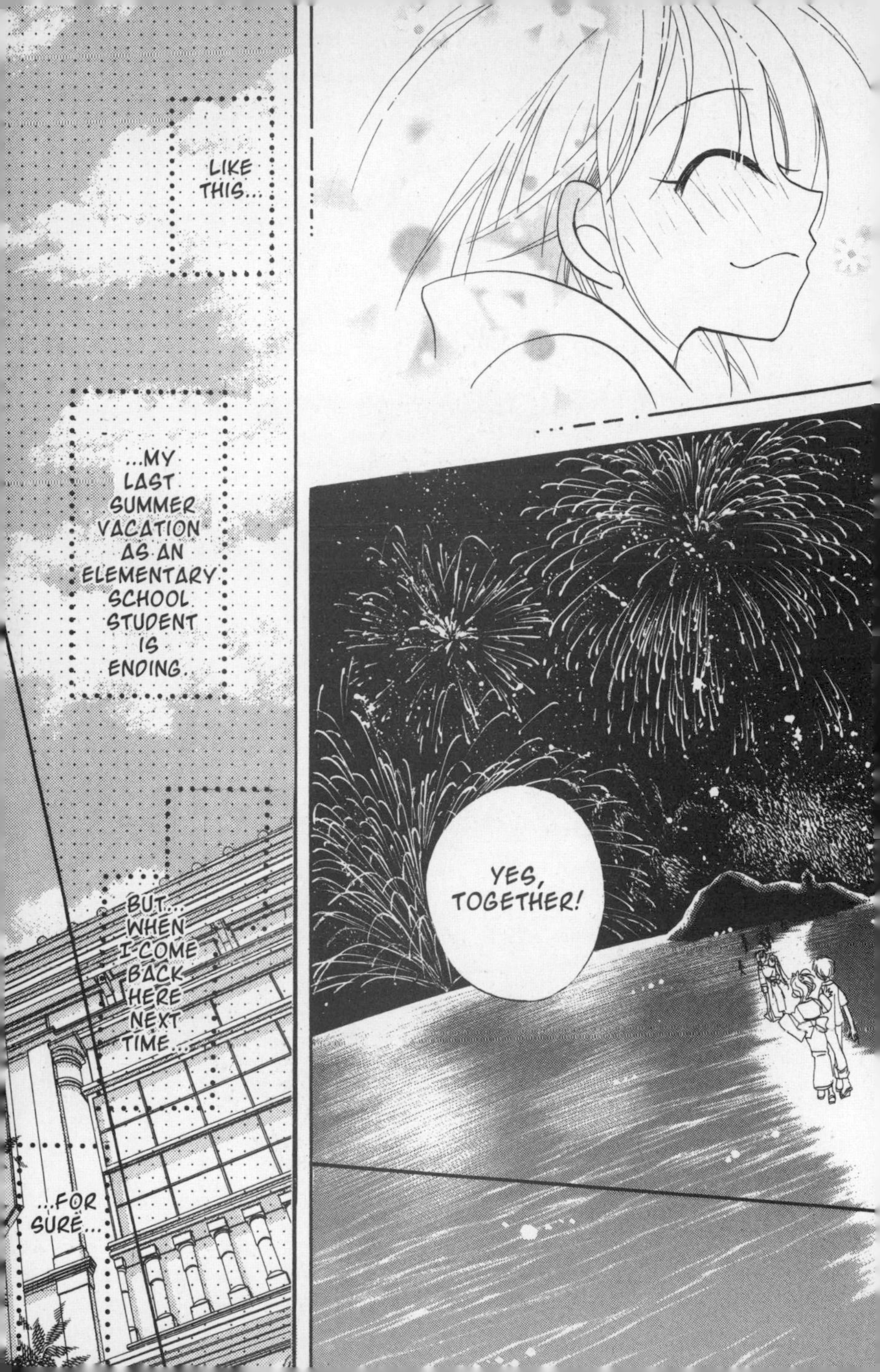
YES, TOGETHER!
LIKE THIS...
...MY LAST SUMMER VACATION AS AN ELEMENTARY SCHOOL STUDENT IS ENDING.
BUT... WHEN I COME BACK HERE NEXT TIME...
...FOR SURE...

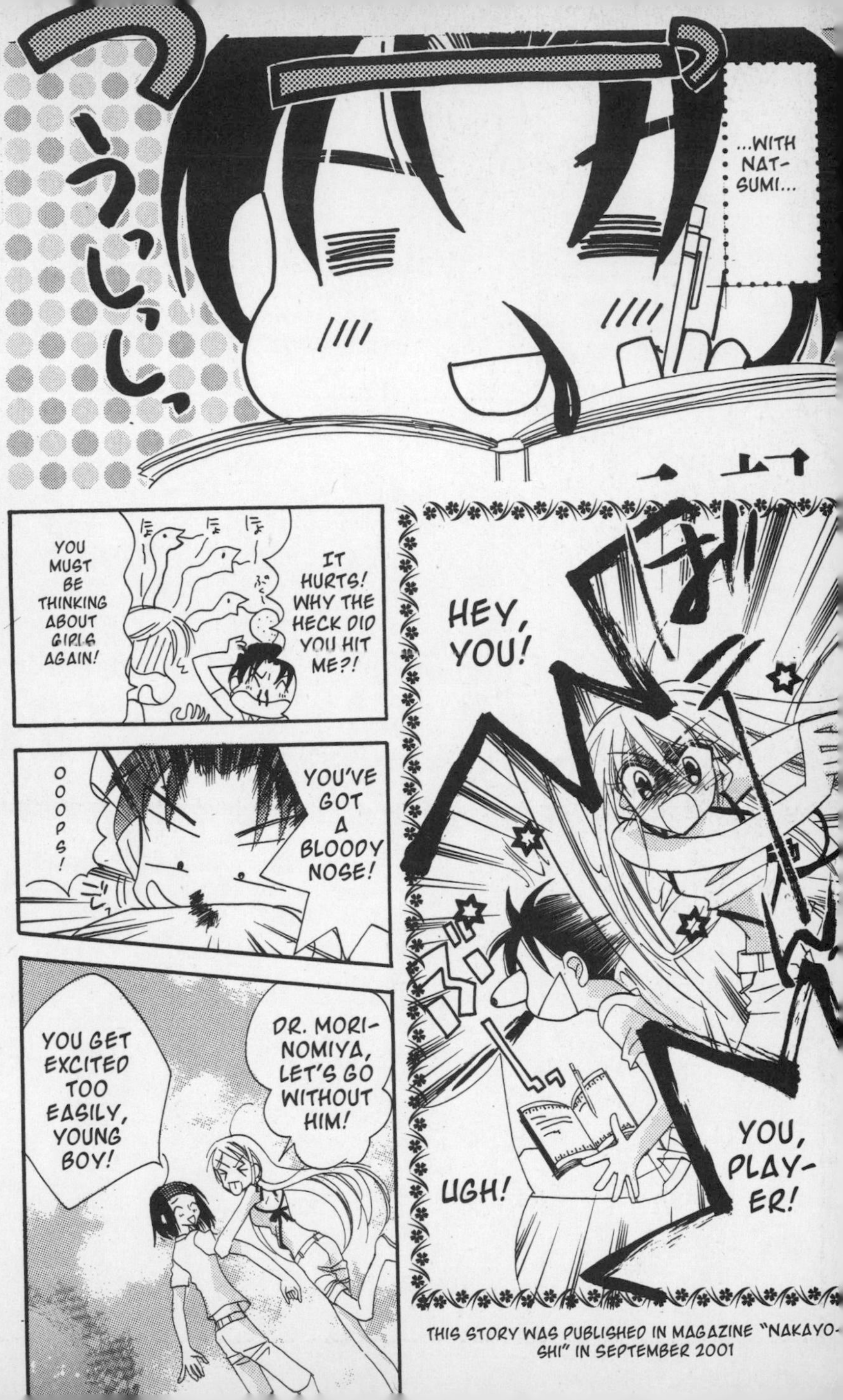
...WITH NAT-SUMI...
うっしっしっ
HEY, YOU!
YOU, PLAY-ER!
UGH!
IT HURTS! WHY THE HECK DID YOU HIT ME?!
YOU MUST BE THINKING ABOUT GIRLS AGAIN!
YOU'VE GOT A BLOODY NOSE!
OOOPS!
DR. MORI-NOMIYA, LET'S GO WITHOUT HIM!
YOU GET EXCITED TOO EASILY, YOUNG BOY!

THIS STORY WAS PUBLISHED IN MAGAZINE "NAKAYOSHI" IN SEPTEMBER 2001

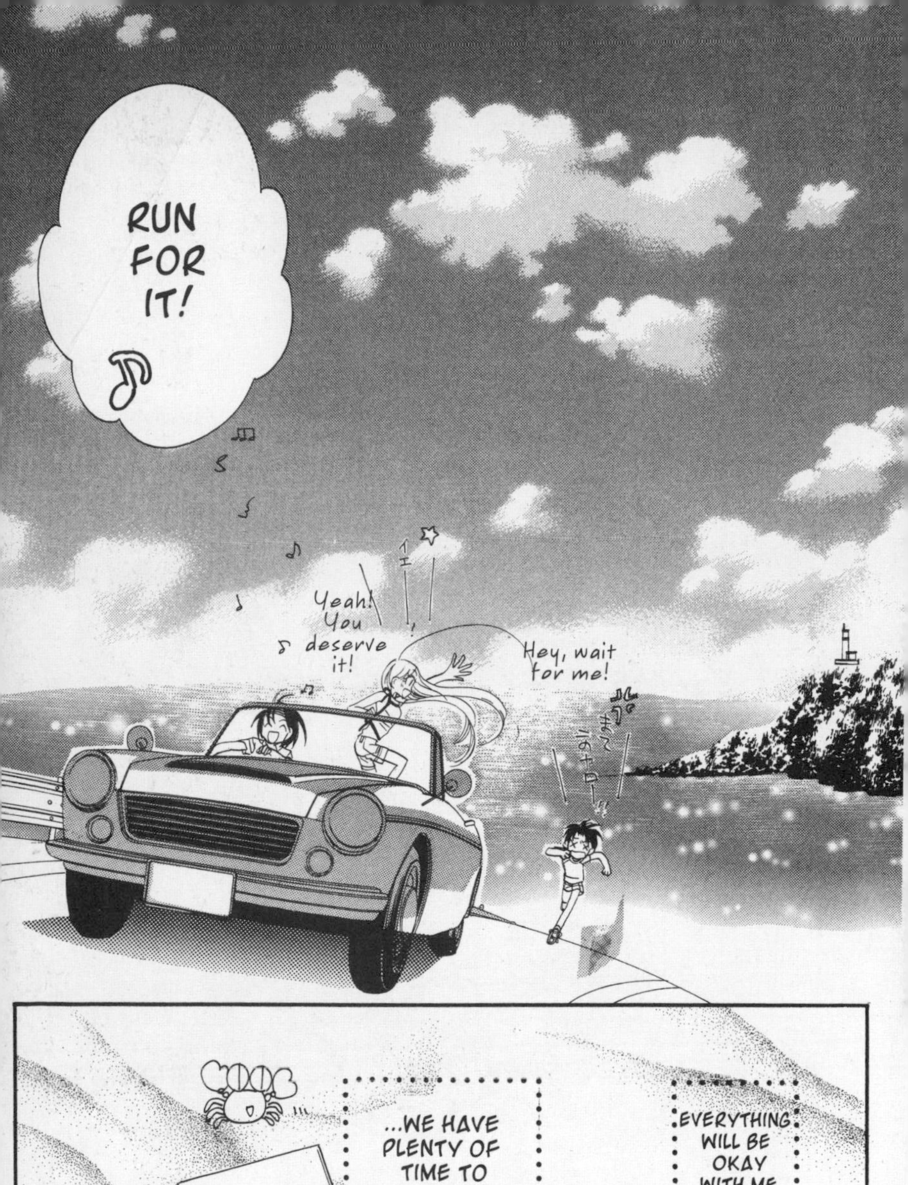
RUN FOR IT!
Yeah! You deserve it!
Hey, wait for me!

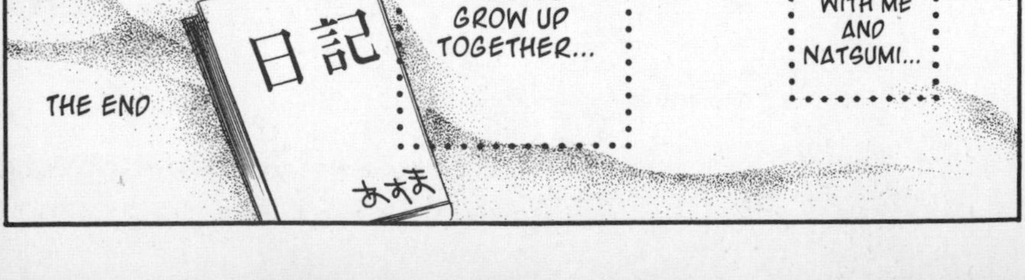
EVERYTHING WILL BE OKAY WITH ME AND NATSUMI...
...WE HAVE PLENTY OF TIME TO GROW UP TOGETHER...
日記
THE END

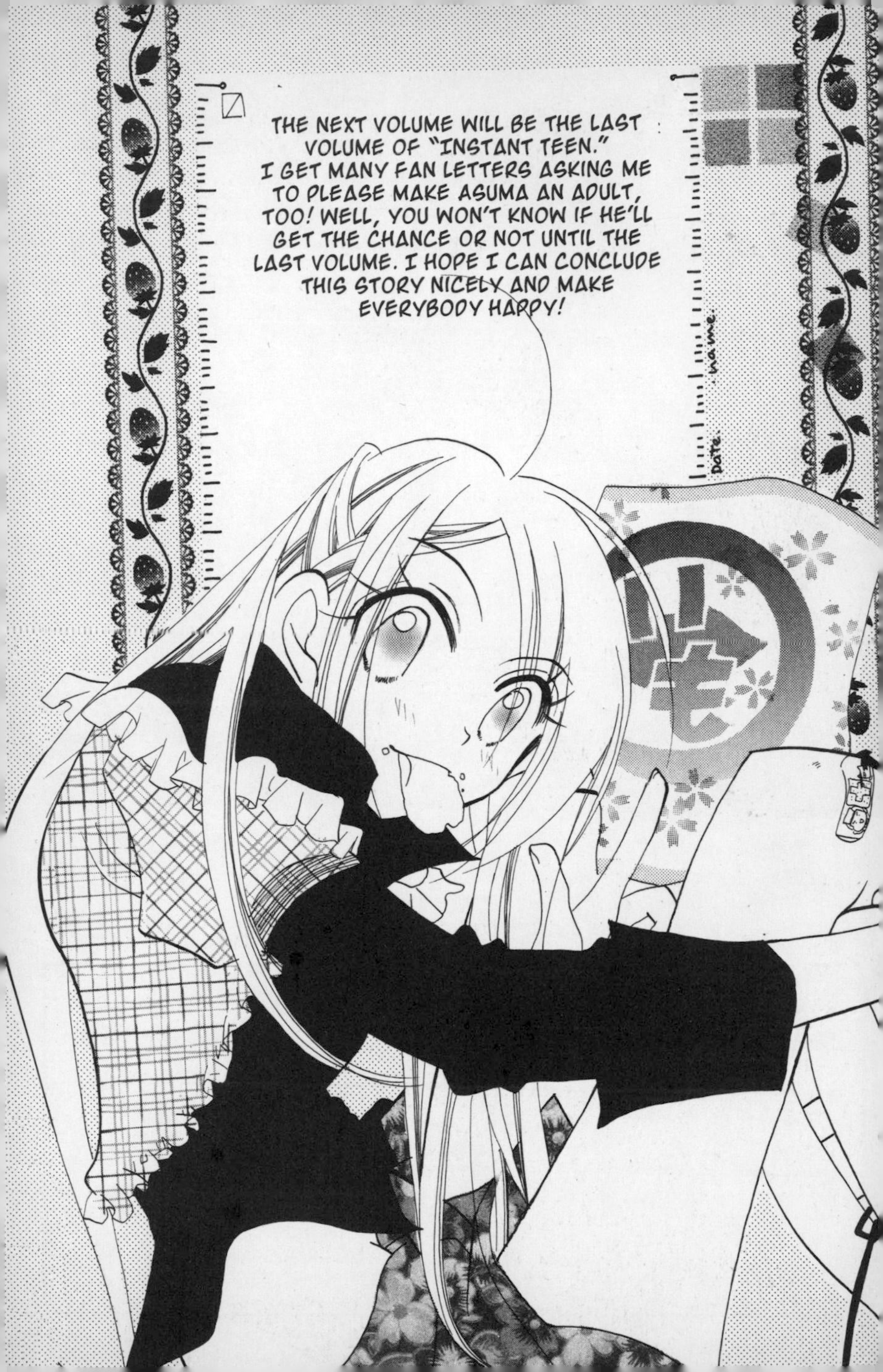
THE NEXT VOLUME WILL BE THE LAST VOLUME OF "INSTANT TEEN." I GET MANY FAN LETTERS ASKING ME TO PLEASE MAKE ASUMA AN ADULT, TOO! WELL, YOU WON'T KNOW IF HE'LL GET THE CHANCE OR NOT UNTIL THE LAST VOLUME. I HOPE I CAN CONCLUDE THIS STORY NICELY AND MAKE EVERYBODY HAPPY!
Date.
name.

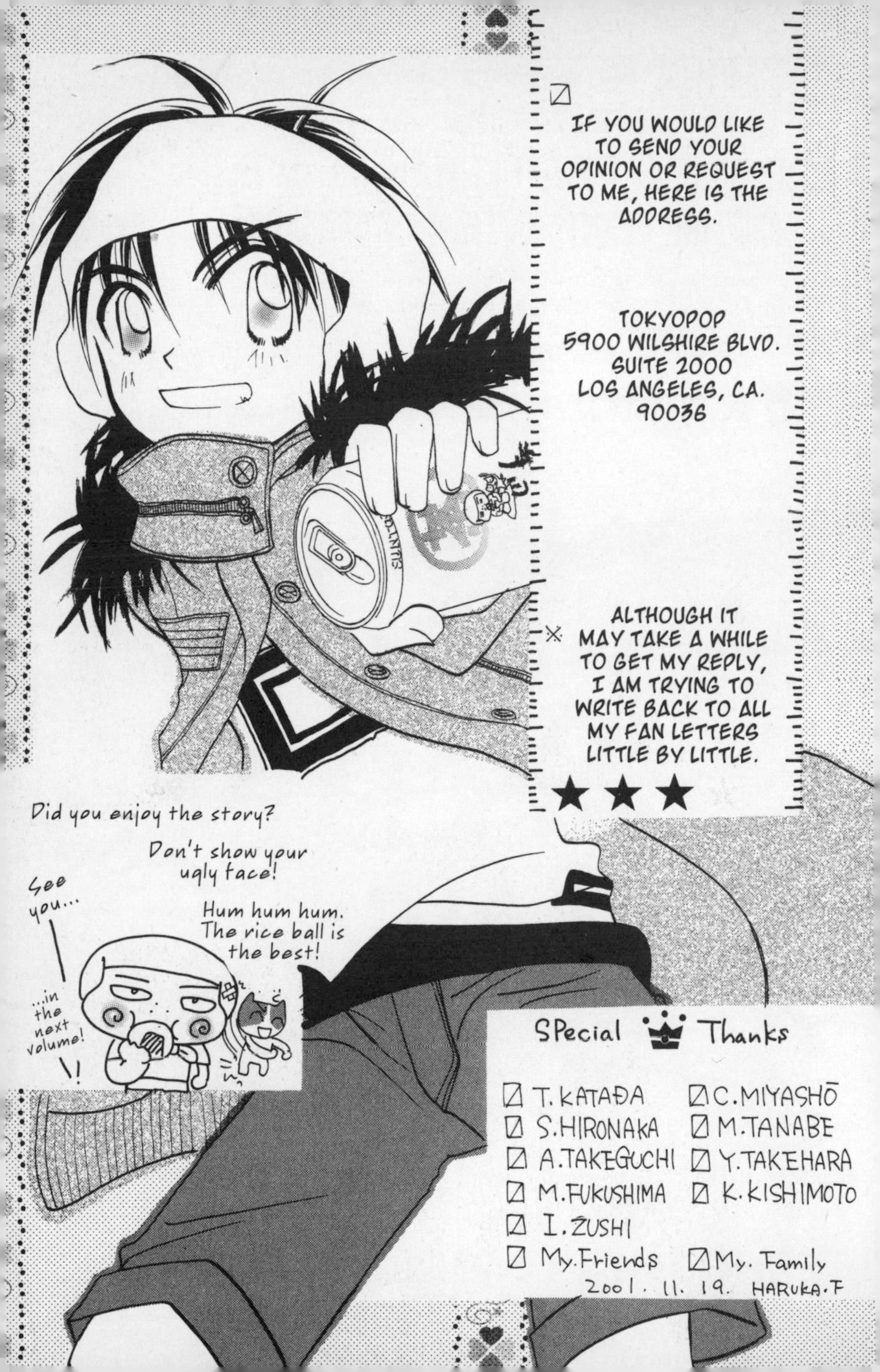
IF YOU WOULD LIKE TO SEND YOUR OPINION OR REQUEST TO ME, HERE IS THE ADDRESS.
TOKYOPOP
5900 WILSHIRE BLVD.
SUITE 2000
LOS ANGELES, CA.
90036
※ ALTHOUGH IT MAY TAKE A WHILE TO GET MY REPLY, I AM TRYING TO WRITE BACK TO ALL MY FAN LETTERS LITTLE BY LITTLE.
★★★
Did you enjoy the story?
Don't show your ugly face!
Hum hum hum. The rice ball is the best!
See you...
...in the next volume!
Special Thanks
T. KATADA
C. MIYASHŌ
S. HIRONAKA
M. TANABE
A. TAKEGUCHI
Y. TAKEHARA
M. FUKUSHIMA
K. KISHIMOTO
I. ZUSHI
My. Friends
My. Family
2001. 11. 19. HARUKA. F

TOKYOPOP SHOP

SOKORA REFUGEES™

CLEAVE!
CHING!
strip
tense
TWIST

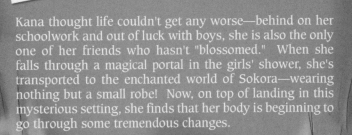

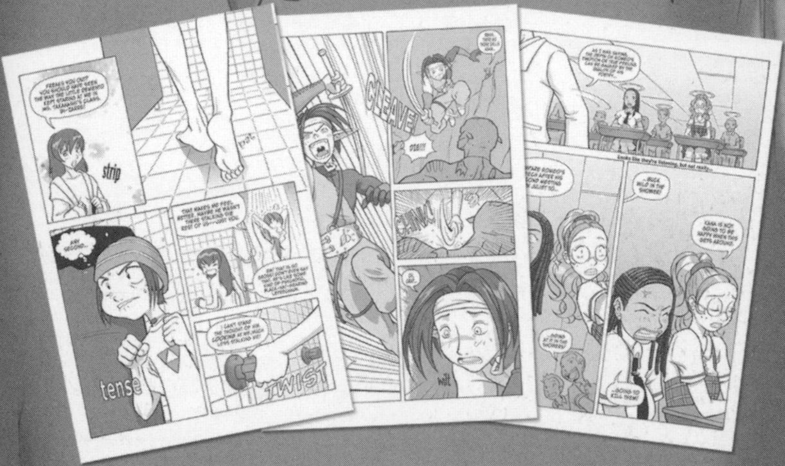

Kana thought life couldn't get any worse—behind on her schoolwork and out of luck with boys, she is also the only one of her friends who hasn't "blossomed." When she falls through a magical portal in the girls' shower, she's transported to the enchanted world of Sokora—wearing nothing but a small robe! Now, on top of landing in this mysterious setting, she finds that her body is beginning to go through some tremendous changes.

Preview the manga at:
www.TOKYOPOP.com/sokora

T
TEEN
AGE 13+

SOKORA REFUGEES

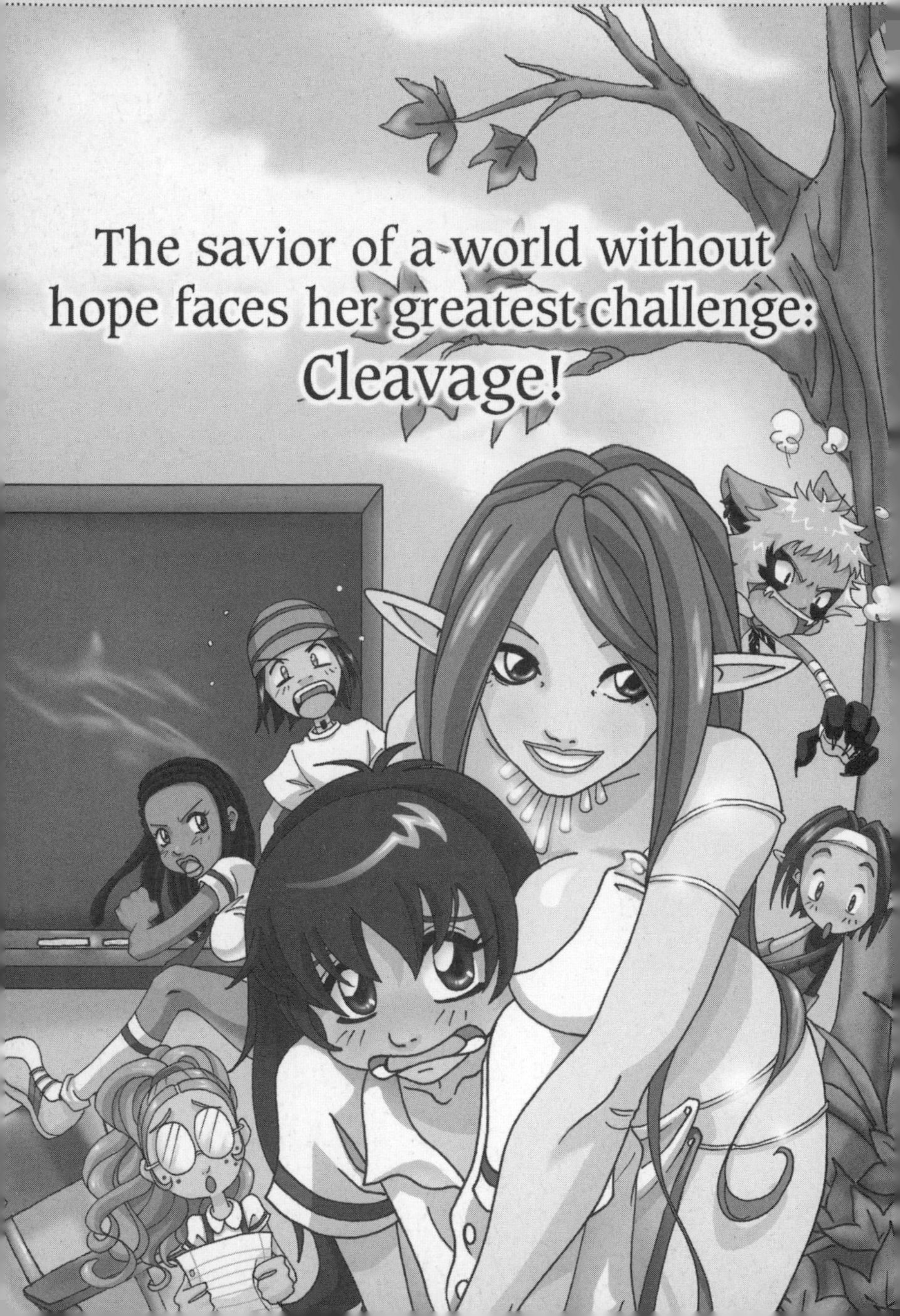
The savior of a world without hope faces her greatest challenge:
Cleavage!

EDITORS' PICKS

DOLL
4

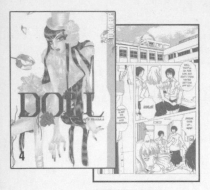

BY MITSUKAZU MIHARA

DOLL

Mitsukazu Mihara's haunting *Doll* uses beautiful androids to examine what it means to be truly human. While the characters in *Doll* are draped in the chic Gothic-Lolita fashions that made Mihara-sensei famous, the themes explored are more universal—all emotions and walks of life have their day in *Doll. Doll* begins as a series of 'one-shot' stories and gradually dovetails into an epic of emotion and intrigue. It's like the *Twilight Zone* meets *Blade Runner!*

~Rob Tokar, Senior Editor

PLANETES
VOLUME 01 | MAKOTO YUKIMURA

BY MAKOTO YUKIMURA

PLANETES

Makoto Yukimura's profoundly moving and graphically arresting *Planetes* posits a near future where mankind's colonization of space has begun. Young Hachimaki yearns to join this exciting new frontier. Instead, he cleans the glut of orbital junk mankind's initial foray into space produced. He works with Fee, a nicotine-addict beauty with an abrasive edge, and Yuri, a veteran spaceman with a tragic past in search of inner peace. *Planetes* combines the scope of Jules Verne (*Around the World in Eighty Days*) and Robert Heinlein (*Starship Troopers*) with the philosophical wonder of *2001: A Space Odyssey.*

~Luis Reyes, Editor

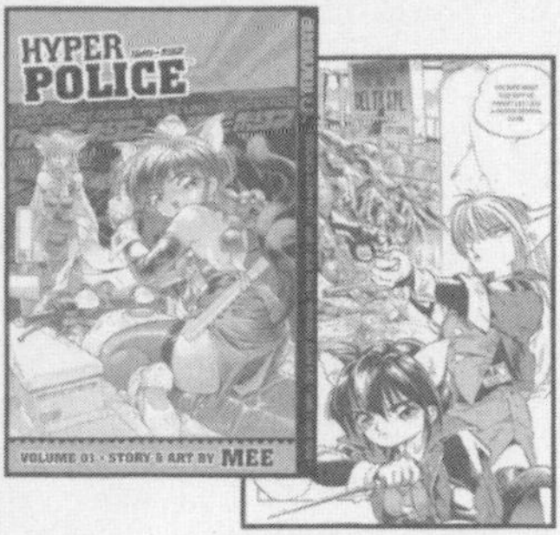
HYPER POLICE
VOLUME 01 · STORY & ART BY MEE

HYPER POLICE

BY MEE

In a future rife with crime, humans are an endangered species—and monsters have taken over! Natsuki is a cat girl who uses magical powers to enforce the law. However, her greatest threat doesn't come from the criminals. Her partner Sakura, a "nine-tailed" fox, plots to eat Natsuki and gobble up her magic! In this dog-eat-dog world, Natsuki fights to stay on top!

OT OLDER TEEN AGE 16+

© MEE

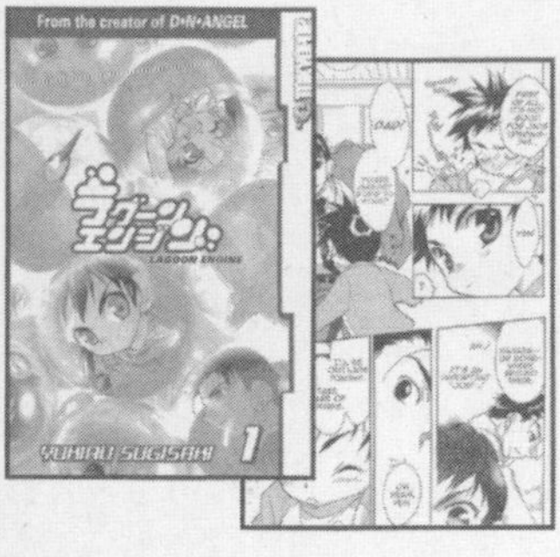
From the creator of D•N•ANGEL
LAGOON ENGINE
YUKIRU SUGISAKI 1

LAGOON ENGINE

BY YUKIRU SUGISAKI

From the best-selling creator of *D·N·Angel!*

Yen and Jin are brothers in elementary school—and successors in the Ragun family craft. They are Gakushi, those who battle ghosts and evil spirits known as "Maga" by guessing their true name. As Yen and Jin train to join the family business, the two boys must keep their identities a secret...or risk death!

T TEEN AGE 13+

© Yukiru SUGISAKI

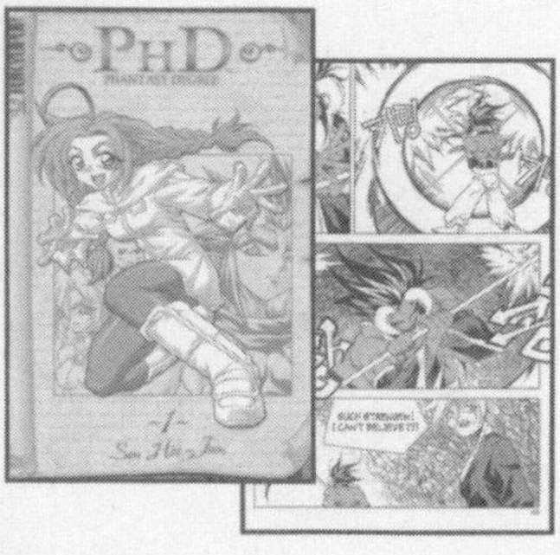
PHD
PHANTASY DEGREE

PhD: PHANTASY DEGREE

BY HEE-JOON SON

Sang is a fearlessly spunky young girl who is about to receive one hell of an education...at the Demon School Hades! She's on a mission to enroll into the monsters-only class. However, monster matriculation is not what is truly on her mind—she wants to acquire the fabled "King's Ring" from the fiancée of the chief commander of hell!

T TEEN AGE 13+

© SON HEE-JOON, DAIWON C.I. Inc.

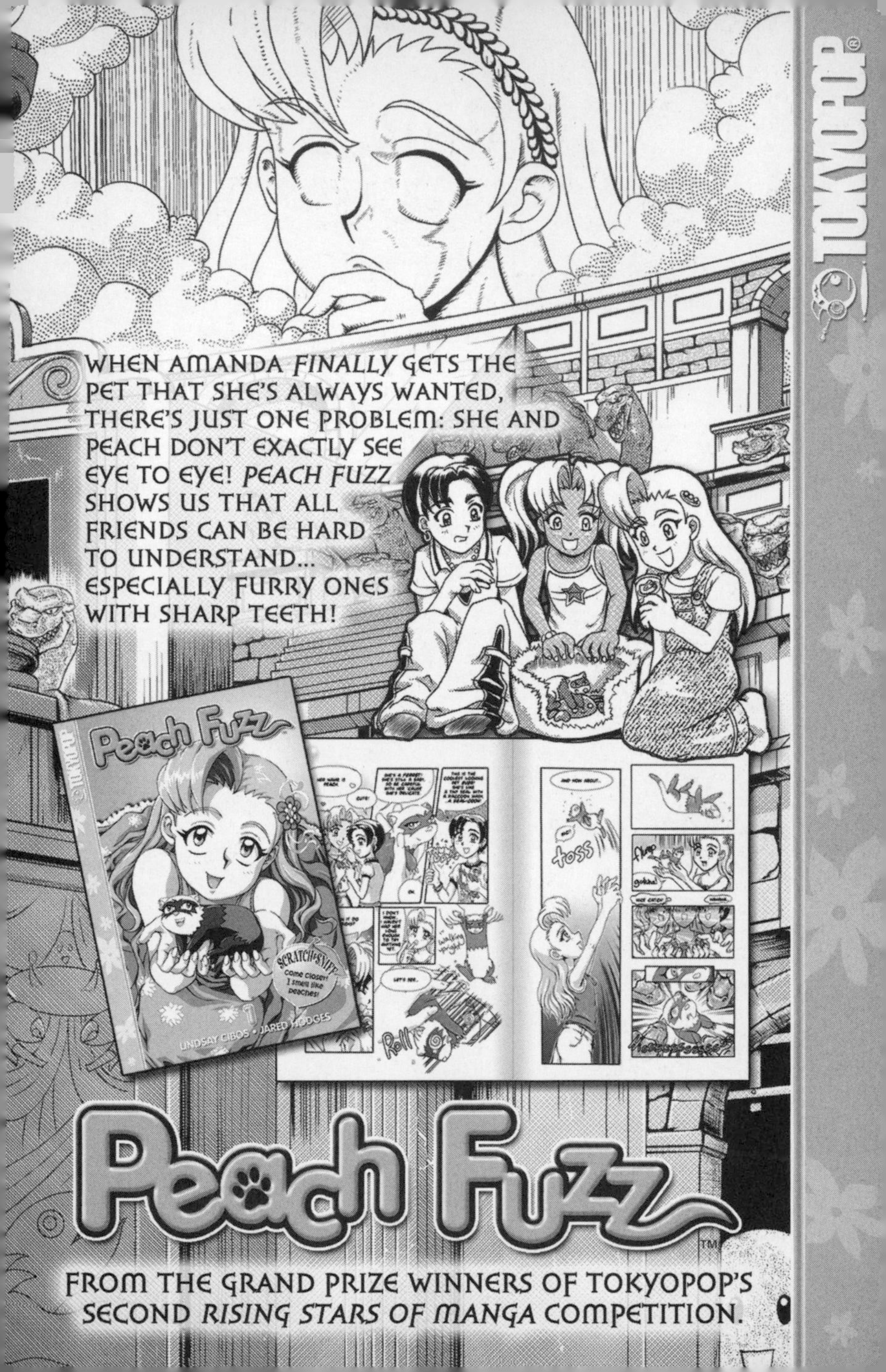
TOKYOPOP
WHEN AMANDA FINALLY GETS THE PET THAT SHE'S ALWAYS WANTED, THERE'S JUST ONE PROBLEM: SHE AND PEACH DON'T EXACTLY SEE EYE TO EYE! PEACH FUZZ SHOWS US THAT ALL FRIENDS CAN BE HARD TO UNDERSTAND... ESPECIALLY FURRY ONES WITH SHARP TEETH!
Peach Fuzz
SCRATCH & SNIFF
Come closer! I smell like peaches!
LINDSAY CIBOS • JARED HODGES
Peach Fuzz™
FROM THE GRAND PRIZE WINNERS OF TOKYOPOP'S SECOND RISING STARS OF MANGA COMPETITION.

TOKYOPOP
A touching story
about a regular guy
with an irregular gift.
HANDS OFF!
TM
T
TEEN
AGE 13+

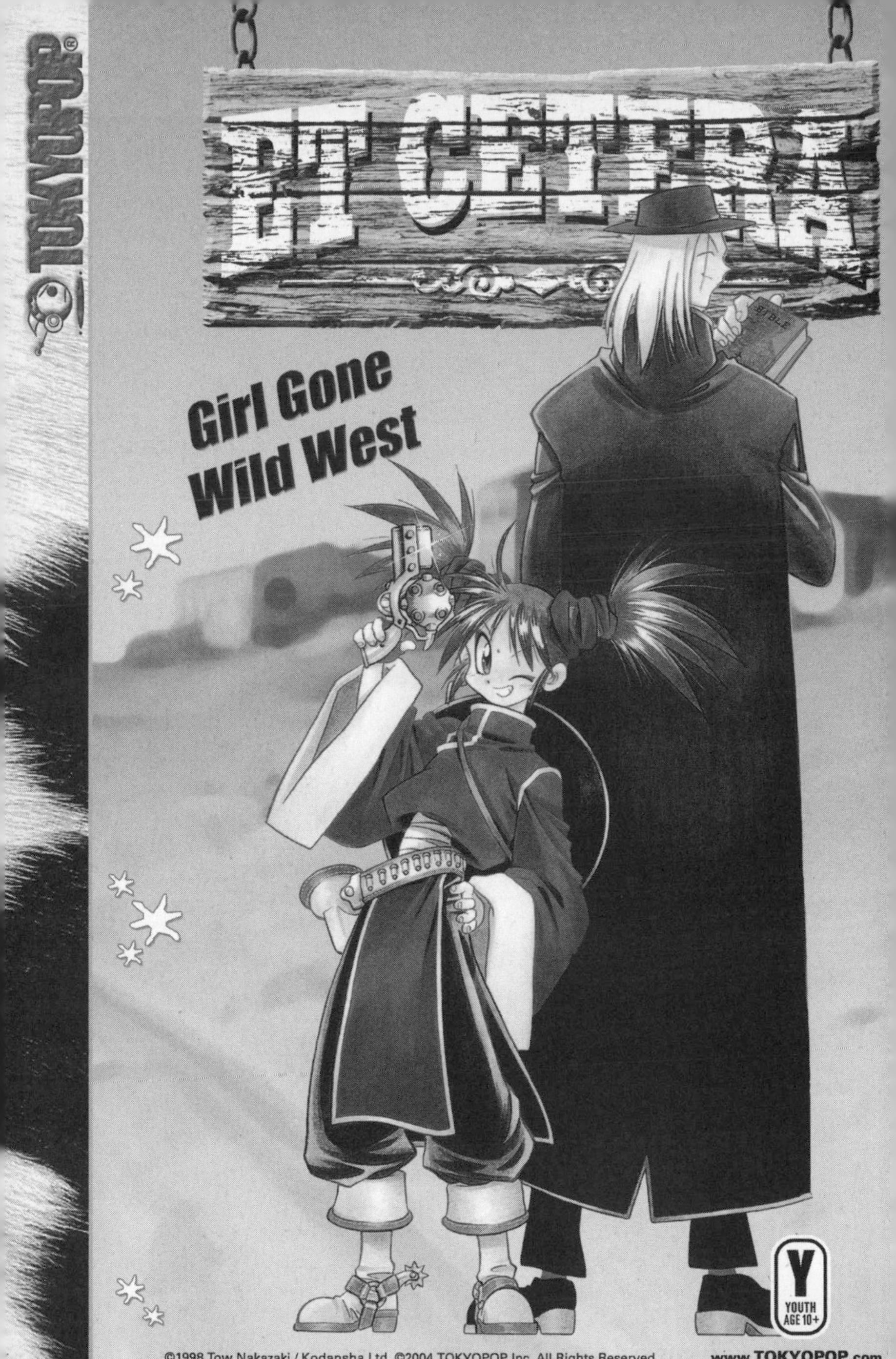
TOKYOPOP
Girl Gone
Wild West
BIBLE
Y
YOUTH
AGE 10+

It's time to teach the boys a lesson...

TOKYOPOP®

★Girl Got Game★ ♡

Let the games begin...

Available Now

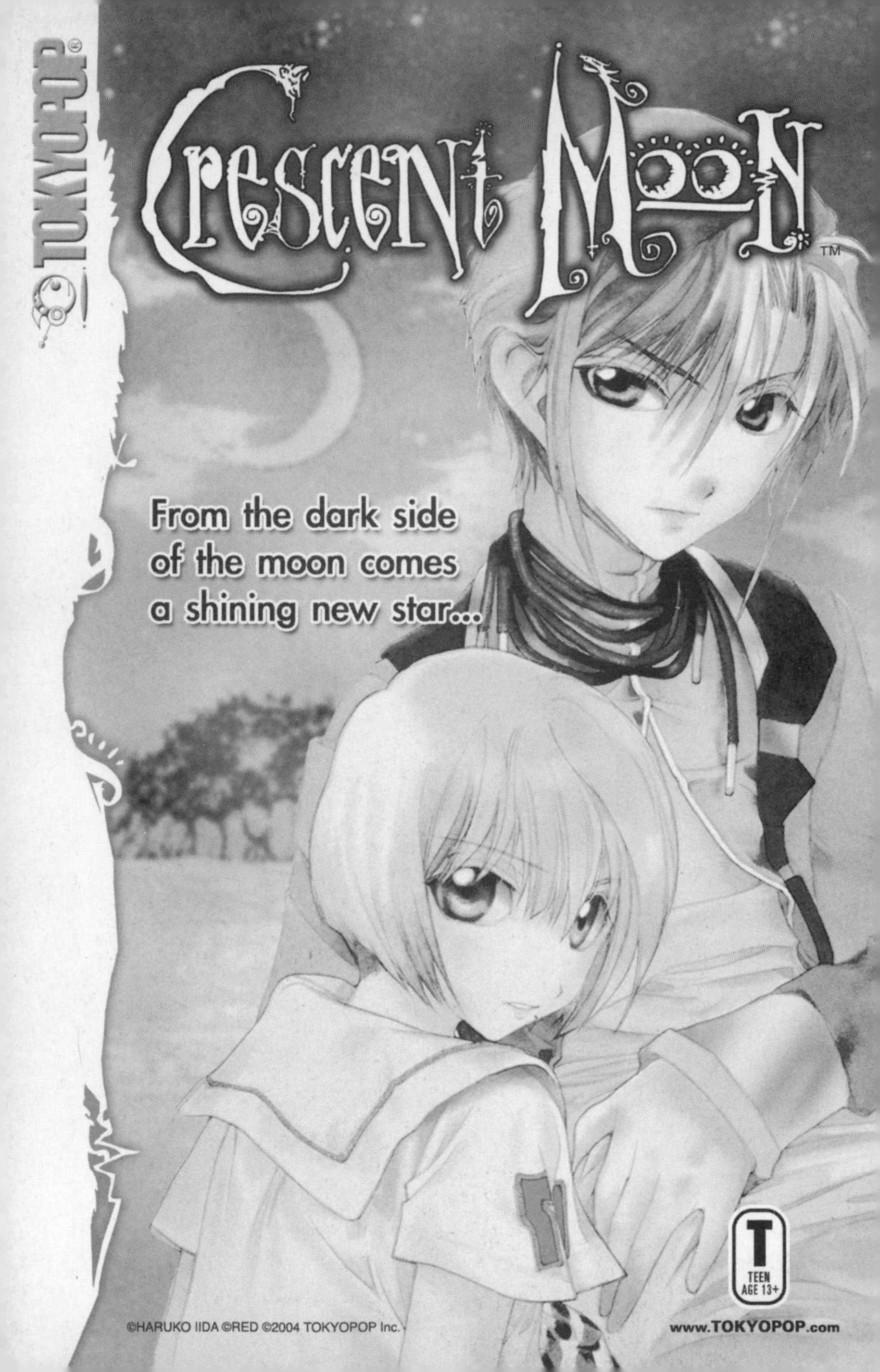

TOKYOPOP
Crescent Moon
TM
From the dark side of the moon comes a shining new star...
T
TEEN
AGE 13+
©HARUKO IIDA ©RED ©2004 TOKYOPOP Inc.
www.TOKYOPOP.com

When darkness is in your genes,
only love can steal it away.

D·N·ANGEL